30.-

D0593267

Marketing Management

The Wiley Marketing Series

WILLIAM LAZER, Advisory Editor
Michigan State University

MARTIN ZOBER, *Marketing Management*

Marketing Management

Martin Zober, *Associate Professor of Marketing*
Department of Industrial Administration
Iowa State University, Ames, Iowa

New York · London · Sydney John Wiley & Sons, Inc.

Library of Congress Catalog Card Number: 64–15002
Printed in the United States of America

To Edith

Preface

Both literature and discussions on marketing management are marked by an emphasis on the interests of the consumer in management decisions. This is a useful way to begin to think about marketing, but it must be enlarged upon by consideration of other factors. For a rounded view of the subject, it becomes necessary to understand the various elements of business management and the techniques that facilitate the solution of business problems. Management covers the planning, organizing, and control of a business, whereas the solving of problems requires a knowledge of both the quantitative and qualitative procedures involved in the making of management decisions. The study of these concepts, how they utilize the methods of the behavioral and quantitative sciences, and their application to the conduct of business activity form the substance of this book, whose central thread is problem solving.

Designed for the second course in marketing at the undergraduate level or the first course at the graduate level, this book concentrates on a discussion of concepts rather than "how to do it." It is concerned with theory and the body of knowledge supporting it. Reading it and absorbing its principles, the student should acquire a firm foundation for meeting the day-to-day problems presented by a career in marketing management.

The book is divided into four parts. First, there is an introduction to marketing management and the marketing concept. Second, the problem areas of marketing are reviewed. Third, the tools that may be used in marketing management are observed. Fourth, the role of organization and anti-trust laws are studied.

In the first section, the scope of marketing management is defined. In the second section, the book considers product development, channels of distribution, pricing, advertising, and personal selling—the problem areas of marketing. Each of them is treated from the approach of marketing management set in a frame of planning, organization, and control. They are all implemented by examples of how the quantitative and behavioral tools may be used to aid in reaching decisions in these several problem areas.

The third section turns to the techniques for solving marketing problems—distribution cost analysis, forecasting, operations research, the behavioral sciences, and marketing theory. The section presents some of the techniques in current use and considers others that may hold promise for solving the marketing problems of tomorrow. Distribution cost analysis and forecasting tend to sharpen both the planning and control decisions made in a company. Operations research and electronic data processing examine the utility of quantitative techniques in problem solving. In contrast, the behavioral sciences deal with the qualitative techniques. Basic to all problem solving, however, is a conceptual framework, and this is supplied by marketing theory. The chapter concerned with theory explores both developments to date and directions for the future.

The fourth section consists of two chapters—one covers the application of three schools of thought on organization to marketing management; the other reviews some of the anti-trust laws that affect marketing.

The material in this book has been tested in the classroom and has been supplemented by actual cases and the playing of the management game. The cases afford the student the opportunity to develop in depth techniques of analysis. The management game familiarizes him with the dynamic aspects of decision making. Their joint use prepares him for the challenges of the real world of commerce.

It is hard to acknowledge the contributions of the many individuals who have played an important role in shaping my point of view or who have influenced my thinking about marketing management. A special debt of gratitude is owed to my teachers, Asher Isaacs, Francis Tyson, and John Maxwell Ferguson. I am also appreciative of the helpful criticisms of William Lazer of Michigan State University and Leonard J. Konopa of the State University of Iowa. My thanks go to William H. Schrampfer, head of the Department of Industrial Administration, Iowa State University, for the freedom to develop my own ideas and to Mrs. Marlene Weisshaar for the many hours spent in typing the manuscript. A final word of acknowledgment is due my children, Norman and Janet, who, by not disturbing their father during his long labor of love, contributed handsomely to the completion of this book.

MARTIN ZOBER

Ames, Iowa
January 1964

Contents

Marketing Management

Chapter One

Science has brought many blessings to the twentieth century. It has
reduced the incidence of illness and premature death. It has improved material well-being through better food, housing, modes of
transportation and communication, recreation facilities, and techniques of education. Through the effort of science we are capable
of maintaining a deterrent military force. Science has been utilized
extensively to probe the secrets of outer space. Science and scientific method have also been applied to the understanding of society
and to the development of more efficient means of producing goods
and services.

Only since the middle of the century have scientific procedures been

Marketing Management

considered feasible for improving the distribution of our goods and services. Encouraged by the gains in physical productivity and the fickle demands of the consumer, marketing management has turned to science to help find the solutions to some of its problems. The disciplines of the behavioral sciences, in particular, have matured sufficiently so that useful generalizations can be applied to problems of managing the various groups controlled by a company. At the same time many theoretical formulations of mathematics have been refined so that they might contribute to the settlement of various types of problems faced by industry.

In one sense science is the god of the twentieth century. It has replaced the role performed by the gods in ancient Greece. If something is scientific it is good; if it is unscientific it is bad. Thus, even in being scientific we develop value judgments.

Although scientists are constantly searching for the answers to why the universe behaves as it does, we are still obliged daily to make many kinds of decisions that science is incapable of handling readily. It is for this reason that in today's world living is not only a science but also an art. Likewise, in the realm of business, in spite of the fact that science has some patent prescriptions for the policy makers, there is still a vast area in which management has to exercise judgment and rely on intuition and instinct. There is no mathematical formula, for instance, for creativity. Yet without creative thinking about such matters as new products, advertising, service to customers, or cost reduction a company would perish.*

But managers must do more than utilize both the science and art of management; they must remain cognizant of the moral and ethical implications of their decisions. Along with its progress toward economic maturity, western civilization has developed a set of important values. These have included the concepts of social justice and

*For a discussion of the subject of creativity see Chapter 6.

freedom. Luxuries of this sort materialize only in high types of civilizations such as our own. Not only must we cherish these values, we must also promote their extension to less fortunate nations than our own. Thus, it is imperative for the leaders of the body politic and of business and industry to do everything possible to preserve these standards and spread them to as much of the world as they can.

Within this milieu scientific marketing management may be of assistance. It is the purpose of this book to explore how science may be utilized by a company's marketing management team as an aid to better decision making for the benefit of civilization at home and around the world.

Interest in Marketing Management

Interest in marketing management is keen, engendered by forces both inside and outside the business enterprise. On the internal side primarily three considerations have stimulated interest in marketing management. These have been the firm's development of a consumer point of view, an emphasis on planning, and the need for improved coordination. On the external side, similarly, three basic forces have sparked interest in marketing management: the development of scientific management, changes in the competitive situation, and the influence of government.

Internal Forces

Consumer Orientation. There was a time in American business history when men rose to positions of top management exclusively through the ranks of the shop, the production end of things. To these men who made the products, marketing was no more than a selling function to be looked upon with disdain. They felt, as top managers, that if the product were good the consumer could not resist it. As a result they tended to downgrade the marketing department whose leadership reflected this general attitude. Marketing decisions, when they were made at all, bore little relation to the demands of the consumers who composed the market. As we can see from Figure 1-1 decisions to produce and market a product were made independently of consumer interests or considerations. Competition, however, forced a change in management views. To compete more effectively for the consumer's dollar, top management had to revise its sights. The results of this change in thinking may be seen in Figure 1-2. Instead

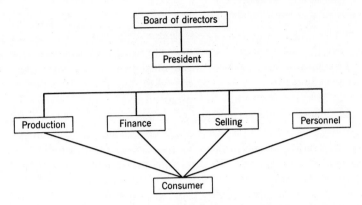

Figure 1-1. Sales approach to marketing.

of giving priority to the product and then considering the needs and desires of the consumer, management reversed itself: now the consumer came first and then the product.

As this change settled over American business, more and more men began to infiltrate top management posts from the marketing department until today many of the country's chief executives are graduates of their organization's sales divisions.

Emphasis on Planning. Before the advent of marketing management a company's top executives consulted their sales manager on problems involving future sales programs or changes in product design. Because of his low status in many instances, the sales manager was often obliged to convince his superiors by forceful argument that certain products were not wanted by the consumer. In addition, the

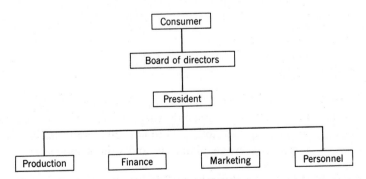

Figure 1-2. Consumer approach to marketing.

sales manager was also sought out frequently by the chief accountant who needed realistic forecasts of next year's sales in order to plot future profits and prepare budgets. These pressures and others like them precipitated the creation of a marketing research department. This new department was charged with gathering the basic facts necessary for sound product planning and sales forecasting, for any top management now recognizes the importance of long-range planning if it is to survive in the competitive struggle. In many companies the marketing research function is lodged in a product planning department. Irrespective of departmental name, the function has become a valuable resource to top management in its weighing of vital business decisions because the staffs of such departments consist of individuals specially trained to solve problems dealing with future circumstances.

Coordination. On many occasions in the past the sales manager was not aware of the activities of other members of the marketing team. For example, no effort was made to consult him on a new advertising campaign, nor did the advertising manager endeavor to relate his campaign to the personal selling effort. Furthermore, there was no basic coordination between a company's production, selling, and advertising departments when new products were ready for introduction to the public. As a matter of fact, Figure 1-1 omits an advertising function altogether. In some cases advertising was a responsibility of the company's president; in others of the sales manager. Clearly, there was need for some type of coordination which had to be centered in the marketing department but which drew on other areas of the enterprise. The man assigned to the function required an unusual combination of analytic and social skills, the former to evaluate some of the tools of the behavioral and quantitative disciplines used in the solution of the company's marketing problems, and the latter to maintain an *esprit de corps* in the department and to interpret its findings to top management.

External Forces

Scientific Management. The first of the forces outside of business to influence marketing management was the scientific management movement launched by Taylor.[1] Through time and motion study programs and incentive wage plans, he and others like him pointed

---

[1] Frederick W. Taylor, *The Principles of Scientific Management,* Harper, New York, 1947.

the way for business and industry to increase levels of productivity. Their findings and recommendations were accepted readily by the business world and incorporated into the body of knowledge forming the principles of industrial management. Then other students of business activity found that they could solve many of the problems of production through the application of mathematics, statistics, and the behavioral sciences. This movement reached its culmination during the second World War as operations research teams, composed of members of different intellectual disciplines, devoted their energies to the easing of problems created by the war effort. After the war, operations research teams extended their interests beyond the area of production to the problems of marketing.

Simultaneously, the thinking of management about the essential nature of the business organization changed. No longer was the worker to be treated as an appendage to the machine; he was now regarded as an individual with needs and desires of his own. And with this change in outlook came a greater emphasis on the place of decision making in the business orbit and the ways in which scientific method could abet it.

Nowadays there are newer problems for industrial society. Management remains faced with growing mechanization and automation. New terms like "cybernetics" and "electronic data processing" continue to gain currency. Mechanization has been applied successfully to production problems. Electronic data processing is being applied to decision making. It has already begun to help in two ways. First, it has made information of vital nature available more quickly than ever before. Second, computers themselves have settled certain routine decisions, freeing management of time-consuming chores to cope with problems of more than routine nature.

Competitive Changes. New products are constantly reaching the market. Many companies are making products that were unknown a decade ago and which may become obsolete in another ten years. Moreover, consumer tastes change all the time. The consumer market, in fact, has been likened to a passing parade rather than a stationary group of individuals that always buys the same products. The market has become more competitive at both pricing and product levels. Then, too, in the wake of mergers and other forms of economic concentration the competition heightens. Fewer concerns come to have control of more of the nation's wealth and of its market areas. All this calls for creative effort and ingenious thinking from those seeking to expand their own marketing horizons in order to increase their sales and revenues. To adapt to the more rigorous competitive conditions, many enterprises have introduced the concept of marketing management into their operations and have taken great care to develop it to perfection.

Influences of Government. Hand in hand with the changes in competition have come increased government influence and regulation. Although specific practices vary with each successive administration, the government has made a notable effort to maintain fair competitive conditions. It is to be assumed that such governmental action will continue in the future. Similarly, the proclivity of government to protect private property and the health and welfare of the nation will go on. With the economic and military commitments abroad, an increasing portion of the gross national product seems likely to be directed toward this end. In addition, the government role in the race for space has created a whole new industry dependent on government. Already the magnitude of the space endeavor approximates the pourings of private capital into the automobile industry,[2] and its implications for the private sector of the economy are vast. How, for example, will government investment in the economy affect decision making in the private sphere? Will this dislocate the allocation of resources to be devoted to raising the standard of living? Questions of this kind, in the light of government's growing influence on the economy, require reliance on scientific procedures in marketing management, in particular, for effective answers. They may indeed necessitate some readjustment in the thinking of the men in top managerial posts as well as among marketing management.

Definition of Marketing Management

As we shall employ the term throughout this study, *"marketing management" is the use of the interdisciplinary sciences in the coordinative effort of planning, organizing, and controlling business activities that direct the flow of goods and services from producer to consumer so that the consumer is fully satisfied and the objectives of the enterprise are achieved.* There seems to be some confusion and overlap in the use of "marketing management" and "marketing concept." In the literature the latter term covers a score of functions ranging from operations research to the coordinating role of manage-

[2] Gilbert Burck, "Hitching the Economy to the Infinite," *Fortune,* June 1962, p. 123 ff.

ment. Advocates of the operations research function believe that the marketing concept should be developed as a staff endeavor under the direction of the head of the marketing department. The operations research group presumably would be able to apply the skills of the interdisciplinary sciences—the social and behavioral sciences, mathematics, and statistics—to the solution of marketing problems, concentrating more on the long-range planning tasks than on the settlement of day-to-day problems.

At the other extreme, Felton has stressed the coordinating nature of the marketing concept in defining it as "a corporate state of mind that insists on the integration and coordination of all the marketing functions which, in turn, are melded with all other corporate functions, for the basic objective of producing maximum long-range profits." [3] This same sort of definition appeared some years ago in a magazine article dealing with marketing management.[4] It said that marketing management essentially was a coordination of functions in the marketing department to achieve efficient and economic operation. A more recent article, considering the marketing concept, emphasized the role of creating markets.[5] This view held the customer as king and stressed his influence on the nature of the business organization and operation. The enterprise, however, had to possess the ability to create a customer and be prepared to cope with innovation in the market place.

These varied definitions illustrate the lack of uniformity and consistency in the use of the two terms, marketing management and marketing concept. The need for standardization of the two is apparent.

Discussion of the Definition

Measuring Objectives

Many companies state clearly the objectives of their operations. In a typical sense these may be to operate at a profit. Nevertheless,

[3] Arthur P. Felton, "Making the Marketing Concept Work," *Harvard Business Review,* Vol. 37, No. 4, July–August 1959, pp. 55–65.
[4] "Marketing Management, Real and Unreal," *Management Review,* September 1939, pp. 290–291.
[5] Garwood R. Wolff, "The Case for the Marketing Manager," *Sales Management,* Vol. 78, No. 2, Jan. 18, 1957, pp. 52–56.

not all managements take the time to think through their over-all objectives for either the long run or the short run. Too often they veer from composing a formal statement of objectives to reevaluating the company's past performance and to laying a basis for future courses to pursue.

One explanation for the failure to develop and issue a statement of objectives is that many of the goals cannot be phrased in quantitative terms. Such matters as enhancing the "good will" of the company, increasing its share of the market, improving service, or providing security for members of the community are all elusive to measurement. One proposal advanced for the handling of these difficulties is the creation of a quantitative system of relative weights for each objective. These weights can then be assigned by a group of individuals entrusted with the responsibility for policy making. Their evaluations either may be averaged or ranked in order of their importance.

Let us assume management's unanimity on the enterprise's most important objective, which, for the sake of discussion, might be considered as the desire to maximize the discounted value of the long-run return on the investment. This might be assigned a weight of 1. Other objectives would then be evaluated in relation to it and assigned weights in ratio to 1. Thus, increasing the share of the market, for example, might be rated at .8. Some objectives even may be rated 0 if it is believed that they have no importance at all.

The following is a list of objectives a company might use.[6]

O_1 Continuation of existing management.

O_2 Guaranteed 6 per cent return to the owners in their original investment.

O_3 Company should be in a position to make a 15 per cent return on investment if market for product stayed in the range of 100 to 200 per cent of current demand.

O_4 No firing and reasonable promotion of key personnel of company.

O_5 Stable labor relations.

O_6 Technological leadership.

O_7 Community service over and above legal requirements.

In preparing a comparison of these, let us assume quantitatively that $O_1 = 1$. Other ratings may have been:

[6] C. West Churchman, Russell L. Ackoff, and E. Leonard Arnoff, *Introduction to Operations Research,* Wiley, New York, 1957, p. 151.

$$O_1 = 1.0$$
$$O_2 = .9$$
$$O_3 = .6$$
$$O_4 = .4$$
$$O_5 = .7$$
$$O_6 = .8$$
$$O_7 = \underline{.3}$$
$$4.7$$

All these ratings may then be totaled and a normalized comparison developed by dividing each rating by the total of O_1 through O_7, namely, 4.7. Thus we obtain:

$$O_1 = .21$$
$$O_2 = .19$$
$$O_3 = .13$$
$$O_4 = .09$$
$$O_5 = .15$$
$$O_6 = .17$$
$$O_7 = \underline{.06}$$
$$1.00$$

The executives responsible for the rating might wish to check the consistency of the evaluations by comparing one weight to another. For example, they may wish to see whether

$$O_1 > (O_2 + O_3)$$
$$O_1 > (O_2 + O_4)$$
$$O_1 > (O_2 + O_5)$$
$$O_1 > (O_2 + O_6)$$
$$O_1 > (O_2 + O_7)$$
$$O_1 > (O_3 + O_4)$$
$$O_1 > (O_3 + O_5)$$
$$O_1 > (O_3 + O_6)$$
$$O_1 > (O_3 + O_7)$$
$$O_1 > (O_2 + O_3 + O_4)$$
$$O_1 > (O_2 + O_3 + O_5)$$

$$\cdot$$
$$\cdot$$
$$\cdot$$

$$O_i > (O_j + \cdots O_k)$$

On the basis of this reevaluation they may change the ratings. One problem of this type of measurement is the absence of a common standard on which to base comparisons. This may be solved perhaps by fixing every value as part of a profit estimate. In the foregoing problem a profit calculation may be made for O_2. If this amount equaled, say, $1000, one might apply the weights to this base. For example, if the revised weights were $O_1 = .18$, $O_2 = .25$, and $O_3 = .10$, these weights we would have the following values:

$$(.18/.25)\ 1000 = 720$$
$$(.10/.25)\ 1000 = 400$$

The total effectiveness of objectives O_1, O_2, and O_3 would thus be:

$$720 + 1000 + 400 = 2120$$

Return on Investment

As we have assumed, one of the major objectives of any business is to maximize the long-range return on its investment discounted to the present. Figure 1-3 represents the kind of projections a marketing department might develop. It plots estimated revenues and costs over the life of the product.

The cost curve rises from t_1 to t_2 because of initial investment in

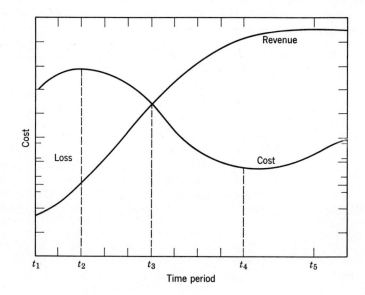

Figure 1-3. Expected revenue and cost.

such areas as advertising, product development, establishment of a new sales force, acquisition of new dealers, and special introductory discounts. Other costs remain fixed during the product's life; these might include plant and equipment, sales administration, sales force, and continuing advertising, although some aspects of the latter two might fluctuate with competitive conditions. Some of the advertising and sales costs do not have to be repeated. These are known as sunken costs. Once they have been incurred, advertising and sales costs may be reduced. At the same time, because of economies of scale, production costs drop. Thus, the graph shows a decline in costs from t_2 to t_4. After t_4 they turn upward again because, in order to maintain its share of the market, a business must expand its advertising outlays and provide additional services for its dealers.

From t_1 to t_3 the operation plotted in Figure 1-3 loses money. The period from t_3 to t_5 is one in which a profit is realized. The question in this case is finding the return on the investment discounted to the present.

Suppose we assume for purposes of illustration the costs, revenues, and profits represented in Table 1-1.

Table 1-1. Costs, Revenues, and Profits

Costs	Revenues	Profits
6	3	−3
7	5	−2
8	7	−1
7	9	2
6	12	6
5	13	8
4	14	10
3	14	11
4	14	10

Now let us say we could obtain a return of 5 per cent on an investment in the current market, and that the cost of acquiring money from lending or investing sources is also 5 per cent. The discounted return may be found by application of the following formula:

$$\sum_{i=i_0}^{T} \frac{P_i}{(1.05)^i} \bigg/ \sum_{i=-t}^{T} \frac{C_i}{(1.05)^i}$$

According to the formula, the sum of the discounted profits (P_i) for a particular year is divided by the sum of the discounted costs (C_i). The number 1.05 which is divided into (P_i) and (C_i) represents the return on investment for (P_i) and the cost of acquiring money for (C_i) multiplied by the exponent (i) which represents the ordinal sequence of years. The summation in costs (C_i) extends from the start of development to the end T of marketing. In profits (P_i) it extends from the beginning i_0 to the end T of marketing.* Applying the formula to the figures specified in Table 1-1 we obtain the following calculation:

$$\frac{-3/1.05 - 2/1.10 - 1/1.16 + 2/1.22 + 6/1.28 + 8/1.34}{6/1.05 + 7/1.10 + 8/1.16 + 7/1.22 + 6/1.28 + 5/1.34}$$

$$\frac{+\ 10/1.40 + 11/1.47 + 10/1.54}{+\ 4/1.40 + 3/1.47 + 4/1.54} = \frac{27.25}{40.23} = 68\%$$

The discounted return on this particular investment is thus 68 per cent.

The Consumer

Not only must a business retain a consumer point of view in developing and marketing its products, it must also maintain effective public relations with others on whom its success depends. It has to enjoy the support of its employees, stockholders, and suppliers, and also of legislators. Without the loyalty of the consumer and these other forces, a business may well suffer extinction.

Planning

The Use of Models. Planning, in essence, requires the logical construction of future expectations into a formal document. To complete a plan about the future one needs to construct a model, a device which may be said to constitute a simplified version of reality. As the human mind is not capable of grasping the many aspects of a complex situation all at once, one begins with very simple assumptions and adds to them, noting the effect of the additions on the simple model.† As an illustration of what could be used in planning,

---

* Formula suggested by Dr. Herbert T. David, professor of statistics, Iowa State University.
† For further discussion on models see Chapter 9 on operations research and Chapter 11 on marketing theory.

one might try a triangular planning model.[7] Table 1-2 depicts a development of this type of model.[8]

The model in Table 1-2 lists the activities across the top of each column and the items resulting from them at the start of each row. Thus, the activity *market delineation* contains the item *potential purchasers*. Where the two cross, the letter *"O"* appears to signify output. Since it is necessary to measure customer potentiality before it becomes possible to communicate with an eventual prospect either through advertising or personal selling, the letter *"I"* representing input occupies the intersection of *communication* and *potential purchasers*. By observing the markings on the remainder of the model, one can see both the input and output combinations and the relations among them.

A model of this kind may also be developed for the classical functions of marketing—the exchange, physical, and facilitating functions. Or it may be applied to the major decision areas of marketing—pricing, advertising, personal selling, product development, and channels of distribution. Furthermore, the reader or any practitioner of the science of marketing might develop other areas in which the triangular model might prove useful.

Long-Range Planning. A study of 400 companies covering the period 1935–1939 showed that most high-growth concerns maintained long-range plans in contrast to low-growth companies which had no such plans.[9] Corporations like General Electric Company have prepared forecasts of what consumer expenditures might be in 1980, and the United States Steel Corporation is already estimating the amount of iron ore it will need in the year 2000. General Mills has indicated that by 1966 at least 7 per cent of its gross investment, 9 per cent of its sales, and 18 per cent of its profit will arise from new products developed by that date.[10]

The director of planning for the Martin Company said his company's five-year plans became obsolete the day after printing, but

---

[7] See article by Robert S. Weinberg, "The Uses and Limitations of Mathematical Models," in Frank Bass et al. (Eds.), *Mathematical Models and Methods of Marketing,* Irwin, Homewood, Ill., 1961, pp. 31–32.

[8] List of functions from Thomas A. Staudt, "The Managerial Functions of Marketing," in Eugene J. Kelley and William Lazer (Eds.), *Managerial Marketing Perspectives and Viewpoints: A Source Book,* rev. ed., Irwin, Homewood, Ill., 1962, p. 392.

[9] William J. Platt and N. Robert Maines, "Pretest Your Long-Range Plans," *Harvard Business Review,* January–February 1959.

[10] *Wall Street Journal,* Oct. 25, 1961, p. 1.

Table 1-2. A Triangular Planning Model [a]

Item Produced	Activity						
	Market delineation	Purchase motivation	Product adjustment	Physical distribution	Communication	Transaction	Post-transaction
Potential purchasers	O				I		
Direct and indirect factors that influence purchase behavior	I	O	I		I	I	I
Product matched with market	I	I	O	I	I	I	I
Movement of goods from producer to consumer	I		I	O		I	
Transmission of information and messages between buyer and seller	I	I	I		O	I	I
Activities that go on in exchange of title	I	I	I	I	I	O	I
Assurance of satisfaction in use and follow-through		I	I	I	I	I	O

[a] O = output; I = input.

added that his staff revised them every six months.[11] At Martin, 200 executives send reports to the planning director, who employs the data to compose the long-range plan. The necessity to prepare amended plans every half-year compels key management executives to concentrate on the future, an activity many individuals tend to put off.

Generally, it is imperative for top-line management to participate in long-range planning, for long-range considerations may indicate certain steps to be taken in present situations. For example, U.S. Steel, to meet its estimated needs for the year 2000, is now prospecting for new sources of ore. At International Business Machines, officials are beginning to train personnel as "systems analysts" so that they may aid in the tapping of the future market for computers.

Organization for Planning. In many companies the sales manager has been brought into the planning activity. Many times, however, having risen through the sales organization, he lacks any experience in planning. Moreover, as business organizations grow, their marketing executives find that pressures of conferences, solving urgent problems, traveling, keeping up with mail and reports, and supervising subordinates leave little time for the thinking necessary for planning. Planning is hard work. It requires rigorous mental activity which many individuals abhor as burdensome. Finally, some companies have operated in industries whose natural growth has carried them along with little planning. Nevertheless, when the conditions fostering growth change, these enterprises become vulnerable to economic disturbances.[12]

For these several reasons many businesses have instituted departments of long-range planning with a director of long-range planning activities in charge. Frequently, these positions carry with them vice-presidential status.[13] To abet this development, the Institute of Management Sciences has created a college of long-range planning.

The newest approach to planning is based on the use of systems. A system may be considered an array of components arranged to accomplish a particular objective according to a specific plan.[14] How systems fit into the structure of a business may be judged from Figure 1-4.

[11] *Ibid.*
[12] Victor P. Buell, "Organizing for Marketing Planning," *Journal of Marketing,* July 1956, pp. 68–71.
[13] *Ibid.*
[14] Richard A. Johnson, Fremont E. Kast, and James E. Rosenzweig, *The Theory and Management of Systems,* McGraw-Hill, New York, 1963, p. 91.

The key planning force in the organization, as Figure 1-4 illustrates, is the master planning council which makes the vital decisions relating to products or services supplied or to be supplied by the enterprise. It is entrusted with establishing limits for operating—or major project —systems, with choosing general policy to govern their design, and with selecting a director to run each new project. The council renders decisions on new products with the assistance and advice of the product research and development, market research, and financial groups. Once the council has approved a project, the resources allocation committee provides the manpower, the facilities, and technical assistance on the design of systems. When a system has been designed, it is placed under the management of the operations committee as either a facilitating system or a major project system. The facilitating systems provide services to the company rather than finished

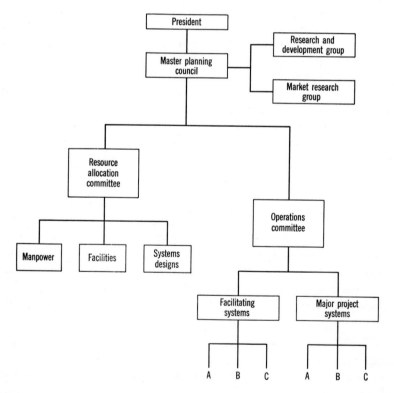

Figure 1-4. Systems organization of top management. (Richard A. Johnson, Fremont E. Kast, and James E. Rosenzweig, *The Theory and Management of Systems*, McGraw-Hill, New York, 1963, p. 96.)

products for the market. Each project system, on the other hand, is designed to yield a marketable end product.

In the case of a product manager, for example, the facilitating system comes to his aid as he supervises the major project system. If we assume that the objective of a particular project system is to manufacture several new products, the facilitating system may comprise a production unit that supplies intermediate products, say containers, for all end products.

The Marketing Development Department. Theodore Levitt has suggested that a marketing development department should report to top management.[15] Most line supervision concerns itself with day-to-day problems. Both the marketing research and product development departments believe they must function within the existing structure of the company and of the market. Levitt has proposed the creation of a new group to develop radical ideas which do not conform to the present organization of the company or of its known distribution pattern. He would call this group the "Blue Skies" committee.

The individuals selected for this committee should be strong in imagination, audacity, cosmopolitan interests, and competence. With an outside consultant or two, the committee should serve as a separate appendage of top management and make creative thinking its prime, full-time task. Working hand in hand with the "Blue Skies" committee, which would constitute the leadership of the marketing development department, there would be a staff composed of individuals drawn from the operating side, who are comfortable in the world of abstractions and ideas.

The committee should be responsible for perceiving and capitalizing on the numerous social, technological, political, and competitive changes in progress. For it to succeed, it must rigidly define its objectives, and then identify and understand the major factors of the competitive world with which it must cope. The committee must realize that the company needs to create new satisfactions for the consumer. It must therefore know both the customer and society, and the dynamic changes sweeping both today.

For example, there is more leisure time than ever before. More activities take place outside the home. Living is more casual. Most housewives are not interested in spending numbers of hours shopping and preparing foods. They prefer simplicity and convenience; they want speedy service. Besides, there is a widespread feeling of im-

---

[15] Theodore Levitt, *Innovation in Marketing,* McGraw-Hill, New York, 1962.

personality with less face-to-face contact in commercial transactions as a result of self-service. All this, which helps mold the customer's psychological make-up, influences his or her behavior. Guilt feelings among wives over not having prepared a fresh, hot cup of coffee for the husband before he leaves home for work are known to have blocked the sale of instant coffee. These feelings were assuaged by advertising showing males contentedly drinking instant coffee. Or take the automobile. It is no longer merely a vehicle for transportation. It is an extension of one's personality—representing the freedom to move.

The marketing development department has to contend with these ideas and attitudes. It should be authorized to consider entirely new or modified ways to market the company's products with special emphasis on any one of them or a group of them to meet the demands borne of these consumer and societal developments. No course of possible action should be ignored, no matter how radical.

One problem in evaluating the efforts of this committee will be the lack of substantiating, quantifiable evidence. Management has to be willing to assume risks and try out new ideas on a test-market basis. The company must beware of thinking that buying habits and motives are static; as we have noted, they change constantly. Yet many companies do not take full advantage of their public images in introducing new products. This is particularly true of large corporations. That is why so many innovations in marketing have come from medium- and small-sized companies.

Three distinct forces in a company should be concerned with marketing innovations: the marketing innovation group, the operating tactics and standards group, and the marketing investment planning group. It is advantageous to separate the functions of innovation in this manner because operating personnel who are concerned with the day-to-day tactical problems cannot grasp the long-term point of view required by innovation. Moreover, any radical departure from the status quo may upset the operators' vested interests. The investment planners figure in the plot by their work on the long-run potential return of the new project.

In a large number of instances, companies have compiled outstanding records of growth through expert use of their marketing development staffs. Some of the specific reasons for their successes have been advanced by the Stanford Research Institute as follows: [16]

1. The companies seek, find, and reach for growth products and growth markets.

---

[16] *Ibid.,* pp. 176–177.

2. They have organized programs to scout new business opportunities.

3. They are constantly self-critical of their present operation and thus have demonstrated superior competitive ability.

4. Their top management is staffed by courageous, adventurous high-spirited executives who are leaders.

5. Formal systems have been established to uncover opportunities.

6. The chief executive establishes an environment of self-examination and effervescent high adventure.

The marketing development department is not to be confused with the corporate planning department. The latter should deal with short- and long-range capital budgeting, and with a variety of specific studies such as acquisition and merger prospects, plant location studies, and the like.

PERT and PEP. Developed by United States Navy, PERT stands for program evaluation and review technique. The Navy calls PERT a statistical technique—diagnostic and prognostic—for quantifying knowledge about the uncertainties faced in competing intellectual and physical activities that are essential for meeting program deadlines on schedule. It is a technique that focuses management's attention on danger signals alerting it to the need for remedial decisions, and on areas of effort in which switches in time, resources (personnel, facilities, funds), or technical performance might improve the capacity to meet major deadlines.[17] The term PEP, developed by the United States Air Force, signifies program evaluation procedure.[18]

PERT is basically a visual process which describes the interaction of three variables in a program—time, resources, and performance specifications. Figure 1-5, a network example of a test-market operation, illustrates how PERT may be applied. In it, each circle represents an activity listed in Table 1-3. The solid, arrow-tipped lines signify units of time. Although the lengths of the lines do not indicate duration, they do show the logical sequence of activities. Thus, ½ indicates that activity 1 must be completed before activity 2 is undertaken. The broken line signifies that activity 25 will be completed at the same time as activity 24. The estimated times for performing the various activities are supplied by the individuals responsible for each one. These estimates are provided as often as every two weeks

[17] Willard Fazar, "Progress Reporting in the Special Projects Office," *Navy Management Review,* April 1959, p. 2.
[18] Johnson et al., *op. cit.,* p. 247.

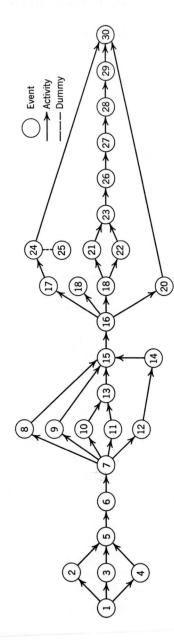

Figure 1-5. Network example of test-market operation.

and revisions of the projected completion times are made constantly.

The estimates include the optimistic, pessimistic, and most likely opinions on when a project will be completed. From these, the expected time of completion may be calculated by use of the following formula:

Where
$$t_e = \left(\frac{a + 4c + b}{6}\right)$$

t_e = expected time
a = optimistic value
b = most likely estimate
c = pessimistic estimate

the variance measure of t_e is:

$$\sigma^2 t_e = \left(\frac{b - a}{6}\right)^2$$

In the computation, the computer calculates the expected time for each activity and identifies those requiring the longest sequence to meet the ultimate objective. This is called the *critical path*. Activities not on this path may experience a certain amount of slack time at their disposal. The amount of slack time available is determined by the latest time at which these activities may be performed. Thus some of the resources on the noncritical paths may be shifted to the critical path to help accomplish the complete job more effectively.

Programmed and Nonprogrammed Decisions in Planning. Because of their routine character, many decisions may be programmed recurrently on a computer, as we have remarked, to solve daily business problems. One such example of programming a decision is the economic order quantity formula

$$\text{E.O.Q.} = \sqrt{\frac{2AC}{B}}$$

in which E.O.Q. represents the economic order quantity, A the cost of procurement, C the annual usage in dollars, and B the cost of carrying inventory. This formula attempts to relate holding costs to ordering costs. Many companies use it repeatedly for ordering supplies for maintenance, repair, and operations.

Unprogrammed decisions do not recur. The problem of introducing a new product or of locating a warehouse exemplifies this sort of

Table 1-3.   Events in Test-Market Operation

1. Marketing research
2. Finance evaluation
3. Production evaluation
4. Marketing evaluation
5. Committee evaluation
6. President's evaluation
7. Evaluation of board of directors
8. Assignment of personnel by sales manager
9. Contacts of agency by advertising manager
10. Personnel needs for project
11. Development of budget for project by finance
12. Work on package design and name
13. Development of model by engineering
14. Evaluation of name and package by package committee
15. Development of marketing strategy by product development committee
16. Development of research design by market research
17. Sales training
18. Work with agency by advertising manager
19. Production plan set up
20. Contact with outside market research agency
21. Tooling
22. Training personnel
23. Assembly line in production
24. Selling activity
25. Billing
26. Warehousing and handling
27. Transportation
28. Retail, wholesale handling
29. Consumer purchase
30. Evaluation of test

decision. Herbert Simon [19] has suggested, however, that heuristic techniques may be useful in situations of this kind. Generally, these techniques attempt to reason by analogy and, within logical contexts, to apply some of the procedures employed by experienced managers. Alfred A. Kuehn and Michael J. Hamburger tried to solve the problem of locating a warehouse by heuristic programming.[20]   The program

[19] See Herbert A. Simon, *The New Science of Management Decision,* Harper, New York, 1960, p. 8.

[20] Alfred A. Kuehn and Michael J. Hamburger, "A Heuristic Program for Lo-

was divided into two parts: first, the main program, which located warehouses one at a time until no additional ones could be added to the distribution system without increasing total costs, and second, the bump and shift routine, which was used after the main program had been completed. The latter routine modified solutions to the main program by evaluating the profit implications of dropping individual warehouses from the system or of shifting them from one place to another. The three principles used in this program were:

1. Most geographical locations do not offer promise as a site for a regional warehouse; locations containing promise are at or near concentrations of demand.

2. Near optimum warehousing systems can be developed by locating warehouses one at a time, adding at each stage of the analysis the warehouse that produces the greatest cost saving for the entire system.

3. Only a small part of all possible warehouse locations need be evaluated in detail at each stage of the analysis to determine the next site to be added.

Market Planning and Corporate Goals. These are some of the ways in which market planning can assist management by matching opportunity with resources.

1. It can free sales executives. By relying on staff personnel to handle the planning phases of the sales management job, market planning releases line sales executives to concentrate on activities designed to increase sales volume.

2. It can improve company profits. In a tough, competitive industry, a company cannot rely on decisions by hunch if it is to have a secure and profitable future. Analysis of the possible courses to pursue is the only method of ascertaining which one will produce more profit than others.

3. It can enhance the company's long-range competitive position. Busy line executives, as we have said, burdened with day-to-day activities, rarely have the time for reflection about the long-range effects of new developments.

Areas for Marketing Planning. Most companies could doubtless improve their profits by a systematic approach to planning for marketing in the following areas.

cating Warehouses," in Ronald E. Frank, Alfred A. Kuehn, and William F. Massy (Eds.), *Quantitative Techniques in Marketing Analysis,* Irwin, Homewood, Ill., 1962, pp. 523–545.

1. SALES AND ADVERTISING. This planning activity is concerned primarily with short-range plans—usually not more than a year ahead—for such things as promotion, contests, advertising media and schedules, new markets to be entered, and sales and advertising budgets. Many companies engage effectively in this type of planning, apparently because it has to be performed to prepare marketing budgets for top management.

2. MARKET RESEARCH. Widespread activities in this area are already scouting potentials for present and proposed products market by market. Companies are also plotting changes in markets, measuring their share of the market compared with their competitors' share, determining customer uses of products, and testing new products and evaluating the findings.

3. DISTRIBUTION. This kind of planning is concerned with channels of distribution. As markets and distribution patterns within industries change, and as new products are added, a company has to be alert to the impact of these developments on its own distributive methods and plans. Distribution planning may also affect production planning, location of plants and warehouses, packaging, and other phases of the manufacturing process.

4. SALES FORECASTING. The foundation for most other planning is supplied by sales forecasting. Short-range sales forecasts provide the basis for manufacturing schedules, manpower needs, sales controls, purchasing and inventory requirements, working capital, and profit estimates. The planning of facilities, capital investment, research needs, organization, and personnel rest on long-range sales forecasts.

5. PRODUCT LINE. Because of its proximity to both customers and competitors, the sales department is acutely sensitive to situations that call for adjustments in the product line. Unless the chief marketing executive establishes a procedure for continuous market research and planning of product line, the long-range sales volume and profit potentiality of his company might be endangered.

6. INVENTORY. Finished inventories are properly the province of the marketing departments of any business. They must make certain that inventories are available in the right place at the right time to render satisfactory service to the company's customers. Yet inventories in excess of actual requirements are costly. They immobilize capital—capital for which the company is paying interest or capital that could be invested elsewhere at a profit.

7. PRICING. Recent marketing developments have uprooted long-established pricing policies. The widespread discount pricing practices for consumer goods by retailers and discount houses is a well-known

illustration. The decision of General Electric to discontinue list prices on its major appliances and to reduce prices and margins on its mail appliances, the Radio Corporation of America's dramatic reductions of up to 40 per cent on its traditional prices for long-playing phonograph records, and the Westinghouse abandonment of fair-trade pricing on its appliances are also examples of this trend.

8. CREDIT. The increasing use of consumer credit has brought about a need for planning in an area formerly of interest to only a handful of industries. In the oil industry, for example, until recently consumer credit was only a minor factor. Now the number of credit accounts for the larger companies runs into the millions. Whether to use credit, how far to extend it, and whether to finance through company funds or through lending institutions all pose questions that open gates to important areas for study.

9. PROFIT. Too often only the financial officer or the company's chief executive officer undertakes profit planning. But the marketing area offers many opportunities to influence a company's profit prospects. For this reason, marketing staff planning personnel should be trained to apply the test of profitability to all programs they develop, and to assess the effects of marketing plans on capital requirements and the operations of other departments of the company.

Improving Marketing Planning. Basically, planning is a problem of organization. Any business may employ the following six-step approach to improving marketing planning.

1. Review and clarify company objectives and policies.
2. Identify major areas in need of organized planning.
3. Determine activities to be performed.
4. Group activities into positions and choose an organization plan.
5. Staff the new positions.
6. See that planning works.

Control

When the recording instruments for the flight of a missile indicate that the vehicle is proceeding on the path previously planned for it, the missile is said to be in control. If the missile veers out of range and thus out of control, a prearranged procedure destroys it.

Some systems of control require complete destruction of a project that runs amuck, while others demand that adjustments be made, and finally there are some that automatically return errant objects to control. In marketing, a product might not prove to be as profitable as anticipated and therefore might be withdrawn from the market. On the other hand, a minor modification in the product or its packaging might bring it back into control in order to realize its anticipated performance. Or an automatic type of control, such as the thermostat on a furnace, might take over the function of restoring the product to control by automatic decisions designed to put the product back on its planned course of action.

Definition. Control is that function of a system that provides direction in conformance with a plan, or, within allowable limits, the maintenance of deviations from the objectives of the system.[21] The elements of control are fourfold: a controlled characteristic or condition; a device for measuring the characteristic or condition; a control group which compares measured data with planned performance and directs a correcting mechanism in response to need; and an activating group or mechanism that is capable of bringing about a change in the operating system.

Characteristics. There are two characteristics of control. One is that large amounts of input may be controlled by a switch. Thus, a small quantity of power may be needed to release the basic inputs of a system—information, materials, and energy. For example, a salesman's order slip may galvanize a whole series of operations. The second type of control unit may be distantly located from the operating system, such as the sales manager who controls the sales force in the field.

Kinds of Control. Two kinds of control systems exist: open sequence and closed sequence. In the former the control unit is not part of the system. For instance, if an individual desires additional light he presses the light switch. Under a closed-sequence system, when the light diminishes to a certain intensity, a photoelectric cell automatically turns on the light. This is the system in which a thermostat acts, and which is of special interest to our discussion.

The thermostat adjusts the output of the furnace so that the temperature will reach the level desired. This results from feedback which occurs in the closed system. Forrester has defined the information-feedback system as one in which the environment stimulates a decision that results in action which, in turn, affects the environment and thereby influences future decisions.[22] It is, in effect,

---

[21] Johnson et al., *op. cit.,* p. 58.
[22] Jay W. Forrester, *Industrial Dynamics,* Massachusetts Institute of Technology Press, Cambridge, Mass., 1961, pp. 14–16.

a continuous circular process, much like a loop. This loop principle appears in business affairs: it turns up in order and inventory levels which lead to manufacturing decisions which fill orders, correct inventories, and yield further manufacturing decisions. The principle also applies to the profitable industry which lures competitors until profit margins are reduced to equilibrium with other economic forces so that competitors cease entering the field. Or it could apply to the competitive need for a new product which inspires research and development expenditure which, in turn, produces technological change.

To convey the nature of a typical system one might find in business, Forrester has used the analogy of a person who, trying to drive an automobile while blindfolded, obtains information from someone sitting in the back seat. Top management does not see the salesman on his selling job, nor does it see the prospects viewing its advertisements. It does not attend board meetings of its competitors. The only thing of which it is certain is past performance. However, a company may resort nowadays to a computer to simulate reality, noting the impact of various actions on the market through a system of loops.

The Systems Approach

Rhochromatics. The systems, or the rhochromatics,[23] approach to the science of marketing regards marketing activity as part of the whole economic process of producing goods and services and delivering them to the consumer. This approach begins by reviewing the function of marketing in relation to the objectives of the business, and then ascertains the marketing costs and results vis à vis other functions of the business. It might be possible, for example, to pare the cost of packaging by using new types of material or new packaging machinery. However, the more basic problem would be to investigate the cost of packaging relative to costs of handling, transportation, and advertising. This may disclose changes that take place in these other functions.

In another area this approach might prove useful when fluctuating production prevents the realization of economies of scale; in such instances economies of marketing might offset this additional cost.

[23] From the Greek *rho,* meaning to flow, as a river or stream; *chrema,* meaning products, materials, or things; and the abstract *-ies* for any of the sciences; see also Stanley H. Brewer, *Rhochromatics: A Scientific Approach to Management of Material and Material Flows,* University of Washington, Bureau of Business Research, Seattle, 1960.

More specifically, the manager views the business as a flow of various resources: information, materials, manpower, capital equipment, and money. Every one of these elements is regarded as a component of the total system, and efficiency becomes the measure of this input in relation to output.

Handling of Inventory. One area to which rhochromatics has been applied is the handling of inventory. Because of the increasing line of products they handle, manufacturers tend to decrease the total volume of each item, thereby increasing the individual handling costs. It has been found, for instance, that increasing the variety from one item to three expands the field inventories by 60 per cent. If total sales rise 50 per cent, the inventory requirement doubles.[24] Moreover, a small percentage of the total inventory, 10 to 20 per cent, accounts for 80 per cent of the sales.[25]

Flow Cycle. The flow cycle is also aided by the rhochromatics approach. This is the cycle in effect from the time management decides to manufacture the product until the product is distributed. All materials have to be ordered in advance, and it takes time for them to be transported and processed. This time gains in significance when it is known that competitors may turn out the same product. Another problem is the phasing out of obsolete inventory which has certain costs associated with it. Who shall assume the burden of these costs —the retailer, the wholesaler, or the manufacturer?

Industrial Dynamics. Because of the complexity of many systems there is a need for the development of models that can be used for simulation. A great amount of work has been done in this area under the general descriptive title of *industrial dynamics.*[26] The elements of industrial dynamics are the following: (1) information-feedback control theory; (2) the decision-making process; (3) experimental approach to systems analysis (model building); (4) the use of digital computers. Under this system, inputs vary with their impacts noted in the output.

It has been suggested that a company's share of the market depends in part on its service.[27] As its service increases so may its share of the market. One way of increasing the service factor is to reduce the

[24] John F. Magee, "The Logistics of Distribution," *Harvard Business Review,* July–August 1960, pp. 90–91.

[25] *Ibid.,* p. 91.

[26] Forrester, *op. cit.*

[27] Johnson, *op. cit.*

time of delivery by locating inventory closer to the customer. The amount of inventory that should be stored in a regional warehouse is governed by the estimated demand of customers in the region. This is difficult to estimate accurately and consequently imposes a certain amount of risk. However, a company may minimize the amount of risk by estimating the probability of the number of times out of 100 in which it might be feasible to run out of stock.

A company, for example, may wish to maintain enough inventory so that it will run out of stock only ten times out of 100. The additional cost of maintaining a stock large enough to satisfy all the customers all the time would be prohibitive. In certain instances it might be feasible to add to the service the inventory located at a central distribution point rather than to increase the regional inventories. This would apply where the costs of handling and servicing offsets the increased costs of transportation.

Management might do well to measure the time it takes to move inventory from the warehouse to the customer. The time element in this delivery cycle may be minimized through the use of mechanical devices for handling materials and the use of computers to bill and control the inventory. In some instances it has been found practical to use air freight to increase service. This increased value of the service plus the cost savings in inventory has proved attractive for many kinds of products.

Summary

Forces both inside and outside a company have been responsible for advancing the science of marketing and the concept of marketing management as we know them today. Some of the internal forces have been consumer orientation, greater emphasis on planning, and a need for better coordination of the elements of marketing activity with the production process. Some of the external forces known to have influenced the marketing science are the scientific management movement, competitive changes in the economy, and the newer role of government in the field of investment.

The major objective of most companies is to maximize the return on their investments discounted to the present moment.

A logical approach to planning is the development of a model of the activities under consideration. Planning is no longer confined to a period of a year but extends over much greater units of time. In an organizational sense, an enterprise must arrange for more staff assistance at top management levels if its planning endeavors are to be successful. One of the newer ideas in planning is the creation of a marketing development department to concentrate on innovations for use in determining the marketing program of the future.

Planning activity has been developed to a considerable extent by the armed forces to expedite the production of space equipment. Both PERT and PEP have been useful in the elimination of bottlenecks and the speeding up of the over-all operation. One may distinguish between routine decisions amenable to programming and those of a more than routine character which cannot be programmed.

Along with planning there is need for some sort of control to assist in future planning. The newest approach to both planning and control is the systems approach. Applied to the science of marketing, this approach has been called rhochromatics.

Suggested Cases

Ralph L. Westfall and Harper W. Boyd, *Cases in Marketing Management,* Irwin, Homewood, Ill., 1961.

Union Carbide Consumer Products Company—*Antifreeze Manufacturer* —General Marketing Plan, pp. 7–16.

United Air Lines—*Airline*—Defining Market Niche for Service Firm, pp. 41–48.

Milton P. Brown, Wilbur B. England, and John B. Matthews, Jr., *Problems in Marketing,* 3rd ed., McGraw-Hill, New York, 1961.

Marlin Firearm Company, pp. 99–103.

Regulus Clock Company (a), pp. 61–78.

Harry L. Hansen, *Marketing: Text, Cases, and Readings,* rev. ed., Irwin, Homewood, Ill., 1961.

Benjamin Corporation, pp. 862–875.

Anthony, Inc., pp. 876–893.

Kenneth R. Davis, *Marketing Management,* Ronald Press, New York, 1961.

General Electric Company, pp. 798–807.

Intercollegiate Case Clearing House, Soldiers Field, Boston 63, Massachusetts.

ICH 3G27—Precision Electronic Corporation.

ICH 3M41—The Dow Chemical Company (b).

Chapter Two

A company justifies its existence by its ability to supply its customers
or clientele with the utility of its product or service. To the extent
that it provides this utility, a company is likely to profit in return.
The product's utility encompasses more than the physical object
alone. It is an aspect of the imagery surrounding a product or service.
For example, the fact that a product is manufactured by a well-known
company rather than some unknown one adds extra value to it. Similarly, other factors affect the imagery evoked by a product. These
may include the size, shape, and color of its container as well as of
the product itself; the style and size of the print on its label; the
placement and environment of the product on the shelf; its price;
what personal salesmanship has to say about it; the advertising program; and finally, the quality of the store that stocks the product.
All these considerations occupy the attention of the forces in a company concerned with product management.

Product Management

Product management embraces the planning and control of every phase of a product or product line from the inception of the original idea to the demise of demand for the object. It begins with the encouragement of research on new product ideas conceived by engineers and marketing men and tests these ideas to learn whether they should be subjected to further exploration and development. Sometimes the product managers themselves may engage in research to acquire leads for new products. Either way, once an idea is deemed feasible, plans are made to expose it to a pilot testing. In preparation for the pilot, the financial, production, and personnel arms of the company are consulted. If the pilot proves satisfactory, further plans are perfected to permit the formal introduction of the product to a large market.

The experience obtained during the pilot phase is extended to the wider undertaking, although various new ideas may be suggested by the test and applied to the project. Now the product is ready for mass marketing, behooving the product manager to coordinate the advertising, personal selling, and sales promotional programs. If sales develop suitably, the product manager has to make his product profitable without reducing its competitiveness. He may find it necessary to experiment with price, advertising, distribution channels, packaging, and in some instances with minor modifications of the product itself. If the rate of profit fails to keep step with the additional costs of these adjustments, it may be prudent to withdraw the product from the market.

In this chapter we shall deal with managerial functions as they apply to product management. We shall begin with a study of the planning and control of products, discussing both the controllable and uncontrollable aspects of product planning. Then we shall consider the organization of forces for product management.

Planning and Control

Controllable Aspects

The planning of a merchandisable product covers a variety of tasks. Selecting the product to be manufactured or stocked, deciding on size, form, and appearance, choosing the packaging, setting the quantities to be made or bought, picking the time to produce or purchase, settling on the price line to be processed or carried—all these, and more, are manifestations of *product planning*.

Product planning is the anticipation by a company of products that will answer a consumer's needs and desires before he is consciously aware of them. The consumer may have certain latent desires for new products and services, which he cannot communicate formally to the company. Only by approaching the consumer directly can the manufacturer hope to uncover what some of these hidden desires might be. At his command are formal quantitative research and motivational research; or he may rely on intuition. The "hula-hoop" craze represents a product based on a manufacturer's intuitive feeling. Often product and fashion designers operate in this manner, working on "hunches" or a "feel" about what will please the consumer. The late Christian Dior, for example, excited the consuming market with his "new look." Yet there is no assurance of success from intuitive action; Dior also created designs, such as his "H," which failed to titillate the public.

The crux of modern planning is adaptability to change. Changes occur rapidly, especially in matters of taste. It is estimated among food companies that nine out of ten products currently on the shelves were unknown or not available a dozen years ago. And there are many companies in all sorts of industrial activity now working on products to be sold to the public ten to fifteen years hence. Not every product introduced by a company automatically gains public acceptance. More than half of the new products launched in any year prove failures—largely because of poor planning or lack of foresight, but also because of the speed of product change. No doubt, one of the most dramatic changes in this respect is the role taken by government in demanding new products for military and space use. The magnitude of the space program alone already equals the total expenditure of the automotive industry.

From a Keynesian point of view [1] the development of new products is a source of investment. If the economy is to grow, further investment must take place. Schumpeter [2] pointed out in addition that, for the economy to grow, innovation was imperative. Innovation may occur among both consumer and industrial products, and the new products offer the public a higher standard of living, not only in this country, but also in any other country that does business with the United States. Through broad programs of research and development, American industry expresses its intention to create and perfect these new products.

Specific Incentives

The *specific incentives for product development* may be grouped broadly into three categories: those relating to production, marketing, and the market. [3]

Production. In the case of production, the incentive is often the desire to utilize excess capacity made available by seasonal or cyclical factors, or by anything else that contributes to less than capacity use of productive facilities. It may come also from the wish to make profitable use of waste products or from an awareness of the high manufacturing cost of the old product. On occasion it may be wholly accidental; that is, a research team or a laboratory staff might be exploring one problem and light upon something quite different which lends itself to practical development.

Marketing. The marketing considerations fall into various areas such as the product needs of the consumer, price matters, distribution channels, advertising, personal selling, and purchasing. With respect to consumer needs, the incentive for developing some new product is prompted by many factors. These include complaints, sales returns and allowances, and the need to eliminate unproductive service calls.

---

[1] J. M. Keynes, *The General Theory of Employment, Interest and Money,* Harcourt, Brace, New York, 1936.

[2] Joseph A. Schumpeter, *Business Cycles: A Theoretical, Historical and Statistical Analysis of the Capitalist Process,* Vols. I and II, McGraw-Hill, New York, 1939.

[3] Classified from listings in following sources: Dudley M. Phelps, *Planning The Product,* Irwin, Homewood, Ill., 1947; Gustav E. Larson, *Developing and Selling New Products: A Guidebook for Manufacturers,* 2nd ed., U.S. Dept. of Commerce, Small Business Admin., Washington, D.C., 1955; C. J. Courtney, *A Checklist for Marketing Management Dealing with the Business Functions of Marketing,* College of Commerce, Creighton University, Omaha, Neb., 1955.

They also include tiring of the old product and technological and market changes that render it obsolete. Besides, suitable new things are required for impulse or experimental buying and for point-of-sale purchase, needs still unmet must be recognized, and use of acceptable products must be broadened. As for price matters, rapid increases spur product development such as the shift from regular to instant coffee for reasons of economy. Moreover, price lines may be extended so that additional sales may be effected to spread the fixed costs and put the product into a more favorable price position. In distribution, changes become necessary when, for example, a factory has to carry a greater line of products to reduce costs should it have to replace or drop a wholesaler, or when a company is called on to protect its exclusive dealer arrangements. In advertising, brand loyalty provides an advantage which may be used profitably for marketing a new product. In personal selling, the sales force can take on a new product in established sales territories without damaging sales of existing products. Finally, in purchasing, the inability to obtain supplies from usual sources is the incentive for the development of new ones.

The Market. Here the competitive action of rival companies or some new or improved product generates the incentive for product development. Then, too, the practice of the trade often requires the introduction of new models periodically, and both new markets and new needs open opportunities for new products.

Marketing Research

Quantitative and Qualitative Research. Of the two, quantitative research pertains to the direct approach to a new product. It involves the presentation of a questionnaire to the general public with such straightforward questions as "Will you buy this product if it is put on the market?" Qualitative research, in contrast, endeavors to probe the prospective buyer's attitudes and motivations through depth interviewing or through use of projective devices.

Quantitative research has not been proved foolproof. The first study on portable television sets, a quantitative undertaking, indicated that no market existed for them. But one executive who had an intuitive "hunch" disregarded the findings and decided to produce a portable TV set notwithstanding. It was, of course, an instant success. The Chrysler Corporation had a similar experience. It surveyed consumers and found that they wanted a stripped-down economical car. The following year Chrysler made such a car, but discovered that it would not sell. The year after Chrysler elected to stress styling and chrome, and achieved a banner sales record. In both cases quantitative research gave the wrong answers. Yet this does not imply that research is useless. It means that research must dig beneath the quick, easy answers to questions to uncover an individual's more basic thinking. Motivational research has accomplished many things in this area, as we shall eventually see.

Marketing research often lends a helping hand to the engineer responsible for the design of a product. His challenge is to design something that will perform a particular job. He does not care about the frills that might add other utility. He is concerned with the basic value or combination of values delivered to the consumer. Generally he approaches his task from the point of view of rational behavior in which the individual maximizes a product's utility. His problem is the lack of an adequate theory of rational behavior.[4] One cannot know exactly how a rational man will choose between gambles. No one knows in general how to predict rational behavior under conditions of complex knowledge any more than under conditions of ignorance. Marketing research may aid the engineer, however, to discern those qualities in a product that are visible to the consumer, but that are not necessarily rational in the view of the engineer.

Frequently, the engineering department of a company develops several potential new products which appear to be profitable. The company has to decide whether to pursue the development of all of these or to focus on those that promise the highest return. Through consumer surveys of the likely acceptance of these new products, marketing research can help narrow the area in which the engineers concentrate their efforts.

Testing. Not all products yield easily to a market test. In general it is difficult and expensive to conduct market tests on consumer durable goods. The cost of setting up a pilot operation is considerably more than for nondurable items. But if the change is of a minor nature and does not necessitate a major alteration in the assembly line, a limited model may be developed for testing purposes. Market testing of durable goods in need of large retooling jobs usually is accomplished through information gathered from consumer motivational studies and studies of buying-habit patterns and use.

Other Areas. Essentially, the marketing research department of a company reports to management the changing consumer habits and

[4] C. West Churchman, *Prediction and Optimal Decision,* Prentice-Hall, Englewood Cliffs, N.J., 1961, p. 243.

motives that suggest the direction new product development should take. Ideas for new products may emerge from studies of how products are being used at present as well as from information on customer satisfaction or dissatisfaction with existing items. Some companies maintain experimental kitchens in which they study the daily household tasks of housewives. From their findings they are able to suggest how work in the kitchen can be made easier or more efficient. Sometimes fixed or traveling exhibits elicit consumer reaction to a new product idea. In addition, consumer panels have proven effective in testing products, and consumer "brainstorming" sessions have generated many good ideas for new products.

One interesting idea contained a "do-it-yourself" element. The company involved manufactured kitchen ranges. Seeking a new design for its product, the company invited consumers to assemble different parts of the range themselves into models best suited to their needs and tastes. The result was a variety of tops, fronts, and sides, and also a wide variety of range sizes.

Sources of Information

The sources of ideas for product development are several; they come from members of a company's staff, from distributors, competitors, and government, and from a miscellany of other areas. Within the company itself ideas for new products may spring from the research, engineering, and sales staffs; they may originate in the market research department, in sales reports, in employee or customer suggestions, or from inquiries and complaints. The records of adjustments, sales returns, and allowances in the accounting department, the service department's record of repairs, and analyses of sales records relating to parts are also internal sources of new product ideas.

Among the distributive forces, brokers, wholesale jobbers, manufacturers' agents, and retailers all may contribute to creation of new items. Or the impetus may stem from a company's competitors through their customers, products, catalogs, exhibits, and trade shows, as well as from products manufactured abroad.

The government is also a source of product inspiration. Companies may draw on information gathered by various agencies such as the Department of Commerce, Department of Justice, Department of Agriculture, Government Patents Board, and Small Business Administration. They may call on the Office of Alien Property, the Patent

Office, the Office of Technical Services, the Business and Defense Services Administration, the Bureau of Foreign Commerce, and the National Bureau of Standards for data that could lead to product development.

Finally, there are miscellaneous sources for new product ideas in a score of directions. They may lodge in companies for sale or in companies relinquishing individual lines. They may flow from inventors, patent attorneys and brokers, manufacturers of parts and accessories, or university and institute laboratories. Advertising leads to suggestions from the public or industry; moreover, advertising agencies, trade-magazine writers and editors, trade-association executives and laboratory personnel are all capable of initiating proposals for new things. And ideas are virtually the end product of commercial laboratories, industrial consultants, management engineers, product engineers, market research agencies, and banks and other financial organizations. In sum, just about anybody, everybody, and everything is a potential source of a new product.

Strategy and Policy

Functions of Policy. Product policy serves three main purposes.[5] It helps to supply the information needed to make decisions on the product line. Second, it gives the responsible executives a supplementary check on the usual estimates of profit and loss. Third, it guides and directs the activities of the entire organization toward a single goal.

Steps in Developing Policy. Development of a product policy consists of two major steps. The first calls for the making of a careful inventory of resources; the second is the actual developing of the policy. The following chart [6] suggests the factors to be checked in conducting the inventory.

Inventory of Company Resources

Financial strength	Money available or obtainable for financing research and development, plant construction, inventory, receivables, working capital, and operating losses in the early stages of commercial operation.

---

[5] Charles H. Kline, "The Strategy of Product Policy," *Harvard Business Review,* Vol. 33, No. 4, July–August 1955, pp. 91–100.
[6] *Ibid.*

Raw material reserves	Ownership of, or preferential access to, natural resources such as minerals and ores, brine deposits, natural gas, forests.
Physical plant	Manufacturing plant, research and testing facilities, warehouses, branch offices, trucks, tankers.
Location	Situation of plant or other physical facilities with relation to markets, raw materials, or utilities.
Patents	Ownership or control of a technical monopoly through patents.
Public acceptance	Brand preference, market contracts, and other public support built up by successful performance in the past.
Specialized experience	Unique or uncommon knowledge of manufacturing, distribution, scientific fields, or managerial techniques.
Personnel	Payroll of skilled labor, salesmen, engineers, or other workers with definite specialized abilities.
Management	Professional skill, experience, ambition, and will for growth of the company's leadership.

Some of the matters to be considered in the development of a product policy fall under these headings:

1. Financial investment
2. Sales volume
3. Channels of distribution
4. Effect of new products on old products
5. Effect on competition
6. Cyclical stability
7. Raw materials
8. Value added by new products
9. Effect on manufacturing load
10. Effect on market mix
11. Effect on advertising
12. Effect on pricing
13. Effect on organization

If a large financial investment is required but the company's resources are limited, this circumstance imposes restraints on the operation. Funds available for physical research, testing, and eventual promotion of the product are necessarily limited. In the area of sales volume the company needs to know the present level as well as the volume anticipated with the proposed products. To put it another way, the company has to know the market opportunity or the market potential. Furthermore, the company must decide whether it can continue to employ its existing channels of distribution or whether it will have to open a new one.

To determine the effect of a new product on an old one, a company must question factors of sales, profit, and competition. Will the new product, for instance, impinge on the sales of the old one? How will the new and old products combined affect total sales and profit data? Will the new product invite competitors to enter the market? If it should, what is likely to happen to the size of the market? As for the new product's cyclical stability, the management has to assess how it will help the company at the low end of the business cycle and what its effect is likely to be on the high end.

Turning to raw materials, does the company have access to an adequate supply of them at favorable prices? Then there are questions about the value added by the new product and its effect on the manufacturing load. First of all, does the product add to or detract from the total value of the company's operation? Next, will present manufacturing facilities suffice or will they have to be expanded to accommodate the new venture? Under the latter alternative, will the additional sales revenue justify the expenditure incurred?

As to the remaining matters in developing a product policy, how important is the proposed item in the company's market mix? How much emphasis should be given to innovation, pricing, advertising, and channels of distribution? How will the new product affect the total quantity and quality of advertising used at the present time? How will it fit into the current pricing structure? Finally, what changes in the organization of the company will the new product require so that it can be developed and sold successfully.

Types of Strategies. A company may pursue several strategies in relation to product development. These can pertain to the timing of the product, product obsolescence, simplification and diversification, following or leading competitors, and share of the market. We shall discuss each of these strategies separately.

1. TIMING. The timing of a new product depends on such matters as product acceptance, trends in demand, and growth cycles. When Chrysler first introduced the automatic gear shift it failed to increase the sales of its cars because the public was not ready for this kind of mechanical improvement. Similarly, farmers did not immediately accept hybrid seed corn; it took them ten years to come around to it.

But once they accepted the idea, it was no longer difficult to win positive support for many other types of hybrid seeds.

The process of acceptance of something new follows a clearly defined progression. The concept is taken up first by a person called an *innovator*. In the case of new farming practices this type of individual has enough resources to engage in experimentation. The next person to fall into line is the *leader*, a well-informed individual who is always seeking new ways to do things. He takes the calculated risk of using the new product. If the product proves useful to him, the *local adopter* begins to employ it. A natural leader in his own right at the local scene, this individual is active in civic organizations and enjoys the confidence of many people. After the local adopter joins the users, the mass public follows his lead and the product wins its consuming market.

If a company could predict the rate of acceptance, it could adjust its resources and manufacturing output on the basis of this rate. To be able to do so, however, it would have to identify the various leaders and estimate their acceptance by studying the experience of similar products in times past. The buyers of different classes of products, of course, are likely to be influenced by different types of leaders.[7] One type of woman might influence the purchase of washing machines and another type the buying of baking mixes. In each case the various leaders after they have been identified might be formed into panels to test the degree of acceptance of new product ideas in their particular areas.

Besides the matter of acceptance, the company must discern whether there is a favorable trend of demand for the projected product. If there is not, the company ordinarily cannot "buck" a trend.[8] At the present time there is a favorable trend of demand for automatic washing machines, but an unfavorable one for the wringer type. If fewer and fewer companies manufacture and sell a product when its demand trend is declining, any single company may receive an increasing share of this falling trend or it may devote its resources to a smaller share of the rising trend of some other product.

[7] Elihu Katz, "The Social Itinerary of Technical Change; Two Studies on the Diffusion of Innovation," *Human Organization*, Vol. 20, No. 2, 1961, pp. 70–82.
[8] Bucking a trend is defined as marketing a product or service that does not conform to the existing psychological and social needs and habit patterns of the consumer. It may be thought of in terms of primary demand trends versus selective demand trends. In the latter case the consumer may be manipulated. George Romney recognized this possibility and marketed the first of the American compact cars.

Also bearing on the question of timing is that a product, like any living organism, has a cycle of growth.[9] The product is introduced to the public, and a slow period of growth ensues. This is followed by a more rapid term of growth until the maximum growth rate begins to taper off.

The rate of growth may be calculated on the basis of the share of the potential market which the company expects to possess in the future—say, three, four, or five years later. This kind of analysis indicates how a company's operation relates to a normal rate of expansion. If the company fails to keep abreast of its predicted share of the market this might be attributed to the actions of competitors, whereas if it exceeds its predicted share this may mean that external conditions have made the product more acceptable than anticipated.

A company's strategy for any product will vary according to the stage of the growth cycle. In the early phase of the cycle the company is concerned mainly with production problems and obtaining outlets for its product. In the next phase it dwells on advertising and personal selling effort to increase its share of the market. At the mature stage it occupies itself with market research to find where its most profitable share lies and with whatever management reorganization might be necessary to achieve better coordination of its handling of the product.

Some products have a remarkably short growth period. This is particularly true of style or fashion merchandise, drug preparations, and some cosmetics. When a company knows that its product has this limitation, it has to adjust its expenditure in such a way as to be able to recover it in a very short time. The Toni company, for example, hopes to recoup its investment in its products within a year. The automobile industry, on the other hand, likes to get its investment back over a period of years, especially in the area of compact cars.

For these product growth cycles, estimates of sales volume may be derived from comparisons of past data on similar or related products. A model developed for styled merchandise might apply in this case.[10] First, a company must estimate a series of growth curves

[9] Ralph Butler, "Growth Pattern for New Specialty Products: A Case Study," *Journal of Marketing,* Vol. 11, No. 1, July 1946, pp. 27–34.

[10] D. B. Hertz and K. H. Schaffir, "A Forecasting Method for Management of Seasonal Style—Goods Inventories," *Operations Research,* Vol. 8, No. 1, January–February 1960, pp. 45–52.

for products similar to the one under consideration. Figure 2-1 illustrates such a curve. In the illustration the percentage of the complete time cycle appears along the horizontal axis and the percentage of cumulative sales along the vertical axis. If the company knows the average duration of the cycle it can estimate the total sales volume. For example, let us assume that a product has reached point A of the complete growth cycle on the diagram in Figure 2-1. Point A represents 10 per cent of total sales. If sales were 1000 units at point A, total sales over the whole cycle would be 1000/.20 or 5000 units.

2. PRODUCT OBSOLESCENCE. A leading automobile manufacturer has said that the principal objective of his industry is to promote rapid obsolescence. Just as nothing is staler than yesterday's newspaper, so, in his opinion, is last year's car a relic. Anyone wanting to keep up with the crowd has to have a new automobile annually. The industry relies on all sorts of appeals to reinforce this impression. The status symbol claim has a persuasive influence on many members of the consuming public. What the automobile industry has taught by

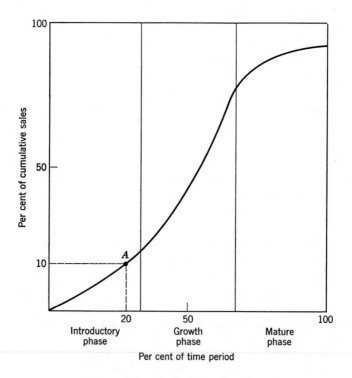

Figure 2-1. Product growth cycle.

its techniques to boost sales has been well learned by appliance manufacturers and other industries.

Some economists view with alarm this glaring waste of the nation's resources. Rather than proliferate products, they contend, it would be preferable to create more leisure time. This argument seems to ignore the economic truth that if factories did not manufacture new products their markets would be limited. Production would then suffer, and a condition of "forced" leisure—unemployment—would eventuate. Nevertheless, two-thirds of a group of businessmen have said there is too much product obsolescence.[11]

In the automotive field rapid obsolescence has created the used-car market. If a person of limited income cannot afford a bright, shiny, new automobile he can wait a year or two and buy the model at a substantial reduction. As most automobiles, despite the blandishments of their makers, are built to last more than two years, the purchaser of a used car may very well acquire satisfactory and attractive transportation for several years to come. To a lesser extent, the same thing holds for the appliance industry. However, there has been little encouragement in the past among appliance dealers of trading in used products for new ones. The industry should support this practice because it will achieve the same economic effect as the sale of used cars. It will permit individuals in the lower-income brackets to enjoy some of the comforts of contemporary life without having to pay the full price of a new appliance. Simultaneously, it will protect the production lines from enforced slow downs.

3. SIMPLIFICATION AND DIVERSIFICATION. Simplifying the product line means reducing the variety of items sold by a company. Diversification refers to the converse—an expansion of the variety of goods sold by the company to the public. For the latter to take place some degree of product differentiation also must occur. This requires one to consider the segmentation of the market, as we shall shortly see.

Mass merchandising nowadays attempts to appeal to the average consumer. Companies that concentrate on the average consumer do not stock as broad a line in sizes and quality as those that tend to reach a wider market. Many discount houses, for example, are able to undersell traditional competitors handling the same merchandise because of the reduced number of items carried by the discounters. The consumer benefits from the savings in distribution and production costs which are passed on to him. In endeavoring

[11] John B. Stewart, "Planned Obsolescence," *Harvard Business Review,* Vol. 37, No. 5, 1959, pp. 14–28, 168–174.

to concentrate on the average consumer, a company has to consider some of these factors:

Consumer use	Shape
Consumer buying habits	Design and styling
Distributive buying	Design obsolescence
Competition	Color
Selling methods	Texture
Sales promotion	Typography
Value	Production costs
Relation to a line	Trade marking
Appearance strategy	Installation and service
Performance	Shipping
Materials	Legal problems
Size	

Generally, a company with a large variety of products will find that a preponderance of its sales occur among a few items. Most of its income derives from this limited portion of its line. It is only natural for companies to wonder often whether it is profitable to carry all their lines. An analysis of the cost of distribution may indicate the profitability of the various products. However, profitability is not the only criterion for retaining a product. A company may have to market a product, even at a loss, to provide customers with service they expect. Thus, a company must weigh the advantages of good will and continued patronage for its unprofitable lines against the larger profits that may eventuate from the addition of new products to the line. Long-run profits rather than short-run contribution to total profits should be the criterion.

In the literature of marketing the policy of simplification has been referred to as the *drop* policy. Products may be dropped because they were mistakenly added to the line or were unavoidable acquisitions. Or they may be dropped because of obsolescence or improvements in rival products. When a product shows a poor record of performance in the market place, its manufacturer may follow one of four courses. The company may improve production techniques and keep the product. It may continue to manufacture the product but sell it to others in bulk for them to market. It may continue the sale of the product but turn over the manufacturing phase to some other company that can produce it more efficiently. Or it can drop the product altogether by ceasing to make and sell it.

Before choosing to discontinue either the manufacture or marketing of the product, a company can consider three possible areas for improvement—increased marketing efficiency, reduced production costs, and better product. To raise the efficiency of the marketing operation necessitates a determined effort by management to keep adequate records of distribution costs and to make a periodic analysis of these data. Although reduction of productive costs presumably is the concern of a company's production managers, a conflict generally emerges between marketing and production forces over the matter of quality. The producers as a rule are more cost minded, whereas the marketing personnel are always preoccupied with the quality of the product to enhance its salability. These differences are usually compromised in such a way that reductions in distribution costs often more than offset the additional production costs for the resulting product. As to product improvement, efforts should be concentrated on products that are currently in an inferior competitive position, or that relate to the company's existing resources, or in which a small amount of research may accomplish great improvement; the governing factor is profitability.

Before a product is dropped because of apparent unprofitability, a company might wish to examine whether the product is meeting overhead. If, in fact, the product does contribute to overhead, the company may feel justified in keeping it alive as it may enable economies of scale which can be passed along to other of its products. It may pay to weigh the advantages to the over-all profit objective of either continuing or dropping a particular product. In many instances a company will discover that by dropping one product and shifting its attention to some more profitable one, its total net profit may show an increase.

Once a company chooses to simplify by paring its line of products, it runs greater risks. Some of these risks relate to competing with the wider variety of products offered by rivals who proffer complete lines of merchandise to distributors and retailers. The cost benefits of simplification, however, may provide a price advantage in competitive situations. Another sort of risk brought on by simplification is design obsolescence. If a competitor designs a superior product or a practical substitute, a company may lose its leadership position in the particular field.

Diversification, as we have remarked, is the opposite of simplification. One impetus to diversification is the discovery of products that enjoy some superiority over competing ones. There are three broad but distinct areas in which a manufacturer may search for this advantage—geography, technology, and the marketing apparatus.[12] These three possible areas must be considered in terms of basic economic opportunities and also in relation to competitive operating factors.

Geography may contribute to a successful diversification of the product line if there is an inadequate number of suppliers in a specific market to meet the existing demand. Making succotash available to the southern market would be a case in point. Advanced technology may help a company to gain a foothold over its competitors in a field selected for diversification—for example, the ability to apply the oxygen process to the smelting of steel. Finally, a company with well-organized, effective channels of distribution might find them particularly suited to new products and capitalize on them to establish a strong position in the market, while rival efforts and strategy remain in a state of general confusion. A food manufacturer, it is evident, would have little difficulty with any product sold in a food store.

Broadly speaking, the cost of acquiring a specific share of the market through diversification should not exceed a reasonable purchase price for a company already operating successfully in the selected field. Moreover, the cost of entry into and the anticipated profit from the new field should present at least as favorable a prospect as might be expected from directing the additional effort toward increasing the company's efficiency or share of the market in its present endeavors. That is to say, the costs and profit outlook of going into new fields should be compared to the costs and outlook of expanding the sales of existing lines.

Whether to engage in diversification should rest on several criteria. A company should have a clear conception of its product line as a whole as a result of diversifying. Then it should screen the prospective product from various vantage points. Next, management should have some appreciation of the problems of introducing the new product and understand whether it satisfies the conditions of product differentiation. Finally, it must look into the consequent segmentation of the market.

The kind of product line to which a company aspires depends on its ultimate conception of itself. A new product which seems to offer promise of profitability may have to be rejected because it conflicts with the successful sale of the current line. Perhaps the better way

---

[12] Wroe Alderson and Robert E. Sessions, "A Program of Product Line Diversification," *Cost and Profit Outlook*, Vol. VII, No. 8, August 1954.

to approach a potential new product is to begin with the market and add those products that serve end purposes similar to those of existing products or that can be distributed through the same channels of trade. Extension of the product line has to fit the company's own view of its capacity to sell, produce, and organize for change.

The first step in screening the product is to develop a profile of the market for the proposed item. Usually it is possible to estimate the size of the total market in relation to both dollar volume and physical units. The structure of the market should be studied. Then the nature and extent of advertising and personal selling expenditures may provide some insight into the cost of entry and the likelihood of long-term survival. The degree of potential competitors' market and financial strength is also of importance. And the physical characteristics and market acceptance of products available at the current time need to be reviewed and evaluated.

If the product passes the screening test, the company studies how to bring it to the market. Here it should follow a standard outline or check list covering all aspects of product introduction even though they may vary from one product to another. Even if the product moves directly from the manufacturer to its ultimate consumer, an analysis of trade practices is necessary. A wide variety of trade information has to be collected and weighed to enable an appraisal of existing competitive conditions, trade data, and potential opportunity. The most fundamental source of this information is the channels of distribution utilized for currently available products. Over and above the number, location, and trade status of outlets, the appraiser has to determine the markets and geographic area served by each type of outlet as well as the relative importance and effectiveness of each channel of trade. If the existing channels are monopolized by its competitors, a company must either build an entirely new system of distribution or refrain from entering the market.

Both profit margins and the structure of discounts to the trade figure prominently in this phase of the study. The manufacturer also must assess the significance of indirect contributions to the profits of the trade through price guarantees, or discounts and allowances in special circumstances or for special services. If the estimate of potential volume is the important factor, the research staff has the difficult task of projecting a sales trend for the new product, which starts from zero. It may often solve the problem by considering itself engaged in a study of the effects of substituting one product for another. Past sales trends of products used in the same way as the prospective one may shed some light on sales potentialities. The unknown element is how fast the new product can be substituted for its predecessor under the existing assumptions about price and promotion. As a starting point one might refer to the market potential indicated by the screening study.

For some manufactured products the market is characterized by imperfect competition. In such cases product differentiation assumes more importance than competing through prices. Differentiation may take the form of minor variations in the product, such as the swinging shelves in a refrigerator, filter-flow in an automatic washing machine, or halo-light in a television set. Differentiation also may take place in the package, the color of the product, its name, or sensory appeal. Through the product and the accompanying promotional effort, a company endeavors to create in the mind of the consumer an image that differentiates its product from others. This image may be associated with either the product itself or the company that manufactures it. Some products may be considered masculine, others feminine; some may give the housewife the feeling that she is more efficient; some may inspire a feeling of esteem or a sense of status. Some companies may evoke an image of friendliness; others may be thought of as authoritarian, big, local, or progressive. When Betty Furness says "you can be sure," one has confidence in the brand of product she is promoting. When Ronald Reagan says "progress is our most important product," one feels one is dealing with a progressive company when buying the brand he promotes.

In developing product differentiation a company must be aware of the growing interest in esthetic products, the convenience needs of the consumer, and the quality of product available on the market. Product planners must recognize that the public is interested in an item that not only serves a functional purpose but also has esthetic appeal. With larger amounts of spendable income, the public prefers a product that both does the job and is pleasing to the eye. This applies to the container and the packaging of the product as well as to the product itself.

The consumer's desire for convenience has presented management with many new opportunities for differentiating its products. But managers must remain flexible to shift their decisions with the changing markets and the changing habits and desires of the consumer. Good product-planning strategy requires a repertoire of possible actions, for sound decision making in the world of business is not hasty but careful and deliberate, based on the anticipation of needs and the application of appropriate action to meet each need.

There is a trend toward purchasing more convenience. We have

conveniences in ready mixes, and frozen, dehydrated, and cold prepared foods. We have convenience in driving automobiles, washing
and ironing clothes, and cooking foods. This has enabled women
to join the labor force more easily. In the 1950's every other new
worker was a woman and now women constitute one-third of the total
labor force. Working women and those who will be working in the
future do not have as much time as others for household chores.
Conveniences save valuable time for them. It also creates greater
leisure opportunities for all, and business and industry have responded
to this development with several new goods and services. Boating
and the do-it-yourself movement both exemplify industries that have
grown phenomenally on the back of increased leisure time.

Quality does not always require the best quality of any particular
product. The average individual, for example, cannot hear sounds
beyond a specific range of frequency. Therefore, it is absurd to build
a "hi-fi" set that exceeds the average perception of sound. A company
may, of course, wish to manufacture a few highly priced units for the
discriminating minority who can encompass a broader frequency
range than the ordinary man. But the mass market lies among those
of average hearing ability.

4. SEGMENTATION OF THE MARKET. Often differentiation may be
accompanied by segmentation of the market. There are several reasons for this sort of diversity.[13] For instance, manufacturers may use
different types of equipment and processes in turning out products for
the same purpose. One manufacturer may have superior resources or
a more favorable location to exploit. Among competitors progress in
the design and development of new products may not be equal. Moreover, some manufacturers may find it hard to eliminate product
variation even under conditions of strict quality control. In addition,
producers do not tend to make like estimates of the tastes of consumers with respect to color, material, and other aspects of manufactured objects.

An individual consumer may have a wide range of ideas in mind
when he shops. It is the objective of the manufacturer to narrow
this range to the limited selection it offers the public. To achieve
a convergence of the two ranges, the company employs advertising
in an endeavor to create additional images on behalf of its particular
products. Sometimes companies decide to accept the divergent demand and adjust their product offerings to the desires of the consumer.

[13] Wendell R. Smith, "Product Differentiation and Market Segmentation as
Alternative Marketing Strategies," *Journal of Marketing,* July 1956, pp. 3–8.

In these cases they base their strategies on the measurement and definition of the market differences.

The strategies of market segmentation and product differentiation vary over time. Any given strategy has to be based on the degree of acceptability of a product or product line. Some products losing out in popularity might be eased out of existence while newer ones are worked into the market. For a rational selection of strategies the total costs of introducing, producing, and marketing a product must be considered rather than a minimization of production and marketing costs alone.

Product differentiation attempts to bring demand into line with supply. It tries to change the slope of the demand curve. Segmentation, in contrast, is the adjustment of a company's procedures to the conditions of demand. Market segmentation tries to increase a company's penetration in areas where its product is already acceptable. A company that relies on differentiation is seeking to acquire a single layer of the market cake, whereas a company engaging in segmentation desires one or more wedges (or shares) of all the layers.

As a matter of strategy, product differentiation is an attempt to distinguish the product through advertising—that is, to create differentiation through imagery. The consumer, it is hoped, will be disposed by the imagery to purchase, despite a higher price for the product. Necessarily, a great deal of promotional effort is required. This results in a price above the equilibrium level of perfect competition. The Mead Johnson Company illustrates the practice. A producer of only drug products, the company decided to differentiate its line and developed the diet food "Metrecal."

Market segmentation, which splits a large market into many sub-markets, caters to the more precise demand of consumers' varying wants. As a strategy, it has given rise to the development of the compact car, the higher-cost soaps that contain antibacterial ingredients, and the use of push-button in place of tube toothpaste and shaving-cream containers, among other products.

The production planners of any company must ascertain the amount of segmentation that may be exploited at a profit. For a number of reasons the planners are eager to spot this prospect for profitability. One of the most important of these reasons is that segmentation enables a company to reduce the minimum size of its production runs. On long runs the need lessens for additional markets for identical items. The planners know that a competitive balance obtains when varied products achieve maximum market potentials among the market segments.

Segmentation may be viewed as a cost of growth. The core market may have reached the point at which further promotional efforts may not prove profitable. Attention may then be directed to the market segments on the fringe of the core. Individually these segments may offer slight potential promise, but combined with other markets or parts of markets they may truly enhance the profit record. For example, the Chevrolet Division's introduction of the Corvair resulted in an increased total demand for all Chevrolet models. As a rule, by catering to the different segments of the market, a company assures greater consumer satisfaction and secures its hold on the complete market. Many of the costs of marketing, which may become fixed costs, may then be allocated among the new products thus introduced, much to the credit of the total profit prospect.

Most companies will survey a market and develop a product to please the average consumer. Suppose we assume that a study was made by companies in the soap industry to discover the degree of sudsiness desired in a soap product. Figure 2-2 indicates the amount of sudsiness favored by most of the population. Presumably all soap manufacturers would direct their efforts toward market area A. In consequence, many different companies would vie for the average market. In order to hold a fair share of this average market any single company would have to invest large sums of money in promotion, advertising, and personal selling. However, there is an alternate strategy. The B market (Figure 2-2) does not desire a high degree of sudsing because of the character of automatic washing machines; the C market, on the other hand, does desire a higher than average sudsing because women prefer a high suds detergent for washing dishes. In this instance a company might pursue the alter-

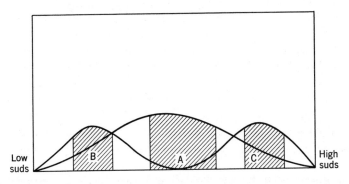

Figure 2-2. The amount of sudsiness desired in a soap product.

nate policy of going after the two smaller segments of the market, B and C, rather than A. The cost of maintaining the market and increasing shares of it under this course would be less than competing for A.[14]

5. FOLLOWER OR LEADER. Some companies seek to maintain their reputations by being first to market a new product or idea. Other companies do not want to risk their resources on something new; they wait until the new product idea catches on before they move into the market. The latter strategy is not necessarily confined to small companies. One major soap producer always sits back until one of its competitors tries out some virgin product. Once consumer acceptance develops for the product, the less venturesome manufacturer steps in with a comparable or better product and promotes heavily to acquire a substantial share of the market.

Sometimes a company must weigh the advantage of being the leader in the field against the costs of winning consumer acceptance for a new idea and the lack of distribution facilities to channel the goods to the customer. The Monsanto Chemical Company faced precisely such a problem when it developed its soil conditioner, Kirilium. The company was uncertain about whether to introduce the product before it had developed full production and marketing mechanisms or to take the risk of launching the product and incurring the animosity of its dealers for lack of supply. Monsanto's decision was crystallized by the discovery that a paint company had hit upon the same type of soil conditioner. Rather than allow a rival to gain a foothold in the market, Monsanto decided it had more to gain in being the leader in the field than in waiting until it could satisfy its dealers with an adequate supply of the new product.

A number of small companies may be committed to a follower strategy because of their limited resources to promote a new idea. Several of them fail to exploit their new ideas because they overestimate the magnitude of the promotional requirements to sell them. Nevertheless, this does not restrict the small company to old, proven ideas and products. Often small producers create the new ideas taken on by larger companies after their manufacture has proven feasible. Such was the case of the jet engine. Only after considerable research and experimentation by small companies in England, Germany, and the United States did the giants of the aircraft industry decide to perfect what appeared to be a practical development pioneered by

[14] A. A. Kuehn and R. L. Day, "Strategy of Product Quality," *Harvard Business Review,* November–December 1962, p. 100.

someone else. Unfortunately, many small companies cannot afford
to keep up with rapid changes of style or product design; the investment in facilities is beyond their means. This is particularly true
in the American automobile industry.[15]

6. SHARE OF MARKET. Several companies have bound themselves
to the idea that they must gain an increasing share of the existing
market. As a company obtains a larger and larger share of the market, it becomes ever more difficult for it to expand without committing
vast resources to this end. The Toni Company has about 80 per cent
of the home-permanent market in the United States. Many competitors have been attracted to this highly profitable area. As a
result Toni must commit extra funds to retain its leadership. Simultaneously, Toni has decided to enter other markets in which the
company may gain a small but certain share. These markets can
be maintained at relatively smaller cost. One item introduced by
Toni is a shampoo. Although the field is highly competitive, Toni's
objective is only a small share of the market.

Market share has become a major strategy for many companies.
Applied to an individual market, it is only a suitable indicator of
managerial performance.[16] Those down the managerial line, however,
must not lose sight of the more substantial objectives of a business,
such as its profitability and the continuity of its market share.

Profit Criteria

Since a company ordinarily would not be likely to engage in unprofitable ventures, individual managements need some kind of yardsticks against which to project the potential profitability of contemplated products. Ideally a company would like to be able to measure
incremental profits against incremental costs when adding new products to its line. Then it could array the prospective additions according to their profit possibilities. But this luxury is still beyond its
grasp. The current state of science prohibits an accurate calculation
of this kind. Lacking such precision, many companies try to get at
profitability by some other route. They ask themselves as an alternative what they should choose as a relevant concept of profit, what
they might use as a standard of profit, and what they should set as
a level for rejection of proposed ideas.

[15] John A. Menge, "Style Changes as a Competitive Weapon," *Quarterly Journal of Economics,* November 1962, pp. 632–647.
[16] Alfred R. Oxenfeldt, "How to Use Market-Share Measurement," *Harvard Business Review,* January–February 1959, pp. 59–68.

One relevant concept of profit is incremental profit. This can be projected easily if costs are estimated for the full life of the new product. The pattern of a growth cycle may prove useful here in seeking the probable size of the incremental profit. By using as an analogy the history of similar products it has marketed or the experience of a competitor's product, a company may reach some valid hypothesis about the profitability of its proposed item.

In some cases the profit added to the full cost of productive operations is more relevant. This applies particularly to durable goods. Since many unforeseen costs usually arise with each new product, the product should assume its full share of the common overhead burden. Incremental profits of the new products must be measured against other uses of capital and the resources of the company.

As a standard of profit a company might rely on total income from a product in relation to its cost, including the cost of the full investment over the product's entire life. This is a "return on investment" concept. If the new products are not permanent additions to the company's line, their costs may be calculated on the basis of various fixed bottleneck factors such as executive time consumed, machine time required, or the availability of materials. For large products financed by retained company earnings, the return on incremental investment is a better profit standard.

In any event prospective profits should be estimated over the life span of a product. As a practical matter a company may not be able to project its expectations more than three to five years ahead. Moreover, as we have observed, products often fail to make the grade because of inadequate marketing research or an underestimation of selling costs. The costs of both development and selling are the hardest to foresee, which frustrates any effort to obtain a reasonably close forecast of a product's profitability.

Whether a product should be accepted or rejected depends on the returns from investment in competing opportunities. If money invested in an alternate endeavor yields a higher return, it is fairly certain that the product may never see the light of day. Although not widely used as a basis for comparison, a company may consider the market cost of new capital as one kind of standard. A better course might be to compare the return on the investment in the new product to what might be achieved if the same resources were invested in other products or were put to other uses. Or a company might establish some long-range standard of investment return, such as the average for a ten-year period as a criterion for whether to adopt or reject a new product idea. Some companies without any rationale for doing so operate on the principle of a minimum level of profit, rejecting any product whose prospective profit fails to reach that level. And some set the level of rejection on the basis of their unit net profit margin at what they regard as their normal rate of output.

Uncontrollable Forces

Having reviewed the controllable aspects of product planning, let us turn now to the uncontrollable forces that beleaguer a product manager. The state of technology, changes in population, the rate of productivity, the shifting psychological and social nature of the consumer, the distribution and expenditure of income, and various social and economic trends—all these bear on planning, but none of them can be manipulated by the planners.

Technology. During the 1960's several of the following developments may eventuate.[17] Electronic refrigerators without moving parts may be manufactured. There may be waterless dishwashers that clean dishes by means of sonics. Vertical take-off and landing (VTOL) equipment may be put into use for short runs by commercial aircraft. Nuclear explosives may be used to create a harbor or desalinize water. It may become possible to control the genetic composition of plants. New devices may permit astronomers to study the "edge" of the universe. Prospective parents may be able to choose a boy or girl offspring. By 1970 a man may be on the moon.

Not all research, of course, necessarily bears fruit immediately. Among the projects whose realization seems still far off are the creation of living cells from inert matter and the use of rockets to carry mail and freight. The control of hurricanes and tornadoes and the accurate forecasting of weather with the aid of satellite-borne instruments are also developments not likely to occur in the near future. And we are a long way from the construction of computers that may learn and make judgments.

For product planning the implications are broad. In view of the present state of technology, companies have to decide whether they can afford to allocate funds and other resources to both applied and long-range basic research. Some companies can undertake basic research more readily than others because they have the trained personnel and resources to assign to "long-shot" studies. The other com-

---

[17] See Francis Bello, "The 1960's: A Forecast of the Technology," *Fortune*, Vol. 59, No. 1, January 1959, p. 74 ff.

panies may have to content themselves with research activities limited to minor modifications of existing products. These latter organizations may keep abreast of changing technology by attending exhibitions and reading and studying the basic-research literature.

Population. From 1947 to 1951 the population of the United States grew by ten million. In the 1950's it grew by another 30 million and in the 1960's was expected to gain at about the same rate. After 1970 the rate of growth will accelerate again.[18] We are entering a period that will be dominated by teenagers and senior citizens, both belonging to the dependent part of the population. In this period the number of persons between the ages of 15 and 19 will increase almost 63 per cent. The implication of the growing teenage and senior citizen markets is that the product planner must be cognizant of how purchase decisions are made by these two groups—how they use a product, what media command their attention, and where and how they shop.

Are the forces in the distribution system adequately prepared to handle merchandise for these two groups? If they are not, what changes have to be made in the channels of distribution? What pricing policies should be followed in merchandise for the teenage set? What appeals should be made to it? Similarly, what tactics should be pursued to attract the interest of older people? These and questions like them require investigation and answers now if companies are to be ready for the buyers of the future.

Productivity. The rate of productivity is yet another elusive factor that affects product planning. In the 1958–1960 biennial, man-hour output increased by about 10 per cent. This has been the sharpest rise of the postwar era.[19] During 1956 and 1957, in contrast, American productivity rose only 1.5 per cent a year. Part of the increase in productivity may be imputed to rapidly changing technology which some call automation.

Marketing has not been immune to this. Technology continues to raise the productivity of marketing workers. For example, vast strides have been made in reducing the cost of shipment of goods by water. The Pan-Atlantic Steamship Company now loads cargo in truck-trailer bodies. The complete cargo may be unloaded and reloaded by two crews in 15 hours compared to seven crews working a full

---

[18] See Daniel Seligman and Lawrence A. Mayer, "The Future Population 'Mix,'" *Fortune,* Vol. 59, No. 2, February 1959, p. 94 ff.

[19] See Charles E. Silberman and Sanford S. Parker, "How the U.S. Can Get 50 Percent Richer," *Fortune,* Vol. 59, No. 3, March 1959, p. 107 ff.; Joint Economic Committee, *Higher Unemployment Rates, 1957–60;* Washington, D.C., 1961, p. 31.

week. Retail stores such as Allied Stores now move their sales clerks to where customers are seeking merchandise rather than confine them to a single department. This has increased sales per man-hour by as much as 20 per cent. And office mechanization has continued to be transferred to computers. In the Bank of America's mortgage and installment-loan section, 100 employees aided by computers now perform work done formerly by 300 persons.

Growing productivity per man-hour means that product planners can look toward lower production costs which lead to lower prices and wider markets. Where a challenge still remains in increasing the output per man-hour is in the area of distribution costs. We have already seen what can be accomplished through the reduction of shipping and handling costs. Similar improvements must be made in decreasing the costs of personal selling, storage, billing procedures, warehousing, purchasing, standardization, and simplification. The product planner should be just as interested in the cost side of the equation as in the demand side.

Consumer. The changing psychological and social nature of the consumer is another concern of the product planner which is hard to pin down. The new American consumer is partial to homogeneity but at the same time seeks uniqueness to differentiate him from the masses.[20] Rising income has been a strong prod toward homogeneity. At the present time 43 per cent of all nonfarm families have disposable incomes of $5,000 to $10,000 a year after income taxes.

The core of the current middle-income group is the blue-collar worker, who has the same wants as the white-collar worker. He is interested in living in the suburbs and participating in community affairs. He is just as concerned as his white-collar counterpart about status symbols. Status, however, is attained by subtle distinctions rather than through conspicuous consumption.

Consumer tastes are changing in America.[21] Some of the factors behind this change are an increase in real income, wider educational opportunities, the old American tradition of striving for self-betterment, and a desire to imitate persons of good taste. The product planner, of course, must be aware of any change in consumer tastes. Items that were once luxuries have become necessities. Some things such as buggy whips have vanished from the market altogether. In general, the product planner may lean on motivation research for

[20] See Daniel Seligman, "The New Masses," *Fortune,* Vol. 59, No. 5, May 1959, p. 10 ff.
[21] See Gilbert Burck, "How American Taste Is Changing," *Fortune,* Vol. 60, No. 1, July 1959, p. 114 ff.

clues about the importance of product symbols and on social psychological research for data on the changing class structure of the market. All this information, though by no means infallible, can help him to define the product to process and the segment of the market to exploit.

Income. Income has become more evenly distributed in recent years.[22] By 1970, *Fortune* predicts, 45 per cent of all families will earn after taxes more than $7,500 a year in 1959 dollars, while another 39 per cent will fall between $4,000 and $7,500. Only 16 per cent will have less than $4,000 annually after taxes. More than half of all disposable income is expected to be discretionary by 1970.

Present estimates for expenditures by 1970 on food, clothing, liquor, tobacco, and a variety of other goods and services run to about $175 billion.[23] This may be compared to an equivalent expenditure of $125 billion in 1959; it represents an increase of 40 per cent. On an annual basis this signifies a rise in per capita spending of 1.5 per cent a year. Because income will be mounting more rapidly than consumption, the proportion of income to be spent on consumption will decline from 37 per cent in 1959 to 35 per cent in 1970. This surplus income will go into recreation, charity, private education, savings, and "personal business" such as interest payments.[24] It is not expected that outlays for movies, sports, books, and travel will increase any more rapidly than income. However, expenditures for medical and educational needs are likely to double in the current decade. And there may very well be a trend toward investing more money in securities.

Social and Economic Trends

In addition to the foregoing uncontrollable forces, there are several other social and economic trends of an elusive nature to haunt the product planner. He or his company may consult with a sociologist for some light on these various considerations that will influence product development.[25]

---

[22] See Sanford S. Parker and Lawrence A. Mayer, "The Decade of the 'Discretionary' Dollar," *Fortune,* Vol. 59, No. 6, June 1959, p. 136 ff.

[23] "The 'Ordinary' $125 Billion Market," *Fortune,* Vol. 60, No. 3, September 1959, p. 132 ff.

[24] See Charles E. Silberman, "The Money Left Over for the Good Life," *Fortune,* Vol. 60, No. 4, November 1959, p. 134 ff.

[25] J. Gordon Lippincott, "Matching Products With Customers," *Research Management,* Vol. 5, No. 2, March 1962, p. 81; Theodore Levitt, *Innovation in Marketing,* McGraw-Hill, New York, 1962, p. 135.

1. New concepts in education.
2. Trend toward rentals.
3. Communications explosion.
4. Growing importance of corporate image.
5. Growth of world corporations and world brands.
6. Increasing difficulty of maintaining and building brand equities.
7. Escape from megalopolis, suburbanization.
8. Major changes in distribution.
9. Growing importance of developing products and services for specialized markets.
10. Casualness and informality.
11. Convenience.
12. Simplicity oriented behavior.
13. The desire for efficiency and speed in all areas of activity.
14. Extension of leisure.
15. Peoples' growing preoccupation with security.
16. Upgrading of taste.
17. Perpetual prosperity.

Organization for Product Development

Product development is usually assigned to a single department, a company committee, or both. Yet even when the responsibility rests with a product development department, there is close cooperation with all departments of a company that may have any concern with new products. The following remark was made by a company having a product development department: [26]

We have a product development department which reports to the Marketing Vice President. The Sales Manager works closely with the Manager of the product development department.

One company, which uses two routes for channeling product development, advised:

[26] Remarks taken from questionnaires submitted to author. This was a mail questionnaire survey. One thousand questionnaires were sent out in 1954 to a systematic sample of companies reported in *Moody's Industrial Manual*. There were 50 returns. The returns were roughly proportional to the percentage of industries listed in the Census of Manufacturers for 1950. In addition to the chief executive in charge of marketing, questionnaires were filled out by the following department heads: sales, market research, advertising. Unless stated otherwise, any further reference to the author's survey will relate the results of this study.

There are two general routes for handling product development. The first concerns the performance of products in customers' equipment and in having products available to meet the requirements of newly developed equipment. This information is obtained from field-sales units and various equipment manufacturers, and is evaluated by the Sales Engineering Division, a unit of the headquarters' office. After evaluation, the necessary information is given to the Product Division so that it may include it in its over-all research program. The Research Division upon completion of development work for a new product or product quality improvement will then evaluate performance of the product in a field-test program in co-operation with the Sales Engineering Division if it is an automotive product. If it is an industrial product, the field testing will be done completely under the direction of the Sales Engineering Division.

In the other channel in which products are developed a new product will originate from the Research Division as a result of its continuing research programs. Such products are tested in much the same manner as described previously. Upon satisfactory completion of the field-test work, the product is given a brand name and arrangements are made for promoting its sale.

This is a report on use of the committee method:

Product development is handled in a committee for product quality control throughout our complete distribution system. This committee is composed of two marketing department representatives, one of whom is chairman of the committee; two members from the manufacturing department; one member from the pipe line department. This committee may take final action in all cases except where the introduction of a new product or change of present design results in increased manufacturing costs in excess of $10,000 per year. In this case, the committee submits the recommendation to the Vice Presidents of Manufacturing and Marketing, whose joint approval must be secured before action is taken.

Role of the Sales Manager

One of the key individuals in product planning is the sales manager. He is in a prime position to obtain direct information from the sales force regarding the acceptability of old products and the need for new ones. Sales managers participate in product planning in the following ways.[27] They make recommendations and require surveys for proposed products and possible markets. They suggest to the designers and superintendent new things that they feel are important to the company. They join in committee planning, lend a hand in research and development, approve recommendations of the product planners, and help determine the engineering program.

[27] *Ibid.*

Formal Approach to Product Development

The formal approach to the development of new products usually takes one of four courses.[28]

1. MANUFACTURING. New products are still the prime responsibility, most often, of the manufacturing department, particularly in companies that lay great stress on engineering. An aircraft builder, for example, places the responsibility for new products along with market research and forecasts on its engineering staff.

2. MARKETING. Many companies in diversified manufacturing activities have recently put new product development near or under their marketing forces.

3. COMMITTEE. Many companies do not believe that new products can be handled effectively by any one division—engineering, manufacturing, or marketing. They hold instead that only committee action with all groups cooperating can achieve a sound new product program.

4. INDEPENDENT. New product development as a separate function, often headed by its own vice president, is the most recent approach to the problem. It is used in consumer and producer goods enterprises alike, in metals and in paper, among large and medium-sized companies. But it is not yet accepted on a broad basis. It is feasible only in large, complex operations.

When the variety of products handled by a company becomes substantial, management needs guidance on many matters. How much of the sales force's time, for example, should be allocated to each specific product? How should the advertising budget be spread over the several product lines? Which lines have the greatest potential in terms of new, related products that might be added? No marketing manager or general sales manager alone can control and develop individual products which, in effect, are competing against each other for attention.

The concept of the product or product planning manager has been one attempt developed to cope with these problems. But there are many significant variations to it. Essentially one man, who is a staff manager for each major product or product line, fights for his particular line—for sales-force time, for advertising dollars, for promotional support. He coordinates and plans all aspects of the program, acting simultaneously as a watchdog, a clearing house for in-

[28] Henry Bund and James W. Carroll, "The Changing Role of the Marketing Function," *Journal of Marketing*, Vol. 21, No. 3, January 1959, p. 318.

formation, and a source of new ideas for promotional efforts and marketing tactics. Sometimes separate product managers may be designated for individual markets.

Functionally, product planning covers a broad range of activities. It may be confined to the development of new products only. More often, however, the product planning manager plans a line but does not supervise its current performance. His concern is with the future changes that may be necessary in models, prices, discounts, features, quality, or timing. But some managers assume total responsibility for a product line—both future planning and current performance. In such cases their job encompasses the full obligation of guarding the product line, identifying problem areas, recommending action, devising new promotions, keeping alert on competitive undertakings, exploring new markets, guiding new product development, and weeding out unprofitable items. Final action may depend on the marketing manager or the top sales executive, but the initiative comes from the manager of product planning.

Organizationally, most product planning managers operate within their company's marketing department. A few of them are one level removed from the marketing manager, although the majority are directly responsible to him. In some companies, however, product planning shares the same level as marketing, manufacturing, and finance. Thus, we see quite clearly that as our lives and social order grow more complex and there appears a corresponding increase in the complexity of our business and industrial organizations, product management, product planning, and product development take on a greater significance. The understanding of their role in the marketing scheme is one of the essentials of modern marketing management.

Summary

Product management embraces the planning, organizing, and control of a company's product line. Product planning generally fits into a company's budget for research and development.

There are two aspects of planning and control. One consists of controllable and the other of uncontrollable forces. Among the uncontrollable areas are the state of technology, population changes, the rate of productivity, the changing psychological and social nature of the consumer, and the distribution and expenditure of income.

The controllable aspects include specific incentives for product development which relate to production, marketing, and market considerations. Actually, the door to successful product planning is often market research. However, such research is no panacea, although both quantitative and qualitative marketing research may chart the direction for new products. One important phase of marketing research is the testing of new products before their introduction to the public.

A most important controllable element is the development of strategy and policy. In developing policy one must first analyze a company's resources and then formulate policy. The strategies on which a company may rely include the timing of new products, minimization of risk, product obsolescence, the choice of simplification or diversification, whether to be a leader or follower, and the obtaining of a share of the market. On top of all these, planning and control must evaluate long-run profit prospects.

Product development may be handled by a single department, by a committee, or by both. The sales manager frequently is a key factor in product development. But the trend in organizing for product development has run toward the creation of a separate product development function within the company.

Suggested Cases

Ralph L. Westfall and Harper W. Boyd, *Cases in Marketing Management*, Irwin, Homewood, Ill., 1961.

Parker Printing Company—*Publisher of Guide Books*—Adoption of Product to Changing Market, pp. 155–156.

Household Laundry Products Company—*Manufacturer of Household Products*—Addition of Product Line of Household Items, pp. 175–177.

Milton P. Brown, Wilbur B. England, and John B. Matthews, Jr., *Problems in Marketing*, 3rd ed., McGraw-Hill, New York, 1961.

General Motors Corporation—Oldsmobile Division, pp. 206–209.

Bradmore-Owen Company, pp. 120–130.

Harry L. Hansen, *Marketing: Text, Cases, and Readings*, rev. ed., Irwin, Homewood, Ill., 1961.

Van Wart Chemicals, Inc., pp. 404–418.

Hector Lazo and Arnold Corbin, *Management in Marketing*, McGraw-Hill, New York, 1961.

Motor Makers, Inc., Adjusting the Product Line to Changing Market Demands, pp. 389–391.

Kenneth R. Davis, *Marketing Management*, Ronald Press, New York, 1961.

Hansen Company, pp. 399–412.

Carrols, Inc., pp. 420–430.

Intercollegiate Case Clearing House, Soldiers Field, Boston 63, Massachusetts.

ICH 2M55 MA27—The Jenny Manufacturing Company.

ICH 2M35—American Sisal Kraft Corporation.

Chapter Three

From Adam Smith onward classical economists viewed the action of the market as shaped largely by price-making forces. In this century the classical assumption has been challenged by the works of Chamberlin [1] and Robinson.[2] These contemporary economists have suggested that other forces operate in the market place to put a company in a monopolistic position. The forces to which they refer lie mainly in the area of product differentiation. Since the breakthrough there have

[1] E. H. Chamberlin, *The Theory of Monopolistic Competition*, 7th ed., Harvard University Press, Cambridge, Mass., 1956.
[2] Joan Robinson, *The Economics of Imperfect Competition*, Macmillan, London, 1933.

Pricing

been various efforts to relate the other elements of market-place competition in some systematic manner.[3]

Current marketing literature is fully aware of these developments and has termed the manipulation of price along with the other competitive forces the market mix. But there has not been much of an attempt to perfect a conceptual model of how these various forces interact. It is in this particular domain that some interesting ideas have been advanced by economists.

Elasticity Concepts

One group of concepts that have borne fruit in economic analysis deals with elasticity. Economists speak of price elasticity and income elasticity. The former $(\Delta Q/\Delta P)$ concerns the change in the quantity of a product or service demanded as a result of a change in price. The latter $(\Delta Q/\Delta Y)$ pertains to the change in the quantity demanded in response to a change in income. The notion of elasticity may be used also with other means of competition $(\Delta Q/\Delta C)$; in this case the change in the quantity demanded is conditioned by a change in the means of competition. These means may include advertising, product quality, pricing, or services.

Price Elasticity. The amount of money that an individual has available for expenditures on consumption affects price elasticity. The higher the price the larger the portion of his budget it absorbs. The greater the portion of the budget absorbed the greater the elasticity. Thus, elasticity of demand in relation to price varies directly with price, as Figure 3-1 illustrates through a logarithmic curve of demand. A decline in price from p_1 to p_2 precipitates an increase in demand from

[3] See references cited in Gösta Mickwitz, *Marketing and Competition,* Centraltry-ckeriet, Helsingford, Finland, 1959.

x_1 to x_2. This is a substantially greater change than when the quantity demanded rises from x_3 to x_4 as the price falls from p_3 to p_4.

Conventions and customs also bear on elasticity of demand. For instance, if the price of a candy bar were to mount to 50 cents consumers would tend to pass it by as they would regard the price as exorbitant. Yet a slight increase in price might not affect the amount purchased at all. Thus, price elasticity of demand may vary with the degree of price change.

Price Elasticity Community Demand. The demand for a product in any community will change from one income group to another. What may severely affect the action of one group may have little or no bearing on other groups. For example, a very great price decrease might reduce the elasticity of demand for persons in the top income bracket but actually increase it for those in the bracket immediately below. Thus, we see that the elasticity of demand does not necessarily decrease when prices drop sharply. Such a pattern would apply only to goods for which there is no new class of buyers. As a matter of fact, the average of elasticity demand in a community tends to move counter to prices. One may plot a series of curves (Figure 3-2) for each buying class plus an envelope curve to cover the entire set, which shows that it is possible to have low elasticity at both high and low prices and high elasticity in a medium price range. Moreover, a large price change will generate more attention than a small one. This elasticity may be less marked for a series of small price changes than for a single, large one.

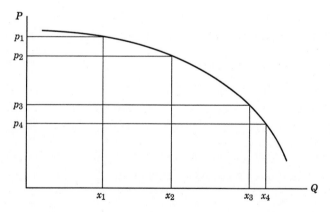

Figure 3-1. Elasticity of demand varies directly with price.

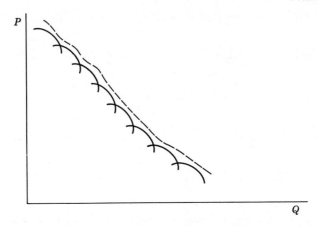

Figure 3-2. The average of elasticity demand in a community tends to move counter to prices.

The possibility of substituting one product for another also influences elasticity of demand. If the difference in price between the two is wide there is not much possibility of making a substitution. As the price difference narrows substitution may occur, such as margarine for butter, or aluminum for copper. Modern pricing theory indicates that calculation of elasticity holds only for small changes in price. Changes of as little as 10 to 15 per cent show unusual results.[4]

From a company's point of view, elasticity of demand relates to the increasing of its share of the market.[5] A price reduction by one company alone may not only increase the demand for its products but also affect an entire industry. Norris maintained that goods purchased regularly might become sensitive to prices because they require so large an amount of outlay.[6] Mickwitz, on the other hand, contended that habitual buying might eliminate price sensitivity.[7] Both arguments, of course, assumed a rather high price as requisite for price elasticity.

Cross Elasticity. There are two types of cross elasticity. One is between two individual enterprises; the other is between one company

[4] Herman Wold and Lars Jureen, *Demand Analysis,* Wiley, New York, 1953, p. 98.
[5] J. Dean, *Managerial Economics,* Prentice-Hall, Englewood Cliffs, N.J., 1951, p. 162.
[6] Ruby Turner Norris, *The Theory of Consumer's Demand,* rev. ed., Yale University Press, New Haven, Conn., 1952, p. 100.
[7] Mickwitz, *op. cit.,* p. 34.

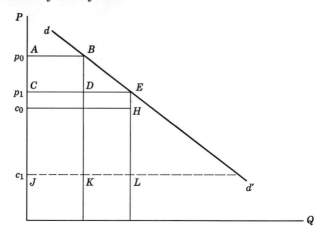

Figure 3-3. Effect of a reduced variable cost on profit structure.

and several other companies in its industry. In either case the formula for cross elasticity may be expressed as follows:

$$\text{Price cross elasticity} = \frac{\text{Relative change in A's sales volume}}{\text{Relative change in B's selling price}}$$

Relative changes in A's share of the market, according to the formula, depend on changes in B's selling price.

Equilibrium Elasticity. This is the demand elasticity necessary for a company's price to be profitable. It is a matter of how much of the price corresponds to variable costs and how much to gross profit $(p - c)$, leaving enough of a margin to cover fixed costs. In a profitable price reduction, the price elasticity is greater than the quotient of the sales price and the gross profit. Thus, the smaller the margin of profit the greater is the elasticity required. Figure 3-3 shows the effect on the profit structure of a reduced variable cost that accompanies a change in price. In dropping the price from p_0 to p_1, the profit at $p_0 = ABCD$. This is greater than the additional profit at p_1, which is $DEHG$. However, trimming the costs from c_0 to c_1 makes the price p_1 more profitable than the price p_0, as $DELK$ is greater than $ABCD$. We can find equilibrium elasticity through application of the following formula: [8]

$$e = \left(1 + \frac{c}{p - c}\right) = -\frac{p}{p - c}$$

[8] For proof see Mickwitz, *op. cit.,* pp. 37–38.

Elasticity and Other Competitive Means. The analysis of price elasticity has been developed on the assumption that other things remain equal. This cannot be done so easily with the other means of competition. Measurement of these means requires use of the costs of advertising, product quality, or services. The elasticity concept is useful, however, in discussing the incremental changes related to the other means of competition.

Total Elasticities. Do the elasticities of the other competitive means follow the same pattern as pricing? As a rule, elasticity correlates with the capacity to find substitute goods or services. Although better quality may result in either increased or lesser elasticity of demand, a great change in quality will not increase elasticity if it becomes harder to make substitutions. As a product gains versatility, however, the chances for substitution improve and elasticity increases. Bettering the quality also creates a problem of lesser utility. One may conclude from this that a similarity exists between quality and elasticity. Of the two, quality is the more heterogeneous.

Advertising attempts to increase the substitutability of commodities and at the same time make the use of any single product more specialized. A large expansion of advertising will likely influence most buyers. However, there is always some saturation point after which the effect of advertising diminishes and diminishing returns take over.

Advertising elasticity may grow more rapidly than price elasticity because of its appeal to a broader sector of the population. As more and more segments of the population are reached by it, advertising may be able to persuade additional members of the public to buy the products or services it advocates. How well it succeeds depends on how sensitive the various population segments are to different doses of advertising.

The continuous use of price to attract customers cuts down the price elasticity of demand; by and large, a particular purchase tends to require less and less of the buyer's budget. The tendency is reversed in the case of quality, advertising, or service elasticity; here the elasticity of demand is likely to increase. The many variations in quality, advertising, and service make this almost inevitable. Nevertheless, variation in only one quality may touch off a diminishing return.

To summarize the foregoing observations, price elasticity might be considered negative and the other elements of marketing competition positive. The quantities sold increase when prices are lowered, but not when quality, service, or advertising are reduced. That is to say, dropping prices will always decrease price elasticity, but not quality, service, or advertising elasticity.

Although saturation may set in from excessive advertising, the elasticity of advertising is greater than that of price because it is still possible to vary the former considerably. As to service, some forms will attract more buyers than other forms. Yet in many instances service saturation is reached at a very early stage. Service elasticity, in fact, is the closest to price, as we may observe in Figure 3-4. The curves show the quantities demanded (x) as various changes take place in price (p), service (s), advertising (a), and quality (q). Competitors' activities, these curves indicate, may vary continuously. In the graph, the elasticity of the price curve is negative, sloping downward to the right, whereas the other curves are positive, sloping upward and right.

Besides varying individually, all of the elements are interdependent. A change in one type of elasticity affects all the other types. Thus, if price elasticity looms important in a buyer's mind, quality, advertising, and service elasticity decline. If quality were predominant, price elasticity would join those that diminish.

The correlation between price and advertising elasticity is negative. For example, low-priced merchandise is much more amenable to impulse buying created by advertising. On the other hand, some elasticities, such as those of price and quality, are complementary. A rise in price will tend to increase quality elasticity. Elasticities of quality and advertising may also be grouped together. An increase quality may expand the advertising elasticity. This may, however,

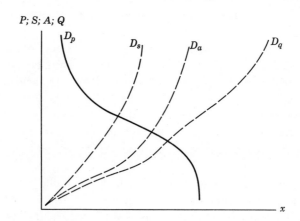

Figure 3-4.   Elasticity of price, service, advertising, and quality.

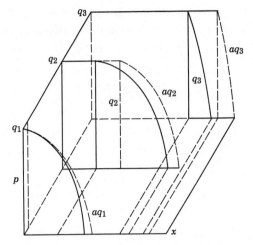

Figure 3-5. Price quality and advertising combinations.

reduce the sensitivity of the elasticity of price. Service and quality also may support each other in items like appliances.

Figure 3-5 illustrates that as quality increases price elasticity diminishes. Advertising shifts the curve to the right; the higher the quality the greater is the shift. Moreover, the better the quality of the product the more likely that price elasticities will be reduced by advertising. The assumption, of course, is that advertising becomes more effective as the quality of the product improves. The model in the illustration represents one simplified, conceptual approach to the problem of the interaction of the several elasticities. It is not the only approach. Other possible combinations exist. For example, if only advertising were expanded while price were dropped, it is possible that price elasticity might increase.

Ordinarily, the elasticities of price, advertising, service, and quality tend to be greater for a company than for its industry. This applies especially to advertising and, to some extent, to quality. Service elasticity, on the other hand, does not tend to be very large. Having thus taken a bird's eye view of the elasticity concepts, let us now shift attention to the problem of making pricing decisions.

Factors in Pricing Decisions

In any pricing decision four basic factors require consideration.[9] These factors, of which all marketing managers are fully aware, are

[9] E. Raymond Corey, *Industrial Marketing: Cases and Concepts,* Prentice-Hall, Englewood Cliffs, N.J., 1962, pp. 215–234.

the nature and extent of customer demand, the action of competitors, the cost of making and selling the product, and the company's basic objective.

Customer Demand. A company may wish first to classify the various segments of the market to set an appropriate price for each portion. Potential customers may be grouped according to the nature of the market they serve, the prospective uses they have for the product, their size, and geographic location. This data may then be utilized to estimate the likely sales volume at various price levels. Competing products in each market segment may be noted and a forecast made of the potential volume of each. Finally, the company must appraise the extent to which the new product may displace those already on the market.

In theory it would be desirable to fix a specific price for each group of customers based on what the members would pay. But there are legal and practical limitations which prohibit such action. A company, nevertheless, may distinguish among its customers by granting either functional or quantity discounts. It may also schedule different prices for different locations. Price differentiation shows two tendencies. One is for prices to reflect competitive conditions within market segments rather than differences in cost to the manufacturer. The other is a tendency for prices to deteriorate to the point at which the lowest price becomes the market price.

Action of Competitors. Competition by its very nature tends to set an upper limit on pricing. Whenever a company desires to make any price move it must anticipate the action of its competitors. Generally competitors will meet a price cut rather than risk a loss of revenue. They refrain from paring prices, however, when the lowered price falls below the out-of-pocket cost, or when a reduction tends to harm other items in their product line. Moreover, a large company may not match a price cut made by a competitor who sells only a small volume; it would rather absorb the loss of revenue.

Similarly, plans to increase prices must be weighed against the probable course of competitors. If a company raises its prices and its competitors fail to follow, it may experience a lowering of sales volume. Many industries, however, recognize a price leader and trail along its path when market conditions are favorable. Usually the company with the greatest market share is the leader. Invariably it is concerned with the health of the entire industry.

Cost Considerations. Factors of cost, in contrast to competition, tend to set lower limits on pricing policy. As a rule of thumb, cost plus pricing should be avoided. It is more practical to calculate price on the basis of the customer's evaluation of the product or service. Even so, one must not ignore the element of cost in establishing price.

Unit costs are not necessarily constant. They may fluctuate with volume and over time. In addition, there may be different views of what constitutes cost, according to what has been included or left out as cost items. Consequently, several choices become necessary in analyzing costs. Should a company, for example, consider full cost or only incremental cost? Should it choose current or anticipated cost? In keenly competitive situations, the costs may tend to be restricted to the incremental level. In this case the incremental cost becomes the lower limit for calculating overhead and profit, and for setting price.

Basic Objectives. Occasionally a company may forego maximizing short-run profits in deference to its long-term objectives. Its relations with customers over the long pull is one of these influences. Customers may not like arbitrary price increases. But they are likely to accept as justified those increases shown to be essential to cover rising costs or support product improvement.

Another deterrent to short-term profit is the impact of price changes on a whole product line. A change up or down that affects the prices of a company's entire line may easily jeopardize its long-range profit objectives. Moreover, if a company discriminates in its prices to customers in competition with each other it may damage its ultimate ends. It has to be careful also lest its pricing policy drive small competitors out of business. Yet many companies price their products conservatively to reduce the industry's power of attraction to other business organizations.

Pricing policy reflects a company's marketing objectives. Thus, a company may wish to be known as a leader in style and price and keep introducing new products to the market on an appealing price basis. Maintenance of its market share and its views on product promotion also may influence a company's pricing policy.

Market Penetration and Market Shares.[10] Various companies have tried different tactics to expand into new markets. A & P, for example, seeks a maximum market share through maintaining a downward pressure on prices. Other companies prefer steady prices to a larger share of the market. When Esso and U.S. Steel have sought to expand

[10] A. D. H. Kaplan, Joel B. Dirlam, and Robert F. Lanzillotti, *Pricing in Big Business,* The Brookings Institution, Washington, D.C., 1958, pp. 259–266.

their markets they have done so without trimming prices. Yet when their smaller competitors have cut prices to move into new markets the larger producers often have matched them. Recently, however, penetration of new markets has depended on assurances of supply and dependable quality and services rather than on price.

Some companies have no fixed policy on fixed market shares. Swift & Company, for example, attempts to maintain a steady supply of meat to its retail outlets despite the meager margins of its prices. Companies like Reynolds Metals, on the other hand, have tried to raise prices and simultaneously increase their market share by special features in their finished products. And in 1948 General Electric Company reduced prices in a rising market in order to combat inflation and better its competitive position.

Planning and Control of Pricing

This section of the chapter falls into four distinct divisions, each of which will be discussed in detail. The first is the relation of price to the market mix. This will be followed by an analysis of the role of research in pricing. We shall then consider the uncontrollable aspects of pricing and end the section with an inspection of the controllable elements. In this final category we shall also examine closely the methods of pricing and pricing policy.

Price and Marketing Mix

Quality Service and Price Competition. In selling their products a great number of companies stress engineering and sales service while playing down their price. They do so because they are marketing products of a differentiated character. Although American Can Corporation, for example, passes on all savings in the cost of tin plate and in wages to its customers, it really emphasizes its routine special services. The DuPont Corporation knows that heavy chemicals sell on a price basis but realizes that missionary work among dealers and first-hand demonstrations to farmers enable it to compete effectively in the field of agricultural chemicals. Nonprice competition in the form of development of new products and product improvement may succeed without reference to price, at least for a while, and is quite common in the chemical industry. It is introduced, as are the other emphases on service and engineering, to bring better satisfaction to customers.

Among consumer goods, General Foods has developed several food novelties that sell at high profit margins but nevertheless pick up sales and contribute heavily to profits because of their quality. Minute Rice, Swan's Down, and the newer Jell-o flavors are products fitting this description. In the search for a suitable metal for automobile transmissions, the competition narrowed to aluminum and steel. Although a cheaper metal, aluminum was more expensive to cast. With the development of new techniques for casting, aluminum won out, despite its still higher cost. In the rubber-tire industry the attempt was made to achieve product differentiation by special treads, and low-pressure and tubeless tires. And the over-all strategy of the automobile industry has been to accent style over pricing.

International Harvester, which attaches great importance to the durability, economical operation, and dealer service built into its units, also has always felt that credit terms were more significant than price. The Kroger Company, in addition to stocking nationally branded merchandise selling at higher prices, also carries tenderized meats. This has given an impression of quality to the customer and has created the image that Kroger patrons trade in high-quality stores. Often, large retailing companies such as A & P will make quality differentiation the distinction among several of their own privately packed brands. Similarly, oil companies have been able to command higher prices for gasolines having higher octane ratings or the presence of special additives.

Varieties in Quality and Style. There are many varieties among competitive qualities and styles. In one category, which includes automobiles and appliances, nonprice competition is used to divert attention from price. In another category, typical of the competition in the chemical industry, research expenditures are expected to attract new customers. A third category stresses engineering, sales, and service. Companies like American Can, Johns Manville, and Union Carbide pursue such a policy. DuPont, International Harvester, and General Electric follow still another path. They pass improvements on old products along to their customers without increasing prices.

According to the authors of *Pricing in Big Business*,[11] few respondents to a survey they conducted on reactions to pricing practices mentioned advertising or superficial changes of style as optional to pricing policy. The reason for this, they said, was that advertising

[11] *Ibid.*

and product changes were seldom regarded as separate matters of policy independent of price.

Product Promotion. Examples are numerous of companies having taken products from small enterprises for further development and having promoted them to great success. These larger companies have built up a primary demand for these products. General Motors' venture in diesel engines is one case, and DuPont's promotion of cellophane is another. Cellophane was an inferior product before DuPont became interested in it.

Pricing Research

Research into pricing usually goes into analyses of cost or studies of competition. Several different types of information have been gathered by a number of companies, and one set of businessmen has listed various areas as ones into which their organizations have dug for pertinent pricing data. These areas include studies of current costs, analyses of past records and competitive price schedules, continuing competitive price analysis, freight and delivery cost analysis, distribution cost analysis, wholesale and retail price surveys on continuing and periodic bases, maintenance of information on competitive prices, studies of effects of price changes, analyses of competing products and of competitive prices on the basis of projecting costs, and comparative pricing with similar products of other manufacturers.

Other types of pricing research relate to studies of price elasticity, experimentation, and what the consumer is willing to pay. Survey work is useful also in trying to identify the utilities inherent in each product or service offered to the public. Motivation research and studies of a product's use have bared many of the underlying reasons why consumers may favor a particular product.

Experimental Methods. Different controlled experiments have yielded substantial assistance in developing pricing policies. One technique has been to select similar markets and alter the price from one to another while keeping the other elements in the market mix constant. The problem in this type of experimentation is the choice of markets and the freezing of the rest of the market mix. A company cannot count on its competitor to refrain from acting; nor can it be confident that such external factors as weather, employment, and the political climate will remain constant.

An experimental technique employed to price new goods permits consumers to select from a table familiar items similar to the one being newly produced. The consumer is asked to specify which familiar item most nearly has the same value as the new one. Thus, a new paring knife may be comparable to an old-fashioned paring knife, a carrot peeler, or a cheese cutter. The prospective purchaser expresses his evaluation of the new knife in relation to an implement he knows, which is a superior method to asking him how much he is willing to pay for a new product. If the consumer were given a list of prices, the chances are that he would select the middle one. If no list were provided, he would be likely to choose a very low price. Since he is not really in a purchasing mood under the experimental conditions, he does not truly know how much he is prepared to pay for the product.

Statistical analysis of the relation between a change in price and a change in demand is fruitful in estimating potential revenue at various price levels. But here again, as in the experiment of altering price, the problem is to control all other variables bearing on demand so that the outcome of the statistical analysis pertains solely to a change in price. Ultimately a company will find its demand function by direct communication with the market. It sets its price for a product, which the market either will confirm or reject. By its reaction the market will advise the company whether its price decision has been sound.

Uncontrollable Elements

The uncontrollable factors in pricing arise from four different sources. They relate to competition, to institutional differences in pricing, to the elements of supply and demand, and to economic and other forces.

Competition. Among various industries, Triffin observed, competition takes place in substitute products.[12] Thus, Triffin appeared to broaden the concept of competition in one respect by disregarding the border lines between industries but to narrow the concept in another sense by insisting on tight product classifications. Under pure competition, he felt, a company's sales depended on prices of all other companies. Yet the company is not capable of affecting the prices of its competitors. For Triffin the governing factor is cross elasticity.

To Rasmussen competition depended on the parameter of action of one or more companies. This becomes apparent as one or more

---

[12] R. Triffin, *Monopolistic Competition and General Equilibrium Theory,* Harvard University Press, Cambridge, Mass., 1940.

cross elasticities deviate from zero in numerical value. He defined monopoly as a condition obtaining when sales were completely independent of the parameters of action of other companies in which cross elasticities held at zero. However, one could speak of the effect of rising income on prices.[13] The Rasmussen definition has run into criticism on grounds that the cross elasticities reflect the appraisal of buyers but not the policy of sellers, especially where competition has ceased.

In a narrow definition, J. M. Clark has asserted that competition was a form of independent action by an entrepreneur in the hope of increasing his profit or protecting it against encroaching forces. The entrepreneur offers advantages to a buyer to win his patronage.[14]

Less extreme than the foregoing definitions of competition was the definition of Abbott who held that competition was a contest in which rival sellers entered products of their independent choice, at prices they themselves established, for appraisal and purchase by independent buyers. These products substitute for each other through being optional means of obtaining utility or satisfaction. The buyer is free to accept or reject whatever is offered. Rival products and prices may supplant each other, with the opportunity to exercise a substantial amount of freedom, including the freedom to alter the quality of products,[15] the essential condition for a truly competitive situation. And, finally, Salonen has defined competition as all the conflicts and compromises of individual members of the community and corporate bodies who strive to promote their own objectives through economic influence and activity.[16]

Now Mickwitz has distinguished "commodity competition" from "entrepreneur competition." He used the term "commodity competition" to signify competition among various goods [17] and preferred "entrepreneur competition" where others would speak of competition. The latter might be measured by the strength of competitive activity, which rests on cross elasticity or substitutability. Although no active measures are taken by an entrepreneur in adapting to the market place, entrepreneur competition is considered active by Mickwitz whereas commodity competition is regarded as passive. The passive

[13] Mickwitz, *op. cit.,* p. 9.
[14] J. M. Clark, "Toward a Concept of Workable Competition," *The American Economic Review,* Vol. 30, No. 2, June 1940, pp. 241–256.
[15] L. Abbott, *Quality and Competition,* Columbia University Press, New York, 1955.
[16] Mickwitz, *op. cit.,* p. 57.
[17] *Ibid.,* p. 60 ff.

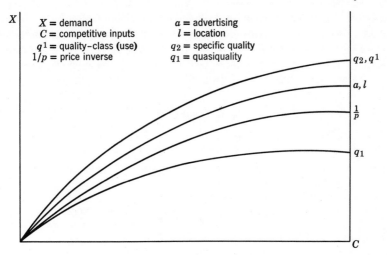

Figure 3-6. The static level effect.

form, which results from buyers' needs and evaluations, is character-
ized by cross elasticity; the active form presupposes action by sellers.[18]
The greater the elasticity is, the sharper the commodity competition.
This relationship applies as much to price as to other parameters.
The largest elasticity exists between commodities in the same industry.

When the sales or market shares of one company increase or decrease the competition is said to be *specific*. When the total demand
for a particular product increases or decreases the competition becomes
generic. Through generic competition sellers endeavor to expand their
shares of national income. Entrepreneur and commodity competition
can be either specific or generic.

Figure 3-6 demonstrates the static level of competition in markets
unexposed to violent fluctuations of demand and big differences in
price. It shows that quality-class (use) competition has the greatest
amount of elasticity, followed by price, advertising, and specific quality (such as easy to mix), and quasiquality (package). These elements affect a buyer's choice at a particular moment in time.

Figure 3-7, showing the elements of competition over the various
zones of development, illustrates the dynamism of advertising. Area
1 and half of area 2 form a generic zone. Here the new product is
being introduced and the total market is being expanded. Competitive activity for the moment centers around considerations of quality.

[18] *Ibid.*

In area 2 quality slips behind advertising which becomes the major force developing the market. At this juncture competition enters the field with the accent shifting from advertising activity to competitive pricing. This moves the seller into the specific zone where shares of the market are won or lost. Price competition is short-lived, yielding to quasiquality or minor product differences. In areas 1 through 4 the elasticity of the elements of competition heads toward inelasticity. But in area 5 advertising restores elasticity and generic competition returns to enlarge the total market.

Institutional Differences. Wholesale prices tend to fluctuate more than retail and manufactured prices because of the wholesalers' close association with supply and demand. Manufacturers' prices follow wholesale patterns. Retailers' prices are more stable than those of the other two institutions in the marketing orbit.

Forces of Demand. The consumer takes concrete views of price versus nonprice competitive activity. For certain products he is

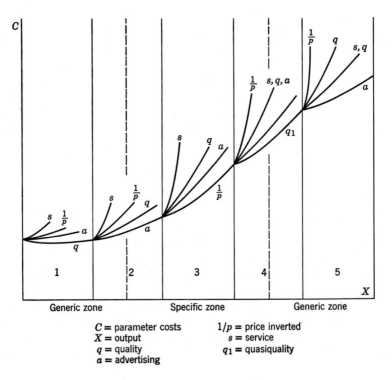

Figure 3-7. Dynamic level effect.

more interested in pricing than in product differentiation created by advertising. This is true of standardized items like coffee and butter, but does not apply to meat and vegetables which are chosen for quality.[19] On the other hand, the consumer is fairly convinced that Kellogg's Corn Flakes represent a superior quality to rival brands, despite Kellogg's selling twice the quantity as its competitors. The same may be said to hold for consumer attitudes toward certain detergents, soaps, and dentifrices.

The consumer is a constantly changing individual and pricing will not alter his habits. No amount of price reduction will foster a revival of the wagon industry. But if a favorable demand exists for some product it may be possible to manipulate that demand within limits. In such cases forces that affect the habits and motives of consumers, such as the amount of leisure time, the degree of family togetherness, the size of the family and its income, living in the suburbs, or membership in the church, have a more profound influence on buying behavior than price manipulation. Ostentation or conformity may play a more important part than price.

There is also the psychological role of price in determining value. Many persons believe that the higher the price the greater is the value and vice versa. To the extent that such an image persists, it may be difficult to manipulate demand through price reduction. To the contrary, raising prices for items like perfumes has tended to increase rather than diminish demand. Higher quality is assumed for higher-priced fashion clothing. One reason for this assumption is the consumer's lack of knowledge of what, in fact, constitutes good quality. A company, however, may be able to maneuver the demand for certain staple items such as shorts or stockings because consumers feel there are no appreciable differences in the high-priced lines of these commodities.

Economic Forces. Income and price elasticities of goods are also uncontrollable pricing elements. By cutting the price of a loaf of bread in half, a baker does not precipitate a doubling of the demand for bread, which is an inelastic product. But cutting the price of automobiles by 10 per cent may release an additional demand for them of perhaps 20 per cent. This would hold true, as well, for changes in incomes. A 10 per cent rise of income may yield a 20 per cent increase in the purchasing of expensive products like automobiles and "big-ticket" appliances. At the root of both income

[19] See Bob R. Holdren, *The Structure of a Retail Market and the Market Behavior of Retail Units,* Prentice-Hall, Englewood Cliffs, N.J., 1960.

and price elasticities lie psychological reactions of consumers to changes in these areas. The reactions may also be modified by the consumer's expectations for the future.

Controllable Aspects

In this portion of the chapter, devoted to the controllable aspects of pricing, we shall discuss the optional methods of pricing available to an administrator of prices. This will be followed by a look at the policies a company may pursue in the pricing area.

Basic Methods. Essentially, basic methods of pricing fall into three categories. Not necessarily mutually exclusive, these categories are analytical, cost plus, and competitive. Companies may use any one of the three or a combination of them. Most of a group of companies questioned by the author use some mixture of the three methods. In the words of one of them:

Our company prices its products essentially on a single price system. The primary wholesale market for each group of products is soundly evaluated. Prices are then calculated by adjusting expenses from the location of the primary market to each point of sale, including a reasonable profit, preferably expressed in terms of return on investment. Competition often does not allow us to attain our desired prices, causing us to make adjustments upon recommendation of our local people and approval of management in the home office. Our procedure generally follows the marketing principle of selling products at competitive prices, after allowing for quality differences, limited on the low side by the necessity of at least covering our costs.

1. ANALYTICAL. In applying the analytical method one would try to equate marginal revenue with marginal cost at the point where profits would be largest or try to use a break-even analysis. Under the latter alternative, a company would postulate a price that would retrieve fixed costs and yield the profit sought. Table 3-1 illustrates

Table 3-1. Break-even Analysis

Price	Cost of Goods Sold	Gross Margin	Estimated Units to Be Sold	Total Margin	Overhead	Contribution to Profit
$ 8	$5	$3	1,000	$3,000	$2,400	$600
9	5	4	800	3,200	2,400	800
10	5	5	550	2,750	2,400	350
11	5	6	400	2,400	2,400	0

Table 3-2. Effects of Price on Profits

Unit Price	Expected Volume Units	Unit Gross Margin	Total Margin	Fixed Overhead	Contribution of Margin to Expense and Profit	Expense	Net Profit
$10	1,000	$5	$5,000	$3,000	$2,000	$1,000	$1,000
9	2,000	4	8,000	3,000	5,000	1,100	3,900
8	3,000	3	9,000	3,000	6,000	1,200	4,800
7	4,000	2	8,000	3,000	5,000	1,300	3,700
6	5,000	1	5,000	3,000	2,000	1,400	600

this method. The table shows that a price of $9 yields the greatest contribution to profit, whereas a price of $11 contributes no profit at all. The lowest price of $8, it may be noted, does not produce the largest profit contribution even though it generates the largest volume.

In using the break-even analysis one may estimate the volume of sales at each price level and then compute the contribution to profit at this price. This method of pricing may be employed for a single product or a line of products. By going a step further and subtracting the expenses from the contribution to profit, we may obtain the net profit, as Table 3-2 indicates. By examining Table 3-2 we can see immediately that $8 is the most profitable price. The total margin is more than sufficient to cover overhead; where total margin first covers overhead is the break-even point. In the foregoing example it is assumed that expenses tend to mount with volume. In fact, a company may use an example of this kind at first and later stabilize expenses at some specific level of volume. To obtain more realistic cost figures, however, a company needs data on the relation of cost to the rate of output, plant size, and technology.

Figure 3-8 is a graphic representation of a break-even analysis. The area $ADXE$ constitutes the company's fixed charges. The triangular area enclosed by ACD represents the variable costs, and the straight line XY signifies sales volume. Assuming that the cost of goods sold at $3 were $2, a gross margin of profit of $1 would remain. To break even in this case, the company would have to sell 3000 units at $9,000. Thus, point B becomes the break-even point, beyond which lies the area of profit symbolized by the triangle BYC.

Regression analysis may help to understand cost relationships over a period of time and also to appreciate their influence on price.

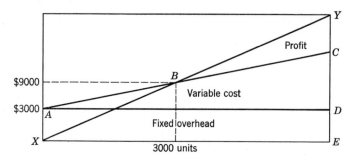

Figure 3-8. A graphic representation of a break-even analysis.

One may plot a regression equation with a number of independent variables to discern the forces that do, in fact, influence price.[20]   Or one may use a linear regression to ascertain separable costs. We shall discuss these matters in a subsequent chapter on distribution costs.

2. COST PLUS. Under a cost-plus calculation, a company adds a specific predetermined margin or percentage to its costs. One company reported its use of cost plus as follows:

The price of goods is based solely on basic raw material costs plus fundamental expenditures applicable to the product, plus the profit we desire for the company.

This is the most prevalent method of pricing. The "plus" mark-up may be flexible. It may be intuitive or it may be a matter of trial and error. If it is flexible, a company changes its mark-up relative to demand. If it is an intuitive mark-up, the company tends to rely on its "feel" of the market. With trial and error, the company attempts to test consumer reactions to different prices. Before a company can turn its attention to the plus element in pricing, however, it needs to know the pertinent cost factors. Although they may be secondary to mark-up considerations, costs are useful in measuring the effects of different prices on profit. They are useful also in anticipating the reaction of consumers to projected prices. They justify a course of price action and enable a company to design a product to price.

The businessman, of course, is primarily concerned with future costs. What happened in the past is relevant to him only because

[20] See Milton H. Spencer Colin G. Clark, and Peter W. Hoguet, *Business and Economic Forecasting,* Irwin, Homewood, Ill., 1961.

it might outline the probable pattern of change ahead. The past is valuable for a knowledge of the forces underlying change and any variation from the basic course. The insight gained from the past should explain why variation has occurred and indicate whether it is likely to recur in the future.

To be able to make appropriate decisions in the light of changing patterns, a company should develop a repertoire of demand and cost conditions. For instance, it might construct a table of estimates of demand ranging from the most pessimistic to the most optimistic circumstances. This table might include several subjective estimates of probable demand. In planning for the future, the company's executives would choose the estimate with highest probability. As to estimates of cost, they may be made for different production volumes and for changes in technology. Here again subjective estimates of probable changes in the composition of costs may be made. What, for example, are the probabilities of a 10 per cent, 15 per cent, or 20 per cent increase in labor costs? And, correspondingly, what is the likelihood that output per man-hour would show an increase in efficiency of 10 per cent, 15 per cent, or 20 per cent?

Costs of individual products are determined by the production and marketing situations.[21] Four such situations are pertinent to calculating costs. First, can the proportion of products be varied? Second, is long-run or short-run cost adjustment required? Third, are costs traceable to individual products? Fourth, are costs variable or fixed for the short run?

When the proportions of a product line cannot be varied in the production lanes, the allocation of costs of its individual items is difficult if not impossible. One may, however, approximate the cost by examining the demand for the product, particularly where demand is unaffected by pricing or advertising. For example, in the case of a dining set composed of a table and four chairs, the demand for the table and chairs is a function of the demand for dining-room sets. The relative prices of chairs and tables would affect neither the ratio of chairs nor the total number of sets. Under these circumstances the total cost remains impervious to the relative prices of chairs and tables because the product mix does not change. This is, therefore, a joint cost situation stemming from demand rather than from production costs.

[21] Joel Dean, "Pricing Policies," *Industrial Accountant's Handbook,* Prentice-Hall, Englewood C iffs, N.J., 1955, pp. 599–644; also Joel Dean, *Managerial Economics,* Prentice-Hall, Englewood Cliffs, N.J., 1951; also Joel Dean, *Pricing from the Seller's Standpoint,* Columbia University Press, New York, 1949.

Allocation of fixed costs is a short-run problem. In the long run costs become variable; hence, the long run requires some other approach than normal cost allocation. As a result, studies of cost allocation may be restricted to short-run matters.

Traceable costs are the costs that can be identified with particular products. How well costs may be traced depends on the accounting system used by the company. This is no apparent difficulty in tracing short-run costs. The question is whether the accounting system may be comprehensive enough to keep an accurate record of the diverse costs that may be deemed traceable.

The problem that does arise relates to the establishment of a cost for the common, nontraceable, short-run costs. These costs may be fixed or variable. But fixed costs are really irrelevant for pricing because in the long run all costs tend to be variable. Short-run, nontraceable costs, therefore, may be allocated among products by a systematic varying of both the volume of output and the proportions of the several products. One should take note of the effect of this on common variable costs, although this may be difficult to do. It could perhaps be accomplished by isolating the common variable costs as a function of total output and then allocating them among the items in the product line according to the proportion of incremental costs traceable to each item.

Costs are important in demonstrating to the government that price reductions have not been granted on a discriminatory basis, but on savings in distribution. In this way a company can comply with the requirement of the Robinson-Patman Act. Half of the cases dealing with violations of the Act, in which cost is raised as a defense, have been declared invalid by the United States Supreme Court.[22] Besides, many investigations by the Federal Trade Commission, which is charged with administration of the Act, have been settled out of court upon proper presentation of cost data. Costs should also be recorded and kept on file by a company because they are often required by other regulatory bodies of government.

As we know, there are economies of scale in manufacturing. There are also economies of lot sizes, and these may very well influence pricing in developing volume markets, quantity discounts, differentials in package size, and differences in models. Table 3-3 illustrates the effect of set-up costs on unit volume cost. Initially there is a

[22] Herbert F. Taggart, *Cost Justification*, Michigan Business Studies, Vol. 14, No. 3, Bureau of Business Research, School of Business Administration, University of Michigan, Ann Arbor, 1959, p. 544.

Table 3-3. The Effect of Set-up Costs on Unit Volume Cost

Other Costs	Set-up Cost	Total Cost	Units per Lot	Unit Cost
$ 1,000	$1,000	$ 2,000	50	$40
2,000	1,000	3,000	100	30
3,000	1,000	4,000	200	20
4,000	1,000	6,000	300	20
11,000	1,000	12,000	600	20

rapid decline in unit costs which then tend to become stabilized. The increase in lot sizes from 300 to 600 in the illustration does not, as we can note, result in any savings in unit cost. The profit per unit on 600 units is the same as for 300 units. But if we may assume a constant price, the sale of 600 units would yield twice the amount of profit as the sale of 300 units.

Since rate of output curves relate to plants with fixed capacity, what happens to the cost pattern when the capacity is varied? As the size of the plant increases, possibilities arise for economies of scale. When decisions are made to expand capacity, one may want to investigate the effect of the costs on the profit margin and the relationship of price to volume. Let us suppose, for example, that a company is producing at full capacity at a cost of $1 per unit. If the capacity is doubled the unit cost may be reduced by 25 per cent to 75 cents. Then by assuming a selling price of $2 for the item, the margin of income under the new capacity becomes 25 per cent larger—or the increase in margin is equal to the decrease in cost.

Technological changes also effect reductions in cost. A company does well to anticipate the technological changes of the future and the steps to be taken in altering the price structure accordingly. This may be done in two ways. One is to review present technological advances and assess their possible application to the enterprise. Another is to trace technological developments within the company and project them into the future. The effect of these innovations may be gleaned from a measurement of man-hour productivity. Where output has increased the result may be imputed to technological progress. Specifically in the area of marketing, one might check any advances in order handling, material handling, and billing in this manner. Companies with histories of technological change, such as those in the steel, automobile, and mining industries, may extrapolate from their own past experience.

Finally, one must employ incremental costs with care. These costs for a short-run increase in volume may be quite different from corresponding costs in long-run increases in volume. Short-run marginal increases are likely to be less than those of the long run. This is the same thing as saying that variable costs will go up over the long run. For example, labor costs will tend to rise as fewer and fewer efficient workers remain available for hire. Moreover, on the upswing of the business cycle it is also likely that raw material costs will increase.

The size of the increase in volume will also influence incremental costs. For a small, gradual increase in volume incremental costs will differ from equivalent costs for large, abrupt increases in volume. The latter would make greater demands on overhead and greater utilization of excess capacity. Thus, the size of the increase in volume must be borne in mind in estimating incremental costs. We must also recognize the risks related to accepting a price level at or near incremental costs. One of these risks may be the spoilage of the market by tearing down the whole price structure or by converting a high price into a low one.

Classical economic concepts of maximizing profit do not seem to apply in pricing policy. Companies may strive for reasonable or normal profits because of concern over good will; they want the public to feel confident that it will not be exploited even when supplies are scarce and demand is high. This sort of thinking reflects a long-run point of view rather than a short-run, short-sighted view.

What, then, may a company use as criteria for determining reasonable profits? To begin with, it must consider total profits rather than profits from any single product. Moreover, it should compute rate of return on the basis of its investment rather than on its sales. To ascertain reasonable earnings, it may be guided by the earnings of some normal period in its past. Another criterion might well be the average earnings for its industry, while still another might be the rate of return most popular with the government. Railroads, for example, usually look for 6 per cent.

Some companies resort to public-opinion polls to learn the public view of what constitutes a reasonable profit. The weakness of such surveys is that most people do not have any opinions, whereas those who do reply give a wide range of answers. Other methods through which companies may try to reach reasonable profit include the maintenance of traditional margins on individual products or on total sales, the calculation of profit on the basis of variable costs rather than on full cost, and comparison with the break-even point in a period of depression or recession. It is important for companies to consider not only these criteria for profit but also the cost of borrowing money to finance the products on which the profit is sought.

Before we move on from this discussion of the cost-plus approach, let us note its weaknesses. First of all, it does not take demand into consideration, nor does it weigh what consumers are willing to pay. Moreover, the reasoning is circular; unit cost depends on volume but volume depends on the price charged. Next, this method of pricing does not pay attention to the influence of competitors, to substitute products, nor to potential competition. Finally, the cost-plus method is based on past costs, whereas in dynamic pricing a company should concern itself with the future and costs anticipated in days to come.

3. COMPETITIVE. Where competition dominates the approach to pricing a company observes the prices established by its rivals. One company responding to the author's survey advised:

Price is determined on the basis of competitive value of the item in relation to other similar items in the line. Profit margin varies widely type by type, and "loss leaders" must be carried.

Variations on competitive pricing include some of these following practices: adaptation of the product to establish prices, price leadership, competitive circumstances, what the traffic will bear, and customary or conventional prices. At the established price the company will offer goods for sale at either the prevailing competitive price or at some existing retail price line. In a price leadership situation one company sets the pattern for the others to follow. And there also may be competition through consumer identification with a particular brand and the substitution of other brands or products for it.

Cost considerations become secondary to a competitor's reaction to price. This reaction is governed by the degree of competition among companies and to a lesser extent by the competition in the channels of distribution. In a typical oligopolistic industry, price retaliation at the manufacturing level is virtually nonexistent. Each company in the oligopoly knows that if it should price its product above the market, its competitors would not follow its lead. Thus, the company would lose its portion of the market. Yet were any company in the group to cut its price the others would follow along, thereby shaving the profit for all of them. In theory, at least, a company in an oligopoly will tend to price its products at a level that maximizes its profits. Knowing how much competition is likely to exist will be the pivotal factor in determining what a rival's reaction may be in response to a particular price. The more the number of companies in an industry, the greater will be the chance for a price reaction.

Pricing may be a way of enticing competitors into the market because of the prospects of profit, or it may be a way of discouraging them from entering the field if the profits are small. The latter policy is known as "stay-out" pricing. In establishing a price for a product, companies must be sure to estimate accurately the costs of their potential competitors. It is not uncommon for competitors to move into a market with newer technologies and undercut someone else's price.

Policy. The establishment of predetermined prices among the components of a related product line is known as *price lining.* For example, a schedule of prices might be prepared for the various models of an automobile maker's line. Some buyers may prefer more chrome; others may desire engines of a different style or seat covers, or some other embellishment. The attempt to acknowledge many of these preferences and tastes gives rise to the differentiation among the models in the line and to the practice of price lining. The objectives of price lining are threefold: to appeal to the many different income brackets and tastes in the market place; to achieve market segmentation and profitable sale of the product line by facilitating buyers' decisions with respect to goods that satisfy their needs; and to keep the variety of products within economical boundaries so that there may be savings in production and inventory.

The manufacturer begins to consider pricing the line at the time of product design and selection. But he is obliged to work backward from what is likely to happen in the marketing phase when he indulges his thinking about pricing. First, he asks himself, what will the ultimate consumer be willing to pay? Then he estimates the margins both the retailer and the wholesaler will require, and finally the margin he will need to obtain a satisfactory return on his investment. All products and prices must take into consideration the needs of the consumer, the intermediaries involved in reaching him, and the manufacturer.

Most companies have more than a single product to price. Where a line of products contains several different models, as among automobile makers, some rationale is needed for pricing the products within the line—or *product-line pricing.* Factors contributing to this rationale are types of product relationships, optional policies of price relationship, special problems, policy for new product, market segmentation and pricing, and trading up and trading down.

1. TYPES OF PRODUCT RELATIONSHIPS. The main factor distinguish-

ing the pricing of a product line from the pricing of unrelated items is the demand relationship among the components of a particular product line. If the products in a group have similar demand characteristics they compose a related line. The demand relationship itself may be viewed first from the buyer's standpoint and then as a matter of over-all sales strategy. The buyer may consider certain products to be in competition with each other, such as Chevrolet's Biscayne and Bel Air; yet these models roughly serve as substitutes for one another. Or the buyer may consider that one of them includes supplementary items or "extras" that constitute a more complete or more elegant product.

From the point of view of sales strategy, the company has to note the position the product occupies in the acceptance cycle. When first introduced a product may command a higher price. Another strategy is for one product in a line to be priced high to lend prestige to the other products in the line. The presence of the Cadillac in the General Motors family certainly brings prestige to other General Motors products. Loss leaders also may be used to attract attention to a line. This is a common practice among grocery stores in selling butter and coffee. And during off season, it is not unusual to price products at or below cost to equalize the production load.

2. OPTIONAL POLICIES OF PRICE RELATIONSHIP. A company may choose among various pricing policies, evaluating each in relation to its product line and the characteristics of its industry. Some policies worthy of consideration include the following seven: first, prices that produce the same net percentage of profit for all products; second, prices that achieve the same percentage of margin over incremental costs for every product; third, prices that contribute margins related to stages of development; fourth, prices that provide equal service to buyers of all products; fifth, prices that generate margins proportional to conversion costs of various products; sixth, prices that differ systematically among products, depending on competition; and seventh, prices that depend on the elasticity of demand of each market segment.

For prices to produce equal percentages of net profit, a uniform percentage of net profit is added to the cost of each product. This is a form of cost-plus pricing with each product bearing a similar proportion of the common and overhead expense. The allocation of common costs among all products has to be arbitrary. Moreover, this policy fails to assess the nature of demand or the amount of competition.

For prices to yield the same margin over incremental costs, a fixed mark-up such as 20 per cent of the selling price is tacked onto the cost of goods sold. This additional fixed margin is equivalent to adding to the marginal cost. The margin is the difference between the variable costs or cost of goods sold and the selling price. Thus, a company must continually check the relationship of the margin to the marginal costs. In essence this policy is a minor variation of the cost-plus approach based on profit objectives.

When prices are related to stages of development, companies find that as they grow and add new products to their lines some additions contribute more to profits than others. Some of these may be wholly new products while others may be by-products of existing items. Frequently, new products may become more important than older ones. For this policy, therefore, the presumption is made that prices should be chosen in relation to their ability to carry the common costs of the enterprise. Consequently, a company must analyze its products continuously to ascertain their relationship to each other and their potentialities for contributing to profit. Here again arises the question of allocating common costs.

For prices to provide equal service value, they must be chosen in a manner that assures the buyer the same service value for each dollar spent on the various products in the product line. In the case of producer goods the determining factor in setting a price might be the measurable capacity of the company or the savings in cost. With consumer goods, it would be a subjective estimate of value in relation to price. For example, the motivating force in the purchase of extras in an automobile must be the consumer's opinion that they will make driving more enjoyable. If the consumer believes that back-up lights and windshield wipers offer him the same utility, these items must carry the same price tag.

When prices generate margins that are proportional to conversion costs, they become proportionately higher as the cost of conversion increases. Conversion costs generally approximate the *value-added* concept found in the census of manufacturers. These costs include the labor and overhead necessary to convert raw material into finished products, reflecting a company's economic contribution. But in adopting this policy of choosing prices that are proportional to the conversion costs, a company ignores the differences of competition among products, price elasticity, substitutes, and potential competition.

When prices differ systematically among products in relation to competition, they are affected by the degree of differentiation in a company's product line. If there are few products in the line which are highly differentiated and protected by monopoly patents or by the imagery in the consumer's mind, they may be priced higher than less differentiated products. This policy, of course, requires an assessment of the extent of product differentiation and the intensity of competition in the market. It may be applied through experience, systematic experimentation, or market research.

Prices may be established to appeal to different segments of the market if a company is able to learn the elasticity of demand in each one; it can then formulate a pricing policy for each segment. The pricing of compact cars in comparison to standard makes, or of paperback books in contrast to clothbound books, or of ball-point pens in distinction to expensive, gold-plated pens all represent instances of this policy. At lower prices, companies expect to achieve substantial sales volume, but in pursuing this policy they must differentiate their product lines so that the distinctions among the components of any line are clear-cut and effective. Under this policy margins should be added to the incremental costs and should be inversely related to the price elasticity of the various market segments.

3. SPECIAL PROBLEMS. Product-line pricing entails various special problems. Four of them, in particular, command attention. These are the problems of pricing ephemeral goods, load-factor price differentials, goals of price differentials, and trade channel discounts.

Ephemeral goods are those that perish easily with respect to style cycles or novelty. Changes in the style cycle, expiration of patents, and progressive imitation contribute to this perishability. In response to these ephemeral factors two courses may be pursued. One is to set pricing high in order to recover developmental costs rapidly even though this may attract competitors to the field. The converse is to adopt a low or "stay-out" price policy which discourages competitors, encourages rapid expansion of the market, and thus enables economies of scale. Choice of the correct policy depends on some of the following considerations:

Whether prestige pricing has a significant role in developing demand;

Whether it is better to restrict production and sell the inelastic sector first;

Whether there is a high elasticity of demand for nonstyle items in the early phases of the style cycle;

Whether the elasticity of demand increases over the style cycle;

Whether there are great economies of scale in marketing and production as the product advances in the style cycle;

Whether there are substantial barriers to entry.

On the whole there has not been much quantitative information available on the foregoing questions. Experimentation may offer some answers for those charged with determining price policy.

In response to changing load factors some companies choose to alter prices as fluctuations occur in the demand for a product. This sort of policy is reflected in off-peak rates for electricity, off-season discounts on power mowers, August fur sales, and advance dating of merchandise. Off-peak pricing policies also may be used with supplementary products in a company's line to keep their sales on a par with the sale of regular merchandise. Private branding may take place during the off season to move goods at reduced prices. Nevertheless, some stable products may be manufactured in the off season because of the minimal risk of holding them in inventory.

The question then arises as to what kind of differential may be used in different localities. Its answer lies in demand, cost, and competition. No one can predict how quickly a price change will affect demand. Some clues may come from previous experience with other products and from experimentation. But to detect the limits, costs, and risks of shifting demand one really has to study the circumstances of consumption, purchase, and resale. Ordinarily a smaller price change then is needed to generate a shift in consumer demand will induce wholesalers and retailers to take on inventory.

Actually, the load consideration offers a company the choice between opening new markets to increase total demand and waiting for off-peak or off-season opportunities. As we know, demand elasticity varies greatly among products. Off-season sales may bring in customers who may remain out of the market when normal prices exist. On the other hand, anticipation of off-season reductions may cause buyers to postpone purchases until the reductions become effective, as in the case of summer prices on coal.

These various price differentials based on load factors need not necessarily be proportional to differentials in cost. Cost analysis, in fact, should suggest their limits and lead to creation of an optimal pattern of discount and reduction policies. Both economies of large lot production and stable production schedules are sources of cost differentials. By comparing the present load to some other, more favorable one, it becomes possible to ferret out possible savings in costs. If discounting the price, for example, were to result in increased business, the off-season incremental costs could guide a company in setting a course of price cutting. But if the effect of a price decrease were to defer business from periods of normal demand to off-peak periods, the company would have to compare the incremental costs of the normal season to those of the off-peak season in planning a price-reduction program. Indeed it might be advisable to estimate total costs before and after the shift in loads so that in both instances the incremental costs could become the basis for computing the dollar contributions to profit. For competitive reasons there seems to be a disinclination to pursue off-peak pricing policies, except in the style and fashion goods industry where sales on seasonal merchandise seem quite common.

The goals of price differentials change in accordance with diversities found among buyers and sellers. A company enacts differentials for such varied purposes as market strategy, market segmentation, market expansion, and cyclical adjustments. Its discount policy implements its over-all strategy. To participate in diverse types of markets, a company must coordinate its discount structure with other parts of total strategy which include the complete marketing mix, advertising, personal selling effort, and proper channels of distribution. The discount structure may be used also to fractionate the market into segments of differing price elasticities. To the extent that each of these segments may be sealed off from one another, volume of sales and profits may be enhanced. In addition, the discount structure may open new uses for the product or attract new types of customers to expand the market, and finally, discounts are a flexible means of adjusting a list price to short-run changes in demand. The discount, of course, is the principal vehicle for adapting price to changes in economic conditions and the competitive scene. One response to falling demand is the secret adjustment of quantity discounts and product classifications. Competitors whose brands do not command preference or whose product is of lower quality compensate for these weaknesses through their discount structures.

Generally trade channel discounts are reflected in the different concessions to diverse types of buyers. The discount to buyers who link the manufacturer with wholesalers who, in turn, sell to retailers is likely to differ from the discount to those buying directly for retail distribution. In both cases the objective of the trade channel discount is to cover operating costs and normal profits of the intermediaries between producer and consumer. The producer must keep these costs in mind as well as the size of a just margin. If the margin is too great overselling may result. Conversely, if it is too small the selling effort exerted may be insufficient.

Discounts must vary also according to the functions performed by the intermediary. For example, a wholesaler who both stocks inventory and makes deliveries should receive a larger discount for executing these functions than one who does not. The manufacturer may consider, however, the varying costs among buyers performing the same functions. Some companies may be more efficient than others and the discount rate may reflect these differences.

Clearly, a company must evaluate the impact of a competitor's discount structure. Discounts are a method of winning support from dealers and the allowance of a greater one than offered by competitors may be a prudent action on the part of a manufacturer. The ability of larger discounts to increase volume, however, depends on whether the concession merely compensates for low turnover without providing any incentive to push the product, whether the margin inspires greater selling effort by the dealer, or whether competitors will match the discounts. This problem is often circumvented by offering larger discounts to dealers who agree to handle the brand on an exclusive basis.

Opportunities for market segmentation depend on the price elasticities of the ultimate buyer. Such elasticity is greatest among large buyers who are mainly interested in price. The ultimate consumer, on the other hand, may be willing to pay an extra price because of the product differentiation built up in his own mind. Thus, discounts must be directed to the large buyer rather than the ultimate consumer. Market segmentation may be enhanced also by a wide enough discount to dealers to permit them to favor some of their customers. Under fair trade principles, of course, this is prohibited.

4. POLICY FOR NEW PRODUCTS. In relation to new products a company may use a "skimming" policy which endeavors to sell at a high price. The opposite is a policy of "penetration" which is based on a low price. Some companies, however, prefer to slide down the demand curve, starting with a skimming policy and then lowering the price in view of potential competition. Some companies follow an "expansionist" policy; they assume that a lower price will enable them to tap a broader market. This, in turn, permits economies in production. Two other policies are more extreme. One of them, "preemptive" pricing, prices the product low enough to discourage competition from entering the market. The other, "extinction" pricing, involves a price so low that marginal producers will be lucky to break even.

5. MARKET SEGMENTATION AND PRICING. Market segmentation is the splitting of the market into segments on the basis of price and product considerations. The more successful it proves, the greater the possible sales volume and profits. There are numerous illustrations of market segmentation. We have seen some of them in the automobile industry. Others may be found in the deluxe and stand-

ard models of appliances. Segmenting the market is a three-part process: first, the differences in elasticity and their degrees among the markets are determined; next, devices for sealing off the market segments are selected and developed; and finally, the appropriate price for each segment is established.

Once a company determines the degree of elasticity in each market segment it may be able to arrange its prices in a way to improve its over-all profit potentiality. For example, in segments of high elasticity the increased revenue from price reductions may be added to the price increases in other segments where price is not nearly as elastic.

Generally it is difficult for a company to obtain information about the precise conditions of elasticity of demand in the various segments of the market. It also may be difficult to maintain the boundaries between different segments of the market. Consumers are not noted for loyalty to brands. They may shift among brands of a single company or to those of a competitor. The practical pricing problem relates to consumer acceptance and the shifting that takes place because of price differentials between ordinary and deluxe models. Experimentation with various price levels will give some hint of the shift and leakage. For each segment products must be differentiated so that consumers may be able to distinguish effectively among the products in a line.

The ideal for market segmentation is either a leasing or licensing arrangement. Users then pay an additional premium for access to the product. There can be no substituting among products in the product line, and the price charged relates to the benefits received by the consumer. Thus, there is a substantial price barrier between those who use equipment and those who do not. The charging of a uniform price to all provides an unearned advantage but deters the patronage of those whose benefits do not come up to the price asked.

In computing a royalty price for a leased or licensed product, the important factor is what the public is willing to pay. This, of course, relates to expected benefits. Production costs, although of lesser significance than public willingness to pay, are also relevant to determination of the royalty. The governing factor is the marginal, not average, production cost. Moreover, the cost of selling and servicing the product must be considered in the calculation. These various costs add up to a minimum rental which repels consumers who may not be able to use the product profitably. Price is therefore a means of selection. It selects those customers who may benefit most from use of the product and therefore may be willing to pay the royalty.

6. TRADING UP AND TRADING DOWN. To trade down means to sell

a related product at a lower price. To trade up means to sell a similar product or the same one with different features at a higher price. When a company decides to increase the number of price-quality varieties, it can either gain sales by catering to a new segment of the market, or it can gain sales in the existing market by trading up or down. If a new price variety is added to exploit a new consumer group, a company must strive to keep the different varieties distinct in the consumer's mind. Otherwise, the consumer may purchase the lower-priced goods.

The limitations to trading up or trading down are several. Three of them are preeminent. First, the carry-over of prestige based on quality occurs primarily when the customer has no tangible measure of quality to guide him. Second, when the customer habitually demands a particular product, perhaps conforming to certain specifications, no attempt should be made to divert his demand to some other class of merchandise. Third, the addition of a new price variety must be preceded by a clear understanding of its purpose, and this must be predicated on knowing the character of the market demand for a new variety and how much carry-over of prestige is likely to occur because of quality.

Organization for Pricing

In many large concerns, no single official is charged with the responsibility for deciding price changes or price policy.[23] Price setting is generally left to a committee composed of top management and heads of the sales, production, credit, and accounting departments. Not infrequently, the research and legal departments are also represented in price conferences.[24] In a small company the procedure is less elaborate.

Practices in Large and Small Businesses

The chief executives of all large corporations are responsible for some price decisions.[25] Generally they must approve major changes in price policy. But companies selling a multiplicity of products often

[23] Temporary National Economic Committee, Monograph No. 5, p. 81.
[24] R. A. Gordon, *Business Leadership in the Large Corporation*, Brookings Institution, Washington, D.C., 1945, p. 83.
[25] Alfred R. Oxenfeldt, *Industrial Pricing and Market Practice*, Prentice-Hall, Englewood Cliffs, N.J., 1951, p. 112.

entrust price making to officials of relatively lower rank—typically the buyer for a group of related products.[26] Top executives set the policy for the guidance of the lower echelons, to which the buyers adhere. Deviations from policy generally require review by a group of top executives.[27] Subordinates, including individual salesmen, may adjust prices, if necessary, to match reductions initiated by rival organizations.[28] Many companies maintain procedures for speedy adjustments of price on individual orders. They set "quoted prices" in conference but provide latitude for departure from them by individual company officials to save a large order from being lost to a competitor. This delegation of price-making authority on individual orders is a frequently used device to speed up price adjustments.[29]

In small businesses, irrespective of the number of products sold, the owner either sets prices himself or lays down specific rules for those who set prices for him.[30] Because of laws governing the maintenance of resale prices, increasing numbers of distributors do not set price at all, but carry out the instructions of manufacturers.[31]

Generally the organization of pricing policy begins with a broad dictum from the board of directors or the president of the company. Their objective is to use price to yield either a better profit or a higher return on investment. Following the issuance of the dictum, product managers often take over the responsibility for pricing. As in the case of General Electric, the divisional manager inherits this function. The actual administration of the pricing program usually is left to the sales manager. His discretion, however, lies largely in the modification of prices on old products. In the creation of prices for new products top management and representatives of the finance and production divisions often step in. Although in most cases salesmen have little price-making authority, except as already noted, they report competitive price situations to their superiors so that management may review the circumstances and act on them accordingly. The exception to this pervasive rule is General Foods which usually faces excessively keen competition and short-term changes.

Among companies marketing a homogeneous product line or a variety of standardized products pricing tends to be administered from the organization's central headquarters. This is the practice of both American Can and National Steel. Companies whose product line is less homogeneous tend, to the contrary, toward decentralizing

[26] *Ibid.*
[27] Gordon, *loc. cit.*
[28] *Ibid.*, p. 84.

[29] Oxenfeldt, *op. cit.*, p. 113.
[30] *Ibid.*
[31] *Ibid.*

price responsibility among their several product managers. Such is the practice of General Mills, which sells everything from cereals to aircraft instruments.[32]

Background and Training of Price Setters [33]

Most price setters are trained and experienced in business rather than in economics, financing, or engineering. However, they tend as top executives to be familiar with economic concepts. Generally the man who makes the decisions on pricing has the advice of his accounting department on costs and his research department on business conditions and the state of demand. In smaller companies the price setter receives little advice from anyone, but trade associations also make information available on pricing conditions.

The price setter has many forces besides demand and cost considerations to cope with in calculating prices. First, there is risk. Certain pricing policies may court great risk of retaliation or loss of business if the price is too high. Then there is a constant concern over the company's liquidity. Low pricing policies tend to keep the cash flow and state of liquidity high, whereas high prices accomplish the opposite. Next, in seeking larger profits, management must exert greater effort. Executives must study and explore new methods and techniques of expanding their facilities. Finally, there seems to be a strong disposition among businessmen to maintain ethical standards even at the cost of relinquishing profits. However, when survival is threatened, ethical practices may be the first to totter.

The manner in which the price-setting executive is compensated may also have some bearing on his activities. Oxenfeldt has presented evidence of stock ownership in a corporation to show its possible influence on price policy.[34] He concludes that the income of a top executive is not really affected by fluctuating prices and profits, but rather tends to be fairly stable. From this it may be felt that perhaps top executives would be better off if their incomes reflected the changing price level. But this might be a hazardous course. Decisions on pricing might be colored by emotional factors if the income of the price setter depended on the choice of price. Short-sighted thinking might cause decisions of desperation. The individual whose major source of income remains relatively constant is likely to be more

[32] Kaplan et al., *op. cit.*
[33] Oxenfeldt, *op. cit.*, pp. 113–150.
[34] *Ibid.*

objective in choosing prices and to think of long-run rather than short-run goals. Oxenfeldt points out that where executive income has been related to profits the tendency in a declining market has been for management to cut costs. On the other hand, there is nothing to indicate that the same practice does not occur where the income of executives is more stable.

On the whole, price setters are woefully uninformed about conditions of supply and demand.[35] They scale their prices on the degree of product distribution, competitive considerations, and the character of demand. This last includes sensitivity of demand to price changes, the number of buyers and their influence on price, and the effect of the size of the buyer's order on price.

Ideal Organization

Ideally, the organization for price-making decisions should encourage adequate communication, allow for flexibility in decision making, and make provision for long-range planning.

Communication. Clear and rapid communication among the members of the marketing team is of utmost importance. Advertising men should know the pricing plans and vice versa. There should be communication between the marketing department and the other functional areas. The production staff should be apprised of pricing changes so that it may think of cost reduction. The accounting department should not only be advised of price changes but should also inform the marketing management of the effect of various price changes on the profit position of the company. Purchasing should know about price changes, too, so that it may reassess the types of material it buys. Communication must flow also on the pricing policies of companies in direct competition. Information is desirable not only on price changes but also on any competitive action that functions in the same manner as a price reduction. These actions may include special discounts, advertising allowances, premium deals to consumers, coupons, and similar inducements. Both wholesale and retail levels should communicate this information to the producer as quickly as possible for instant referral to the decision centers.

Flexibility. Organizations in which decision making on prices is decentralized will tend to be more flexible in facing competition. The men on the scene see what has to be done and do it. If the decision

[35] *Ibid.*

making is centralized some system of rapid authorization is necessary. Responsibility for pricing should be clearly specified so that authority and responsibility are commensurate, leaving no doubt in anyone's mind that the individual in a particular job has the duty and power to make crucial pricing decisions.

Long-Range Studies. A company's price-making process should not operate on a crisis basis. Someone in the management hierarchy should have the responsibility for studying previous pricing practices and envisaging the forces that might influence pricing in the future. This is best handled as a staff position, and to assure a careful, well-thought-out pricing program, it should be lodged preferably in the marketing research department or in someone attached to the executive in charge of pricing decisions. In any case, pricing should be approached as scientifically as possible, for it may very well constitute the heart of marketing management.

Summary

Various concepts of elasticity are useful in analyzing pricing behavior. Five factors that should be considered in pricing decisions are customer demand, action of competitors, cost considerations, a company's basic objectives, and market penetration and market shares.

The uncontrollable elements in pricing are the market structure, institutional structure, forces of demand, and other broad economic forces. There are three basic methods of pricing: the analytic method, the cost-plus method, and the competitive method. In planning pricing policy one should consider product-line pricing, optional policies, special problems relating to product-line pricing, policy for new products, market segmentation and pricing, and trading up and trading down.

Generally, in large firms there is no official in charge of pricing. In the analysis of pricing behavior one should keep in mind the background and training of price setters. Ideally an organization should provide for rapid and adequate communication, flexibility of decision making, and long-range planning when dealing with pricing problems. In planning for pricing one must consider the relationship of pricing to the market mix. Pricing research is a vital means of gathering information on market reactions to price.

Suggested Cases

Ralph L. Westfall and Harper W. Boyd, *Cases in Marketing Management,* Irwin, Homewood, Ill., 1961.

Haloid Xerox, Inc.—*Manufacturer of Office Copying Equipment*—Pricing When Costs Far Exceed Costs of Competitive Products, pp. 252–255.

Oklahoma Oil Company—*Gasoline Marketer*—Pricing of Non-leader in Price Leadership Industry, pp. 264–269.

Milton P. Brown, Wilbur B. England, and John B. Matthews, Jr., *Problems in Marketing*, 3rd ed., McGraw-Hill, New York, 1961.

G. H. Nelsor. Company, pp. 602–607.

Polaroid Corporation, pp. 608–614.

Harry L. Hansen, *Marketing: Text, Cases, and Readings*, rev. ed., Irwin, Homewood, Ill., 1961.

Wynn Company, pp. 783–784.

DeLuxe Record Company, Inc., pp. 789–790.

Kenneth R. Davis, *Marketing Management*, Ronald Press, New York, 1961.

Bristol-Meyers, Inc., pp. 703–705.

Adele Advertising Agency, pp. 712–716.

Intercollegiate Case Clearing House, Soldiers Field, Boston 63, Massachusetts.

ICH 3C12—Belton Woolen Mills, Incorporated.

ICH 231—Seneca Paper Company.

Chapter Four

Friday is market day in Toluca, Mexico. From miles around Indian
men and women stream into the city's market place, their backs laden
with produce, poultry, and a wide assortment of homemade arts and
handicrafts. Quietly they stake out pieces of ground, spread their
blankets, and set out their products to await the weekly flow of tourists
and visitors from Mexico City, an hour away, and other neighboring
communities. In a simple, face-to-face negotiation, barely one step
removed from barter, producers and consumers bargain over wares and
edibles. Here one of the most direct channels of distribution transfers
products from those who make or raise them to those who wish to
consume them, without the intervention of a vast array of middlemen.
But in the shops of Toluca or Mexico City, as in any sophisticated trade
center throughout the world, a whole army of intermediaries joins in

Channels of Distribution

the complex process of moving goods and services from their originators to the people who ultimately use them. These intermediaries, the inanimate, impersonal organizations and the chains of individuals who compose the wholesale and retail trades, constitute the multiple channels of distribution which form the substance of the present chapter.

The management of these channels is a challenging job. Like other parts of the marketing operation, it necessitates many exacting decisions pertaining to planning and controlling the flow of goods from point of origin through exchange of title to final consumption. As in the planning and control of other phases of marketing, a company must understand both the controllable and uncontrollable elements and organize itself to carry out the policies it develops relative to distribution. The distribution policies of any one company form part of the policies of all companies involved in the channels of distribution, and various theories drawing on scientific and quantitative findings have been advanced to provide a better understanding of these channels. This chapter, therefore, will discuss the planning and control of distribution channels, the organization of a company for this purpose, and various theories about distribution mechanisms.

Planning and Control

Uncontrollable Elements

As a company enters the business arena it has virtually no control over the institutional organization of the channels of distribution. It cannot control the quantity or the quality of middlemen and merchants available to distribute its goods. The number of wholesalers or retailers servicing any area is governed by the size of the area's population. Their quality depends on the keenness of the competition and the attractiveness of the opportunity the company presents to them. Another handicap may be the manner in which goods are distributed at the time, although on occasion it is possible for a new company with sufficient resources to by-pass traditional channels and wait for the rewards of patience.

A second uncontrollable force is the level of economic development. In underdeveloped countries channels of distribution are poorly organized because of the lack of capital and the lack of efficient production. Trading may be even cruder than the market-place activity at Toluca or at best a rather primitive type of wholesaling and retailing. In some underdeveloped countries many individuals are drawn to retailing as a source of income. This has created overcapacity and inefficiency, and one explanation for it has been the relative ease of eking out a living in this way.

The local political system may be a third unyielding element in the attempt to plan and control the channels of distribution. In a monolithic state such as the Soviet Union, the state owns and controls the channels of distribution. In many European countries, cooperatives control them, regulating the flow of goods from producer to consumer. Under the private enterprise system, however, the channels of distribution are free, and when a profitable opportunity presents itself to a company, it will avail itself of these channels.

A fourth element is technological advance, especially changes in transportation. The railroad opened the markets of the western United States. The automobile concentrated local trade in county seat shopping centers and cities. Now the revolution in road and highway construction has taken over. Jay Gould, the railroad empire builder, once vowed to make grass grow in the streets of towns that did not offer him concessions. Nowadays grass may grow in towns by-passed by superhighways and turnpikes. Although federal legislation requires states to conduct studies that show the economic impact of highway relocation, much of the effort is perfunctory and is undertaken with poor market guidance.

Population movements, a fifth uncontrollable factor, have perhaps exercised the greatest recent influence on channels of distribution. The movement to the suburbs, in particular, has prompted a whole development of new shopping facilities in the shape of shopping centers. And qualitative changes in urban population resulting from the flight of so many families to the suburbs have been responsible for changes in market segments. To fit the purchasing capacity of those now inhabiting the cities new types of outlets are required in old locations.

Then there is social change. This is best exemplified by the era following the Second World War with its trend toward higher incomes and more leisure time. This development has influenced not only the types of products sought by consumers but also the method of shopping. Current emphasis on one-stop shopping includes informality in the actual shopping activity and lays greater stress on the physical attractiveness of the store, which now entices patronage with modern architectural design, flowers, and music. The revolution in convenience, a part of this change, has led to vending machines and telephone-ordering services, and one aspect of it, the fetish of self-service, reflects the wish of consumers to maintain their individuality. They like to feel they are making their own choices without anyone telling them what to do. In consequence, there is an increased sale of impulse items. Self-service has already moved beyond the grocery store to the clothing store and the gasoline stations, and the full sweep of this revolution has yet to be felt.

Factor number seven is the level of education. It has made the consumer able to shop more rationally than ever. He is greatly interested in the quality of the product and its price. This interest, particularly after the postwar demand had been satiated, has resulted in the emergence of the discount house, of which there are two types. One is the open type in which any individual may shop. The other is the closed type which sells appliances, soft goods, and grocery items to a restricted clientele of government employees.

Still another uncontrollable element is recession or depression. These have been stimuli to innovations in distribution. The department store, the mail-order house, and lately the supermarket have been responses to depressed conditions and have flourished after their inception. Future cyclical fluctuations may bring forth other new types of retailing endeavors.

A ninth and final uncontrollable element that affects the channels of distribution is the changing habits and customs of consumers. The move to the suburbs following the end of the Second World War had a profound impact, as we have seen, on social change, the living habits of the consumer, and the way he shops. Casual dress and the yearning for convenience have hastened the perfection of the shopping center. The craving to accelerate the rise on the social ladder through buying and more buying of material goods has contributed to the growth of discount houses. To what extent, we may ask then, is the consumer encouraged to join in decision making on the problems of the channels of distribution? These and a number of other nonmaterial considerations may mark the difference between a company's success and failure in distributing its products.

Controllable Aspects

Physical Distribution. The subject that has been very much in the spotlight most recently is physical distribution. Both in the literature of marketing and the top councils of management it has received wide attention. This may result from the fact that many of its aspects respond to mathematical manipulation and computer treatment. Besides, there has been organizational difficulty in a number of instances. Several companies have assigned responsibility for physical distribution to two individuals. One of them deals with the warehouse, and his obligation is to minimize storage costs and increase the rate of turnover. The other deals with transportation and is concerned with minimizing the cost of shipping through shipment of large rather than small units. Thus, the interests of these two men may conflict. The area of conflict tends to be reduced if physical distribution is placed under one person. Under a total physical distribution planning system, the effort is made to provide the quickest and most economical service available. Thus, it may be deemed feasible to ship merchandise by air if the faster service enhances the utility of the product to the customer.

Good management of physical distribution requires control of the movement of raw materials and physical inventories in a way that advances a company's long-run objectives.[1] Physical distribution attempts to bring the right amount of materials or goods to the right place at the right time at the lowest possible cost. To accomplish this objective a group of individuals under effective leadership must work together as a well-knit team. There are two basic parts to the management of distribution, the control of raw materials and the control of finished goods. The control of finished goods inventory necessitates decisions about where, when, and in what quantities products should be located. These decisions are based on marketing research, and it is the duty of a marketing manager to pull them together into a program for finished inventory since it is his assignment to coordinate the marketing effort.

Under certain conditions it may be prudent to increase the number of warehouses while under others it might be more profitable to contract it. If savings on transportation costs exceed the cost of an

---

[1] Donald J. Bowersox, "Forces Influencing Finished Inventory Distribution," *Proceedings of the Winter Conference of the AMA, December, 1961: The Social Responsibilities of Marketing,* edited by William D. Stevens, American Marketing Association, Chicago, 1962, pp. 491–497.

elaborate warehousing system, a company may decide to decentralize its system. Pillsbury, for example, decentralized its warehousing facilities to permit each of its manufacturing plants to concentrate on a smaller number of products and effect economies of scale. Each plant ships its output, even when composed of mixed products, by carload to the nearest warehouse, virtually eliminating storage at the factory. The regional warehouses maintain inventories of products manufactured by all the plants and are so located that a three-day delivery schedule may be maintained to any customer. The net result of this system has been reduction in total inventories and in transportation costs plus improved delivery service.[2]

When companies can offset the expense of transportation by economies in storage, they tend to centralize their warehouse operations. This is the usual practice when there are numerous products in the line, the rates of sale vary, and the values of the products are relatively high. In the Raytheon Company's distributor products division, for example, products are generally sold to wholesale distributors or industrial users. Its distributor customers had been serviced by regional warehouses, which often ran short on various items and had to order them from the factory. This problem was solved by replacing the regional warehouses with a well-stocked central warehouse. As a result, orders received were shipped out by air improving the service and reducing the warehousing costs.[3]

Policies differ among companies on whether to centralize or decentralize their distributive mechanisms. One company that supplies replacement parts to consumers distributes its products from both central and regional facilities. Parts having a slow turnover are stocked in a centralized location, whereas those with a rapid turnover are decentralized. Another company that supplies replacement parts for industrial users pursues a diametrically opposite policy. It meets unexpected demand by retaining slow-moving items in a decentralized warehouse while assigning fast-turning products to a centralized facility.

These differences in policy can be explained by the kind of market served by each company and the degree of product differentiation. The company that decentralizes its slow-moving parts faces extensive competition on replacements for new models, but as parts get older

2 "New-Fangled Routes Deliver the Goods," *Business Week,* November 14, 1959, p. 180 ff.
3 "Why Raytheon Is Dropping Warehouses," *Printer's Ink,* February 5, 1960, p. 48 ff.

it becomes the lone supplier. The other company's decentralized, fast-moving items have only slight style deterioration but many competitive substitutes. Either way, suppliers are judged by how fast they can deliver an item when a production breakdown occurs. The warehousing program a company selects is influenced by environmental, managerial, and competitive forces.[4]

Many companies implement their physical distribution policies through electronic aids. When Westinghouse receives an order for motors, its data-processing equipment plucks out of its memory channels the nearest warehouse that has the motors in stock.[5] The computer adjusts the inventory record of the warehouse, and when the stock shrinks to the reorder point, it instructs the appropriate plant to manufacture additional units of the product. The computer further searches its memory to ascertain the customer's normal trade discount, calculates the sales tax and shipping charges, and prints out the invoice. The order is then transmitted to the proper warehouse for processing. It arrives at the warehouse accompanied by a bill of lading, labels addressed for shipping cartons, and instructions directing the order picker to the correct bin. The complete process takes 15 minutes. Formerly, it required five days on the average.

Control of inventory has been improved in many companies by equating costs of handling to costs of holding. This has proved particularly successful for maintenance and operating supplies. These quantitative techniques of inventory control have also been extended to other items in the inventory but in these cases the mathematical formulations have been more sophisticated. In certain instances models have been developed which not only relate inventory to anticipated sales demand but also refine production schedules to the point at which a plant may be utilized to add inventory in off-seasonal periods.[6] Better controls have resulted in less capital tied up in inventory and a consequent increase on the rate of return on the capital that is invested in rapid turnovers of inventory.

Research. Many companies are ever alert to methods for improving distribution. Research on distribution costs, alternative channels,

---

[4] Bowersox, *op. cit.*

[5] Carl Rieser, "The Short Order Economy," *Fortune,* August 1962, p. 90 ff.

[6] The literature on this subject is extensive. John Magee has done much work in this area. For example, see "Guides to Inventory Policy, Functional and Lot Size," *Harvard Business Review,* Vol. 34, No. 1, January–February 1956, pp. 49–60. This article is followed by two other articles in the *Harvard Business Review,* Vol. 34, No. 2, March–April 1956, pp. 103–116; and Vol. 34, No. 3, May–June 1956, pp. 57–70.

consumer versus dealer attitudes, number and location of outlets, consumer preferences or habits, sales trends and potentials, the effectiveness of present channels, and efforts to extend them has been substantial. Some companies which have analyzed distribution costs have focused on the following areas according to their own reports: [7]

Research that applies to (1) distribution-cost analysis, and (2) profitability studies via various distribution channels.

Transportation costs and times; also scattered studies of transportation time and costs with reference to construction or relocation of existing warehouses.

The real functions performed and the cost of each.

Top marketing executives of these companies expressed strong convictions on the importance of planning in the development of distribution channels and agreed that research was essential to support this planning activity. These are the distribution objectives some of them said they sought to achieve through research:

Sales drives for new wholesale and retail outlets.

The finding of new outlets for present products.

The reaching of new outlets that have not previously handled our type of merchandise.

Establishment of additional outlets, both wholesale and retail.

Revision of the historical tradition of exclusive franchised distribution.

Many companies, of course, know their existing channels of distribution. They learn them by the "invoice-trace method." At random, a manufacturer selects a typical outlet selling directly to an ultimate consumer and traces an invoice back to his shipping department.

Strategy. The choice of a channel of distribution or the course through which an exchange of title to a product flows may be made by either the supplier or the buyer. In this context the term "supplier" refers to the manufacturer and the term "buyer" to a wholesale or retail intermediary who resells the product to the eventual consumer. In the early days of trade the buyer sought out the supplier to purchase luxury items that were readily available to the nobility. Nowadays suppliers seek buyers and, conversely, buyers seek suppliers. There are both powerful suppliers and powerful buyers trying in each case to influence their opposite numbers. Automobile manufacturers, for ex-

---

[7] From author's survey, *op. cit.* (see footnote 26 in Chapter 2).

ample, are in a position to select retailers. They not only grant franchises but also specify the kind of facilities the retailer should possess. Large buyers like Sears Roebuck, on the other hand, not only choose their suppliers but also may dictate how products should be made and how much profit the suppliers are entitled to earn. Between these extremes exists a constant struggle for power. Both suppliers and buyers contend they are the principal force in the distribution system.

Essentially the dispute runs something like this: The buyer maintains that the reason people patronize his store is its location in the right place and its offer of the right assortment of merchandise at the right prices. The supplier counters that people choose a particular store because it stocks nationally advertised brands. The truth is probably somewhere between. The retailer is able to reach the market directly through the sale of goods to the consuming public. He can gauge ultimate needs and desires. But as a rule he lacks the machinery to conduct marketing research in depth and assess the anticipated needs of his customers. This is a job for the manufacturer whose position becomes superior because of his marketing research department.

Both supplier and buyer complement each other. The supplier has the quality of his product and the equity in his brand image created by national advertising and numerous services such as repair, credit, and merchandising information. He has developed a unique product which may attract people to a retailer. The buyer, for his part, has a monopoly location, his established clientele, and a knowledge of the goods his clientele is willing to buy. In a sense when the buyer patronizes the supplier he is granting the latter a franchise just as the supplier is granting him one.[8]

Nevertheless, legislation has been devised to regulate the conflict between supplier and buyer. Maintenance of resale prices is one attempt by the manufacturer to control the channel of distribution and thereby protect his margin. The Robinson-Patman Act, on the other hand, requires fair play among manufacturers to prevent discrimination against small retailers. The Clayton Act also prohibits suppliers from exclusive dealings which compel a retailer to carry only one manufacturer's products.

Search and Assortments. Each intermediate link in the distribution process searches for both suppliers and customers. In searching for

---

[8] See Phillip McVey, "Are Channels of Distribution What Textbooks Say?" *Journal of Marketing,* January 1960, pp. 61–65.

customers the intermediary endeavors to discover the needs of prospects so that the prospects may be converted into customers. In searching for suppliers he tries to collect an assortment of merchandise that will appeal to potential customers. The search involves the effort to establish communication with both supplier and customer. Communication may be developed through suppliers' salesmen, telephone or mail inquiries by potential customers, or through a broker. Ordinarily, there would be two-way communication on the state of the market. This would include knowledge of supplies available from other sources, terms of sale, and condition of demand among the consuming public. When the needs of a customer and supplier correspond a transaction takes place and arrangements are made for the physical movement of merchandise.

After a supplier seeks out various assortments of merchandise he settles on a relatively fixed one. To the extent that he clings to his assortment as demands among buyers change he encourages other suppliers to provide the newly desired items. The do-it-yourself supplier was a response to consumer demand for a complete assortment of goods for repair work or improvement around the house. The discount house, as noted earlier, came about through a decision to satisfy the price-conscious portion of the public. The teen shop sprang from the need for an outlet to cater to this growing segment of the population.

Criteria for Channels. The perfect channel of distribution minimizes cost and maximizes long-run profit. In devising such a channel, a company must be cognizant not only of its own profits but also of the profits of the intermediaries and the final price to the ultimate consumer. In other words, a manufacturer must allow for adequate margins all along the line as incentives to push his merchandise through the distribution mill. Before this may be done, however, two things are required: an adequate knowledge of the distribution cost and a communication system that immediately reports any change in the structure of inventories and prices. We shall explore distribution costs later in the chapter.

The problem of communication is difficult because the retailer does not maintain constant contact with the supplier. Services like the A. C. Nielsen Company and the Market Research Corporation of America can provide the manufacturer with some data on the sale of goods to ultimate consumers. Warranty cards also have been used for appliances, but many purchasers fail to send them in. Some companies have been able to obtain partial information from sampling dealers' reports of sales, which are made every month or every two weeks. Sales representatives of companies can determine the size of the stock on hand, a general rate of sale, and the competitive pressure on the market. All these at best are only approximations which leave the retailer and manufacturer without complete quantitative information.

Turnover is a second and important quantitative criterion of return on investment. However, a company must compare the advantages of turnover with the additional costs it incurs. Some of the costs engendered by a high turnover rate include increased handling, billing, and transportation charges.

Another quantitative criterion for choosing a channel of distribution is the financial resources available to a company. When a company's financial resources are limited, its distribution choices like its production choices are restricted to the existing institutional structure. Companies that are stronger financially may develop new institutional structures of their own or may decide to integrate those they have at their command.

There are also qualitative criteria for the selection of a channel of distribution.[9] By their nature products may be perishable or durable, necessities or luxuries; they may have a high unit value or a low one, and consumers by habit may expect to find them in a particular type of retail outlet. In their manufacture, such matters as the degree of manufacturing concentration, the location of the plant in relation to the centers of consumption, and the breadth of the product line all bear on choice of a distribution channel. In retailing them the number of stores that sell a particular product and their location with respect to manufacturers and consumers both influence the selection of channels.

Where the product is perishable companies tend to seek more direct than indirect contacts in the channels; for durable products the reverse is the common practice. Luxury items such as jewelry and furs are usually distributed directly whereas canned soups are distributed indirectly. Products of extremely high value are normally sold directly. If consumers habitually expect to purchase toothpaste in a supermarket, that is one logical place for its distribution. The single factor that seems to influence consumer purchasing habits most is one-stop shopping convenience.

Where there is a concentration of manufacturing activity, industries incline toward assuming the middleman functions themselves. If

[9] John A. Howard, *Marketing Management,* rev. ed., Irwin, Homewood, Ill., 1963, p. 338.

manufacturing is dispersed over a wide geographic area the general practice is to employ wholesale intermediaries. And the broader the product line the greater is the tendency toward selling directly to the retailer.

When many retailers carry a particular product a manufacturer finds it easier to sell it through these retail outlets than directly to the ultimate consumer. It is also simpler to use the retailer when the location of this store makes it more convenient for him to buy from the manufacturer.

Dealer Policy Boards. One new form of communication between elements in the channel of distribution is the dealer policy board whose role and method of operation were described in a speech by Walker A. Williams.[10]

We established our dealer councils back in 1945 to provide a clear channel of communications between our dealers and our top management. Since 1950, the members of the dealer councils of our Company's Ford Division have been elected by the dealers themselves.

This democratic policy has not been adopted by other companies in the industry. For the past 11 years since the creation of the councils, both our company and our dealers have worked to improve them and make them more useful. We now have a national dealer council for each of our car divisions.

Let me tell you briefly how the council operates at the Ford Division. Members are elected annually by the dealers on a national basis. All of the dealers in each zone, who comprise a zone council, elect two representatives to the district council. The district council, in turn, elects two representatives to the regional council; and each of the regional councils elects representatives to the national council. The two representatives elected at each level are usually a small dealer and a large dealer.

The national council presents to management of the company the views and recommendations of all dealers. These views and recommendations are discussed, first at the zone level, then at the district and regional levels, and finally at the national level.

There is no limitation on the subjects for discussion at the council meetings. They embrace every conceivable area—dealer-company relations, engineering and design, quality, the competitive situation, distribution problems, wholesale prices, and advertising programs, to name a few. Both dealers and the company recognize the necessity of advancing their common interests, and the discussions proceed with complete freedom.

The principal purpose of the board—the principal responsibility of its members—is to establish better communications and improved relations between the company and its dealers. In carrying out that function, we

---

[10] Walker A. Williams, Vice President, Vice Chairman, Dealer Policy Board, Ford Motor Company, National Association of Manufacturers 61st Congress of American Industry, Dec. 7, 1956.

members of the board represent the company's conscience in its relations with the dealers. When policies affecting dealers are made, we help to initiate and formulate these policies from the beginning, and we constantly review the administration of these policies after they have been established.

Intensive and Extensive Distribution. Distribution may be either intensive or extensive. Intensive distribution involves getting the product into every outlet handling that type of goods. Extensive distribution permits a choice of outlets based on such matters as selling ability or financial status. Moreover, this method of distribution may be subdivided into those outlets that are given an exclusive franchise and those that are not. Exclusive franchises are in a sense a monopoly for the product in the particular territory. Many manufacturing companies have switched from them to nonexclusive dealership. They have done so because of the way in which consumers shop and the type of assortments they expect to find in any retail outlet. If a woman is contemplating the purchase of a washing machine she may wish to inspect more than one brand. Rather than visit several stores she may want to go to only one or a few. The store with the widest selection is more likely to make a sale than the one carrying only a single brand. However, a manufacturer cannot count on as much selling effort for his particular product if the retail outlet operates on a nonexclusive basis.

Practices vary with the type of market. In a sellers' market there is a tendency toward exclusive dealerships whereas in a buyers' market the nonexclusive method prevails. However, some manufacturers have successfully maintained either alternative irrespective of the type of market. When a product is backed by strong national advertising, its manufacturer is in a better position to establish exclusive distribution than otherwise. Mass merchandising by its very nature moves away from the exclusive to the nonexclusive form of distribution.

The Best Channel. There is no such thing as a single channel of distribution that works best for any specific product. The telling factor is how efficiently a company manages its particular distribution channel. Ovaltine offers a case in point. Most producers of chocolate products distribute their lines through the customary wholesale grocery channels. Ovaltine, however, has its own sales force to call directly on retail stores, vie for an adequate position on their shelves, and obtain information on the stocks on hand. The Ovaltine salesmen can fight for a proper shelf position, report the movement of stocks, prepare the retailer for future promotions, check that point of purchase advertising is used, and note the action of competitors. Wholesalers carrying many different food products cannot give any one of them as complete attention as the Ovaltine man accords his. Frequently, however, many manufacturers and processers supplement their existing organization of distribution with their own merchandising men to do the kind of job the Ovaltine man performs.

Opening Channels. Two general methods, the push method and the pull method, have been used to open new channels of distribution. In the former the manufacturer sends his own representatives to buying offices to point out the vigorous promotional effort about to be launched on behalf of the product. Deals are made to entice the intermediary with several free cases of merchandise. Sometimes push money is offered to move the product. If the buyer is sufficiently impressed, he will respond to the blandishments and order the merchandise.

The pull method is used when the manufacturer cannot get immediate distribution in retail stores. His tactic is to initiate a broad campaign to induce the consumer to ask his local merchant for the manufacturer's product. If the requests are numerous enough, the retailer is forced to carry the line of goods, usually gaining some kind of concession for doing so.

Basis for Choice. Finally, it should be remembered that consumer buying motives and habits are fundamental factors in the choice and maintenance of distribution channels. A company must remain aware at all times, therefore, of the aspirations of all the elements in the distribution process—the consumer, the wholesaler, and the retailer. The wholesaler and retailer are both interested in an assurance of profit and in knowing that their risks are minimal. The consumer's interest lies in obtaining a good value for his money at a convenient location. A company that is alert to these various concerns may find itself better able to select the most prosperous channels of distribution.

Organization and Channels

The purpose of organization among the distribution channels is to foster cooperation in facilitating exchanges of title and the physical movement of goods. A company must consider not only the exchange of title from itself to its closest intermediary but also the further exchanges from the intermediary en route to the consumer of its particular product. Physical movement of the goods includes billing and inventory control activities as well as warehousing and transportation.

Formal and Informal Organization

The organization for distribution may be considered as being divided into formal and informal aspects. Both of these can be viewed from standpoints inside and outside a company. The internal formal organization embraces those charged with decision-making responsibility for channels of distribution, although in some companies this does not necessarily include the individual designated on the organization chart as nominally responsible for such decisions. The sales manager or the market manager is the likeliest person responsible for selecting the proper channel of distribution and instituting changes when they appear necessitated or justified by new conditions. He would expect cooperation from the traffic, inventory control, service, legal, and accounting departments. Members of the marketing, market research, sales, advertising, and product development departments usually collaborate on the problems of maintaining present channels of distribution and developing new ones. Externally, the formal organization consists of the franchise arrangements in existence. It also includes the commitment of specific resources by all forces in the distribution process to the task of expediting the flow of goods through the channels. As we have seen, dealers have a newer form of formal organization, which enables them to communicate their desires to the manufacturer and the manufacturer his to them.

The internal informal organization consists of how decisions are made and carried out. It may be that the production manager takes the initiative to see that the warehouse is adequately stocked. Or the advertising manager may spot the need for a change in a channel and bring it to the attention of the sales manager. Things get done through these internal informal organizations. The external informal organization comprises all the personal contacts and communications occurring outside the formal organization. The salesman is the principal agent of this association. Through his efforts and personality, cooperation is encouraged and the image of the company is largely transmitted.

Leadership, Motivation, Cooperation

Someone in the distribution channel must take the lead in organizing it and maintaining continuous cooperation among its elements. This leadership may come from the manufacturer, a wholesale intermediary, or a retailer. It may stem from the power or size of the institution in the distribution channel. In some instances a group of smaller companies may join forces to equalize the power of the large concern, whereupon leadership passes to the group. Inside the manufacturing company the sales manager or market manager should supply the leadership. Given formal responsibility for maintaining the channels, he should take the lead in assuring their continuity.

Cooperation is not self-propelled but has to be motivated. Although one might believe that the motive of profit were sufficient to elicit full cooperation, other motives might very well have equal force. The prospect of material gain is not the only incentive to cooperate in maintaining effective channels of distribution. There are such things as recognition and tribute for the job performed. And guarantees of security and opportunities for self-expression also motivate intermediaries to cooperate.

Organization for Physical Distribution

Control of physical distribution rests with several departments of a company.[11] To maintain a smooth flow of goods through the distribution channels, it is therefore necessary to eliminate as many of the intramural conflicts as possible. For example, the traffic department arranges the transportation required. In its effort to reduce expenses it may instinctively concentrate on shipments to intercity plants and certain customers ignoring others in its cost-saving drive. The sales department, on the other hand, is desirous of the speediest delivery possible to all the company's customers. The purchasing department may wish to control traffic to economize on transportation costs and increase purchasing allotments, but the production department may seek to control both traffic and purchasing to assure itself an adequate supply of materials.

Actually it is possible to handle physical distribution in two different ways. One is to centralize the planning phase and let the operation proceed at existing departmental levels. This method creates less chaos in effecting any change in organization. The other way of handling distribution is to centralize the control not only of the planning but also of the operations. Such centralized control is best located in the marketing organization. The company may appoint a manager of physical distribution who is responsible to the head of the marketing department. This manager would take over the planning of all intercity movement and the control of the remain-

[11] Edward W. Smykay, Donald J. Bowersox, and Frank H. Mossman, *Physical Distribution Management,* Macmillan, New York, 1961, pp. 274–277.

ing distribution facilities. He would undertake the necessary co-ordination among appropriate departments to perform the task of physical distribution and also concern himself with incoming goods and supplies.

The distribution manager should control the company's traffic department and supervise its warehouse system, aided by two staff departments. One of these would deal with coordination of the marketing, production, and purchasing organizations, and its activities would consist of analyses of distribution costs, distribution systems, internal warehouse operations, and choice of locations, the last function assigned to a special real-estate group. The other staff department would coordinate all traffic affairs including import and export activities and rate and claim analyses.

Theory and Channels

By and large the economist has not occupied himself with theories about channels of distribution. His main interest appears to have run to the area of pricing. What sparse literature exists on distribution channels has been developed by teachers and practitioners of marketing. Most of this writing has been of a descriptive nature, with useful empirical generalizations drawn from the Census of Business, Barger's study,[12] and Clewett's book on marketing channels.[13] In the development of a priori models for channels, even less source material has been available. This portion of the chapter will examine various empirical and a priori models that may offer some guidance to the student and the market manager.

A Priori Models

Market Structure. Wroe Alderson has pointed out that the essential problem in marketing has been the allocation of varying assortments of merchandise in the most efficient manner possible. This allocation has to be made on the basis of existing consumer demand. The assortments are built up and then broken down through the channels of distribution. Alderson has also pursued the idea that a channel of distribution is a behavioral system very much like the organic

[12] Harold Barger, *Distribution's Place in the American Economy Since 1869,* Princeton University Press, Princeton, N. J., 1955.
[13] Richard M. Clewett (Ed.), *Marketing Channels,* Irwin, Homewood, Ill., 1954.

structure of nature. In his view, individuals grouped together as manufacturers must perform in the behavioral context in which groups of wholesalers and large retailers exist. Their behavior is shaped by the institutional environment as it, in turn, adjusts to the changing behavior of the consumer. In working through the channels of distribution, manufacturers establish systems of routinization in order to increase the efficiency of their distributive mechanisms. To sort their merchandise effectively, they search for buyers among the various channels available.

From theories of organization have come insights that may give the marketer a better understanding of the channels of distribution.[14] Chester Barnard has observed that both suppliers and customers are part of the organization of a company.[15] On the basis of organization theory, Berg has designed models of distribution comprising the following five interrelated states:

(1) factoring the companywide strategic situation, (2) converting key factors into functional prerequisites for the system, (3) grouping individual tasks into work units, (4) allocating tasks for appropriate functionaries, and (5) designing a structure of relationships to provide loci of distributive authority and responsibility within the work structure erected in previous stages.[16]

Stage 1: At the start, in factoring the companywide strategic situation, efforts are made to discover differences among companies in distribution practices. The two variables examined are the environment as it is interpreted by management and factors pertaining to the company's base of resources. Marketing strategy relates both environment and resources as a unit to the functional necessities and structural features of the distribution system. The environment includes stockholders, employees and their unions, the interests of suppliers, trade associations, divisions of government, competitors, and ultimate consumers. The base of resources includes finances, manpower, material, and spatial, temporal, and other facilities. Berg's exercise offers to apply all these factors to the channels of distribution.

Stage 2: Few producers can answer the question of what they wish their distribution set-ups to accomplish for them in converting key

---

[14] Thomas L. Berg, "Designing the Distribution System," *Proceedings of the Winter Conference of the American Marketing Association, Dec. 27–29, 1961, The Social Responsibilities of Marketing,* edited by William D. Stevens, American Marketing Association, Chicago, 1962, pp. 481–490.

[15] Chester I. Barnard, *Organization and Management,* Harvard University Press, Cambridge, Mass., 1948, pp. 112–113.

[16] Berg, *op. cit.*

factors into prerequisites for their systems. Yet it is possible to infer some of the factors they might desire from a study of Stage 1.

Stage 3: This stage applies organization theory which describes the distribution process in a meaningful way as one of division of labor or the grouping of tasks. In utilizing organization theory to group individual tasks into work units, one deals with other methods of specialization, such as by-product, customer, time, location, or process, or by some combination of these categories. Organization theory focuses attention on the need for coordination and cooperation among the forces in the distribution structure to select the proper kinds of specialization. Some types of organization theory concentrate first on the work and then on the worker.

Stage 4: In trying to select the appropriate functionaries for the various tasks the best procedure seems to be to fractionate the ultimate markets to be served, namely, the consumers, and then move backward to the intermediate markets until the whole structure links up directly with the producing organization. Each middleman must be recognized as a candidate for a specific task. The distribution manager must choose for each task the middleman who best fits the key factors, meets the functional requirements, and passes the preliminary screening as to specialization. He then arrays the other candidates in order of suitability. By asking several additional questions about possible economies of scale at each type of outlet, about how many of each type of outlet will be required, and about what pattern of area coverage should be chosen, he can effectively match men to jobs. Computers help him find the answers to many of his questions.

Stage 5: In designating a structure of appropriate relationships a manufacturer must first know which activities are to be controlled in order to comply with law, ensure profits, generate good will and repeat business for brands, keep risks within limits, and provide for effective coordination of the over-all marketing program. Then he must identify the areas in which he can influence the balance of power in the distribution system. There are two alternatives for structural action. The manufacturer may try to accumulate market power and dispense it unilaterally to exact compliance from intermediaries or he may create conditions whereunder authority may be safely dispersed throughout the system. Thus, the alternatives are to reserve distribution authority for the manufacturer or to delegate it to the tradesmen. According to Berg, reservation of authority includes outright ownership of facilities, existence of concubine outlets, preretailing practices, widespread consumer deals, and fair-trade agreements.

Customer   Supplier

Figure 4-1. Single communication link.

The alternative includes specification by contract of what is to be delegated. This may be supplemented by the provision of auxiliary service units such as distributor training groups and dealer advisory councils. It may be facilitated by efforts of all the groups involved to hold the exercise of authority within reasonable bounds. The actual pattern of delegation depends on how the power has been acquired, on the relative bargaining strengths of manufacturer and middleman, and on past history of cooperation.

Communication Networks. In a sense the channel of distribution may be considered as being composed of levels of communication,[17] and this hypothesis may be pursued analytically. Figure 4-1, for example, shows a single communication link between a customer and a supplier. Where no intermediaries exist each customer is also a supplier and each supplier is a customer. Thus, the number of communication links is the product of the number of suppliers and customers, expressed by the formula

$$LINKS = SC$$

This may be seen clearly in Figure 4-2 which contains three suppliers (S) and an equal number of customers (C).

The number of links, it may be clearly seen, is nine. If one wished to calculate the cost of linkage, the number of links would be multiplied by a quantity (q). Without intermediaries, then, the cost of linkage would be

$$T_2 = q(SC)$$

where T_2 represents this kind of linkage cost.

The number of links *with* an intermediary, however, is simply the sum of the total number of suppliers and customers:

$$n = S + C$$

This may be seen in Figure 4-3. In this case the number of links is reduced to six. But as the number of wholesalers (W) increases so

[17] Frederick E. Balderston, "Communication Networks, A Theory of Vertical Market Structure," unpublished paper presented at the Ford Foundation Seminar, Williams College, Williams, Mass., 1957.

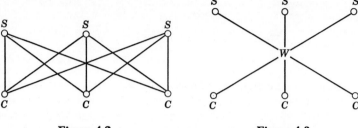

Figure 4-2   Figure 4-3

does the linkage by a multiple of the number of wholesalers.   The formula changes to

$$n = W(S + C)$$

This may be seen in Figure 4-4.   The number of links, it may now be noted, has increased to 12.   The cost of such linkage with an intermediary may be expressed by the formula

$$T_4 = qW(S + C)$$

in which T_4 represents the cost of intermediary linkage.

To the community the advantage of having or not having a wholesaler in the distribution process would be determined by the formula

$$\hat{M} = T_2 - T_4$$

One could then establish a point at which it would no longer pay to increase the number of wholesalers.   This point would fall as a rule where the cost of not having intermediaries equaled the cost of

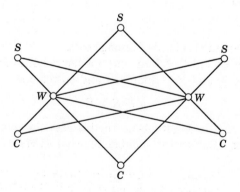

Figure 4-4

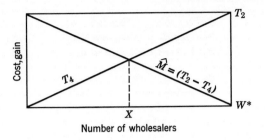

Figure 4-5

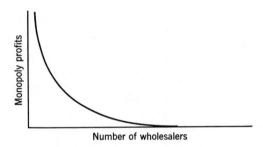

Figure 4-6. Monopoly profits.

having them, or where $T_2 = T_4$, or $W^* = \frac{1}{2}C$, as demonstrated by Figure 4-5.[18] We can see that the cost of adding wholesalers T_4 equals zero advantage $\hat{M}$ at X number of wholesalers. The upper limit on adding wholesalers is fixed by T_2, the cost of nonintermediary linkage.

If a community has only one wholesaler he is in a position to obtain monopoly profits. As the number of wholesalers grows monopoly profits fall. Put another way, monopoly profits are a function of the number of wholesalers and are formulated as

$$M = J(M)$$

which is demonstrated by Figure 4-6. From the community's point of view it becomes necessary to add the cost of monopoly profits to the cost of communication links with intermediaries, and this is expressed in the following manner:

$$T_5 = qW(S + C) + M$$

[18] See Balderston, *ibid.*, for proof.

Table 4-1.   Number of Wholesalers Necessary to Minimize Cost to Community

W	T_4	M	T_5
1	20	80	100
2	40	18	58
3	60	7	67
4	80	0	80
5	100	0	100

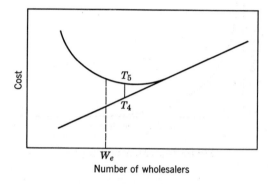

Number of wholesalers

Figure 4-7.   Cost of wholesaler to community.

This raises the question as to how many wholesalers would be necessary to minimize the cost to the community. For the answer, we turn to Table 4-1. The lowest cost of wholesaling to the community occurs, it will be seen from the table, when there are two wholesalers available. In graphic form this may be studied in Figure 4-7, in which point W_e signifies the number of wholesaling establishments that provide the lowest cost to the community. The difference between T_5 and T_4 in the illustration represents the monopoly profits.

Institutional Structure. "The wheel of retailing" [19] is the name suggested by Professor Malcolm P. McNair for a hypothesis pertaining to patterns of retail development. This hypothesis postulates that new types of retailers enter the market as low-status, low-margin, low-price operators. Gradually they acquire more elaborate estab-

[19] Stanley C. Hollander, "The Wheel of Retailing," *Journal of Marketing*, Vol. 25, No. 1, July 1960, pp. 37–42.

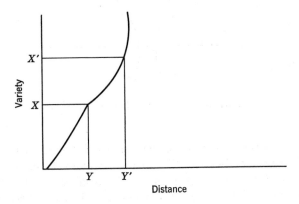

Figure 4-8. Diminishing returns in variety.

lishments and facilities that require increased investments and higher operating costs. Finally, they become high-cost, high-price merchants, vulnerable to newer entrants who, in turn, follow the same course. Department store merchants who were originally competitors to the smaller retailers and who have become targets of discount houses and supermarkets exemplify the progress capsulized in this wheel pattern.

Baumol and Ide expressed the view that among retail establishments variety is an advantage to the consumer only to a point.[20] Ultimately a store may stock so large a variety of items that shopping costs become prohibitive. This suggests why a mail-order company like Sears, Roebuck may find it profitable to catalog many lines that a store like Marshall Field's or Macy's will not carry. By issuing separate catalogs for different lines some mail-order houses have been able to reduce the varieties in each issue and yet increase their total assortments.

The minimum number of items necessary to draw a consumer into any store increases with his distance from that store. A distant consumer's high shopping cost can be justified only by a high probability of a successful shopping trip. For every value of article, there is a maximum distance from a store beyond which it does not pay the consumer to patronize it. Similarly, the benefit of shopping in this store is a function of the consumer's place of residence. Figure 4-8 shows that a consumer may willingly travel distance Y to shop for variety X. By increasing the variety to X' a retailer may extend

[20] William J. Baumol and Edward A. Ide, "Variety in Retailing," *Management Science*, Vol. 3, No. 1, October 1956, pp. 93–101.

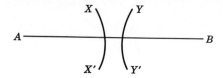

Figure 4-9.   Maximum distance traveled.

to Y' the periphery from which he can attract customers. But increasing the variety beyond X' will not be likely to draw customers from beyond distance Y'. A point of diminishing return sets in, and increasing the variety of goods beyond it will not induce consumers to travel as far as they would for the variety available to that point.

Consumers are attracted to competing stores very much as iron filings are drawn to a magnet. The maximum distance a consumer will travel to any particular store is as far as that point at which the forces of attraction of competing stores equal each other, or where there is no benefit in shopping in either store. In Figure 4-9, for example, consumers between XX' and A will derive some advantage in shopping at A, whereas those between YY' and B will gain from shopping at B. However, consumers between XX' and YY' will gain no advantage in shopping at either A or B. The maximum shopping distances are therefore from XX' to A and from YY' to B. This leads to the following economic conclusions: first, an increased number of items will yield increasing average returns to begin with, then decreasing marginal and average returns, and finally, negative and marginal returns, as may be seen in Figure 4-10. The maximum revenue to be derived from increasing variety is Y for X items. Be-

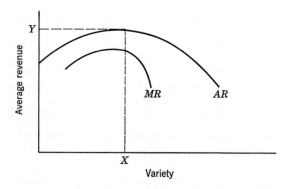

Figure 4-10.   Average marginal revenue of variety.

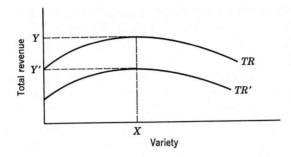

Figure 4-11. Revenue from total sales and single line.

yond this point the average and marginal revenues become negative. Second, as Figure 4-11 demonstrates, it does not pay a store to increase its variety of items interminably even if consideration of the retailing costs is neglected. Third, not only will total sales rise up to a point through an increase in the variety stocked, but the sales *per item carried* also will improve. In Figure 4-11 we can see that as the variety increases to point X total line sales rise to Y. Sales for one item in the line rise to Y'. But if the variety is extended beyond X, there is no additional increase in revenue for the total line (TR) nor for a single item in the line (TR'). Further variety will then attract a disproportionate number of supplementary customers. The Baumol-Ide model, on which the foregoing assumptions are based, is predicated on Reilly's Law of Retail Gravitation, which will be discussed presently.

Empirical Models

Generalizations. When fabrication of semifinished or raw materials is postponed, other things being equal, marketing costs are economized. Under this principle, the commitment of a unit of material to a specific use is deferred as long as possible. In practice, as observed in a study of housebuilding,[21] a piece of material moves successively into narrower and narrower marketing areas and into forms that reduce the range of uses to which it is to be put. Each narrowing choice imposes a penalty in that it either cannot be reversed at all, as when a log is made into plywood or boards are cut into stairways, or can

---

[21] Reavis Cox and Charles Goodman, "Marketing of Housebuilding Materials," *Journal of Marketing,* July 1956, pp. 36–61.

be reversed only at a considerable expense, such as when a girder is melted down and reworked into sheet steel or wire.

This principle of postponement holds that each successive narrowing commitment should be deferred as long as possible to avoid the likelihood and cost of a mistake. In postponing the manufacture of a fuel tank fabricated from sheet steel until shortly before the time to install it, the company delays assigning the sheet to fuel tanks in general and to specific sizes and kinds of such tanks in particular, keeping it available for optional uses in the meantime. Besides reducing the risks of commitment, postponement offers the advantage that plain sheet is less expensive to store and transport than sheet shaped into fuel tanks.

Another principle derived from the housebuilding study is that marketing methods are flexible. For example, the techniques used to build a house shift in response to more favorable turns in costs and price. When the cost and setting of stone rose appreciably, builders promptly and easily changed to some other type of foundation. Other examples of flexibility may be found in changes that have taken place in the functions of wholesalers. Jobbers of mineral wool applicators have taken over the tasks of their customers for the insulation of old housing. As a result, transactions, loadings, and unloadings have been reduced.

This flexibility extends to the willingness of enterprises within any distribution system to realign functions among themselves. The widespread adoption of drop shipping is a conspicuous case in point. Essentially a device to separate the flow of goods, this practice turns up whenever it is advantageous to vest ownership and the responsibility for buying and selling in a middleman without having the goods pass physically through his hands. There is also what may be described as the opposite of drop shipping, although there is no generally accepted name for it. This situation exists when the flow of title is more direct than the flow of goods. It may be observed in the controversial arrangement whereby plumbers and other contractors work for builders on a "labor-only" basis. The builder buys the materials, by-passing the contractor in the flow of title while the contractor receives the materials and installs them.

All the participating companies in a distribution system actually have an assortment of choices at their disposal. Any one of them desirous of assuming a task ordinarily performed by some other company usually can complete the kind of transaction of its choice through appropriate adjustments in price. For every function performed by an intermediary there is a cost. The question to be answered is, "who

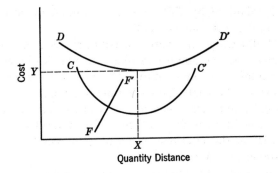

Figure 4-12. Control distribution economies of a single plant company.

can perform this function most efficiently at the lowest cost?" Thus, competition for greater efficiency tends to keep prices in line within the channel of distribution. Price competition is so close and continuous for most products and services required in the housebuilding industry that it leads to a willingness of buyers and sellers to bargain for any arrangements that yield even small advantages.

Large-Company Advantages.[22] Do large companies have advantages in physical distribution? Do they have an edge in freight costs, handling, taking and filling orders, storage, and administration of the distribution functions? Do such advantages increase so that a company can realize them more fully by growing in size? Let us look for the answers in three sorts of economies in physical distribution: control distribution economies, nodal distribution economies, and economies of scale.

1. CONTROL DISTRIBUTION ECONOMIES. These reflect the economies of conducting a distribution system from a single plant. They include the economies of mass, or bulk, transactions—that is, handling and shipping from the plant—offset by rising average freight shipping costs as volume increases and products travel to more distant customers. They will result in an optimum scale of distribution for the plant and may be reinforced by the central economies practiced in a multiplant company through more efficient administration of its central distribution functions.

In Figure 4-12, pertaining to a single plant company, the costs of handling bulk is represented by CC'. The rising costs of shipping

[22] Joe S. Bain, "Advantages of the Large Firm: Production, Distribution, and Sales Promotion," *Journal of Marketing*, Vol. 20, No. 4, April 1956, pp. 343–345.

freight are symbolized by *FF'* with the optimum quantity and distance at *X* and the optimum cost at *Y*.

Figure 4-13 illustrates the control distribution economies of a multiplant company. As the number of plants increases, the control costs at central headquarters are reduced because there is more efficient administration of the control distribution function.

As additional plants are added to *AA'*, control costs vary from *AA'* to *DD'* with freight costs from *II'* to *LL'* and total costs from *EE'* to *HH'*. *MM'* is the envelope curve of total cost. The optimum quantity distance is at *X* with cost *Y*.

2. NODAL DISTRIBUTION ECONOMIES. These economies are realized in the performance of distribution functions at and through particular geographical nodes, such as wholesaling and retailing centers throughout the country. These are the economies of mass or bulk in the volume passing through any node.

In Figure 4-14, an example of nodal distribution economies, the curves *AA'*, *BB'*, and *CC'* represent the cost of handling goods at various combinations of wholesale and retail centers. All these costs may be enclosed in the envelope curve *JJ'*. Bulk and distance costs are indicated by *DD'*, *EE'*, and *FF'* with the best combination of geographic wholesale and retail centers falling at the point where bulk and distance costs intersect the envelope curve *JJ'* yielding an optimum bulk and distance *X* and cost *Y*.

3. ECONOMIES OF SCALE. This type of economy is possible only

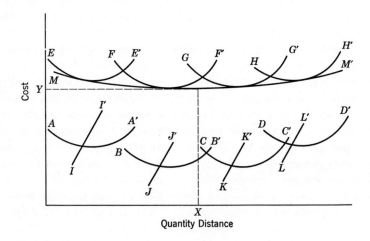

Figure 4-13. Control distribution economies of a multiplant company.

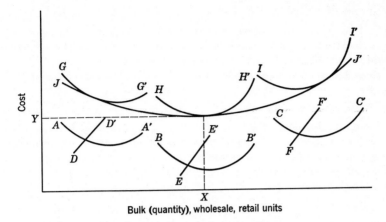

Figure 4-14. Nodal distribution.

when a single company must for some reason reach two or more distribution nodes and the shipping cost is a significant factor. The economy of scale reflects a reduction in the costs of shipping freight to the individual nodes that must be reached. This is achieved by shipping greater bulk to regional dispersal points. Figure 4-15 is an example of economies of bulk freight at three distribution nodes. AA', BB', and CC' represent the wholesaling retail distribution economies; DD', EE', and FF' are freight costs with total costs of GG', HH', and II'. Envelope JJ' is tangent to the minimum points of total costs. At node AA', when freight costs change from DD' to KK', the bulk shipped changes from X to X' and cost savings from Y to Y'. The

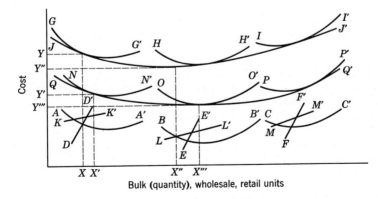

Figure 4-15. Economies of scale on freight at various distribution nodes.

optimum point before reduced freight costs would be at bulk X'' and cost Y'''. Reduced freight costs KK', LL', and MM' contribute to lower cost curves NN', OO', PP', and envelope QQ'. The new optimum is at bulk quantity X'''' and cost Y''''.

Bain found that neither nodal nor scale economies were critical in industries in which product differentiation was unimportant or sales promotion was conducted locally to the exclusion of the possible advantages of broader promotion, or in companies able to concentrate their distribution in a single region.[23] Control distribution economies, however, were critical in these same industries. The optimal scale of production (Figure 4-12) would not exceed the scale for central plant economies, nor would the distribution optimums for plants be any greater than the production optimums. Thus, the scales and the requirements of concentration would not be increased by the factor of distribution.

In industries requiring product differentiation and national promotion, companies must match their efforts with multinode distribution over a wide geographic area, dispersing their products over great distances. Thus, not only nodal but also scale economies are necessary to maintain the most efficient distribution organization of the company. For maximum efficiency the company would need a total scale of production at least equal to the aggregate of the optimal scales of distribution at all nodes to be reached (see Figure 4-14). Also required for maximum efficiency is a dispersion of plants to minimize total production and freight shipping costs when distances, unit freight costs per unit of distance, and production economies are taken into consideration (see Figure 4-15).

Total scale requirements may exceed the sum of the nodal optimums (Figure 4-14) if freight costs are important and production economies of single plants require large scales. This may be seen in Figure 4-16 where AA' represents the envelope curve of handling nodal economies, and BB' is production cost. The optimum among nodal economies falls at quantity distribution X and cost Y. The optimal manufacturing costs are represented by the marginal cost curve CC' and its intersection with the marginal revenue curve DD'. This yields the quantity X' and the cost Y'. Combining the total costs of nodal and production economies creates the new marginal cost and marginal revenue curves EE' and FF', respectively. The new optimum falls at quantity distance X'' and at a cost of Y''.

[23] *Ibid.*

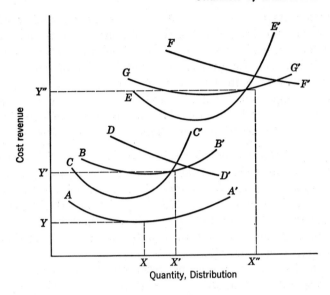

Figure 4-16. Nodal and manufacturing optimums.

For two out of eight industries studied, Bain reported that existing multiplant scales were justified on the basis of their distribution economies.[24] In four other industries the findings suggested that the economies were so great as to permit an excess of distribution scale over the optimum production scale of a single plant (see Figure 4-16), and Bain felt it would be difficult to tell here whether an increasing or decreasing scale were the more efficient. In the two remaining industries Bain noted that nodal economies failed to offset the optimal production scales. He concluded, therefore, that among concentrated industries selling highly differentiated and widely advertised consumer goods economies of distribution were more effective than economies of production in leading to larger-scale operation.

In retailing, the scale of the establishment, apart from telephone and mail ordering, is limited by the customer's need to visit it. Large-scale retailing is therefore associated with a more extensive product mix, although it is by no means certain that this larger and different mix reduces the unit costs of distribution.[25] Besides, as the establish-

---

[24] *Ibid.*
[25] Richard H. Holton, "Scale, Specialization and Costs in Retailing," *Proceedings of Winter Conference of the American Marketing Association*, The American Marketing Association, Chicago, 1960, pp. 459–466.

ment extends its market radius, it increases the probability of new stores entering the field with a special offering of goods and services which diverts a segment of the market from the larger institution.

Over the long run, the average unit cost function of retailing drops off precipitously at quite low rates of output, but for a wide range of output declines only gradually and may eventually turn upward again. In other words, the function has the shape of a reversed J, with the nearly horizontal portions embracing a wide range of output.

Efficiency of Retailing and Division of Labor. In 1954, except for nonstore retailing, more than 30 per cent of the nation's total retail trade in consumer goods was accounted for by establishments in rural areas and in cities of less than 10,000 population. But as sales per establishment in these outlets were only one-third to two-thirds as great as in the larger centers of the country, it would appear that they were not operating at their lowest costs.

Between 1939 and 1954, sales per retail establishment in the United States increased substantially. The net increase in real sales per establishment was about 111 per cent. But of 40 types of retail businesses only six showed greater growth than the weighted mean. Among the six were several of the kinds of activity which accounted for a high percentage of retail trade, namely, gasoline service stations, grocery stores, and both franchised and unfranchised automobile dealers. This group of six has seen its share of instore, consumer goods, retail trade swell from about 40 per cent in 1939 to more than 50 per cent by 1954. The retail trade, it would seem, has been gravitating toward the types of businesses which have experienced the greatest growth per establishment.

Multiple regression analysis of sales-per-establishment data for standard metropolitan areas in 1954 suggested that these areas contained larger shops in only few types of businesses. Women's clothing and specialty shops, for example, decreased in size as incomes rose. The data showed that the scale of establishment expanded markedly between 1939 and 1954. Moreover, increases were also widely evident between 1954 and 1958, even though consumption expenditures for 1958 were below the trend line. Not only were the retail establishments in each kind of business growing in size, but also sales were shifting from kinds of business in which the outlets were small to those in which the outlets were larger. Although the knowledge of cost functions in retailing has continued to be fragmentary and sales per establishment a poor measure of scale, it seems likely that retailing in the United States is now proceeding with less "excess capacity" and closer to the long-run optimum than ever before.

In contending that Adam Smith's theorem about specialization was limited by the extent of the market, Stigler said that as a company became larger it tended to eliminate some of its functions.[26] This is evident in the appliance industry where special service shops have replaced servicing at the regular retail places, in the grocery field where credit and personal selling have been taken over by the consumer, and in consumer durables where financing has been taken over largely by the banks. There also seems to be some evidence that chain organizations are growing because they have been moving into areas where decision making may be routinized.[27]

Reilly's Law of Retail Gravitation. This law, developed after a study of charge accounts in a Texas department store, helps companies select precise locations for retail outlets. Reilly found that the larger the population of a city, the greater would be the number of people outside its area who would be attracted to the business concerns of the city. He observed that the attraction of customers varied directly with the population of the city and inversely with the square of the distance.

Reilly intended his law only for shopping for goods. He also postulated the conditions under which it would not apply, including such natural barriers as mountains or rivers, or the special promotional efforts of merchants in other trading centers. Based on Reilly's Law, P. D. Converse developed the following formula to describe the break-even point between two competing trading areas, which may be called A and B: [28]

$$\text{B.E.P.} = \frac{\text{Distance from } A \text{ to } B}{1 \text{ plus } \sqrt{\dfrac{\text{population of } A}{\text{population of } B}}}$$

The distance is measured over primary roads and the answer is a measure from B. The formula does not apply where the population of B is more than eight times the population of A, but the McGraw-Hill Company has used it as a basis for developing trading areas throughout the United States.

[26] George J. Stigler, "The Division of Labor Is Limited by the Extent of the Market," *Journal of Political Economy,* Vol. 59, No. 3, June 1951, pp. 185–193.
[27] Holton, *op. cit.,* p. 465.
[28] P. D Converse, *A Study of Retail Trade Areas in East Central Illinois,* Bureau of Economic and Business Research, Business Studies No. 2, College of Commerce and Business Administration, University of Illinois, Urbana, 1943.

Many studies have been made of the utility of this formula to define trading areas in comparison with other measures of such areas, such as newspaper circulation. The correlations with the other measures have been quite high.[29]

In planning a shopping center, to cite a case, the promoters were faced with the problem of trying to estimate the volume of business activity they might generate. One analyst, Kenneth Welch,[30] decided that a variation of Reilly's Law might help determine the potential activity. For the population element in the equation, he substituted the presentation of goods. This could be measured in square feet or in dollar volume. For the distance, he substituted driving time, noting that today's shoppers do most of their shopping by automobile. From his amended formula, Welch found that the maximum distance a consumer would travel was approximately 20 to 30 minutes' driving time between his residence and the shopping center.

Applying this formula to projected and existing shopping areas, one can estimate the number of people a center will attract. Although Reilly's Law was perfected chiefly to explain the trading area for consumer goods, it has also been used to define the trading area for food purchases. One study found that the maximum driving distance for food purchases was about six minutes.[31]

Reilly's Law supersedes the concept of an "A" location as one with a high traffic count. Traffic counts are thus only one consideration in the selection of a location. The strength of the competition and the number of persons a business must attract in order to obtain a high sales volume are also to be weighed in picking a store site. The latter problem may be solved through the use of Reilly's Law.

The law does not, however, tell a businessman on what side of the street to locate. It does not consider the impact of highways or of public transportation. It does not inform a developer about the best combination of shops for his shopping center. Nor does Reilly's Law take population trends into account. These and other considerations

[29] Edna Douglas, "Measuring the General Retail Trading Area—A Case Study: I," *Journal of Marketing*, Vol. 13, No. 4, April 1949, pp. 481–497; and Edna Douglas, "Measuring the General Retail Trading Area—A Case Study: II," *Journal of Marketing*, Vol. 15, No. 1, July 1949, pp. 46–60.

[30] James W. Rouse, "Estimating Productivity for Planned Regional Shopping Centers," *Urban Land New and Trends in City Development*, Vol. 12, No. 10, November 1953, p. 2, Urban Land Institute.

[31] A. M. Voorhees, G. B. Sharpe, and J. T. Stegmaier, *Shopping Habits and Travel Patterns*, Technical Bulletin No. 24, Urban Land Institute, pp. 22–23.

require another type of analysis along with the lessons of Reilly's Law.

All in all, theory and practice, experimentation and experience, and the application of some scientific and quantitative procedures enable companies to develop their most profitable channels of distribution. To make money, they must sell their products, and to sell their goods they must get them to the people who want them as inexpensively and as expeditiously as possible.

Summary

The management of the channels of distribution involves the planning, control, and organizing of the resources of the company. Market managers should first be aware of the uncontrollable aspects of the environment that may influence planning, organizing, and control. Some of the controllable aspects of channels of distribution include physical distribution, research on channels of distribution, strategy, evaluation of optional choices, application of the principles of search and assortments, development of quantitative and qualitative criteria for choice of channels, thinking in terms of the classification of goods, maintaining channels, utilization of dealer policy boards, consideration of the policy of intensive versus extensive distribution, evaluation of the best channel for the company, the opening up of channels, and finally developing a basis for the choice of the channel of distribution.

In perfecting an organization for channels of distribution the company should consider the purpose of the organization, distinguish between formal and informal organization, develop leadership, motivation, and communication, and an organization for physical distribution.

Finally, a company may wish to develop some type of theory of channels of distribution. It may examine either the a priori models or the empirical models. Some of the a priori models are concerned with market structure and organization theory. Other a priori conceptual approaches are expressed under the "wheel of *retailing*" and variety in retailing. The empirical studies have added to the insights that may be gained on channels. Certain generalizations have been developed from a study of housebuilding. The advantages of the large company in distribution has also been studied and Reilly's Law of Retail Gravitation has been developed to explain the influences of population and distance on trade.

Suggested Cases

Ralph L. Westfall and Harper W. Boyd, *Cases in Marketing Management*, Irwin, Homewood, Ill., 1961.

International Harvester Farm Equipment, Division (B)—*Farm Equipment Manufacturer*—Selecting Channel for New Market, pp. 190–194.

Kitchens of Sarah Lee—*Specialty Baker*—Selecting Channels for Move from Local to National Market—pp. 195–199.

The Maytag Company—*Major Appliance Manufacturer*—Determining Number and Location of Warehouses, pp. 481–487.

Milton P. Brown, Wilbur B. England, and John B. Matthews, Jr., *Problems in Marketing*, 3rd ed., McGraw-Hill, New York, 1961.

Educational Electronics, Inc., pp. 286–298.

Crerier O'Shea Company, pp. 258–266.

Harry L. Hansen, *Marketing: Text, Cases, and Readings*, rev. ed., Irwin, Homewood, Ill., 1961.

Minute Maid Corporation, pp. 445–449.

General Mills, pp. 481–482.

Kenneth R. Davis, *Marketing Management*, Ronald Press, New York, 1961.

Fuller Brush Company, pp. 166–170.

Kirkwood Company, pp. 182–188.

Intercollegiate Case Clearing House, Soldiers Field, Boston 63, Massachusetts.

ICH 2M8 EA-M—Mayo Satellite System.

ICH 3F21—Norwalk Square Shopping Center.

Chapter Five

Without revenue no company is likely to survive very long. And without sales there is no such thing as revenue. No matter how desirable a product may be, it only begins to collect revenue when some consumer actually purchases it. The price may be right, the quality acceptable, and the channel chosen for distribution the appropriate one, but it still takes another force or two to get the product into the consumer's hands. These forces are advertising and personal selling effort. We shall review them individually in this and the succeeding chapters, the selling function taking precedence in the discussion. First, we shall explore the impact of the marketing concept on sales management and then view the principle of learning as it applies to selling. This will be followed by a survey of the factors involved in planning and controlling the sales force. The final section of the chapter will deal with the organization problems of managing the force.

Managing the Sales Force

Sales Management and Marketing Concept [1]

Under the marketing concept the responsibilities of a company's sales department increase vastly as both sales management and field salesmen are asked to raise their sights and broaden the scope of their activity. Salesmen are invited to expand their horizons beyond quotas and the number of calls per customer, and to assist others in achieving the long-range, clearly defined objectives of the company. In other words, the marketing concept stresses the interaction and interrelationship of selling with the other phases of marketing. Sales management, for its part, must demonstrate an ability to plan and execute strategy in the field with a view toward integrating selling activity with the other elements of the marketing mix. The sales manager, responsible for the total sales effort, must concern himself with more than the recruiting, selecting, and training of salesmen. His major duty is to create a conducive atmosphere to growth, and to plan and coordinate the strategy of the sales force in a way that advances the company's objectives.

Before the development of the marketing concept, a salesman was regarded simply as an individual who pushed a particular product or product line. Now, however, he is concerned with the complete distribution process. His involvement begins with the designing of the product to fit consumer needs and continues through promotion and advertising to final delivery.

As technology advances, the salesman's role assumes greater importance. Marketing no longer means only the sale of a product; it becomes the sale of a system of services. A customer does not seek, for example, to purchase just a machine; he is interested in acquiring greater production. The seller, therefore, must be prepared

[1] Eugene Kelley and William Lazer, "Basic Duties of the Modern Sales Department," *Industrial Marketing,* April 1960, pp. 69–78; Carl Rieser, "The Salesman Isn't Dead—He's Different," *Fortune,* Nov. 2, 1962, p. 124 ff.

not only to sell the machine but also to install it and service it after it has been installed. Selling concentrates on the needs of the seller, whereas marketing focuses on the needs of the buyer and covers all of them, including the services that may be required to enhance the utility of the product.

Formerly, the manufacturer would fabricate his product and instruct his salesmen to go out among the public to sell it. Following the line of least resistance, the salesmen would sell those products easiest to move. But as a rule the easily sold products were not the most profitable items. The bulk of the profit derived from a small percentage of the line. Under the newer marketing concept, the sales manager knows from distribution cost-analysis reports which products are the most profitable and encourages his salesmen to concentrate their selling effort on these items.

One casualty in all this is the sales manager's autonomy. Many of the coordinating activities performed by him in the past are now carried out by the vice president for marketing, to whom he reports instead of to the president of the company. Generally, the sales manager has less to say than previously on credit and pricing policies. Moreover, he finds that his sales force has to work within the confines of the company's over-all marketing policy. Finally, he notes that new specializations have been created which overlap his authority. For example, as we have seen in an earlier chapter, the product manager frequently has both staff and line authority for a specific product and may coordinate productive activity with advertising, research, and personal selling.

At the General Electric Company, salesmen used to be product specialists on one or a few products. Different salesmen on the company's staff selling different products called on the same customer. Then the procedure was changed from products to markets. Instead of selling a single product, the salesman is now responsible for a group of products. For example, one man sells all the components of an air-conditioning system rather than having individual salesmen vend push buttons, fan motors, car sets, and the like. In selling to the government, GE uses the same pattern. Unlike its previous practice of having many company departments canvass the government, it now coordinates sales to the government under a single force.

The Systems Approach and Specialization. At Westinghouse Company, top management refers to its "province concept." The company wants to be represented by a "Mr. Westinghouse" rather than by a group of salesmen each calling on the same customer for another

Westinghouse product. The management also felt it was important for salesmen to meet their customers personally and therefore eliminated a whole collection of staff sales managers. In the same way, American Optical Company has pursued a province method. Salesmen who formerly sold only a single product are now responsible for the whole line from heavy furniture to lenses.

This new type of salesman must be a generalist instead of a specialist. He must be capable of absorbing a vast amount of information about many products from the marketing department for application to individual customer problems. He requires data on his customers' needs, their products, corporate organization, and delivery schedules. As a rule he shows more executive ability than his predecessor and is given broader authority to make a larger number of important decisions in the field without referring to company headquarters. General Foods, for example, calls its salesmen account executives.

Nevertheless, the need remains for hard and aggressive selling in opening new accounts, in introducing new and untried products, and in marketing the products of companies lacking a national reputation. A new kind of sales specialist has thus been created—one who concentrates on new accounts. For a fee a New York firm catering to this need assigns its own salesmen to open new accounts for others in new territories. After it has opened the accounts it turns them over to the sales organization of the manufacturing concern that engaged its special services. Some manufacturing companies, however, have established special units within their own sales departments to concentrate on selling new products or penetrating new territories. Eventually, they turn the new business over to the regular sales force.

Service. Today's salesmen are buttressed by a great support of service and information. The Food Machinery and Chemical Corporation, for example, has increased by 20 per cent the number of technical people in its inorganic sales division. There is now one technical man for every four salesmen. DuPont has been doing this for a long time. The company now employs 1700 scientists, technicians, and others to prepare sales literature, solve technical problems, and provide services for the customers and potential buyers of DuPont products. Steel companies are storing their products in advance of customers' orders so that they can provide more rapid service. Similarly, distributors of industrial goods are stocking wider lines to offer additional service. In this respect, a new type of electronics distributor has entered the scene. He sells not only parts but also component systems for missiles, communication, and other massive undertakings. Moreover, several recent mergers have been motivated by a desire to consolidate in order to supply greater service to the consumer.[2]

Electronic data processing has relieved the modern salesman of the detail of writing up orders and reports, checking on the availability of goods, and inquiring when they might be delivered. Besides, many customers also have their own inventory control systems which signal when to reorder. In such instances no salesman is actually needed, some companies having teletype machines in their offices for direct ordering as required. This frees the salesman from the more routine tasks of selling to devote time and energy to its creative aspects. For example, salesmen at Allis Chalmers have more time to perform the service and communication functions of selling.

Another thing has changed. Business tends to be concentrated among fewer customers. Some 300 buying offices throughout the country, for example, account for 80 per cent of all food bought from wholesalers. Small buyers have grouped together through many of these offices to enjoy the advantages of large-scale purchasing. This is true of schools consolidating on a county basis, associations of independent hardware stores, grocery stores, and hospitals. Moreover, individual buyers in food chains are becoming less and less important. Decisions are being made in committee. The salesman, therefore, has to find out the identity of the principal decision maker among the committee members and cultivate this individual to further a sale.

As part of this pattern, emphasis in industrial purchasing has changed from buying a single item to buying a complete system. This may include the following combinations: heating and air conditioning, fire and theft protection, or automating a whole production line or a materials-handling process. Companies prefer to sell an entire system where they can. Salesmen need to know, however, that decisions for buying such systems are usually diffused through an organization rather than made by a single individual.

Top Executive Selling. More and more top executives have become involved directly in selling activity, but generally they endeavor to limit their calls to big customers. Once the practice in the sale of expensive equipment, this has become common procedure among companies selling less expensive products. For example, Raytheon has divided its large customers among the officers and managers of the company. Their task is to bolster the salesman's effort.

---

[2] *Duns Review and Modern Industry,* Vol. 81, No. 1, January 1963, pp. 37–38.

The president of General Foods, accompanied by a team of his executives, visits large customers personally. Customers are requested to have all their key personnel on hand for these visits. The appearance is preceded by a questionnaire designed to elicit comments on the performance of General Foods products and on the company's image as well as to stimulate suggestions for topics to be discussed. The customers enjoy this type of conference which improves relations as General Foods understands its customers more fully and vice versa.

Thus, there are many ways in which the marketing concept has affected the role of sales management. Selling is no longer solely a "get out and hustle" affair. Hustle continues to be necessary but it is a more thoughtful, perceptive type of solicitation governed by the desire to satisfy the customer's total wants. For example, at the National Cash Register Company, personal selling effort now takes place on all sorts of levels. To facilitate this departure in its computer division, the company has changed the system of compensation for the sales force from a draw against commission to a salary plus bonus and has created a technical organization to back up the salesmen. This new staff helps customers define their problems, trains computer operators for customers, sets up the data-processing systems, and develops the programming for them. Internally, the technicians get into the selling act by preparing manuals and training salesmen. Wherever the marketing concept has flourished, selling has become a demanding taskmaster.

Learning and Selling

A politician courting votes, a teacher lecturing to students, a salesman trying to persuade consumers to buy his product or service all are engaged in the same endeavor. They are trying to change the behavior of the individuals with whom they are communicating. When behavior changes learning occurs. Behavior has been changed through communication, which may be written or spoken. Thus, advertising and personal selling are both part of the process of communicating ideas in order to change the behavior of consumers.

This change in behavior, or learning, may eventuate if there is repetition, response, motivation, and a minimum of interference. The basic ingredient in learning is motivation. If there is no motive to learn, no amount of repetition will affect behavior. Similarly, if there is no awareness of a need, no amount of selling effort will change an individual's lack of interest in buying. An individual's need to purchase an item may spring from biological or social stimuli. Biological needs are expressed in the form of hunger, thirst, or sex. Social needs may be expressed in the form of "keeping up with the Joneses," being the leader in the community, or merely showing off.

In selling situations the salesman must discover the needs of his prospect. In the case of the washing machine, the need might be for a product that enables the housewife to perform her wifely and motherly roles in a superior manner. In the purchase of clothing, the need might be to accentuate extreme individuality. In selling to an intermediary it might be the amount of profit the product will yield to him. In any case, this is an area for research. A company's research department should be able to provide a salesman with information on the types of needs his product might satisfy.

Once the need is known, a certain amount of repetition is necessary to establish the idea of the product's capacity to meet it. If the prospect has already been exposed to advertising and has talked to other persons who have the product, the personal selling task is minimized. But when a person has not heard of the product the salesman must impress its salient features on him by repeating them in as many different ways as possible. The repetition, of course, should relate to the needs of the prospect.

Each person approached in a selling situation will have objections to the purchase of the product or service. This is interference. It may be reduced by relating the selling points again to the need of the individual. This necessitates eradicating the "noise" of communicating. Noise may develop from the fears of an individual or from erroneous information. It is also created by conflicting statements about a product which may impede the process of choice. The salesman must counteract the "noise" and overcome all objections of the prospect.

If a student in the classroom is thinking about last night's date, no communication can occur between teacher and student. However, if the teacher can appeal to the student's basic motivations, he may be able to reduce this "noise." Similarly, the salesman must always return to the basic motivations of the consumer if he wishes to generate interest in the product or service.

Once communication has been established, a response has to occur. In personal selling it is ultimately the sale of the product or service to the consumer. This would indicate that a change in the behavior of the consumer and learning have taken place. In the event no sale is concluded various gradients of response may exist. At the opposite extreme the person refuses to buy. Between the two are consumers who are still uncertain and cannot see how this particular product or service fits into their needs.

Psychologists have demonstrated that learning takes place more rapidly when there is an advance introduction to the concepts to be studied.[3] Thus, before a salesman approaches a prospective customer, it is advisable for him to precondition the prospect through various media. Advertisements may be placed in journals likely to be read by the prospect. This may be followed by a direct mail campaign. These devices should acclimatize the prospect for the salesman.

The role of the salesman is to assist the individual faced with the necessity of making a choice. Some believe that the salesman may help in these situations by offering inducements or rewards. Nevertheless, evidence has been developed to support the view that one is better able to predict choice by concentrating on what might be lost rather than on what might be gained.[4]

Communication in Small Groups

Communication theory pertinent to small groups offers some insights that may apply to sales situations. Theorists talk of one-way and two-way communication. The former is exemplified by a radio or television set talking to a consumer. The latter may be seen in a customer asking a question of a salesman and the salesman replying. This would be a communication link in which A communicates to B and B responds to A.

$$A \leftrightarrow B$$

In most selling situations one may presume there is two-way communication. However, a salesman may be so overwhelming that he does not permit the customer to respond. Thus, he gets no feedback from the customer. Or "noise" may develop so that the symbols of communication are not clearly received by the customer. The customer may be concentrating on a problem wholly unrelated to the selling effort. Howsoever, the salesman has to determine the individual's motivation and direct his message in a way that provokes a response.

In very general terms there are two poles of communication in

[3] David P. Ausubel, "The Use of Advance Organizers in the Learning and Retention of Meaningful Verbal Material," *Journal of Educational Psychology*, Vol. 51, No. 6, 1960, pp. 267–272.

[4] Harvy A. Taub, Jerome L. Myers, and Raymond E. Reilly, "Differential Monetary Gains in a Two Choice Situation," *Journal of Experimental Psychology*, Vol. 62, No. 4, October 1961, pp. 357–360.

small groups. At one extreme is the authoritarian type of communication and at the other extreme the democratic form. Most individuals fit somewhere between these poles.

democratic • _____ • authoritarian

The salesman must assess whether the customer is susceptible to authoritarian or democratic forms of communication. Many types of individuals like to be told what to do. These would respond to authoritarian communication. Others, more mature, feel they are capable of making up their own minds if supplied with the right sort of information. Not only must the salesman recognize the character of his customer, but he must also be aware of his own authoritarian or democratic behavior. He may have to modify his behavior before he can influence the behavior of others.

Planning and Control

Uncontrollable Elements

Various forces impinge on management's ability to plan and control the direction of its sales force. Among those forces beyond its control are the internal characteristics of the business, physical limitations, lack of materials, amounts of available finance, and the manpower situation. The sales manager must indicate to his salesmen that it is their function to introduce the product to the consumer rather than expect the consumer to request the product from them. Salesmen must know how to compete with their product or service for the attention of consumers. All this is to say that sales take place within a free-enterprise system in which the consumer exerts a vast degree of choice.

The numbers of consumers of various age levels, the composition of their income, and their geographic location cannot be controlled by sales management. Nor can consumer attitudes and motivation be controlled. These may be understood, and a sales force may work within the framework of existing attitudes and motives, but it can never control them. Also beyond the control of the market manager are the state of competition and the growth rate of the industry. Moreover, he can do nothing about government regulations affecting sales. Let us turn, therefore, to those aspects or planning and control that lie within marketing management's power to manipulate.

Controllable Elements

Planned Selling. Prior to the appearance of marketing management, salesmen were given their packs of samples, their order books, and told to take them out and sell their products. This method is obsolete among companies that practice modern marketing management. Sales planning in the current sense begins with proper selection of potential salesmen. After these candidates have been chosen in accordance with a company's concept of what constitutes desirable sales-force material, they are trained. When they are finally assigned to a territory, the sales manager has some idea of the area's potential volume and each salesman is given a quota for a specific period. The quota is the goal set by sales management for each salesman. It is the amount of volume for which he is responsible in a stipulated sales period.

In addition to predetermined potentials and quotas, companies often supply their salesmen with planned routes of operation and systems for reporting to the central office on market conditions. They also back up their men with advertising designed to facilitate the personal selling effort, and they endeavor to improve the product and package so that the salesmen will be able to offer additional value to customers. Modern marketing management has seized upon many new mathematical techniques and some of the sophisticated tools of the behavioral sciences. These implements have fortified the salesman with more detailed information so that he can seek out the customer. Newer developments such as linear programming [5] and application of probability theory,[6] although bearing much promise, need additional refinement before they can be applied to the average company's needs. For the present, therefore, the ordinary company has to rely on marketing research to help pinpoint the market for its salesmen.

Accounting and Selling. The accountant has been showing a greater interest in the planning and control of the selling function.[7] Some of the questions he has been raising include the following.

1. IS A SALES FORCE NEEDED AT ALL? Some types of products require

[5] G. Dantzig, R. Fulkerson, and S. Johnson, "Solution of a Large-Scale Traveling-Salesman's Problem," *Journal of the Operations Research Society of America,* Vol. 2, No. 4, November 1954, pp. 393–410.

[6] Arthur A. Brown, Frank T. Hulswit, and John D. Kettelle, "A Study of Sales Operations," *Operations Research,* Vol. 4, No. 3, June 1956, pp. 296–308.

[7] "Marketing, the Accountants Frontier," *The Price Waterhouse Review,* Vol. 7, No. 4, Winter 1962, pp. 14–18.

little selling effort because of the amount of advertising heralding them. Moreover, many companies have begun to reconsider the value of the territorial method of operation and have instructed their salesmen to call in person only on larger accounts. In such cases, the salesmen solicit other customers by phone.

2. HOW ARE TERRITORIES DESIGNED? In general, there should be some rationale about their size, which should be related to potential volume and the amounts of time spent with accounts of different statures.

3. HOW MANY CUSTOMERS? A company not only wants to increase its number of customers; it also wants customers who are profitable.

4. HOW MUCH SERVICE CAN THE COMPANY AFFORD? The amount of service should be related not only to present volume of sales but also to the volume anticipated in the future.

5. USE OF "LEADERS." The drug industry is constantly bringing out new products and therefore the speed with which these new products are accepted is a problem. To expedite their acceptance, the industry has conducted intensive campaigns to find "leaders" among the medical profession. Although not necessarily the presidents of the local medical associations, when these leaders speak out at meetings other members of the profession seem to follow them. Thus, once the leaders have been persuaded to prescribe the drug and they find that it performs as promised, their good word will encourage further prescription of this same product by other doctors.

Executive Planning. In companies having a vice president for marketing and a sales manager, both participate in planning and control activities. The chief executive in charge of marketing interests himself in the broad aspects of selling and the marketing mix, whereas the sales manager dwells on the actual management of his sales force. The following material on the role of the executive in planning and control of sales activities has been drawn from the responses of sales managers and chief marketing executives to a survey conducted by the author.[8]

Both chief marketing men and sales managers indicate that planning and controlling the sales area is their primary responsibility.[9] The activity most frequently cited by them is the development of sales potentials and quotas. In some companies in which the sales manager is the chief marketing executive, he is charged with both development and administration of potentials and quotas; in companies where he

[8] Author's survey, *op. cit.*
[9] *Ibid.*

reports to a market manager, the superior officer may review the potentials and quotas periodically. The sales manager is held responsible for attaining the goals embodied in the quotas. Thus, the amount of managerial activity performed by the chief executive in charge of marketing depends on the degree of specialization existing within the marketing department. The more the specialization, the less the chief marketing executive is directly involved in sales management activity and vice versa.

The chief marketing executive includes the development of sales plans under his planning activities. The sales plan requires coordination of the affairs of the sales, advertising, sales promotion, credit, warehouse and transportation, pricing, and product development departments. The principal marketing executive is responsible for the timing, integration, and coordination of these activities. The sales manager is expected to provide the details of the personal selling effort and to suggest other areas to which the effort may be extended.

Both officials adhere to the strictures of the budget. The chief marketing executive prepares the master budget for the entire marketing operation. It consists of the budgetary requests of his various department heads including the sales manager. It represents the final plan as it is presented to top management and contains the quantities of volume for which the marketing department is responsible. It also contains anticipated expenses and profits. The budget is top management's principal vehicle for judging the performance of its chief marketing executive. Correspondingly, it is the device through which the chief marketing executive evaluates the performance of his sales manager. Very careful planning must be undertaken, therefore, to develop the budget. The close collaboration of the marketing research, sales, and all other departments engaged in the marketing effort is essential for a realistic appraisal of the amount of effort to be expended in relation to potentiality.

The budgetary criterion by which the chief marketing executive is measured is the amount of profit he produces for the company. Thus, we find him making studies of cost, competition, buying habits, and population growth, and developing a profit plan that reflects revenue and expenditure. In some companies he is responsible for the development of sales territories although normally this is a duty of the sales manager to free the chief marketing executive for coordination of the total marketing effort. The analysis of sales territories demands the establishment of realistic territorial boundaries on the basis of the number of salesmen and the potential volume available. It is also concerned with developing new territories, which necessitates defining the territory, breaking down or expanding existing territories, and demarcating new ones.

The chief marketing executive is concerned, moreover, with substandard performance. Frequently, he will ask the sales manager to explain the deficiencies or request that special studies be initiated to discover the reasons for them. In this respect staff specialists and marketing research facilities lend valuable assistance.

Alertness to possible markets for goods and services that are presently available or that may be anticipated for the future is yet another duty of the chief marketing man. Then, too, he must bear the responsibilities for maintaining the sales organization, appointing the sales manager, planning material for salesmen, reviewing monthly field notes of salesmen, and developing arresting sales displays and local promotion and publicity. To assist him in deciding whether to enter new markets, he may have at his disposal special staff studies on such subjects as channels of distribution or consumer acceptance.

Second in importance to development of sales potentials and sales quotas, chief marketing executives rate coordination of intra- and intermarketing departmental activities. Many executives carry out this coordination through a committee composed of both intra- and intermarketing departmental personnel. The marketing chief also serves as the company's liaison with industry organizations which assist in planning.

The third area of importance as seen by the responses to the survey is the implementation of strategy. This includes approval of merchandise changes in the organization, capital outlays, new products, and price changes. It further includes decisions on new markets and training within the organization. Much of the implementation work is abetted by the marketing research department which can conduct consumer surveys and market tests, and collect reports from dealers. In some companies the chief marketing executive also implements strategy by setting finished inventory, and at times he will also study credits.

As for the sales manager, his planning and control activities are shaped by the size of the company, the degree of specialization achieved in the marketing department, and the amount of coordination undertaken by his superior in the marketing operation. As a rule he deals primarily with administration of the sales program. His responsibilities entail recruiting and training a supervisory staff, setting up a sales organization, conferring with branch managers on planning of sales quotas, conducting meetings of sales supervisors and salesmen, maintaining instore activities, administering sales plans for large accounts, and pricing.

Like the chief executive in marketing the sales manager coordinates the activities within his own department with those outside the department. Some of these activities consist of working with various individuals on sales campaigns and educational programs for dealers, maintaining a balance in the distribution organization, devising the general sales approach for field managers, and reviewing production forecasts. For his diverse responsibilities the sales manager requires abundant information, far more than he obtains from the marketing research department. He needs an accurate impression of the world in which he operates, and to get it, in some instances, he actually conducts his own market research, as we have previously remarked. At other times he may collect data for analysis by staff executives. He also acquires a great deal of information through personal contacts and trade journals. All this fund of knowledge equips the sales manager for the decisions he is called on to render and for the coordination of activities he is obliged to undertake.

In planning sales coverage, the sales manager considers the minimum and maximum degrees of effort needed for the company's cash customers. Some customers require relatively little service while others demand more. The sales manager therefore allows time for travel, preparation of calls, and visits with customers. The intensity of the sales coverage relates as well to the company's growth objectives and to the responsiveness of the market to sales campaigns and advertising.

As part of his planning of sales coverage, the sales manager groups sales territories into districts and gives his district managers authority commensurate with responsibility. The size of the district must be no greater than can be managed effectively. Contacts should be maintained by supervisors with the men in the field who must always feel there is a district representative to whom they can talk if they require advice on some problem. If more than one level of supervision is needed in a district, this means that it is probably too large.

A sales manager assigns his salesmen to territories, product groups, or consuming industries. If his company sells a long line of products the territorial basis of assignment may prove inadvisable. Territorial assignments really work best when the distance factor is minimal. Judicious selection of a headquarters city minimizes the distance factor. Before choosing to assign his men to product groups the sales manager observes whether products tend to be purchased by companies whose line of business is similar to each other's or whether they are distributed through the same trade or channel. Some companies classified as being in the same industry may manufacture products totally unrelated to the product line being sold. In this case the sales manager classifies companies on the basis of their consumption needs, grouping together those companies that make similar use of the product his concern supplies.

Elements of Total Sales.[10] In developing a concept of total sales, a company must view the interaction of marketing elements as a single system. The system has three basic components: input, communication, and output.

1. INPUTS. The inputs of the marketing system are manpower, money, information, and products and service. Manpower should be scheduled to achieve the best possible coverage of the territories and the finest performance of selling and service activities. Supervision should maintain effective communication with those whom it supervises, and staff and advisory assistance should be available to analyze selling problems and aid in planning and control.

The amount of money at the disposal of the sales department depends on the state of liquidity of the company's assets, its ability to borrow, and the stage of its growth. The sales manager has to evolve a program for the most efficient allocation of the company's monetary resources. Generally, various departments compete for the money. In the development of his budget, the sales manager shows how it is more efficient to use the available funds for sales than for other purposes. He must specify the minimum amount necessary to accomplish the job and how much more can be done if sales were allotted the maximum funds on hand.

The problem of evaluating information is to determine the real state of the world in comparison to the world as it is perceived and reported by salesmen, colleagues, competitors, research department personnel, trade journals, and association meetings. Management must strive constantly to achieve a coincidence between the world as it is and this perception of its minions and friends. Information is necessary not only on how one's own product is selling but also on how the competitors' products are faring. It is essential to know both the present situation and what is likely to happen henceforth as well as the future plans of one's competitors.

Although products and services are basic inputs of a company they are subject to alteration with changes in the market. A constant re-

[10] Kelley and Lazer, *op. cit.*

evaluation of these products and services is necessary in relation to market opportunities and the company's production and distribution resources.

All these inputs must be combined so that they will help to achieve the company's objectives. In grouping them, management has to balance the mix. Should more attention, for example, be accorded manpower than money? Should more weight be given to information than to products and services? The proper mix is conditioned by the state of competition, the resources of a company, and the management of these resources.

2. COMMUNICATION. The second element of total sales is communication. This refers to the efforts of the customer and the salesman to overcome the barriers of time, space, and lack of knowledge to obtain sustained, significant information. The sales manager has the responsibility of coordinating the flow of information which links management to the sales force and the customer to management. It is one of the key concepts of marketing management.

A company's customers, as we have seen, include the intermediaries who handle the product as well as the ultimate consumer. In consumer durable goods, the customer may be a distributor. When he speaks to the manufacturer he engages in two-way communication. Noise may intrude to prevent effective discourse. There may be a misreading of the communication symbols or interference from outside sources, but a two-way exchange does exist. When, however, the distributor communicates with a retailer, the arrangement is a one-way deal. The distributor, that is, may know exactly how many units he has sold to the retailer. But the chances are that he does not know the rate of sale at the retail level.

The type of information that may be communicated may include the rate of sale, rate of inventory turnover, competitive prices and margins, news of new products, promotions of competitors, and new personal selling effort. Communication, whatever its content, covers what is going on at present and what may be expected in the future. It assesses the risks, details the uncertainties, and reports the probabilities of achieving objectives over the long run.

If market action could be communicated instantly to the decision centers at the time of its occurrence, the barrier of time would be overcome. Unfortunately, there are many blocks to effective communication of sales information at the time of the sale. There is the physical task of counting receipts at day's end, not only by total sales, but also by item, color, shape, size, and other classifications. This may be a costly process for the retailer. He may ask why he has to count these receipts daily to report conditions to the manufacturer. In most cases retailers do not report this information at all. When the manufacturer or wholesaler wants these data, he must engage the services of a marketing research firm to provide them on a sampling basis. What holds true for receipts also applies to the state of his inventory. Thus, there is a time lag between sales on the market and reports back through the channels to the manufacturer.

Even so, it is not enough to know as quickly as possible how sales are progressing. A manufacturer also needs to know how his rate of sale compares with the rates of competitors. Frequently, monthly information indicates that a company's sales position relative to its competitors' positions is sound. However, within this period the competitors may change their tactics. How fast does one know what the changes may be, and how they are likely to affect one's sales? Sometimes it is preferable to obtain a quick impression of the state of the world through a sample study rather than to wait for the full story. Although this information is less accurate than a complete account, it affords a company an advantage of time to counter the actions of its competitors. The essence of timing is to have information on the competitors' intentions before they act. In this way, the company can time its own strategy shrewdly.

Space is very closely linked with time in communication. The message must be communicated not only in a timely manner but also over the physical space separating the parties in communication with each other. Space exists between a company's top command and its lower echelons, between a company and its intermediaries, and finally, between intermediaries and the ultimate consumer. To bridge the distances of space requires the perfection of effective means of personal contact and oral and written communication.

Lack of knowledge may result from either an erroneous perception of a situation or an absence of means of communicating with the real world. Lack of knowledge in the latter case may be overcome through the expenditure of effort on marketing research and making greater utilization of current resources. One of the resources that seems to be overlooked is the sales force. This force is in the market place perpetually and has the potentiality for communicating much information to the decision-making center.

Some information is readily available in such forms as the sales records of customers. Other information may be difficult if not impossible to obtain. This may include information on what a competitor has in mind or on his decision-making process, or it may include projections on the state of the economy. However, approximations may be extrapolated from analytical data which might give a company some guidance for proceeding. Basic to such analytical undertakings is a sound intelligence system.

The customer sends out certain impulses which are indications of his need. They are expressed through purchase behavior, shipping behavior, changes in the way of living, and changes in the quantity and quality of the family. The salesman must know not only how the consumer is expressing contemporary needs but also the changes that may take place in the consumer's future expression of needs. The company, for its part, sends out impulses in the form of advertising, personal selling effort, and the product for sale. It must relate its impulses to the needs of the consumer both for the present and the anticipated changes. Thus, the company constantly experiments with its assortment of merchandise in relation to consumer needs.

The understanding of consumer needs is illustrated by one company that sells to wholesale accounts. Its wholesalers stock so many different items that they cannot concentrate on any one of them. Hence, the manufacturer has developed a set of aids to help the wholesale salesman.[11] These include a list of sales-call openers such as an outline of the history of chemistry. They also include personal sales assistance and advertising support.

From the many sources of information at his disposal, the sales manager has to sift out that intelligence which he feels reflects the true state of the sales world. This is not an easy task. There may be contradictory information. He must therefore establish a standard for verification of his information and continue to observe and experiment. No sales manager will ever have complete information. Thus, his job is to decide how much information is necessary to assess the degree of risk before him. On this information he estimates the probabilities of succeeding and proceeds accordingly.

The goal of information is a coincidence between what the sales manager knows and the real state of the needs and desires of the consumer. This calls for consolidating all sorts of intelligence from the salesmen, from staff reports from the marketing research department, from suggestions by associates, from rumors, data in trade publications, conventions, and outside reading to fashion an accurate impression of customer needs, which then becomes the basis for decision making.

[11] T. Isaacman, "How to Make Advertising, Promotion, and Sales Really Work as a Team," *Industrial Marketing,* March 1963, pp. 67–70.

3. OUTPUT. Top management may appraise its sales manager by the volume and profit standards he achieves and by the type and quality of information he provides for management planning. The sales manager therefore has to develop among his staff mutual areas of interest, and he accomplishes this by applying the "systems" approach. Through this approach the salesmen in the field are more likely to see how their efforts support and supplement the specialist in the home office. The headquarters specialist, conversely, can be shown that it is the salesmen who produce the markets. The idea of teamwork is easier to establish when all components of the sales operation are recognized for contributing certain inputs which yield sales outputs.

The marketing concept in sales is also a means of looking at market opportunity. It applies a systems approach to selling. This means that there is an understanding of markets and of the complexities of business systems. It signifies the introduction of new products on a systems basis. Instead of introducing a single product, the company thinks of how this product will fit in with other related products. Finally, in viewing the factors contributing to a total sales concept, the broader marketing notion should extend into manufacturer-dealer relations.

Organization

There seem to be some differing opinions over the extension of the term "marketing management" to the area of sales management. The literature of sales management reflects the evolution of the sales manager's responsibilities into those of a market manager, and yet in an organizational sense there is a tendency for the market manager to rank higher than the sales manager. As we have already noted, the market manager supervises the complete marketing process, whereas the sales manager is responsible only for management of the sales force. In some companies without a titular market manager, the market-managing function is performed either by the sales manager or the vice president in charge of marketing.[12]

[12] John A. Howard, "Marketing Management—Something Old, New or Borrowed?," "Marketing Management: A New Point of View"; and Richard R. Still, "Sales Management and Marketing Management," *Proceedings of American Marketing Association,* December 1958, American Marketing Association, Chicago, pp. 448–457.

Organization for Strategy [13]

Like any other body within a company the sales division requires a hierarchy of authority and a channel of communication up and down the line so that effective decision making may proceed. In addition, it needs flexibility in order to adjust and adapt to changing conditions. One may compare the sales force with an infantry firing line. Fighting on the line may be of the guerilla-warfare variety or it may be highly organized and mechanized. In guerilla-type selling, supervision remains at a minimum. The salesmen take advantage of local circumstances and price levels. Where the market is large relative to the size of the sales force guerilla action may be suitable and salesmen may fend for themselves. When the selling is highly organized, however, the salesmen rely not only on their supervisors but also on the advice of other company staff members regarding areas in which the prospect of sales is strongest. Plans and strategy are handed down to the salesmen from the top. The marketing executive requires control over his organization so that the greatest efforts are directed toward the areas offering the greatest opportunity. He should give salesmen a clear statement of their specific assignments but permit them to use discretion in creating additional sales.

In building a sales organization one must think in terms of the adequacy of the force and the size of the territory. Grouping into branches and districts may be necessary to enable proper supervision. The size of territory assigned to a salesman varies with the number and calibre of customers, the amount of selling effort required in each case, the expense incurred, and the needs of the salesman. Within the organization there are questions of the number of assistants needed and the character of the home office staff units. There is also the problem of setting up the relationships between line and staff, and headquarters and field operations.

The number of salesmen to be employed should be considered in incremental terms. That is, salesmen should be added to the force until the incremental cost of maintaining them is as great as the incremental revenue to be derived from their activities. It is not only a matter of having the right number of salesmen but also of having them well trained to carry out their jobs effectively.

[13] Wroe Alderson, *Marketing Behavior and Executive Action,* Irwin, Homewood, Ill., 1957.

Sales Managerial Duties [14]

Sales Administration. A sales manager's duties under the marketing concept fall into two categories, sales administrative responsibilities and sales-force management. Administration includes such planning and organization functions as determining sales potentials, programming the sales effort, coordinating sales inputs and controlling outputs, sales innovation, sales communication, and sales research.[15]

Sales-Force Management. The management of the sales force includes such tasks as recruiting candidates, selecting, training, and supervising them, and compensating and motivating the field staff.

The selection of salesmen involves the whole hiring process itself. Most companies hire salesmen only by personal interview. An interview may take one of two forms. One is a structured interview in which the interviewer asks the job applicant a series of questions. The other type of interview has no structure but uses discussion in such a way as to uncover the applicant's qualifications. Research into the two methods shows that the latter type of interview places a strong weight on general impression. If the interviewer forms a good general opinion of the applicant, he probably views all his characteristics favorably, including the applicant's capacity to describe a product and close a sale. In a structured interview, the interviewer is able to judge social presence of mind, self-assurance, and maturity, and to receive a general impression from physical appearance.[16]

Some companies hire salesmen through some combination of testing and interview. Testing of salesmen has not been perfected, as a rule, to the point at which its results may be applied universally in hiring procedures. Certain companies, like those in the insurance business, have had more success with tests than others. The major types of tests used are the paper and pencil tests and the projective tests. Paper and pencil tests attempt to abstract the qualities that are desirable in an executive and then test for them. Persons considered good executives score well on these tests. The major objection to this method is that scores work well for groups but not for individuals.

---

[14] Kelley and Lazer, *op. cit.*
[15] Illustrative material on the application of operations research techniques to sales administration may be found in the Appendix at the end of this chapter.
[16] M. A. Lavoegïe, "La Technique de l'interview pour la sélection du personnel commercial," *Travail humain,* 1961, Vol. 24, No. 1-2, pp. 65–142.

Paper and pencil testing, however, does provide a quantitative measure for decision making.

Projective tests seek to elicit information about the basic personality of the potential executive. Depth interviewing may accomplish the same result. Both types of tests shed light on the personality make-up of an individual and how he may react to strain and stress. However, they have not been standardized sufficiently so that any two psychologists can interpret the results in the same way.

Incentives. The major incentive for any salesman is remuneration. Of the many compensatory arrangements available, perhaps the most widely used is the combination of salary and commission. This type of compensation plan permits management to maintain control over salesmen who cannot afford to become too independent or too lax in performing services for their employers. At the same time the prospect of commission spurs the salesmen to increased individual efforts.

Many sales managers have sought to stimulate salesmen through such devices as gimmicks and inspirational meetings. In such cases salesmen tend to believe that their job to sell is less important than the sales manager's job to use magic and gadgetry to make them sell. This kind of stimulation, however, does not necessarily have the desired effect of changing a salesman's personality or of increasing his technical capacity to sell. The more fundamental task of stimulating salesmen necessitates an understanding of their personalities. Understanding of this sort may come from conversations with the salesman or from the results of interviews with a competent psychologist. Once this information has been obtained it becomes possible to manipulate a salesman's behavior so that his own goals may be made to coincide more closely with those of the company.

Morale in the Sales Department.[17] The most important tactic for maintaining morale in the sales department, as in most departments, is salary adjustment. This embodies adequate salary, inducements during special sales-promotion campaigns, bonus plans, and assurance that salaries are as good as or better than those of competitors. The next most important device for maintaining morale is personal supervision, which is accomplished by direct contact with the salesmen in the field and regular reviews of the salesman's performance.

A third means of promoting morale is the staging of national meetings of sales people. Sometimes these consist of sales and refresher training meetings or discussions at various levels. Some companies

[17] Data from survey taken by author (see footnote 26 in Chapter 2).

hold sales meetings frequently. Others prefer to eschew them and maintain morale through yet another device, the welfare program that includes pension, medical care, and insurance plans.

Recognition of the employee as an individual is also a morale builder. The provision of the proper climate for individual development, personal recognition, use of the "golden rule," special tribute for outstanding achievement, delegation of responsibility to each employee at his own level, interviewing each individual at least once a year—all these serve the common end of appreciating the employee as a person.

Or morale may be raised through general communication. It may take the form of a daily printed bulletin, executive newsletter, company newspaper, house organ, or memorandum for general circulation. There may be one such publication dealing with external affairs, namely, the company's customers, and another devoted to the internal life of the company. In this same category may be considered the impact on morale of a sound communications system. This would embrace mutual understanding, provision of useful sales tools, information on research, and keeping the sales force current on all matters of significance to the welfare of the company.

The opportunity to progress in the organization, which also bolsters morale, should be predicated on proven ability and performance. Promotion from within as often as possible and the chance for advancement both add to sales-force spirit. Then there are such additional morale builders as periodic sales competitions, rewards for long service, good and safe working conditions, attitude surveys, job security, recreation groups, social organizations, the right to ask for merchandise in the territory, and seniority advancement.

Yet morale does not always assure exceptional productivity. To the contrary, some companies have maintained high levels of productivity despite the discontent and complaining of its employees. But even among these companies there is probably a point of diminishing returns. Where the salesman finds the situation absolutely intolerable he may quit. A company cannot permit morale to sink so low. Its whole future may be threatened unless it can traverse some sort of middle ground to keep morale high enough to assure itself of maximum productivity.

Since it is part of the sales manager's job, as we have observed, to change the individual salesmen so that their behavior more nearly corresponds to the needs of the company, he must engage in teaching while the salesmen partake of learning. The older view of learning theory maintained that learning occurred on the promise of reward.

Punishment consisted of withholding the reward. The newer conception of learning suggests the existence of a feedback process in which a person who is not rewarded is punished by stimulation of fear.[18] Once the stimulation of fear has become established the stimulus is reduced by offering hope that the cause for fear will not recur.

Applying this concept to the sales-management situation, the sales manager may threaten the salesmen with firing, loss of prestige in the organization, or a reduction in wages. When the threat is removed or the salesman at least has the hope of no longer being threatened, he is inspired to much greater effort. It is, of course, important for the sales manager to know his salesmen so that he can select the situations in which he can encourage them to hope that fear will not reassert itself.

Total Sales Perspective. The sales manager operates in a setting determined by forces beyond his control, such as competition and a changing social and political scene. The behavioral sciences may assist him to understand these forces. Sales management with a total perspective is less likely to view a particular problem as an isolated phenomenon. The effectiveness of personal selling, for instance, may depend on the pricing of the articles for sale, the amount and quantity of promotion conducted by the company, the type of dealer handling the product, and the skill of the selling effort. What is needed are sales managers who think about how the sales force is affected by the systems approach, which for sales covers money, manpower, and the flow of information.

The Salesman's Duties

The systems concept is as important to salesmen as it is to management. A salesman may be regarded as the manager of a market area. Thus, the salesman is concerned not only with selling the product but also with the strategy to be followed by the company and with innovations used to secure a better position in the market. He is involved in the goals of the company and in the planning of long-run market development.

The distinction between a salesman and a manager of a market area is important to note. It is the difference between viewing sales-

---

[18] See O. Hobart Mowrer, *Learning Theory and Behavior,* Wiley, New York, 1960; O. Hobart Mowrer, *Learning Theory and the Symbolic Processes,* Wiley, New York, 1960.

men as employees and as members of management. It affects the way in which the salesman conceives of his job. Under the marketing management concept, the salesman can become creative, strategic, or innovative. For a salesman to become manager of a market area he must identify his goals with those of the company. He must keep in mind the objectives of profit, developing new accounts, and maintaining and expanding the good will of the company through information and service. The salesman is in the best position to see how the planning organization and control effort work in the field. Thus, he is able to point out the efficacy of the effort and to propose suggestions for improving the means of attaining these objectives.

Management must be willing to take the salesman into its confidence and acquaint him with the true profit situation in his market area. It must also discuss with him the future plans and controls and over-all objectives. Research studies frequently provide a real stimuli to the salesman. They persuade him that his company is progressive and growing. Thus, he may believe with enthusiasm and confidence that his company really has the best product or service available on the market.

Management has to assume the initiative in stimulating its salesmen through progressive programs which make them feel that their company outshines its competitors and spur them to protect that position. This requires an *esprit de corps* from top management down through the market manager to the salesman. When management treats the salesman as a market manager for an area it inspires him to higher strategic and planning levels. From the company's point of view, this may provide another bonus for the future; a man's ability to run his own territory indicates his potentiality as management material.

Coordinating Sales and Production

Most companies have a single department or individual to co-ordinate production and sales.[19] Coordination in these concerns may be the responsibility of the president, assistant vice president of marketing, advertising manager, sales manager, or the marketing research department. In other companies informal agreements prevail in which department heads confer with each other. There may be a general liaison between line (product and sales) and staff (advertising and marketing), or managers may meet periodically to plan activities

[19] Author's survey, *op. cit.*

that fit the needs. In still other companies, the committee method rules. Under this procedure production and sales representatives meet formally as a committee at regular intervals. This is what some companies have reported: [20]

> The management committee is the formal part of the organization which ties in the marketing and production end of the business. Communication, however, exists between the production unit and sales department through the latter's processing the paper work on orders directly for the production unit.
>
> Staff meetings are held wherein the production department is informed of the demand for the various products and of their anticipated movement by the sales department. At these meetings, the sales department helps to set up the advertising program for the year and also suggests certain specific items on which to concentrate.
>
> Advertising and selling are linked together in an advertising and sales promotion committee, which is composed of the V.P. and General Sales Manager, Manager of Trademarked Product Sales, and the Advertising Manager. There is no direct link between advertising and production except through the General Management Committee. The link between the sales and production departments is co-ordinated in the manufacturing and sales committee which meets monthly and is composed of the following members: President, V.P.'s of Manufacturing, Marketing, Pipe Line, Crude Oil Procurement and Trading, Production, and Financial. The Comptroller is also a member of this committee.

It is evident that the sales force is a vital element in a company's pursuit of its objectives. Without a well-managed, well-staffed sales organization as a fundamental part of a total marketing operation, a company may find itself compelled to consume its unsold products. This forced feeding can lead only to indigestion, a malady as painful to business enterprise as it is to the human body. To keep the business in a healthy state adding steadily to its accumulation of profits requires the kind of sales operation discussed in this chapter. The salesman invariably finds that his way is eased by another component of the marketing mix, namely, advertising, and that topic is the subject matter of the next chapter.

Summary

Managing the sales force is just one aspect of the marketing mix. In trying to obtain new business, executives consider product, advertising, personal selling effort, and channels of distribution. Under the marketing concept

---

[20] *Ibid.*

the marketing chief executive is concerned with the over-all coordination of all the ingredients of the selling effort, while the sales manager deals with the management and administration of the sales force.

Selling involves communication. If communication is effective learning has taken place.

Management should be aware of both uncontrollable and controllable elements in planning a sales program. The controllable elements of planning and control include the development of sales plans, particularly through the use of marketing research. The planning activities of the chief executive in charge of marketing overlap some of the activities of the sales manager. Both, however, work together as a team.

Some of the elements of total sales are inputs, communication, and output. There seems to be a difference of opinion on the application of the marketing concept to sales management. The sales organization should be organized on a centralized or decentralized basis.

The duties of the sales manager are sales administration and sales-force management. The sales manager must help the salesman solve his problems and consider the total sales perspective rather than a single incident as an isolated entity. The salesman's duties may be viewed as being creative, strategic, and innovative. Many companies have worked out amicable relations in coordinating sales with production.

Suggested Cases

Ralph L. Westfall and Harper W. Boyd, *Cases in Marketing Management,* Irwin, Homewood, Ill., 1961.

> Candy Gram, Inc.—*Developer of Candy-by-Wire Service*—Development of Sales Program, pp. 272–277.
>
> American Hospital Supply Corporation—*Wholesaler of Hospital Supplies*—General Line Salesmen as Product Specialists, pp. 376–383.

Milton P. Brown, Wilbur B. England, and John B. Matthews, Jr., *Problems in Marketing,* 3rd ed., McGraw-Hill, New York, 1961.

> General Foods Corporation, pp. 490–510.
>
> United States Plywood Corporation, pp. 385–400.

Harry L. Hansen, *Marketing: Text, Cases, and Readings,* rev. ed., Irwin, Homewood, Ill., 1961.

> H. J. Heinz Company, pp. 674–683.
>
> John Hancock Mutual Life Insurance Company, pp. 700–705.

Kenneth R. Davis, *Marketing Management,* Ronald Press, New York, 1961.

> Caldwell Hospital Supply Corporation, pp. 515–530.
>
> Simpson Company, pp. 554–560.

Intercollegiate Case Clearing House, Soldiers Field, Boston 63, Massachusetts.

> ICH 3M102—Scott Paper Company, Part I and Part II.
>
> ICH 3M27—The Associated Shoe Company, Ltd.

Appendix

Many techniques generally classified as operations research have applicability for sales administration. For example, the Lamp Division of the General Electric Company was the subject of a study to determine how sales depended on the number of calls that salesmen made.[1] It was found that salesmen were making too many calls and that sales would not drop even if the number of sales calls was drastically reduced. This suggested a reassignment of salesmen so that the same number of salesmen could cover more customers.

A simple analytical technique has been described to determine the number of salesmen to be assigned to territories.[2] First, let us start with the problem of assigning salesmen to two territories. The profit for each of these marketing areas is given as a function of the sales effort expended, as shown in Figures A-1 and A-2.

It can be seen in Figure A-1 that if seven salesmen are assigned to the first marketing area, a profit of $96,000 results. Figure A-1 also shows that if more than eight salesmen are assigned to this marketing area, profits will actually go down. The situation could arise where too many salesmen would antagonize the customers and sales might drop.

As an illustration, let us suppose that a corporation has six salesmen, and that the problem is to allocate these men in two areas so that profit will be maximum. There are seven possibilities: we can allocate no salesmen to area 1 and six salesmen to area 2; we can allocate one salesman to area 1 and five to area 2; and so forth. Therefore, we can prepare the table shown, in which x_1 and x_2 refer to the number of salesmen in territories 1 and 2; $f(x_1)$ and $f(x_2)$ refer to the profit to be earned in areas 1 and 2, and z is the total profit in areas 1 and 2.

x_1	0	1	2	3	4	5	6	
x_2	6	5	4	3	2	1	0	
$f(x_1)$	38	41	48	58	66	72	83	*In thousands*
$f(x_2)$	82	75	66	60	50	42	40	*of*
z	120	116	114	118	116	114	123	*dollars*

[1] R. L. Ackoff, "Allocation of Sales Effort," *Proceedings of the Conference on What Is Operations Research Accomplishing in Industry?* Case Institute of Technology, April 1955.
[2] Andrew Vazsonyi, *Scientific Programming in Business and Industry*, Wiley, New York, 1958, pp. 219–227.

Figure A-1. Profit for first marketing area as function of sales effort.

The last row shows the profit realized corresponding to each of the seven allocation schemes. It can be seen that the best allocation is to assign all of the six salesmen to the first area and no salesmen to the second area, because this results in maximum profit of $123,000.

We can proceed now to determine the maximum profit for 1, 2, 3, . . . , 12 salesmen; in fact, we can determine the maximum profit for any number of salesmen. A somewhat simpler procedure is shown in Table A-1, where the profit is computed by assuming that a certain number of salesmen are assigned to the first area, and a certain

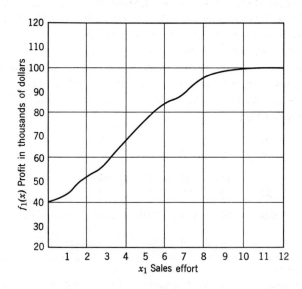

Figure A-2. Profit for second marketing area as function of sales effort.

Table A-1. Optimum Distribution of Sales Effort between Two Marketing Areas ᵃ

Number of Salesmen in First Area

Number of Salesmen in Second Area		0	1	2	3	4	5	6	7	8	9	10	11	12
		38	41	48	60	66	72	83	96	102	100	95	89	92
0	40	78*	81*	88*	100*	106*	112	123*	136*	142*	140	135	129	122
1	42	80	83	90	102	108	114	125	138	144	142	137	131	
2	50	88	91	98	110	116	122	133	146*	152	150	145		
3	58	96	99	106	118	124	130	141	154*	160	158			
4	66	104	107	114	126	132	138	149	162*	168				
5	75	113*	116	123	135	141	147	158	171*					
6	82	120	123	130	142	148	154	165						
7	88	126	129	136	148	154	160							
8	95	133	136	143	155	161								
9	99	137	140	147	159									
10	100	138	141	148										
11	100	138	141											
12	100	138												

(Profit in thousands of dollars)

ᵃ The numbers marked with asterisks are the maxima along each diagonal.

number are assigned to the second area. For instance, it can be seen that if three salesmen are assigned to the first area and two salesmen to the second area the profit realized will be $110,000.

Along the diagonals of Table A-1 the combined number of salesmen assigned to the two areas is the same. For instance, if we assign four salesmen to the two areas we read along the diagonal the following profits: 104, 99, 98, 102, and 106. We see that the best way to allocate these four salesmen is to allocate them all to the first marketing area, the profit in this case being $106,000. Therefore, by using a table of this kind, we can determine when the maximum profit is reached with a combined number of salesmen. The most profitable combinations on the diagonals are indicated by asterisks.

Let us suppose now that there are three marketing areas to consider. The profit as a function of sales effort for the third marketing area is shown in Figure A-3.

The problem with three marketing areas can be solved in exactly the same fashion as the problem for the two marketing areas. In Table A-2, the same method of solution is shown.

The top row shows the combined number of salesmen that are allocated to the first and second areas; the second row shows the

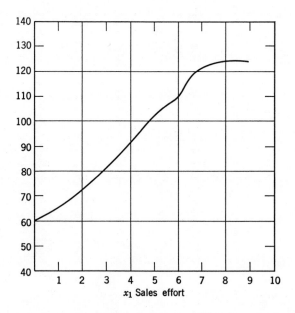

Figure A-3. Profit for third marketing area as function of sales effort.

Table A-2. Optimum Distribution of Sales Effort for Three Marketing Areas [a]

Combined Number of Salesmen in First and Second Areas

		0	1	2	3	4	5	6	7	8	9	10	11	12
		78	81	88	100	106	113	123	136	142	146	154	162	171
0	60	138	141	148	160	166	173	183	196	202*	206	214	222	231
1	64	142*	145	152	164	170	177	187	200	206	210	218	226	235
2	68	146*	149	156	168	174	181	191	204	210	214	222		
3	78	156	159	166	178	184	191	201	214	220	224			
4	90	168*	171	178	190	196	203	213	226	232				
5	102	180*	183	190	202*	208	215*	225	238*					
6	109	187*	190	197	209*	215*	222	232						
7	119	197*	200	207	219	225	232							
8	124	202*	205	212	224	230								
9	125	203	206	213	225									
10	125	203	206	213										
11	125	203	206											
12	125	203												

Number of Salesmen in Third Area

(Profit in thousands of dollars)

[a] The numbers marked with asterisks are the maxima along each diagonal.

maximum profit that can be realized by allocating the salesmen only to the first two areas in the best possible fashion. The first column on the left shows the number of salesmen allocated to the third marketing area, and the next column shows the profit that can be realized by allocating these salesmen to the third area. The table itself shows the combined profit of areas 1, 2, and 3. What we have to do is to follow the diagonals and select the maximum value. In Table A-2, these maxima are shown by asterisks.

This technique, although useful conceptually, may be difficult to apply in terms of defining the amount of profit associated with additional salesmen. At best the company may be able to establish the separable costs and determine the resulting margin which contributes to the nonseparable fixed costs and profits.[3] However, there is still the problem of associating profits only with selling effort. Profits may be due to other variables such as price, product, channels of distribution, action of competitors, changes in economic conditions, and weather. If everything else but personal selling were constant, then we could measure the profits achieved from personal selling effort accurately. Unfortunately, other things being equal does not hold up in real life situations.

[3] See Chapter 7 on distribution costs for discussion of separable costs.

Chapter Six

For some individuals the mere presentation of a product by a salesman may be enough to spark its purchase. As a rule, however, people who respond so directly to personal selling represent a minority of the consuming public. The majority prefer some preparation or ad-

Advertising

vance warning, some softening up, so to speak, before they are willing to entertain thoughts of buying. Thus far, the business community has devised no softener superior to advertising. By heralding new products in newspapers and magazines or on radio or television, by announcing them in leaflets and brochures, by displaying them on wayside signs, and by extolling the virtues of familiar articles in these same media, advertising presents the temptations for consumers to seize when the salesman calls. To judge from the record, "It pays to advertise."

Advertising and the Marketing Concept

As a major aspect of the market mix, advertising attempts to convey a message about the products and services available to satisfy consumer needs. Because of its importance many enterprises, large and small, have instituted organizational changes to enhance the role of advertising in the mix. One step taken by many companies has been to upgrade the advertising manager to vice-presidential level. They have done so because advertising, which devours a large portion of a company's funds, has been poorly coordinated with other aspects of the mix. The higher status accorded to the advertising department has put it on a more equitable footing and enabled better coordination of its activities with the rest of the marketing endeavor. Moreover, this finer enmeshment of advertising with other marketing functions has increased the cross-fertilization of ideas among marketing executives and has stimulated creativity conducive to strengthening the company's performance in the market place.

Electronic Data Processing. Recently advertising entered a new phase. A survey of 100 of the nation's largest advertisers found that while most of them used computers for many accounting and distribution chores, such as billing and inventory control, ten had begun to employ these electronic aids to measure the sales effectiveness of advertising, and four companies were relying on them to determine their advertising budgets.[1] Looking to further areas in which computers may be of help to advertisers companies will require the capacity to translate marketing problems into mathematical symbols.[2] Yet even now companies that use computers must compile a large library of facts for them and a set of assumptions on whose validity they are prepared to stand.

The present impact of this new technique on marketing and advertising strategy was indicated at a recent meeting of the Association of National Advertisers.[3] For the future, however, the computer was expected to hasten an improvement in the planning of marketing activities through an understanding of models, to increase mobility in marketing by speeding up the acquisition of information, and to foster the emergence of professional analysts to manage and evaluate data. In addition, the capacity of the computer to analyze advertising media was expected to suggest more efficient media patterns and a redesigning of the media themselves with a view toward reaching quality rather than mass audiences. The computer was expected also to feed back better marketing intelligence and a more objective appraisal of creative marketing and advertising ideas. It was to review systematically case histories and their outcomes, to aid in research and the development of information and technology, and finally, to generate greater interest in professionalism.

Already one leading advertising agency, Young and Rubicam, is using the computer for selection of media.[4] Into its decision making now enter such considerations as the way in which consumers utilize media, the potential market of any brand according to geographic and demographic factors, and the time of the year that consumers purchase the particular brand. Media schedules already developed can be checked for efficacy against these considerations. Currently, Young and Rubicam does not have enough information to employ a high-speed computer, but the unit it uses can select media at the regional level if required. It can, for example, recommend the media

[1] "Present and Future Use of Computers to Advertising Told," *Industrial Marketing,* August 1962, p. 178.

[2] See discussion in Chapter 9.

[3] "A.N.A. Weighs Issue in Multiplicity of Areas," *Advertising Age,* Nov. 12, 1962, p. 1.

[4] "Advertising: Computers for Picking Media," *New York Times,* Sept. 26, 1962, 60:3.

for an advertiser to choose if he wishes to sell to teenage girls.[5] But it can neither determine the qualitative editorial differences among media nor make space or time available when desired. The latter problem is one for media planners and space buyers.

A Case History.[6] This is the story of a small company, Noxema, turning to a market plan as its weapon to compete against Revlon, a well-established company in its field. First, Noxema reorganized its marketing team. It included in this group the executive vice president, vice president for new products, advertising director, and sales manager to achieve more effective creation, development, testing, and marketing of new products. The company had been supplying the market with products for the skin. Now it wished to introduce a product for women with clear complexions offering the color benefits and beauty of the finest cosmetics but also capable of improving the skin.

Most cosmetics on the market were of two types. There were conventional make-ups which were available in a variety of shades but which did not aid the skin. Then there were the so-called medicated products using sulfur which were sold in only one shade. These latter products were designed to cover blemishes, but they often caked up and appeared unattractive. Market research indicated a need for a product of the type contemplated by Noxema. By the fall of 1959, following laboratory tests, market checks, and consumer testing, the company was ready to submit a new liquid make-up and pressed powder in three different shades to a market test. These three shades, according to market research, accounted for 80 per cent of make-up sales.

The company faced the problem of introducing its product to women whose skins were unblemished. In collaboration with its advertising agency, it decided to accent glamour, and to do so, it engaged the nation's most fashionable cover girls and named the product after them. These cover girls were tied in with the company's marketing program. The models in Noxema's ads were telling American women about "Cover-Girl." They appeared in fashion promotions, publicity films of a woman's typical working day, and were widely photographed and quoted on their beauty advice.

The product was tested for a year in markets in Phoenix, Syracuse, Sacramento, Wichita, Omaha, and Grand Rapids. One of the initial ads showed a leading cover girl saying: "Imagine medicated make-up

[5] "Electronic Buying of Media," *New York Times*, July 15, 1962, Sect. III, 12:1.
[6] "How to Crash a Crowded Industry," *Printer's Ink,* June 29, 1962, pp. 62–68.

that looks so lovely. I love new Cover-Girl." The campaign stressed
a "cover-girl" complexion "so natural you can't believe it's make-up."
By now it was selling well. The tests disclosed that "Cover-Girl"
appealed to women of all ages and women with different types of skin.
Hence, the company extended the strategy used in the test to the
national scene.

Salesmen from all parts of the country were summoned to a meeting and told the full story of "Cover-Girl." The cover girls modeling
the line emerged at the meeting from giant compacts. Within five
months distribution among wholesale and retail outlets—drug stores,
department stores, food and variety stores—was complete. National
advertising appeared the following month. Most of the advertising
funds were allocated to television. The commercial messages stressed
the cover-girl theme, and package covers dramatized the personalities.
This was followed by a space campaign in the women's service, young
fashion, and teenage magazines which emphasized the models and
minimized the copy. Moreover, radio was used to reach the teen
market.

In addition, the company purchased a special four-page promotion
in *Vogue* which linked the cover-girl theme with the high fashion
clothes of a famed designer. To the 40 stores listed in the *Vogue*
spread as vendors of the product complete merchandising kits were
supplied. Other promotional material included miniature samples
of the pressed powder for department store and magazine exploita-
tion. As a result of this total marketing activity with advertising in
a forefront role, "Cover-Girl" soon became one of the three top selling
brands of make-up in the country.

Advertising and the Market Mix

How advertising dovetails with the other elements in the market
mix may be seen from the tactic used by the Toni Company to recap-
ture its share of the home permanent market.[7] Originally Toni controlled 95 per cent of its market. Competition drove this share down
to 21 per cent, but the company has rebuilt its hold to 50 per cent
through the introduction of new products; of these, its Tonette is
the third leading home permanent. Advertising stories were created
around the company's new products. But in 1956 the entire home
permanent industry ceased to grow as the quality of work done in

[7] "Communicate Better to Get Campaigns Okayed, Snyder Tells A. A. Work-
shop," *Advertising Age,* Aug. 6, 1962, p. 1.

beauty shops improved, new hair styles called for fewer curls, and hair sprays helped control the hair.

Toni met this situation by introducing its own hair spray which rapidly took a dominant position in the market. It also attempted to influence changes in hair styles through a series of ads in the women's prestige magazines, but this effort failed. Its biggest idea was "hidden body." This gives fullness to the hair. The smoother a girl wore her hair, the more she needed the hidden body, Toni proclaimed. Although the home permanent market eventually leveled off, Toni's share, as we have said, retrieved some of the ground it had lost.

Future Toni advertising, according to the company, would concentrate on the theme that home permanents were more fun and easier. To put its ideas across the company has invested 70 per cent of its advertising budget, including cooperative advertising with dealers, in television. And the total advertising budget has reached as much as $3.5 million a year.

The two elements of the market mix principally illustrated by Toni's experience were new product development and coordinated advertising and sales promotion. Other elements of the mix which came into play were pricing policy, personal selling effort, and channels of distribution.

Advertising and Related Concepts

The term *advertising* often evokes negative responses from people who charge it with such crimes as selling on the basis of emotional or irrational appeals, enticing the uninformed or ignorant, violating freedom of choice, and duping innocents into buying. This may be seen from the remarks made some years ago by a woman replying to an interviewer's questions. Asked if she ever read any of the advertising in a magazine, she said she did not. However, in thumbing through a magazine in the interviewer's presence, she commented that she always liked to look at the "attractive liquor ads." For this woman the term *advertising* was laden semantically, yet she was willing to acknowledge interest in a certain type of advertising. As a matter of fact, most of us do not know exactly the influence advertising has on our personal behavior. It may affect us at the conscious level or penetrate into our subconscious.

In the development of an advertisement a company has to make all elements in it conform to the central idea. The image of the product must relate to the consumer's need. What single thought or fact distinguishes one product from another for him? To get to the core of the consumer's needs a company conducts depth interviews. These inquiries should locate the common ground on which the premise of the company meets the premise of the consumer. Then the company must persuade the consumer that the premises of both are identical.

Advertising must be aimed at the symbolic image the consumer has of himself.[8] The fundamental motivation of human behavior is preservation of the symbolic self. This is the sum total of the things that we feel we know about ourselves. When a woman reads or hears an advertisement for perfume she asks herself, "Am I the sort of woman who can wear this?" If she does not answer affirmatively she will not buy the product. The advertiser, therefore, has to recognize the individual's concepts of self as well as purchasing habits. Advertising, of course, may alter these concepts.

Bardin Nelson has suggested the following seven principles for advertisers to bear in mind in creating images: [9]

1. Individuals are not exclusively rational.
2. People respond to situations in a way that protects themselves.
3. The researcher must determine the various images and reference points which already exist in the minds of a particular group or society.
4. If an image appears to be stable and the reference groups surrounding the individual support this image, then the individual will resist internal and external forces opposing the image.
5. If an image is marked by doubt, uncertainty, the advertiser should present the new image in a form that would dispel anxiety or doubts.
6. The desired image should be placed in a favorable setting. This may be done by clothing the image with already accepted values of the public.
7. In order to develop a new image a company must attract the attention of large numbers of potential customers.

Advertising and Propaganda. Advertising is not propaganda. Although both may use the same techniques, such as name calling, "getting on the band wagon," or broad generalities, and employ the same media they are not the same thing. One difference between them is that in advertising the individual is aware of the sponsor's identity and objective. The sponsor is trying to get him to buy his product or service. In propaganda, to the contrary, one may not be able to

---

[8] "Professor Hayakawa Says Ad Must Deal Not Only with Consumer's Attitudes toward Products But Also with His Attitude toward Himself," *New York Times,* April 19, 1962, 48:4.

[9] Bardin H. Nelson, "Seven Principles in Image Formation," *Journal of Marketing,* January 1962, pp. 67–71.

identify the sponsor or his purpose. The influence is indirect. Ordinarily, there is a disposition to regard propaganda as evil or bad. Not all propaganda is insidious. There may be propaganda for democracy, freedom, and improvement of social evils as well as the propaganda of special economic and social interests.

Public Relations. Public relations may be considered a form of propaganda. There is little difference between the two since in both instances the identity and motives of the sponsor may not be known. What difference does exist is that in public relations the subject matter pertains to a product or company image and the activities that affect the security of the company's operation.

Though frequently concealed from the public, the manufacturer's public-relations goal is to cultivate a favorable attitude toward his company and the products it sells. Public relations takes the form of news stories that mention the company, its product, or both, in a favorable light. Along with advertising, public relations seeks to form an image of a company and its products. This image is intended to influence not only the potential purchasers of the product, but also the company's stockholders, employees, suppliers, and intermediaries. The ultimate objective of a public-relations program is to encourage cooperation.

If a group of individuals, for example, thinks well of a company, Tucker has found, it will associate favorable attributes and motives with the company. This is particularly true in considering whether a company's attitude is fair or unfair in relation to attitudes of rich versus poor, distant versus friendly, or calm versus nervous.[10] In other studies this has been discussed under the attribute called the "halo" effect.[11] In all this there is a challenge to public relations to create the favorable image.

Not only has public relations become an important function in companies selling products or services but it has also become a vital tool to advertising agencies. In 1962, for example, about 43 per cent of the agencies, with headquarters in New York City and billing more than $1,000,000 a year in advertising, performed public-relations services for their clients. However, the interest of advertising agencies

[10] W. T. Tucker, "How Much of the Corporate Image Is Stereotype?" *Journal of Marketing*, January 1961, pp. 61–75.
[11] See A. O. Bowden, F. F. Caldwell, and G. A. West, "Halo Prestige," *Journal of Abnormal and Social Psychology*, Vol. 28, No. 4, January–March 1934, pp. 400–406; G. J. Dudyeha, "The 'Halo' around Personality," *Teachers College Record*, Vol. 43, No. 7, April 1942, pp. 564–569.

in this technique has waned as the number of wholly public-relations concerns has increased.[12]

Advertising and Communication. Advertising is part of the communication process to influence consumers to purchase the products or services of a company. This influence is built up through persuading the consumer that the product or service will ease tensions and thus satisfy specific needs. To do so, the consumer has to have a favorable impression of the product and its manufacturer. This applies to intermediaries as well as to ultimate consumers.

Sales Promotion. Sales promotion lies somewhere between selling and advertising. It is designed to intensify the pressure directed at one group such as a particular trade or a class of customers. Its devices include point-of-purchase advertising, contests, premiums, and the like. Sales promotion usually falls under the jurisdiction of a company's advertising department and forms a vital part of the total selling effort.

Advertising under Attack

Books such as Vance Packard's *The Hidden Persuaders* and *The Status Seekers* have roundly condemned the advertising profession. Even members of the profession are appalled at the examples cited by Packard of thoughtless and tasteless advertising.[13] Of a more serious character is the criticism leveled against advertising by an economist of the Federal Reserve System, Bernard Shull. He said that the volume of sales generated by each dollar of advertising had declined. It was $116 in 1947 but only $90 in 1960. In manufacturing alone, advertising produced only $50 of business for each dollar spent in 1960 compared to $100 in 1947. Several reasons are advanced for this decline. They include rising competition for the consumer's dollar, lagging demand, and higher media costs.[14] It has been pointed out, for example, that the cost of magazine space rose 20 per cent in 1962, that the cost of advertising in both business publications and newspapers rose 19 per cent, and that the cost of television time increased 19.4 per cent.[15]

---

[12] "Public Relations Aid Agencies Billing over $1 Million Perform Public Relations Services for Clients," *New York Times,* Aug. 22, 1962, 42:5.
[13] "Gossage Excoriates Ad 'Trivia,' Hits Ad's Failure to Entertain Prospects," *Advertising Age,* Aug. 13, 1962, p. 38.
[14] "Advertising Yield Cause for Concern," *New York Times,* May 22, 1962, 47:3.
[15] *Ibid.*

Suggestions for Change. At a meeting of the American Association of Advertising Agencies, Marion Harper, Jr., chairman of McCann-Erickson, a leading agency, proposed the following steps to be taken by the industry to combat some of the criticism against it: [16]

1. Setting up of a program of continuing research to determine which advertisements are considered offensive so that action might be taken to eliminate them.
2. Establishment of an information center to publish material about advertising and to guide research in the field.
3. Promotion of efforts to measure the effectiveness of different types of advertising.
4. Redrafting of the AAAA's membership code to include provisions that would discourage irresponsible advertising by members of the organization.
5. Aiding of agencies to encourage more young men to enter the field.
6. Development of a code governing agencies that establish or acquire overseas outlets to prohibit raiding of accounts and personnel, and other irresponsible acts.

In writing against a proposal to tax advertising, two members of the Northeastern University faculty suggested four functions for advertising.[17] First, they said, advertising stimulates demand and provides the consumer with valuable product information. Second, it helps organize and modify the basic perceptual process of the consumer. Third, it counters the lag among habits. And fourth, it inspires the consumer to seek a higher standard of living.

Businessmen's View. From a study of businessmen's attitudes toward advertising the following opinions were obtained.[18] Four out of five believed that advertising was vital to business and the economy, and as many as nine out of ten thought that the public had more confidence in advertised brands than in those not advertised. Of the total surveyed, 85 per cent felt that advertising raised the standard of living, and 89 per cent considered advertising the most efficient means to stimulate mass buying. Three out of ten said advertising lowered prices. Another 24 per cent said it partially lowered prices. On the other hand, 28 per cent said it raised prices. On the negative side, 78 per cent expressed the view that advertis-

[16] "Program Suggested for AAAA by Marion Harper," *New York Times,* April 30, 1962, 42:3.
[17] "Professors Kibarian and Koons Defend Ad Against Recent Criticisms," *New York Times,* May 14, 1962, 43:5.
[18] Stephen A. Greyser, "Businessmen Re Advertising 'Yes But,'" *Harvard Business Review,* May–June 1962, pp. 20–46.

ing persuaded people to buy things they did not want. To 80 per cent this was a bad practice. Only 41 per cent thought that advertising had an unhealthy influence on children.

Forty per cent considered current standards of advertising to be higher than they had been a decade before. To 36 per cent the standards had not changed, and to 24 per cent they had deteriorated. A total of 36 per cent considered television both the most effective and most objectional medium. As to other choices of the best medium, 22 per cent favored consumer magazines, 17 per cent the trade magazines, and 10 per cent the newspapers. Nearly three out of four—74 per cent—favored an ethical code for the control of advertising.

Advertising in the Marketing Process

Advertising serves a double function in the marketing process. First, it gives the public information about available products and the relative prices. Second, it reduces costs through requiring fewer salesmen and wholesalers.

Mass advertising tends to bring a routine into the transactions of consumers. To begin with, consumers are presold before they enter a store or a salesman calls on them. As a result the attractiveness of rival products narrows the area of negotiation to the special features claimed for a product or service.

Moreover, advertising stimulates cooperation between the consumer and those wishing to sell him their products. Before negotiation for a product begins, a company has to select the appropriate media to command the consumer's attention. While the consumer does his preliminary scouting for what he wants, advertising is busy searching out prospects. The prospects must be persuaded to identify themselves with the product and company advertised. Advertising induces the prospect to make this identification and then take the initiative. This applies equally to suppliers in the trade channels and thus simplifies the task of completing negotiations.

Primary and Selective Demand

The primary difficulty in recognizing what advertising accomplishes for a company results from the frequent use of the expression "advertising creates a demand." If the phrase "creates a demand" means modifying the basic habits and customs of people within a short period of time, advertising's ability to do so is questionable. Cigar advertising was deemphasized to cigarette advertising only after the habits and customs of the consumer began to change. Back in the 1880's the workingman no longer had the time for a long, leisurely smoke. The tempo of industrial activity demanded that he spend long, intense hours on the job. Thus, the shorter cigarette became popular. Prior to this popularity the cigarette had symbolized an effeminate mode of smoking. The same type of change has taken place in recent years with the development of filter-tip and longer cigarettes. The tip was instigated largely by the "cancer scare" and the greater length by the acceptability of longer European cigarettes.

No amount of advertising in the early years of the century could have persuaded people to switch from the horse and buggy to the automobile. The basic product idea had not been accepted. Similarly, if the money spent nowadays on advertising passenger flights were doubled, it is doubtful whether passenger traffic would double. There is still a group of people who feel that if they were supposed to fly God would have given them wings.

All these experiences lead to the generalization that it is difficult for advertising to alter a primary demand. Only when the habits and customs of the people are changing can advertising take profitable advantage of the situation. This is not to suggest, however, that advertising cannot and does not manipulate and modify the values that people place on products and services already accepted by them.

In addition to primary demand there is selective demand. For example, why is it that the consumer may prefer one toilet soap to other similar brands? The competing brands may have exactly the same cleansing power. However, when the consumer selects a particular brand, it promises not only cleanliness but also beauty, romance, and allure—and all this for 15 cents! This is the kind of advertising effort that is directed at selective demand, and it may accomplish much for the company employing it.

Planning and Control

As in so many elements of the market mix, we are confronted once again by the presence of both controllable and uncontrollable factors in the planning and control of advertising. Let us, therefore, examine these two different types of factors to see how they affect advertising outlook and practices.

Uncontrollable Factors

Each year productive efficiency has continued to increase. If the pattern remains undisturbed with production proceeding to expand at the same rate as heretofore, consumers will have to buy more automobiles, more refrigerators, more washing machines, and more clothing to absorb this greater output. This presents a challenge to find creative ways for inducing the consumer to purchase goods before they become obsolete. The automobile industry has met this challenge to some extent through establishment of the used-car market. As noted in an earlier chapter, through the used-car market many persons who cannot afford a new car are able to purchase good transportation at a lower price. This may very well have implications for the appliance makers.

Other uncontrollable factors certain to affect the selling effort of the future will be the growth of population and the burgeoning foreign markets. The population growth starting in 1965 should result in the formation of an increased number of families which should require more goods and services. In the foreign market, only the surface has been scratched. At best the total volume of foreign trade in the early 1960's was about 5 per cent of the country's Gross National Product. The future opportunities in the foreign trade area are enormous.

Controllable Factors

Planning Activities. Most planning activities in the advertising department start with defining the objectives desired and the tasks necessary to accomplish them. Before the defining begins, however, the present market situation must be analyzed. This is how one company said it proceeded with its planning activities: [19]

The over-all marketing picture is reviewed using sales, share of market, distribution, and other data collected over a five-year period to the present time. Careful attention is also given to research data which have been collected on advertising copy, media effectiveness, market profile, etc. In other words, we do our best to determine exactly where we stand at the moment.

We next take a look at our objectives for the coming budget period, estimate as accurately as possible what the marketing climate will be during

[19] Author's survey, *op. cit.*

that period and how much effort we will have to expend in terms of advertising and promotion to achieve our objectives.

Following this general analysis and evaluation, we prepare detailed documents covering marketing objectives, marketing strategy, and the specific copy, media, promotion, and publicity plans by which we propose to accomplish our marketing objectives. These plans are worked out in conjunction with our advertising agency and they prepare a detailed budget covering each of the items.

Thus, the first task of planning is to establish an opportunity in terms of the potentiality of the market. This opportunity is then segmented into the individual areas in which the company wishes to concentrate. The amount of effort to be invested is expressed in the budget, which also reflects the final form of the advertising plan. Generally, the budgetary goals are reviewed monthly or quarterly and amended to cope with shifting market conditions. In essence, the budget is not only a planning tool but also a mechanism for controlling the entire advertising operation.

Long-Range Plans and Models.[20] In planning an advertising program a company has to consider not only the program's immediate benefits but also its long-range aspects. Conceivably a heavy advertising campaign for a short-term period may draw sales from the future, making a steady rate of advertising preferable. Actually, a company may develop a cyclical pattern which shows the effectiveness of advertising. For instance, introduction of an advertising program may increase public awareness of advertising. Since many prospects *buy* the product in response to the advertising, the number of prospects decreases. The amount of time necessary to reach a decision to buy lessens and sales are borrowed from the future, as the experience among consumer durable goods shows. Conversely, when the advertising is curtailed, public awareness of it contracts. The length of time between purchases grows. The number of prospects increases and sales are deferred to the future. Under these latter circumstances, the impact of the retailer's demand for goods from the manufacturer is delayed. Yet it is only when the manufacturer has expanded his sales that he intensifies his advertising which, in turn, may generate further sales. When this happens awareness of advertising becomes proportional to the advertising, and sales are borrowed from the future.

The growth cycle of a product may also be related to advertising.

[20] Jay W. Forrester, "Advertising: A Problem in Industrial Dynamics," *Harvard Business Review,* March–April 1959, pp. 100–110.

At the outset of the cycle the amount of advertising is large. As the product gains acceptance the advertising program is contracted, as we have seen previously. Once the growth curve reaches maturity advertising is again increased. But by this time the rate of the product's profitability has declined. If large sums are invested in advertising at this stage the demise of the product may be hastened. On the other hand, if the advertising appropriation is increased gradually the life of the product is prolonged, and unused manufacturing capacity is minimized.

Advertising should be an integral part of the corporate operation. Its amount, timing, and character should be related to such factors as the status of the product, research, manufacturing, inventories, price, and the moral and ethical standards by which the company wishes to be known.

Planning by the Agency.[21] In distinction to the planning conducted by the advertising personnel of a company, the marketing plan devised by the concern's advertising agency may contain these elements: a statement of facts, a review of the problems and opportunities, a list of objectives, and a series of recommendations. The statement of facts includes everything on sales trends, distribution, seasonal variations, the competitive situation, the location of markets, and the types of people who represent the best prospects, the best consumer attitudes, and the like. The statement of facts informs the company who its customers are, what they want, where they want it, and when they want it.

The review of problems and opportunities defines the existing problems so that they may be recognized and efforts may be made to solve them. The review lists the existing opportunities so that they will not be ignored in the over-all planning. The statement of objectives should consist of a clear exposition of where the company would like to go, how it wants to get there, and what it wants to do that is essential. Finally, the recommendations should contain a proposed copy theme, suggested media strategy, and ideas for such things as promotions and selling activity.

The Advertising Budget and the Marketing Concept. Almost invariably funds are scarce for investment among the various company uses to which they may be put. Each functional division has finan-

---

[21] Paul N. Lideen, "The Marketing Function in a Client Organization and in an Advertising Agency," *Speeches and Articles by BBDO'ers,* Batten Barton Durstine & Osborn, New York, mimeographed, Feb. 13, 1958.

cial needs from one budgetary period to the next. Thus, it becomes the job of top management to reconcile the conflicting aims of the rival divisions and their needs for funds by judicious apportionment of the available resources. Top management may allocate the funds on an opportunity cost basis. That is, it would disperse the funds among those divisions that promise to yield the company the greatest long-run profit. In practice, this necessitates a taxing analysis because of the interrelationships among functions and the difficulty of assigning profits to each function. The return on money invested in selling effort is even harder to assess, particularly because of inadequate measures of advertising effectiveness. Yet it is within this context that the advertising budget must be developed.

The usual formula for the allocation of funds to advertising is a percentage of sales. This method fails to consider changes in competitive conditions, fluctuations in the business cycle, and the differences in the capacity of a company to finance an advertising program in periods of depression and periods of prosperity. Finally, this method looks backward; it bases the allotment of funds on past performance rather than on what may be anticipated for the future.

The most realistic approach to the advertising budget under the total marketing concept is the *task approach* in which the company decides what task the selling effort must perform for it. The company begins by choosing the objective of the task to be undertaken. This objective may be to increase sales by a certain percentage, to expand the number of distributors, to meet or surpass competition, to retain old customers and minimize switching to rival brands, to introduce new products, to change the channels of distribution, to present a new pricing policy, to initiate a new service policy, or any of a number of other similar desires.

The task approach would attempt, for example, to communicate the idea that Brand A automobile is a roomy compact car.[22] This might be called the objective of advertising. The precise goal for the advertising effort might be to increase by one million a year the number of prospects who are exposed to the message that Brand A is the roomiest compact of all competitive makes. The success in meeting this goal may be measured by employing marketing research both before and after the advertising campaign. The marketing objective is to increase sales; the marketing goal is to achieve a 10 per cent increase by next year.

[22] Russell H. Colley, "Squeezing the Waste Out of Advertising," *Harvard Business Review,* September–October 1962, pp. 76–88.

In an advertising campaign to promote the sale of gasoline, the effectiveness of the drive may be judged by two criterion, the number of motorists who are made aware of the differences and features of the brand, and the number of motorists who consider the brand superior or outstanding. The goals may be designated as an increase by a specified amount in the awareness of the brand and the noting of its superiority. If marketing research into attitudes before and after the campaign shows that the desired increase has been achieved, the objective obviously has been reached.

The communication process used to accomplish the task contains five stages, which are, in order of appearance and development: unawareness, awareness, comprehension, conviction, and action. The marketing devices a company may use to nurse this conversion from unawareness to action are advertising and promotion, personal selling and publicity, recommendations from users, product design, availability, display, price, and packaging and exhibits. The countervailing forces to these efforts are competition, memory lapses, sales resistance, and market attrition.

Advertising may contribute to each of the five stages in the communication process. One may define its goal, in fact, as a single step or a combination of steps in the stages of communication to offset the countervailing forces. Sometimes the emphasis in the various stages of communication changes with the different periods of the growth cycle of the product. For example, the objective might be to build a brand name during the introductory period, whereas it might become the establishment of knowledge and preference during the period of rapid growth, and might change to a reminder type of advertising after the brand has grown established. The following guide may be used to achieve desired results.

1. The advertising objective must be distinguished from the marketing objective: marketing may be to increase sales, advertising may be to increase awareness.

2. Executives should distinguish between specific and general aims. This may be done by establishing a goal for specific aims and an objective for general aims.

3. Goals are based on knowledge of market opportunities and buying motives.

4. Goals should be expressed in writing. Nonadvertising people may participate.

5. Bench marks are required if progress is to be made.

6. There must be a method for measuring the accomplishment.

Management may ask its advertising department the following sorts of questions in relation to its objectives and goals.

1. Whom are you trying to reach with advertising?

2. What is the size of the audience for the company's advertising?

3. What are the deciding factors that cause people to buy or not to buy our products?

4. What do we want to communicate to our prospects?

5. What combination of media will do the best job at the lowest cost of registering the intended message with the intended audience?

6. How many of the target audience already know or believe the basic message?

7. How are you going to measure the results of the proposed advertising campaign?

The task method of apportioning funds usually concerns all the executives involved in the marketing effort and also the representatives of the company's advertising agency. The advertising budget is a coordinated effort of all these individuals in and outside the company. Viewing the advertising appropriation as a task to be accomplished sets up a basis for planning. This may lead to changes in the organizational structure of the advertising operation and to suggestions for methods of control.

Economic Analysis and Budgeting. Economic analysis has developed many concepts that may be useful in budgeting for advertising. Although many of these concepts are difficult to measure at present, they should be borne in mind when the over-all advertising budget is prepared.

Economic analysis assumes that advertising is a form of nonprice competition. Instead of decreasing the price to produce a greater amount of sales, a company increases its advertising which results in additional sales. The effect of the advertising is to raise the price to the consumer and make the demand curve relatively inelastic. This is true where greater changes in price would be necessary to increase sales. But this is considered to be a monopolistic influence; that is, it is maintained that prices would have been lower if the product had been sold under purely competitive conditions.

Actually the criticism that advertising causes higher prices does not necessarily hold. When automobiles and refrigerators were first introduced to the public they were too expensive for the average consumer. Today, as everyone knows, they are within the average consumer's price range. Because advertising enlarged the market, lower unit costs of production became possible and were passed along to the consumer in the form of lower prices.

To assume that the demand curve is inelastic in the wake of advertising is to assume that a company knows the shape of its demand curve. It assumes, moreover, that the company knows how the demand curve is affected by the action of competitors. Now, it may be possible for a company to construct a demand curve, but economic theory has not dealt with the way in which the shape of that curve is affected by competition. The assumption of inelasticity presupposes that the company will not engage in price competition. Discount houses and price wars belie this assumption. As a matter of tactic, price competition resorts to such varied devices as premium coupons and even giving money away to induce the consumer to try new products.

The elasticity of demand really depends on the type of product being sold. When a housewife shops in a grocery store the effort to persuade her to buy includes the appearance of the package and the advertising she may recall about the product. When she shops for a refrigerator she may remember that she "can be sure" when she buys a Westinghouse model, but the burden of selling remains on the salesman.

A useful concept of economic analysis, therefore, is the elasticity of advertising. What change may be expected in sales volume from a small change in advertising expenditures? Some products, such as drug items, may have a high promotional elasticity of demand, while others, such as electric motors, may have a very low one.

Related to elasticity is the concept of marginal or incremental returns from an investment in advertising. With each additional amount of advertising how much more should be spent to encourage more sales? Incremental funds for advertising should be appropriated as long as they yield increments in sales and profits, and they should be continued until the incremental increases in advertising cost equal the incremental increases in revenue.[23] The difficulty in applying this concept is the problem of assessing the proportion of sales directly attributable to a company's advertising. Increased sales may be due to a number of other things, such as a total increase of advertising in the industry, changes in the weather, personal salesmanship, price and product changes, or selection of media.

---

[23] For a discussion of the incremental approach see Sidney Hollander, Jr., "A Rationale for Advertising Expenditures," *Harvard Business Review,* Vol. 27, No. 1, January 1949, pp. 79–87; Arne Rasmussen, "The Determination of Advertising Expenditures," *Journal of Marketing,* Vol. 16, No. 4, April 1952, pp. 439–446.

Another pertinent concept is the idea that advertising affects the sales of both the present period and the future.[24] For example, current sales may be influenced by the total quantity of advertising, whereas at some time in the future they may be influenced by only half as much and at some other time by but a fourth of the original amount. This concept suggests applying the investment approach to the advertising budget. The future effects of advertising have been called the lagged effects of advertising, but the difficulty in applying the concept is the problem of measuring the impact on sales and finding the fractional multiplier or coefficient.

Economic analysis, furthermore, has yielded the concept of diminishing return. That is, with each increase of advertising there is at first the prospect of increased sales, but then the rate of sales increase gradually tapers off in relation to expenditures for advertising. The return for the outlay diminishes. Many empirical studies have been conducted on this subject as it relates to advertising, particularly in the field of magazine advertising. The yardstick has been the rate of increase reached by advertising in additional periodicals. After a certain point has been reached the returns quickly diminish.[25] Although this concept has its uses it is difficult to apply to determine the impact of advertising on sales. How much of a sales increase may be due to advertising and how much to nonadvertising factors remains to be answered.

Budgeting and the Business Cycle. As a rule appropriations for advertising fluctuate with the business cycle. When business is good, large sums are spent on advertising; when business wanes, smaller amounts are allocated to advertising. There are some exceptions to this rule in which companies have appropriated larger advertising funds in periods of recession than during recoveries. RCA, for example, introduced the portable radio during the depression of the 1930's. However, this was a case not only of increasing advertising but also of putting a new product on the market.

The effect of increasing advertising during the recovery phase of the business cycle is to raise sales more than they would have been if no further advertising had been authorized. On the other hand, sales fall off more rapidly on the downswing of the cycle if no advertis-

---

[24] See Roy W. Jastram, "A Treatment of Distributed Lags in the Theory of Advertising Expenditure," *Journal of Marketing*, Vol. 20, No. 1, July 1955, pp. 36–46.

[25] Seymour Banks, "The Use of Incremental Analysis of Advertising Media," *Journal of Business*, Vol. 19, No. 4, October 1946, pp. 232–243.

ing effort is exerted in this period. This has led to the suggestion that advertising may be a means of retarding a business decline.

At the outset this proposal seems to have some merit. But upon reexamination it appears unwise to base an advertising policy on the fluctuations of the business cycle. An advertising appropriation should be enlarged mainly when there appears to be a profitable opportunity for sales. When this opportunity does not exist, increasing the advertising appropriation constitutes throwing away good dollars on a poor sales position. Nevertheless, some companies maintain an advertising reserve for depression times.

Irrespective of the phase of the business cycle, advertising cannot make much of an impression if the consumer is strongly disposed not to buy a particular product. This was well illustrated with the marketing of the Edsel, which the Ford Motor Company attempted some years back. The advertising campaign was excellently conceived but the product failed to win consumer acceptance. Factors that may have militated against the sale of the Edsel were that it was introduced during a period of economic recession and that the selling effort put forth by the distributors lacked energy and enthusiasm.

From an economic point of view, wide variations in the advertising appropriation over the cycle relate to the advertising elasticity of demand.[26] Dean maintained that advertising elasticity and income elasticity were both related to the cycle. Products of high elasticity such as appliances tended to demonstrate wider variations in advertising allocations than a product like milk. For the former type of product a company would understandably earmark more advertising funds on the upswing than on the downswing. Products like milk, however, with a low advertising elasticity, would tend to have steadier appropriations for advertising which ignore the changes in size of allotment otherwise associated with swings of the business cycle.

Yet there are some writers who believe that advertising appropriations should remain constant even on the downswings of the business cycle. They reason that by maintaining the level of advertising on the downswing, a company will experience a greater recovery of sales when the cycle swings upward than those companies that contract their advertising during the recessive phases of the cycle.

Budgeting and the Demand Trend. Some products that have been on the market for many years have an unfavorable demand trend. Wringer-type washing machines, for example, are being superseded

[26] Joel Dean, "Cyclical Policy on the Advertising Appropriation," *Journal of Marketing*, Vol. 15, No. 3, January 1959, pp. 265–270.

by the automatic kind. No amount of advertising will reverse this trend. Yet a company may decide to seek an increasing share of a declining market. In such instances it may undertake more advertising than its competitors. However, it would not spend more on advertising wringer washing machines than on automatic washing machines.

The declining demand trend for pork provides another example. The most that advertising might be able to accomplish in this case might be to stave off the downward movement for the short run. A similar fate has befallen white bread, but the baking industry has overcome it by introducing diet breads which conform to demand trends.

It is evident, then, that advertising appropriations have to be adjusted to the cycle of growth of a product. In the early stages, as we have observed, a large amount of money may be spent until the product gains acceptance. Then the company may trim its advertising until competitors begin to enter the field. At this point the company has to fatten its advertising appropriation to hold onto its share of the market. Some products, such as dentifrices and soaps, have long growth patterns while others like automobiles and appliances face obsolescence within a year. Advertising which intensifies the demand for a generic product will probably reflect a longer growth trend than advertising associated with annual product modifications or differences.

Advertising Budgets and Break-Even Analysis. Break-even analysis may be a useful tool in preparing an advertising budget. The first item to be calculated is the gross margin to be earned by the product. This is divided into the advertising appropriation in the following manner:

$$\text{Break-even point} = \frac{\text{Advertising appropriation}}{\text{Gross margin}}$$

The quotient signifies the number of units that have to be sold merely to recover the advertising expenditure. If this sales volume is unattainable because of too limited a market potentiality the advertising appropriation has to be trimmed to size. The potentiality indicated, however, may be greater than it is feasible to anticipate. This, of course, would permit recouping of the outlay for advertising and perhaps enable a profit from the operation.

Amortization of Advertising Costs. When a manufacturer purchases a large machine or piece of equipment he will generally amortize its cost over the life of the unit. With advertising and selling costs it has been the custom to assign them to the period in which they are incurred.[27] By so doing, however, a company does not obtain a true understanding of the expense of advertising as it affects some future period. Thus, income may be overstated in the period following the initial advertising outlay and understated in the period in which the advertising if first used to develop the market.

The accountant, on the other hand, has had difficulty in applying amortization principles to future sales because of the problem of measuring the impact of present advertising on future sales. Some accountants are willing to accept the notion that an amount in excess of the normal advertising expenditure should be charged to future periods. Nevertheless, they still emphasize the complexities of trying to reach agreement on what is normal.

There is still one more drawback to using the concept of amortization in connection with advertising costs. That is the many adverse rulings of the Internal Revenue Service on the deferral of advertising.[28] However, the tax officials have allowed deferral when a company could prove that its advertising cost continued over the life of the product or service. In one case in which advertising was used to win a contract, it was ruled that the advertising cost might be amortized over the life of the contract.[29]

Advertising Research. It is the job of a company's marketing research department to keep tabs on the changing habits and customs of consumers and report these shifts to the advertising department. These changes produce a new set of wants that spring from a new set of needs. Apart from uncovering the changes the research department makes recommendations to top management.

In the years following the Second World War, we have seen many changes in the consumer motivated by the desires for casual living and convenience. Foods, clothing, and even housing have responded to these changing needs. A more recent illustration may be noted in the automobile industry. Following the conclusion of the war there appeared a growing interest in foreign cars and then the compacts.

[27] See Richard S. Woods, "Theory and Practice in the Capitalization of Selling Costs," *The Accounting Review,* October 1959, p. 564 ff.; John Van Pelt, "Giving Attention to Accruals in Deferrals in Interim Reporting," *National Assn. of Accountants Bulletin,* April 1961, p. 18 ff.; H. A. Finney and Herbert E. Miller, *Principles of Accounting,* 5th ed., Prentice-Hall, Englewood Cliffs, N.J., 1958, p. 411.
[28] See CCH, Advertisers' Exchange, Inc., 25 TC 1086, Dec. 21, 583; CCH, Sheldon and Co., (CA-6) 5t-2 USTC Par. 9526, 214 F 2d. 655; CCH, Harper & McIntire Co., D.L. 57-1 USTC, Par. 9627, 151 FSyp. 588.
[29] CCH, United Profit Sharing v. U.S. 1 USTC, Par. 21966, Cl. 171.

Underlying this change was a large-scale shift away from the social status of the automobile to the house, among other things. Right after the war, the symbol of status was the large chrome automobile. But as family living became more important, the values of the consumer swung from transportation to the home. The consumer dollar sought more expensive homes and less expensive automobiles.

The challenge to the advertiser is to discover the existing pattern of public needs. With this as a starting point, he may develop an advertising campaign directed to the needs. Some of these needs may be expressed at the conscious level and others in the subconscious. As previously observed, the needs hidden from view or expression may be detected through motivation research.

Many companies consider advertising research to consist of some sort of pretesting of an advertising theme, followed by testing during the campaign and further tests after the campaign has ended. These tests are generally described in textbooks on advertising and marketing research.[30] We shall deal instead with research on model building in advertising. First, we shall present a model that suggests a general approach to the measurement of advertising's effectiveness. Then, we shall propose a model that measures the contribution of advertising to the total selling effort.[31]

Perhaps one of the most comprehensive efforts to construct a model depicting the effect of advertising through the various media and through a single medium was made by the Advertising Research Foundation.[32] In a study conducted by its Audience Concepts Committee the Foundation put together in broad form a model that could be used productively in future research on the effectiveness of advertising. The committee defined advertising to mean an attempt to influence the public's awareness of and attitude toward a product or service through messages carried by paid media.[33] The media studied by the committee included newspapers, magazines, radio, television, and outdoor advertising.

There are six steps, according to the committee, in the propagation

[30] See Charles H. Sandage and Vernon Fryburger, *Advertising Theory and Practice*, 5th ed., Irwin, Homewood, Ill., 1959; Harper W. Boyd and Ralph L. Westfall, *Marketing Research*, Irwin, Homewood, Ill., 1956, Chap. 14.

[31] More sophisticated mathematical models appear in the Appendix at the end of this chapter.

[32] *Toward Better Media Comparisons: A Report of the Audience Concepts Committee of the Advertising Federation*, Advertising Research Foundation, Inc., New York, 1961.

[33] *Ibid.*, p. 13.

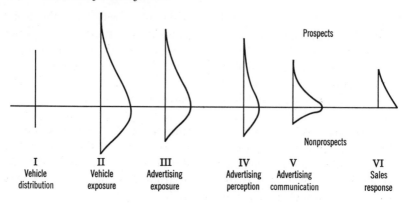

Figure 6-1. A model for evaluating media.

and effect of advertising. The first three of these, concerned with the extent to which individuals are exposed to advertising, are *vehicle distribution, vehicle exposure,* and *advertising exposure.* The final three, dealing with the response to advertising, are *advertising perception, advertising communication,* and *sales response.*

Within each medium is an advertising vehicle that provides advertising opportunities on a continuing basis. For example, there is *The New York Times, Life,* the *Eleventh Hour News,* or all the media in a single city such as Chicago or San Francisco. Conceptually it is possible to describe the effect of each of the six steps on a group of prospects and a group of nonprospects as a frequency distribution for each step. By the time the sixth step is reached only the prospects remain. The chart in Figure 6-1 [34] depicts the process.

In the progression from step I to step VI the variance decreases and the distribution tends to skew toward the prospects. By developing a frequency distribution at each step in the advertising process one can obtain a predictive model. Let us examine the model step by step and the various problems relating to measurement.

1. VEHICLE DISTRIBUTION. This refers to the number of copies circulated by a publication, the number of sets tuned in, or the number of outdoor locations. Newspapers and magazines have an official circulation number that is certified by the Audit Bureau of Circulation. In radio and television there are diverse techniques for ascertaining how many sets are tuned in to a particular station or network. One is the coincidental method in which a sample number

[34] *Ibid.,* p. 15.

of homes are telephoned and asked the station to which each is tuned. Another is a sampling of families that keep diaries of their listening habits. A third method employs the audimeter, a mechanical device attached to a sample of radio and television sets to record the stations to which the owners tune at specific times.

One must be chary of deducing that the effectiveness of advertising is a function of the number of people exposed to the broadcast medium. There is no assurance that everyone owning a radio or television set sees all the advertising, not even those who report watching particular programs. Yet the objective of an advertiser in selecting media is to reach an audience that contains many good prospects for his product or service. Among this group there should be a high probability of buying what is advertised. Thus, the advertiser may understandably wish to know the composition of the audience drawn to a particular medium. Unless the members of the audience form part of the market the advertiser covets, the specific medium has little value to him.

2. VEHICLE EXPOSURE. This alludes to the total number exposed to the media. In vehicle distribution we know the total number of purchasers of a newspaper or magazine, or the number of sets tuned in to a particular radio or television program. However, we lack an accurate count of how many people actually read the magazine or newspaper. Nor do we have a precise count of the number and types of individuals listening to radio or watching television.

For the Advertising Research Foundation the term *exposure* means to open eyes to the vehicle. A technique has to be devised to test whether people actually have been exposed. Some serious problems impinge on the development of a definition of exposure. For example, to consider the case of outdoor billboards, if exposure is defined as the number of people who pass by the billboards, the exposed would also include persons who do not face them. Or if a camera were focused on all the eyes that passed the face of the billboard does this really mean that all these people have been exposed to its message? Is it not possible that even though they may have been looking in the direction of the billboard they may not have seen the advertisement?

In the case of television exposure data have been gathered by asking respondents how many persons were viewing a particular program or station at a certain time. Yet this data would not necessarily constitute an accurate or objective measure of the audience exposed. Besides, there is the problem of a person viewing a program but ignoring the advertising messages. Can anyone maintain that every member of the radio or television audience exposed to a program hears or sees or pays attention to the advertising message? Finally, there is the need to find a common denominator among the different definitions of exposure.

3. ADVERTISING EXPOSURE. Differing from vehicle exposure, advertising exposure deals with only those exposed to the relevant advertising. Ideally a frequency distribution is required of those exposed to a medium over varying intervals of time. Here the frequency may be more important than effective coverage because the advertiser is interested in a particular segment of the population. He should therefore have as much information as is available to discern whether the audience of a particular medium conforms to his market. Most media are able to supply considerable quantitative data on their audiences.

4. ADVERTISING PERCEPTION. Here we are dealing not only with exposure to the medium but also with the ability of the individual to describe the advertising presentation. This, however, introduces the element of memory. How is it possible to measure perception without measuring the ability to remember? It would be desirable to have a frequency distribution of the number of individuals who perceive the message one or more times. This is a difficult figure to obtain because an individual may be able to remember that he has seen or heard the advertisement before but not be able to give the precise number of times he has done so.

5. ADVERTISING COMMUNICATION. Perception either occurs or it does not occur. Communication is more than perception. In communication an advertisement can add to knowledge, change an attitude, and develop a resolve to buy the advertised product. How far advertising can communicate depends on the message as well as the form in which it appears in the medium. There is an element of communication in the fact that a consumer chooses a particular medium. Yet despite their ability to communicate many advertisements do not change beliefs. They may sharpen beliefs and thus influence judgments, or they may evoke moods.

Recall records what has been remembered and is thus an extension of perception. Recall may pertain only to a particular portion of an advertisement. Communication, therefore, is only in part a function of the various media. It is also a function of the person perceiving the advertisement. The data communicated by the person tells something about the kind of sales response that might be expected. And there are studies that indicate that some aspects of recall and attitude change correlate well with sales data.

6. SALES RESPONSE. Ideally, a company might like to hold constant all other factors bearing on sales and vary only the quantity of advertising. This has been done in many types of market tests. Re-

gretably, there is great difficulty in holding everything constant. For example, two test-market areas may be composed of individuals of different psychological characteristics; media habits may differ. The real problem in measuring the impact of advertising in a sales situation is the influence of one bit of advertising. That impact is cumulative.

The most fertile area for research, concluded the Federation study, is the exploration of the concept of perception. The committee seemed to feel that this was the most logical as well as the most convenient place to compare media. A measure of perception, the committee was quick to point out, does not, however, provide an absolute measure of advertising effectiveness. If an advertisement is a positive communication, which puts its message across unambiguously, then the greater the number of people who perceive it, the better will be its effect. But first one must know the kind of effect it will have and how well it is communicated.

Not many manufacturers really grasp advertising's prime purpose and function.[35] Few of them go beyond general statements to the effect that the purpose of advertising is to increase sales. Because of this lack of clear understanding of what advertising can do for them, there is a considerable amount of waste in advertising. To eliminate this waste through improving their knowledge of advertising's role in the manufacturing orbit, companies should draw heavily on their marketing research departments. They might seek to evaluate the contribution of advertising to their selling effort.[36]

One approach to this evaluation is subjective. As a beginning the selling task must be defined. It may be broken down into the following phases: making contact, arousing interest, creating preference, making specific proposals, closing, and keeping the customer sold. Next, one must assign each of these phases of the selling task a percentage of value. For example:

Making contact	5%
Arousing interest	10
Creating preference	30
Making specific proposal	20
Closing	30
Keeping sold	5
	100%

[35] "Efficiency Drive," *New York Times,* Aug. 20, 1962, 35:3.
[36] Cyril Freeman, "How to Evaluate Advertising Contribution," *Harvard Business Review,* July–August 1962, pp. 137–148.

Then, one would evaluate the contribution of advertising to each of the selling tasks by multiplying the contribution by the proportion of the selling task:

	Contribution of Elements of Sales	Contribution of Advertising	Total Promotional Contribution
Making contact	5%	30%	1½%
Arousing interest	10	20	2
Creating preference	30	10	3
Making specific proposals	20	0	0
Closing	30	0	0
Keeping sold	5	5	2½
	100%	65%	6¾%

Thus, the contribution of advertising to the selling effort would be 6¾ per cent. On sales of $1 million, the revenue contribution of advertising would total $67,500.

Using a scaling device, one may apply learning theory to advertising research in a number of ways. For example, one might measure the amount of learning which has occurred between advertising campaigns. This may be done for specific brands or for groups of products. The test may measure the amount of learning with respect to a company's own products in relation to its competitors' products.

One of the foremost problems of advertising is the correct allocation of funds among rival media. Here, too, learning may be the criterion for the apportioning of funds. One might test the amount of learning which has taken place among the different media and appropriate funds according to the learning pattern.

From a small study on the relative amount of learning among competing brands of cigarettes it was found that the brand attaining the highest score in learning was the one that achieved the highest sales volume for the year.[37] This notion is not offered as an invariable rule, but it does warrant experimentation. Recently the field of operations research has developed learning models which may be useful in further exploration of the impact of communication in advertising research.[38]

[37] Unpublished study by author; see example in Chapter 10 on the behavioral sciences.
[38] See R. R. Bush and F. Mosteller, *Stochastic Models for Learning*, Wiley, New York, 1955.

The physical sciences have developed intricate formulae for communication in electronics. It is only recently that communication has received attention in the social sciences. The principal research thus far has dealt largely with group behavior and communication, in particular, with small groups. This research has underscored the complexity of communication as the group grows ever larger. It has also spotlighted the efficiency of the decision making in authoritarian as contrasted with democratic groups. In the latter instance, it may take longer to make a decision, but there is greater cooperation and participation when the decision is reached democratically. The decision is made more expeditiously, if more arbitrarily, in an authoritarian group.

In the marketing department communication occurs within the department and between the department and other departments. It also takes place between the marketing department and the ultimate consumer through personal selling effort and the advertising media. Communication is further carried out, as has been noted, with the company's stockholders, intermediaries, employees, and suppliers.

Actually, communication with the consumer is more difficult now than it was in the past. Consumers are better educated, more critical, and selective; they demand more from the products and services they buy. Brand names have been proliferated; it has become harder to reach the buyers, harder to implant the selling idea tied to a single brand. Fewer larger volume retail outlets are replacing multiple, smaller ones; therefore, the retailer has become more demanding with respect to product, price, merchandising, and advertising. Personal salesmanship in many retail areas is at low ebb; consequently, more goods must be presold. Finally, retail selling is becoming more impersonal and more dependent on mechanization, putting a greater premium on creative advertising and merchandising. All these, and more, are problems for the advertising research teams of companies and their agencies.

Creativity. The advertising manager of a company should be responsible for not only the budget and the maintenance of liaison between the concern and its advertising agency but also the stimulation of creativity within his own department and within the company in general. In the past the agency had usually supplied many creative ideas to the company. It continues to do so in most cases. The advertising manager, of course, evaluates these ideas, but he should also encourage creative effort among his own forces. The premium on creativity is much greater than ever before. In many instances the delicate balance between survival and demise may swing on the company's capacity for creative action. Competition for the consumer's dollar is keen. The major challenge to advertising men is to increase the appeal of advertising. The pressure bears down as consumers are exposed to more advertising than ever and the urge to creativity grows ever stronger.

In science a man who proposes a theory makes an imaginative choice which outruns the facts on many occasions. This creative step in science is the process of induction. Induction imagines more than there is justification for and creates relationships that may not be capable of verification.[39] The scientist finds unity in the variety of nature. The creative mind seeks out unexpected likeness.

Creativity, then, is the ability to transcend conventional patterns of thought.[40] It may comprise achievement through the development of a new pattern to a new problem. More likely it is the application of a known pattern to a problem. Creativity also requires the ability to communicate and is dependent on imagination and initiative in addition to communication. In company situations requiring creative activity six steps are necessary to follow through. These are problem finding, problem defining, problem selling, problem distribution, problem solving, and solution selling.[41]

The General Electric test kitchen represents a device directed at *problem finding.* In it the attempt is made to find the problems encountered by the average housewife in her everyday tasks. Many of these problems may be identified through depth interviews with the consumer. Once the problems are found the second step is *problem defining* so that when solutions are obtained they may be applied to the problems themselves. *Problem selling* must occur not only within the company but also among its intermediaries and even the ultimate consumers. *Problem distribution* is the effort to involve more than one functional area of the enterprise. This is the essence of the marketing concept, for it constitutes an attempt to encourage the entire company to consider the problem from the consumer point of view. It is also advisable to distribute the problem to the intermediaries and the ultimate consumer. In *problem solving* the need arises to evaluate a number of optional possibilities and recommend the one that best solves the problem. Group suggestions may be sought to

[39] J. Bronowski, "The Creative Process," *Printer's Ink*, Jan. 13, 1961, pp. 24–27.
[40] Group 25 Manufacturing Course Class of 1958 of Harvard Graduate School, *Individual Creativity and the Corporation*, Manufacturing Group 25 and Institute of Contemporary Art, 230 Fenway, Boston, Mass., 1959, p. 6.
[41] *Ibid.*, p. 18.

develop the possible approaches. Before the final recommendation is made the solution may be tested on a limited basis. *Solution selling,* the final step, is based on the results of tests. Its problem is one of communication.

In working problems through imaginatively it is important to reduce them to their essentials.[42] Five steps are involved in the process: assessing the situation, defining the problem, using the subconscious, idea-producing sessions, and selection of the best idea.

In assessing the situation one accepts a tentative definition of the problem but avoids seeking solutions at this juncture. For the moment the individual must profess intelligent ignorance. He must be careful lest he overestimate his experience. He must avoid the opinionated, demand numbers instead of adjectives, and search for key factors. Facts tend to reveal themselves; they should be gathered with continuity but accepted with caution. The important pieces of information may be visualized either by recording them on cards or placing them on charts. Then comes the test of time. Is the situation the same today as yesterday? If possible, the individual should conduct a personal investigation of the situation so that he may view it through his own eyes.

Next, the individual should surround himself with the situation so as to get the feel of conditions. He should develop thoughts about where additional research may be needed.

In developing ideas one may draw on one's subconscious.[43] First, the facts are gathered. Then it is advisable to let the problem lie presumably unattended. During this interval the problem is really not ignored for the subconscious is hard at work on it. From time to time, however, the individual consciously rechecks the definition of the problem.

Prior to the idea-producing session, the individual shuts off the subconscious.[44] In this session the individual seeks singleness of purpose—he engages in concentration. Time may be needed. Environment can also prove helpful, especially an environment that best encourages one to work. After an individual believes he has captured the idea, he may want to discuss it with others. Or he may wish to switch subjects and apply himself to something else. Later, he may

[42] Frank Alexander Armstrong, "Idea Tracking: Tool for Decisions," *Printer's Ink,* July 29, 1960, pp. 56–58.
[43] Frank Alexander Armstrong, "Creating with the Subconscious," *Printer's Ink,* Aug. 5, 1960, pp. 44–45.
[44] Frank Alexander Armstrong, "How To Pick the Number One Idea," *Printer's Ink,* Aug. 12, 1960, pp. 50–51.

return to the idea and check it again to see whether it actually relates to the problem at hand.

The best ideas are selected and allowed to jell again in the region of the subconscious. By this time objectivity is required and is sought through outside, detached opinions. Finally, a balance sheet is drawn listing the good and bad points of the ideas so that a choice or choices may be made. Yet the question remains, does the choice actually solve the problem?

Basically, there is agreement that new ideas are born to the individual in isolation. However, there is some belief the ideas may be expanded through group discussion. Two techniques have been used. One of these is called "brainstorming," and the other is known as "operational creativity."

1. BRAINSTORMING. Alex F. Osborn, the founder of brainstorming, has pointed out three ways in which the technique may be used. It may be a supplement to individual ideation, a supplement to conventional conferences, or an adjunct to creative thinking. Its primary advantages are:

1. To aid the individual involved in problem solving to get new approaches and new ideas which he may wish to use in his individual problem-solving work.

2. To give the individual involved in brainstorming the experience of suspended judicial thinking as an aid to training himself in his thinking technique.

The technique of brainstorming includes the following: [45]

1. A session requires eight to twelve people for best results. There should not be in the group anyone formally responsible for the project.

2. Leadership should be held by a person with an understanding of the meanings of words, remarks, and gestures. The leader should act when there is a breach of rules.

3. Rules during the session:
   a. *Critical judgment is prohibited.* Criticism of ideas must be withheld until later.
   b. *"Free-wheeling" is welcomed.* The wilder the ideas are the better; it is easier to tame down than to think up.
   c. *Quantity is desired.* The greater the number of ideas, the more is the likelihood of there being good ones.

[45] Group 25, *op. cit.,* p. 93.

d. Combination and improvement are sought. In addition to contributing ideas of their own, group members should show how suggestions by others can be turned into better ideas, or how two or more ideas can be combined into a still better one.

Before the brainstorming session begins it proves useful to acquaint members of the group with the problem to be considered. The leader of the session may wish to scout some of the possible approaches to it in order to find a practical way to get started. In addition, a method may be developed for evaluating the ideas emanating from a brainstorming session.

2. OPERATIONAL CREATIVITY.[46] This technique may be used either by a leader of a group or by an individual in the development of his own thinking. The process has been divided by its originator, W. J. J. Gordon, into four categories covering six themes. The first category contains the theme of "involvement-detachment." According to this theme there are basically two ways of looking at things. One is to look only at the unique aspects of a problem or object; this might be called the fact-finding stage. The other is the detached or general approach; here one may reason by analogy. The group or the individual, as the case may be, shifts back and forth between the involved and the detached approaches.

In the second category are the two themes of "speculation and deferment." One might be able to defer a definite statement about a problem until other avenues have been explored. This tends to push the individual beyond the limits of his theories, preconceptions, and traditional ways of viewing things.

The third category includes the themes of "autonomy and purposefulness." In this category one relates all the elements of the problem to the result one hopes to achieve. Although the individual should become aware of the interrelationships he must truly wish to create. In work situations, which involve an ever-changing combination of problems, the advantages of purposefulness may be observed. This applies especially to advertising where problem situations change daily and where each situation faced exists in a state of flux.

The final category embraces the theme "use of the commonplace." The theme of involvement provides a fresh, unstructured approach to a problem situation and to observing the elements of possible solution. We therefore use the commonplace as a springboard for new ideas.

[46] W. J. J. Gordon, "An Operational Approach to Creativity," *Harvard Business Review,* Vol. 34, No. 6, November–December 1956, pp. 41–51.

Organization for Advertising

The Advertising Department and the Marketing Concept

Under the marketing concept the advertising manager is on the same corporate level as the sales manager and reports to the chief marketing executive. It has been fully recognized that advertising is a part of the total marketing effort. Advertising begins before the product is sold and continues while it is being sold and after it has been sold. It must be integrated and coordinated with the other aspects of the marketing program, such as product development, pricing, channels of distribution, and personal selling.

Status. The top advertising jobs now enjoy vice-presidential prestige. In 1932 only four among the 250 member companies of the Association of National Advertisers had vice presidents for advertising. Thirty years later nearly 100 of the association's 700 members had such officers.[47] Similar changes have taken place in public relations. A survey of 253 corporations on their public-relations policies found that 34 per cent of the 132 responses said their chief public relations official had vice-presidental status.[48] In the view of 84 per cent of the respondents the function of public relations was of growing importance, and 77 per cent said that the chief public-relations officer had access to policy decisions of management. This change came about only in the late 1950's.

There are important policy implications in these changes in the organizational status of the advertising and public-relations manager. Formerly when advertising was supervised by the product manager, the accent was on the hard sell. With advertising now under the direction of the vice president for advertising there is less pressure for the hard sell and the short-term point of view. The advertising manager may concern himself with the impact of advertising on the corporate image and the product over the long haul. In many companies, therefore, it is inevitable that top management should now involve itself in advertising decisions that are good for both the concern and for advertising.

Contributions. Decisions on product development may reflect the point of view of the advertising department on the size of the package

[47] "Advertising: Industry's Men in High Posts," *New York Times,* July 9, 1962, 40:3.
[48] *Ibid.*

and the advertising it is to contain. It is the responsibility of the advertising department to select the features of the product that lend themselves to good advertising and thus can appeal to the consumer. The advertising staff embodies these features in copy and art work. The ideas for the features may originate in the engineering, production, and marketing research departments.

To attract consumers price information has to appear in the right place. The advertising department assumes the responsibility for placing the price on display where it will do the most good. Frequently, this involves the placement of local advertising which stresses price in conjunction with the product's features. An advertising manager should know whether prices are too high or too low. He should also understand the influence of odd pricing.

As indicated before, the major function of advertising in relation to the intermediaries is to encourage their cooperation. Advertising of this sort not only points out what the company is attempting to do in introducing a new product but also indicates what the dealer has to gain in expected sales volume and gross margins. The advertising also stresses the services performed for the intermediary by the manufacturer.

Actually the burden of advertising in the total selling effort will vary with the product to be sold. For convenience-type goods the burden is greater than for consumer durable goods. Self-service selling and impulse buying also place a heavy responsibility on advertising. With consumer durables, on the other hand, the advertising creates an impression, favorable or otherwise, but the burden of selling falls on the shoulders of the salesman.

Relationships with Other Departments [49]

The advertising department collaborates closely with all other departments by planning and attending meetings at which advertising is coordinated with other activities of other departments. This necessitates the cooperation of the advertising department with other department heads to learn their requirements. Total selling effort requires the advertising department to maintain communication with other departments of the company and to appraise realistically the value of these promotional get-togethers. The meetings are a vehicle through which everyone may be apprised of plans, past performance may be evaluated, and future needs may be anticipated. Some of

[49] Empirical data from author's survey, *op. cit.*

these meetings are designated as committee sessions of groups known as merchandising committees or planning committees.

The advertising department may collaborate with the following other departments: sales training, public relations, legal, sales, service, and marketing research departments. All these exchange ideas and data to help develop a well-informed and efficient marketing organization.

Relation to Sales and Production

To achieve a sound over-all marketing plan for any product or group of products it is particularly necessary for the advertising department to work in close association with both the sales and production departments. In some companies the advertising department participates in the performance of the sales management function in such areas as the development of sales quotas and incentives. And there are instances in which the advertising department supplies a weekly sales analysis to the sales and production departments. More generally, however, the advertising department teams with sales and production to determine the products or models to be featured in the company's advertising and the items which will be available and around which a promotion campaign may be built.

Because of its concern with the features of new products and the timetable for the introduction of these products, the advertising department consults with the sales department on market trends, product acceptance, new markets, and similar matters. The information gathered in these meetings is interpreted and translated into useful advertising material aimed at prospects, customers, stockholders, distributors, salesmen, suppliers, government agencies, prospective employees, and the community. Moreover, information from the sales department, marketing research, and the company's advertising agency provides the advertising department with data that suggest the specific audience on whom the company's marketing efforts should be concentrated.

In some companies the liaison is complete between all product managers and the advertising department. This is achieved through periodic consultation between the advertising staff and the various production managers, as well as the general sales administration. These relations with the production forces are largely individual except for broad cooperation on the technical aspects of products.

As a resource department for sales and production, the advertising department may comb leading publications for pertinent editorial information and reports on the markets they cover, referring such articles to the appropriate executives concerned with them. As reprints are needed, they are distributed by the advertising department. Statistical information may also be provided to sales and production by the advertising department.

Frequently the chief marketing executive is also responsible for advertising. This facilitates the close liaison with sales. Since the marketing chief is concerned with the ways and means for improving strategy, he may constantly review and appraise plans for advertising and merchandising campaigns. Generally, the company's sales manager, as we have seen, designs the merchandising and sales promotion programs. However, top management freezes the budget on which the advertising department's activities are based.

Coordinating Advertising and Personal Selling.[50] The problem of coordinating advertising and selling among companies specializing in packaged products has been solved in many instances by appointment of product managers. This has worked especially well for the Nestlé Company. Some time back field men were responsible to merchandise managers. Now, however, specific product managers supervise the sales force's activities with respect to their particular product, and even the advertising for the product. This form of organization, however, will not serve for every company; it does not seem especially to fit the needs of a rapidly growing company.

The coordination problem has been intensified in many companies by the failure of top management to enforce coordination. Thus, sales and advertising executives may work at cross purposes. District sales managers may not fully understand the role of advertising in selling, and salesmen may be poorly informed as to what is being advertised. Frequently, the sales and advertising departments may be competing with each other, particularly when the advertising budget is bigger than the sales budget. In many cases, besides, there are personality problems—such as, who is king? This kind of rivalry can be averted only through budgetary safeguards.

The responsibility of the product manager is to develop promotional campaigns aimed at a definite profit objective, forecasting sales, pricing, and preparation of the budget. Yet he may not always have control over the total selling situation. For example, he may have to share the responsibility for leadership of the sales force.

[50] "Needed! New Ad-Sales Unity," *Printer's Ink,* March 3, 1961, pp. 21–25.

There are several methods for coordinating sales and advertising efforts [51] and these may be considered among the best of them:

1. Use a field guide for sales managers stating:
   a. Advertising objectives.
   b. Sales review of past promotions.
   c. Information on competitive advertising.
   d. Product information.
   e. Promotion information.
2. Show salesmen how advertising may make them more money by:
   a. Salesmen's past experience.
   b. Records of inquiries from ads.
   c. Results of test markets.
   d. A statement by executives.
3. Describe the origin of advertising ideas—many come from the salesmen in the field.
4. Use company organ to describe advertising campaigns past and future. Tell success stories.
5. Distribute one-page, weekly newsletter.
6. Mail salesmen reprints of business-paper discussions of the company's advertising campaign.
7. Have the right man, such as the market manager or the sales manager, give information.
8. Avoid reliance on older men who cannot be inspired because they do not believe in the effectiveness of advertising.

The Company and Its Agency

The most important reason for the choice of an advertising agency is that the agency is familiar with the markets and products of the company. These are typical comments made by companies who were asked how they selected their agency: [52]

Our advertising agency was selected on the basis of its experience in the appliance industry and its proven ability to produce effective, sales-producing, advertising programs, both national and local, in all media. The agency provides the services of a highly trained staff of experts in all phases of advertising activity.

Our products may broadly be considered instruments. As such, technical knowledge is required in their sales and by the same token in their advertising. Our present advertising agency couples advertising know-how with

[51] *Ibid.*
[52] Author's survey, *op. cit.*

the required technical background—all of the account executives are graduate engineers thoroughly versed in advertising skills.

The second reason for choosing an agency is that it satisfies the service requirements of the client. This was how one company put it:

Our main advertising agency on biscuit and crackers has handled the account for more than 20 years. We have found it well able and willing to satisfy our service requirements. Personnel changes have been made when they seemed necessary.

Other reasons that may influence the selection of an agency include the agency's willingness to handle small accounts, its flexibility in changing its method of operation to meet changes in the over-all marketing picture, and its readiness to expand its staff in response to additional demands from the client. A feeling that an agency is eminently fair and hard working or that it is management minded also sways a company in favor of one agency above others. Some companies have picked agencies that boast top billings while others have chosen agencies because of their personnel, creative thinking, or research and merchandising facilities. Two of the companies surveyed said they selected their agencies because of size and ability to function as the advertising departments of their enterprises.

One furniture manufacturer found a new way to select an agency. The company needed a good one in a hurry. It narrowed the choice down to three agencies, invited each to submit a list of its personnel and clients, and then asked its representatives to drop around for a talk. The company briefed each set of agency men on its background and posed for them the problem of how to open new retail outlets in Cleveland. It gave the agency men 45 minutes to solve the problem. The agency that produced the best solution won the account.[53]

Role of the Agency.[54] There appears to be some argument over the relationship of an agency to its client. One school believes that the agency should not participate in marketing and the other believes that it should. J. Edward Dean, director of advertising for DuPont, maintains that the advertising agency is no more than "a projection machine which flashes the image of the client on the screen of public consciousness." He said the character of advertising would reflect the

[53] "How to Select an Agency Fast," *Printer's Ink,* June 1, 1962, pp. 37–39.
[54] "J. E. Dean Sees Ad Agency Role as Passive with Company Management Setting Policy," *New York Times,* April 17, 1962, 52:3.

stature and responsibility of management and not the agency. He did suggest that joint planning take place between the agency and the company. On the other hand, the advertising vice president of a food company said that "anyone who downgrades the importance of advertising agencies is harking back to the past." The role of the agency is becoming more important in laying out executive marketing strategy. Additional support is given to this point of view in an article in the *Wall Street Journal* pointing out that the clients of advertising agencies are demanding such services as marketing research, package design, public relations, and counseling.[55]

Some agencies have developed a reputation by developing all sorts of specialized services. McCann-Erickson has not only developed a number of these services, but it has also constructed special rooms in which creativity is encouraged. The agency promotes group discussion. The group then divides into smaller groups. Members of each subgroup may look in on other subgroups through glass panels but the insiders are unable to look out.[56] Other agencies in preference to specialized services stress creativity. Papert, Koenig, Lois is such an agency, and among its personnel is the creator of the Volkswagen advertising. Moreover, an unknown product like the pickled string bean was advertised into a success by calling it a "dilly-bean," and it was even promoted for use in cocktails.[57]

The following is a set of suggestions on how a company may get the most out of its advertising agency:[58]

1. Maintain liaison between the company and agency at all times.
2. Give its advertising manager status and authority.
3. Give its agency enough time to work.
4. Hold the agency responsible only for what it controls.
5. Be realistic about the agency's production cost.
6. Expect the agency to make a profit on the account.
7. Treat the agency like a business partner.

Thus, working together a company and its agency may undertake the necessary actions to make advertising serve the total marketing goal. In so doing, the company furthers its own objective of selling the consuming public the products and services it demands to meet

[55] *Wall Street Journal,* Nov. 12, 1958, 1:1.
[56] Spencer Klaw, "What Is Marion Harper Saying?" *Fortune,* January 1961, p. 122 ff.
[57] Stephen Mahoney, "How To Get Ahead in Advertising and Maybe Stay There," *Fortune,* November 1962, p. 145 ff.
[58] William Marsteller, "How To Get the Most Out of Your Ad Agency," *Sales Management,* Nov. 3, 1961, pp. 34–36.

its needs, and thereby assures itself of conducting a profitable enterprise.

Summary

The marketing concept applied to the advertising department means that
organizationally the advertising director plays a more important role. One
of the newer developments in advertising is the electronic computer, which
has helped to solve many of the routine tasks of advertising and has left more
time for creative activity.

Advertising is a part of the marketing mix. As such it must be coordinated
with pricing, product, channels, and personal selling. Advertising is concerned
with the semantic impact of words in developing copy themes. The advertising manager must concern himself with public relations and sales promotion.

Advertising has been criticized by many groups. At the present time
members of the profession are attempting to develop a code of ethics that
will minimize some of this criticism. Advertising enables transactions to be
more routinized and it also encourages cooperation among the members of
the channel of distribution.

In planning advertising the manager must consider the long-range impact
of advertising as it relates to the long-range objectives of the company.

One of the important phases of planning and control is expressed through
the budget. The recommended technique is the task or objective method.
The advertising manager should also be cognizant of the economic aspects
of advertising such as nonprice competition, elasticity concepts, incremental
returns, and the effect of advertising on future sales, and diminishing returns. The manager must decide how he will appropriate funds in relation
to the business cycle. He must also consider the demand trend and the
product's growth cycle. There has been a great deal of interest displayed in
treating advertising as an amortized cost. However, there remains the
problem of measurement of advertising effectiveness.

One of the most important tools of the planner is the use of research to
aid in defining consumer needs. One of the most promising bits of research
that presents the direction that may be followed is the work of the Advertising Research Foundation. An area of planning that needs to be developed
further is the area of creativity.

Organizationally the advertising department is participating in many more
decisions involving the broad area of communication. One of the big problems of the advertising manager is to maintain a relationship with the advertising agency that conforms to the organizational needs and objectives
of the company.

Suggested Cases

Ralph L. Westfall and Harper W. Boyd, *Cases in Marketing Management,*
Irwin, Homewood, Ill., 1961.

   Hallmark Greeting Cards—*Greeting Card Manufacturer*—Advertising
   Strategy with Seasonal Products, pp. 305–308.

Playskool Manufacturing Company—*Toy Manufacturer*—Establishing Advertising and Promotion Program, pp. 292–293.

Milton P. Brown, Wilbur B. England, and John B. Matthews, Jr., *Problems in Marketing*, 3rd ed., McGraw-Hill, New York, 1961.

Armstrong Appliance Company, pp. 357–369.

Hallicrafters Company, pp. 375–384.

Harry L. Hansen, *Marketing: Text, Cases, and Readings*, rev. ed., Irwin, Homewood, Ill., 1961.

Westinghouse Electric Corporation, Elevator Division, pp. 553–562.

Cleveland Industries (1), (2), (3), pp. 596–602.

Hector Lazo and Arnold Corbin, *Management in Marketing*, McGraw-Hill, New York, 1961.

Caldyn Corporation, Organizing and Controlling Advertising, pp. 415–416.

Kenneth R. Davis, *Marketing Management*, Ronald Press, New York, 1961.

Gillette Company, pp. 646–653.

Ad-a-Rater Company, pp. 653–655.

Intercollegiate Case Clearing House, Soldiers Field, Boston 63, Massachusetts.

ICH 3M66—Levi Strauss and Company.

ICH 2M76—Alka Seltzer.

Appendix: Some Useful Quantitative Concepts in Advertising

Traditional economic analysis overlooks the actions of competitors as factors in a company's advertising decisions. Some efforts to weigh these actions have been made in duopoly theory, but thus far the efforts have not been satisfactory. Although game theoretic may not solve the advertising problems of a company, it offers a conceptual framework which may be useful in understanding advertising decisions in relation to the actions of competitors. In Table A-1 we see the amounts of profit earned when a company spends one sum of money on advertising and its competitors spend another sum. For example, if the company spends $150,000 on advertising while a competitor spends $100,000, the profit to be earned from the company's expenditure is $300,000 (column 1, row 1). The remaining rows and columns show the profits that would accrue to the company relative to other competitor's actions.

If a company decides to spend $150,000 on advertising, it cannot be assured whether a competitor will spend $100,000 or $200,000. The amount will influence the profit expectation. If a company decides

Table A-1. Profit and Advertising Expenditure [a] **(Interval Decision)**

Firm Spent on Advertising	Profit Earned by Firm When Competitor Spent on Advertising					Decision Criteria		
	100	125	150	175	200	Min- imum	Per- centile	Average
150	300	360	380	360	340	300	340	350
175	270	380	420	440	430	270	380	390
200	200	370	450	490	500	220	370	410
225	150	330	450	520	550	150	330	400
25	50	280	430	530	590	50	280	380

[a] Tableau suggested by Russell Alterberger and Dr. Herbert T. David of the Statistics Department at Iowa State University.

to spend $150,000, expecting its competitor to spend the same amount, it will expect a profit of $380,000. However, if the competitor spends $200,000, the company will earn a profit of only $340,000. Thus, it seems wise to consider the range of decisions that might be made by the company and choose one based on the range of opponents' possible countermeasures to the company's action. Column six, headed minimum, contains all the minimum row values. The minimum profit earned is $300,000 if the company expends $150,000 on advertising.

The minimum profits in each row show that $300,000 is the highest of them all. This is the maximum of all the minimums. If a company decides to expend $150,000 on advertising it assumes that its rivals will be acting in such a way as to drive it out of business eventually; therefore, the company will take a pessimistic view. The next column contains the assumption that the opponent is not trying to drive the company out of business; the view is not as pessimistic as previously. In this case the company chooses the second lowest profit, or the second quintile from the bottom. Thus, in column 3, row 2, the second lowest profit is $380,000. The maximum of the minimum expressions listed in the percentile column is also a profit of $380,000.

The last column lists the averages of all the profits that may be earned with a specified advertising expenditure. For example, if the company decides to spend $150,000 it might expect an average profit of $350,000. From the average profits in the average column it can be seen that the maximum profit will be earned when the firm spends $200,000 and earns a profit of $410,000.

The major shortcoming of this analysis is the assumption that it is possible to measure the amount of profit associated with each sum spent on advertising. Factors other than advertising may be responsible for this profit. To avoid this situation it would be necessary to build up a tableau showing all profits associated not only with advertising but also with price, amounts spent on personal selling effort, and amounts spent for product development. Corresponding information for competitors would also have to be estimated.

The company has to choose its own criterion for decision. That is, should it follow the rule and choose the maximum of the minimum profits, or should it select the maximum of the percentile profits, or the maximum of the average profits? The state of competition and knowledge of the competitor's strategy will be the determining factors in developing the criterion. If a company is in a cut-throat competitive industry it may assume the worst. On the other hand, if it is in an oligopolistic industry it may be optimistic and choose a more optimistic criterion.

Next, it is possible to construct a box which will show profits based on the allocation of marketing resources in comparison with the allocation of competitors' resources. To make a table of this size would be a formidable task involving the analysis of all the row and column possibilities. To overcome this difficulty one may sample all the possible actions. Then, based on the sample a decision may be made regarding the amount to spend. One may not only estimate what the company has done in the recent past, but also may anticipate profits for the next decision period. The techniques of game theoretic offer some insight into these problems.

Profits may not be computed exactly. However, it may be possible to get reasonable approximations after separable costs have been calculated. This would include the amounts going to nonseparable costs and profits. (See Chapter 7 on distribution costs for discussion of separable costs.) The calculation would include factors that might influence the profit position, such as the state of competition, economic and political conditions, weather, asset position of the company, and competing needs for resources. Perhaps it may be possible to calculate the degree of variation in these factors with respect to profits.

This list is suggestive and does not exhaust the range of possible decision criteria or parameters to be considered. With the advent of large-scale computers it may be possible to simulate the range of possible decisions and their outcomes by varying the assumptions about the competitors' actions and the parameters surrounding these actions.

Use of Markov Process

The "Markov process" applied to advertising is a mathematical technique that describes the changing of a system from one state to another. One interpretation applied to advertising describes the probabilities of some customers becoming noncustomers and of non-customers becoming customers.[1] This technique may be useful when accompanied by an experimental design in which advertising is replicated and the resulting effects are noted. Based on past experience it may be possible to predict the amount of brand switching with a certain quantity and quality of advertising.

Let us assume that we have investigated a sample of 1000 consumers. We find at the time of the first interview that there are 600 customers who buy Brand A and 400 who buy Brand B. One month later we interview the same customers. We now find that Brand A only has 300 customers whereas Brand B has 700 customers. What has happened in terms of transitional probabilities? One explanation might be that Brand A lost 300 customers and this became the gain of Brand B. Another explanation might be that Brand A lost more than 300 customers, say 400, but that some of the customers of Brand B shifted to A, say 100. We may state this latter condition in the following manner:

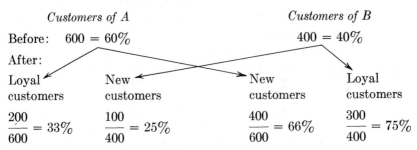

	Customers of A			*Customers of B*
Before:	600 = 60%			400 = 40%

After:

Loyal customers	New customers	New customers	Loyal customers
$\dfrac{200}{600} = 33\%$	$\dfrac{100}{400} = 25\%$	$\dfrac{400}{600} = 66\%$	$\dfrac{300}{400} = 75\%$

We may generalize based on the conditions that may have produced this brand switching, such as an extensive advertising campaign conducted by B. We may say that the probability of customers of A switching to B is 66 per cent while the probability of B customers switching to A is only 25 per cent. It seems apparent that the manufacturer of B's products stands to gain if similar relation-

[1] See Richard B. Maffei, "Brand Preferences and Simple Markov Processes," *Operations Research,* Vol. 8, No. 2, March–April 1960, pp. 210–218; John F. Magee, "Operations Research in Making Marketing Decisions," *Journal of Marketing,* Vol. 25, No. 2, October 1960, pp. 18–24.

ships continue in the future. Where we assume that the probability of transition remains constant in the future we have a stationary Markov process. In advertising we might assume that this condition might maintain itself for a period of, say, six months—assuming that all other elements of the market mix, competition, and economic conditions remain constant.

In the foregoing example Brand B retains 75 per cent of its own market and in addition gains 66 per cent of Brand A's customers. We can see that A is losing customers rapidly to B. Thus, while in zero period Brand A has 60 per cent of the market and Brand B has 40 per cent, in period 1, B's share increases to about 70 per cent while Brand A loses about 30 per cent of the market.

$$(.33) \times (.60) \times (.25) \times (.40) = .2980$$

Continuing on to periods 2 and 3 we see that Brand B increases up to about 72 per cent of the market; continuing on into further periods will not increase Brand B's share substantially. This then is called the steady state—or a tendency toward stability. Assuming the switching rate to be constant we may predict market shares for Brand A and Brand B. The table below shows the brand shares through period 3.

Share of Market

Period	A	B
0	.60	.40
1	.2980	.7020
2	.2738	.7262
3	.2719	.7281

Once the probability rates are known one might wish to learn how quickly the shares of market tend to become stable. This is called convergence time and defined by a symbol C which represents the ratio of the number of customers buying now compared to the steady state. Thus 85 per cent would indicate that the process has moved 85 per cent toward the steady state. This convergence to steady state will vary in time. Some brands will converge rapidly while others will converge slowly.

Finally, once we know what the transitional probabilities are we may also calculate the cumulative gains or losses of a company that may take place over any time period. This type of information may be useful in estimating the period in which fixed charges may be recovered.

The Markov process has been useful in indicating the destination and origin of customers. In one case it was found that brand switching took place among private brands. Therefore, it was felt that it was not profitable to attempt to switch customers from private to manufacturers' brands. The Markov process may also be useful in test marketing to determine both potential market shares and payout period. The Markov process also is useful in pointing up the lack of consumer loyalty to brands.

Sales Response to Advertising

One operations research model has three parameters: sales decay constant, saturation level, and sales response constant.[2]

Sales decay is the rate at which sales decrease if there is no advertising. Sales decrease at a constant rate per year with variations by product.

The saturation level is maximum level of sales that may be achieved by a particular product. Or it may be looked on as achieving the sales potential. Experimental studies show that advertised product sales increase rapidly and then taper off in spite of continued advertising. When a given medium is used the sales response will amount to a fraction of the potential customers reached by that medium. Increased usage of the product by present customers is excluded from the model. Thus, the saturation level includes only present customers and those customers who will be attracted by advertising—or total market potential.

The sales response constant may be defined as the incremental return to sales with a dollar of advertising when sales are zero. Let us assume that a company just starting business has zero sales. It spends $10,000 on advertising and sales go from $0 per month to $20,000 as a result. The sales response constant would be ($20,000 per month)/($10,000 per month) = $2 per month. This tells us for every dollar invested in advertising we may get a $2 increase in sales when sales are at the zero level. Let us see how this fits into the saturation level M.

Suppose we assume that the saturation level is $50,000 per month and the advertising expenditure is $10,000 per month. Sales before

[2] M. L. Vidale and H. B. Wolfe, "An Operations Research Study of Sales Response to Advertising," *Operations Research*, Vol. 5, No. 3, pp. 370–381.

advertising S, we shall assume, are \$30,000 or 60 per cent of the saturation level. The sales increase in response to advertising is \$5000 per month. The response constant is equal to $r =$ (\$5000 per month)$/(.40 + 10,000) = \$1.25$ per month. In other words, since sales are already 60 per cent of saturation level the advertising then only works on the 30 per cent who are not customers. This is the difference between existing sales and saturation level. In formula terms this is $(M - S)/M$. Since the response constant r is defined as sales response per dollar of advertising, R, when sales are at any level above zero must be adjusted to determine r by the fraction $(M - S)/M$. Thus, if R is defined as sales per dollar of advertising created in response to advertising when sales are at a specific level, say S_1, and the saturation level is M_1 then

$$R = \frac{r(M - S)}{M} \quad \text{and} \quad r = \frac{M}{(M - S)} R$$

Thus, in the foregoing example, the actual sales response when sales are at a level of \$30,000 per month is \$5000/\$10,000 $= .5$ per month. This means for every dollar invested in advertising 60 cents in sales were gained through advertising at a sales level of 30,000 per month. This may be calculated using the formula $R = r(M - S)/M$.

We have seen that the sales increase due to advertising when sales were at zero was equal to $r = 1.25$. Let us substitute the quantities in the formula.

$$R = \frac{r(M - S)}{M}$$

$$R = \frac{1.25\,(50,000 - 30,000)}{50,000} = .5$$

$$r = \frac{M}{(M - S)} \quad R = \frac{(50,000)}{(50,000 - 30,000)} .5 = 1.25$$

Thus, while it is assumed that response for potential customers, r, is constant, the observed increase in sales per advertising dollar, R, is assumed to decrease as the level of sales increase. This is so since there are fewer potential customers who may be influenced by advertising. Graphically, the relation between R, the response per advertising dollar when sales are above zero, and the level of sales in shown in Figure A-1. We see here that R decreases at a constant rate of r/M per dollar of sales increase until rates reach the saturation level; then R becomes zero.

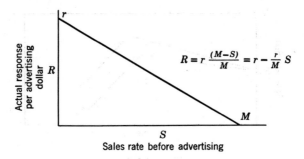

Figure A-1

Mathematical Model

The basic concepts in the mathematical model may be represented by the following equation.[3]

The instantaneous rate of increase of sales at any time, $t =$

$$\text{Response constant} \times \text{Rate of advertising at time } t \times \frac{\text{Saturation level} - \text{Sales rate at time } t}{\text{Saturation level}}$$

$$- \text{Sales decay constant} \times \text{Sales rate at time } t$$

The equation is then solved to determine the relationship among the three parameters, the independent variable advertising, and the rate of sales as [4]

$$S(t) = \frac{rAM}{rA + \lambda M} + \left(S_0 - \frac{rAM}{rA + \lambda M} \right) e^{-\left(\frac{rA + \lambda}{M} \right) t} \quad \text{for } t < T$$

where $S(t)$ = rate of sales at time t
    r = response per advertising dollar when sales are zero
    A = the rate of advertising
    λ = the sales decay constant
    S_0 = sales at the time advertising is started
    M = the saturation level of sales for the product
    e = 2.718
    T = the time at which the advertising is stopped.

[3] Frank M. Bass, Robert D. Buzzell, Mark R. Greene, William Lazer, Edgar A. Pessemier, Donald L. Shawver, Abraham Shuchman, Chris A. Theodore, and George W. Wilson, *Mathematical Models and Methods in Marketing*, Irwin, Homewood, Ill., 1961, p. 359.
[4] *Ibid.*, p. 360.

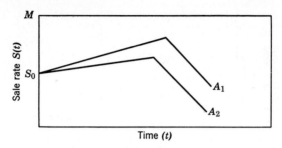

Figure A-2

The only variable in the equation is time t. To solve the equation we need only substitute varying time periods and multiply by the constants. Thus, it is possible to determine the rate of sales at different periods of time. Graphically, sales per time period is illustrated in Figure A-2.

This chart shows us that as greater amounts are expended on advertising, A_1, sales will rise more rapidly at a decreasing rate than with a smaller expenditure, A_2. This solution implies that the law of diminishing utility sets in after the first dollar is expended in advertising and furthermore that greater additional sales can be attained in a long campaign than in a short one. The additional sales in a short campaign can be expressed in the following formula where a is the advertising expenditure:

$$[(ra)/\lambda][(M - S_0)/M]$$

Budget Allocation

The return on advertising is considered as a return on investment. The unsolved variables are:

1. Total cost of advertising campaign for a product.
2. Additional sales from advertising.
3. Incremental expenditures resulting from advertising campaign. These include:
    a. Cost of advertising campaign.
    b. Cost of manufacturing and distributing additional items.

The analysis attempts to equate rate of discount to the incremental expenses, or marginal revenue equal to marginal cost. The rate of discount is defined as the rate of return on the investment for a

product. The solution for expanding advertising funds instantaneously
is based on this formula: [5]

Rate of return on investment for a product

$$= \frac{\text{Instantaneous sales increase} \times \text{Gross profit per cent}}{\text{Total cost of advertising}} - \frac{\text{Sales decay}}{\text{constant}}$$

One may apply this calculation to several products, determine which
ones would yield the greater profitability, and thus form a basis for
the allocation of advertising funds.

The sales decay rate in the absence of advertising seems to be
realistic. The assumption that the sales increase is due to dollars
spent constantly on advertising is not realistic. This assumption does
not take into consideration the action of competitors, changing conditions in the economy, changing tastes, and habit patterns.

The model does not consider the effect of increased customer usage
of the product. Also the model assumes that advertising appeals in
competitive campaigns are equal. This may be overcome by using
different sales response constants for each campaign. In order to
estimate the parameters of the equation experimental data may be
needed.

[5] *Ibid.*, p. 362.

Chapter Seven

Types of Costs *Direct and Indirect · Fixed, Variable, and Semivariable · Controllable and Noncontrollable · Cost Control and Cost Analysis* STANDARDS

Methods of Distribution Cost Analysis CLASSIFICATION · BASIC DOCUMENTS *Classification of Accounts* FUNCTIONAL CLASSIFICATION · HOW DISTRIBUTION EFFORT IS APPLIED · RELATED PRODUCT AND CUSTOMER COST ANALYSIS · ALLOCATION TO ORDER-SIZE GROUPS · ALLOCATION TO TERRITORIES · CHANNELS OF DISTRIBUTION · USE OF SALES POTENTIALS *Physical Distribution · Reducing Distribution Costs* TRANSPORTATION ECONOMIES · WAREHOUSING · SELLING EFFORT · LABOR COST · BUDGET · ORGANIZATION · MANUFACTURING COSTS · PRODUCT QUANTITY AND QUALITY

Organization

Summary

Suggested Cases

As the phrase implies *distribution costs* embrace any and every effort connected with the development and delivery of a product or a service from its source to an ultimate consumer. The payment for auxiliary help or the charge for any internal facility used in developing a product or service for market is truly a cost of this kind and may very well go back to the inception of the product or service idea. The range of these costs is indeed extensive. It includes management time devoted to decision making on the product, on price, on selection of distribution channels, on advertising expenditures, and on physical facilities, as well as the actual expenditures themselves on physical distribution, advertising, personal selling effort, sales promotion, and special price discounts. This chapter contains a detailed discussion of distribution costs. In it we shall review their types, examine their

Distribution Costs

accounting, and observe a thing or two about how a company organizes itself for distribution cost analysis.

Distribution costs, which are also known as marketing costs, are quite different from production costs. Unlike the latter, distribution costs have the capacity to produce revenue for an enterprise. Whether they grow or shrink in size these costs are potential sources of revenue for the businesses incurring them. For example, we may observe in Figure 7-1 that an increase in marketing cost from AC to AC_1 yields the higher revenue AR_1. This, in turn, nets profit $Y_4Y_5Y_6Y_7$, which is larger than $Y_1Y_2Y_3Y_4$. The increased cost of marketing is offset by profit.

Similarly, a drop in marketing costs may increase a company's revenue. As Figure 7-2 illustrates, reducing the cost from AC to AC_1 generates the added profit $Y_1Y_2Y_3Y_4$. Profit development of this

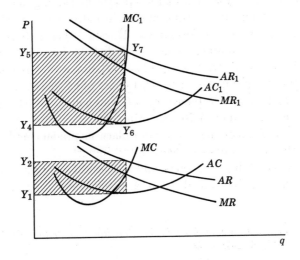

Figure 7-1. Effect of increased cost.

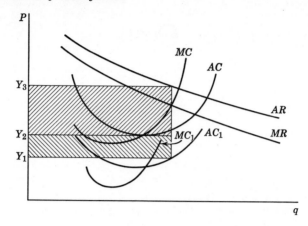

Figure 7-2. Relative profits.

kind may eventuate from a decrease in the costs of handling merchandise in warehousing, from trimming inventory costs, and from instituting economies among delivery costs.

Prior to exploring the various types of distribution costs and their accounting, let us consider for a moment the several advantages of distribution cost accounting.[1] To begin with, it compels a company to review its basic marketing plan and provides management with data on the marketing structure. Next, it shows a company the kinds of expenses incurred for each of its separate marketing activities. It permits the assignment of responsibility to individuals thereby creating accountability for performance. It establishes a basis for objective analysis of optional choices of distribution and points out inefficiencies in the distribution process. It makes it possible to calculate profits by product and by customer, which may suggest ways to reduce costs through relocation of warehouses or changing the order routing on standard items. Moreover, it shows the effect on profits of any changes that may take place in product and customer mix. Finally, it simplifies budgeting and imparts confidence to management by supplying cost facts and a sense of cost control. Thus, there is much to be gained from a careful study of distribution costs.

[1] Donald R. Longman and Michael Schiff, *Practical Distribution Cost Analysis*, Irwin, Homewood, Ill., 1955, p. 72.

Types of Costs

Direct and Indirect

Among the several possibilities for classifying costs the distinction between direct and indirect is one of the most useful. Direct costs are usually associated with some activity. The salary of a salesman, for example, may be allocated directly to the function of selling. The charges for transporting merchandise typifies direct cost as does the price paid for the packing crates in which the merchandise is shipped. In contrast, indirect costs basically cover supporting, necessary, behind-the-scenes efforts such as the supervision of the sales force or clerical work performed at the office. One tends to be more readily apparent to the eye than the other, but both types of costs may be incurred in most phases of a company's marketing program.

Fixed, Variable, and Semivariable

Some marketing costs are fixed. These remain more or less inescapable over the years and do not tend to be influenced by fluctuations in sales volume. Such costs include the salaries of the executives connected in any way with marketing activity. They also include the cost of maintaining the minimum staff required for slack seasons, the nonrecurring costs of introducing a new product, opening up a territory, or developing new distribution channels, and the cost of marketing research.

Variable costs change with fluctuations in output or, in the case of distribution, in sales. They include such things as the increased amount spent on sales promotion, advertising, and personal selling effort. Both fixed and variable costs rise and fall over long periods of time. The difference between them is really the length of the period over which they change. Costs that change within a year generally are considered variable, whereas those that change over a longer period of time are said to be fixed.

A third category of marketing cost falls between the two. This is the category of the semivariable costs. Over the short run part of these costs is fixed and the remainder is variable. Distribution cost analysis tends to relate to many items of a semivariable character. In general it has not been found profitable to allocate many fixed

Table 7-1. *Work Sheet for the Least Square Method*

(1) Month	(2) X (Sales in thousands of dollars)	(3) Y (Salaries in hundreds of dollars)	(4) x Deviations from average of X	(5) y Deviations from average of Y	(6) x^2 (4) × (4)	(7) xy (4) × (5)
January	80	157	−120	−33	14,400	3,960
February	90	170	−110	−20	12,100	2,200
March	110	172	−90	−18	8,100	1,620
April	160	175	−40	−15	1,600	600
May	200	188	0	−2	0	. . .
June	240	202	40	12	1,600	480
July	340	217	140	27	19,600	3,780
August	400	237	200	47	40,000	9,400
September	280	203	80	13	6,400	1,040
October	200	197	0	7	. . .	0
November	120	280	−80	−10	6,400	800
December	180	182	−20	−8	400	160
Totals	2,400	2,280	0	0	110,600	24,040

costs to marketing activities because of the difficulty in applying a uniform measure to them. For this reason most distribution cost accounting deals only with the variable and semivariable costs. Moreover, fixed costs cannot be controlled whereas other costs are amenable to control. Since it is a responsibility of the market manager to determine that part of the business that is not profitable, he must be familiar with the variable and semivariable costs as these show the contribution to net profit and overhead.

Let us pursue a valuable mathematical technique for separating the fixed from the variable costs. This is called the *least square method*.

First, one assigns values from Table 7-1 to the equation for a straight line

$$y = a + bx$$

In this exercise y represents the average of column 3, or the average salaries; a is the fixed component of salaries; b symbolizes the average of column 2, or the average sales; and x signifies the slope of the line

$$\frac{xy \text{ (column 7)}}{x^2 \text{ (column 6)}} \frac{24,040}{110,600} = .021736$$

Then, by computing in the following manner

$$19,000 = a + (200,000 \times 2.1736\%)$$
$$19,000 = a + 4347$$
$$19,000 - 4347 = a$$
$$14,653 = a$$

the fixed component is found to equal $14,653, and the variable component 2.1736 per cent of sales.

Thus, with a sales volume of $200,000 the variable component becomes 2.1736 per cent multiplied by $200,000, or $4347.20. This method of distinguishing the variable from the fixed costs may be used for billing procedures, handling of goods, transportation of goods, or any other aspect of marketing.

As an alternative to the least square formula one may develop the same kind of information by plotting a graph of sales against the expenses incurred. In Figure 7-3 each dot represents the expense for a particular level of activity. A straight line is fitted among the dots. The point at which the line touches the vertical axis, which signifies expenses, marks the fixed costs. For example, in Figure 7-3 the line crosses the axis at $14,653. To compute the semivariable costs requires taking any incremental change in sales and extending dotted lines to both axes. For a change in sales of $10,000, from, say, $200,000 to $210,000, we note that sales expense increases from $14,749 to $14,966.36. This represents an increase of $217.36 on a sales rise of $10,000. That is, there is an increase in sales expense of 2.1736 per cent on every $1000 increase in sales, the same figure obtained from the least square formula.

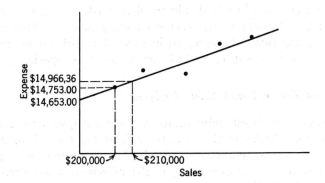

Figure 7-3

Controllable and Noncontrollable

Not all costs are subject to control, as we have remarked. Some of them are influenced by market conditions over which management has no power. Fixed costs, furthermore, go on even when there is no production activity. For the purpose of making decisions, management dwells on the controllable costs but recognizes the existence of noncontrollable items which may spring from the inherent nature of the particular cost, from outside influences, or simply from lack of authority.

Minimal organizations to conduct business, minimal forces to effect sales, minimal advertising, minimal staff organization, minimal appropriations for research and development, and minimal allocations to maintain distribution channels—all these are fixed marketing charges. The changing economic environment, the influences of government activity, the actions of competitors, wars, and disasters are the kinds of outside influences that are impossible to control. No less difficult is the lack of authority among members of an organization to act when discrepancies in costs arise. This latter problem may result from divided authority or lack of specific assigned responsibility.

Turning to the other side of the matter, the controllable factors are those that may be affected by a specific decision of an individual in a company. Here the total cost may be influenced by individual action. Moreover, the individual may exercise partial control when there are induced expenses—that is, fixed expenses, such as those for induced labor—or outside influences, such as changing prices. Under these circumstances, he is held responsible for only the controllable portions of the partially controllable items. In any event the controllable elements of costs should be distinguished from the partially controllable elements in the cost accounting process. This view of controllability should be reflected in account classifications, accumulation of cost information, and all control analysis reports.

Cost Control and Cost Analysis

Longman and Schiff differentiate cost control from cost analysis.[2] Cost control alludes to the measurement of the cost of an activity against some predetermined standard. Let us assume, for example, that the standard cost of making a sales presentation for a particular product is $5.62. This standard may have been established by a time

---

[2] *Ibid.,* p. **71.**

and motion study and influenced by other variables affecting a sales solicitation. If the actual cost runs considerably higher than the standard, a company is justified in investigating the causes for the discrepancy. Cost analysis investigates the choices for performing a task. For example, a company might check the alternative costs of storing its products in a public warehouse and in a private one.

Standards. The whole field of standards comprises one of the newest phases of distribution cost accounting. Much has been learned from the experience of accounting for production costs. In devising standards, accountants have attempted to find the relevant costs to be considered through scouting past performance and estimating the changes likely to take place in the future. Properly chosen standards can become the basis for evaluating marketing performance and for spurring management to inquiry when marked variations from the norms occur.

There are seven ways to establish standards for the analysis and control of distribution costs. They include the use of time and motion study, the study of historical costs and their projection to future situations, the uses of potential analysis, break-even analysis, ratio analysis, averages, and special indices. In addition, special studies may be made of the effectiveness of advertising and of personal selling expenditures—and marketing research may help to predict a product's growth cycle which, in turn, may be a basis for the development of cost standards.

1. TIME AND MOTION STUDY. Time and motion studies have been conducted among the activities of salesmen, warehousing, and transportation and billing procedures. In analyzing salesmen's activities, for example, time standards may be set for traveling between customers, waiting to see customers, selling time, introduction of the product, the sales presentation, closing the sale, and writing the order. Separate standards may be imposed for separate customers buying different volumes of merchandise in separate locations, and even for different lines of merchandise. The development of proper standards is a painstaking job, and to complete it, a company must obtain a comprehensive job audit and then assign a time and motion study man to accompany a salesman. There is considerable precedent on which to draw in the areas of materials-handling and accounting procedures, but the application of time study to sales activity is relatively novel.

2. HISTORICAL METHOD. Under this approach costs are classified into appropriate categories. Then past costs are reviewed and future

costs are projected. From these actions standards for future use evolve.

3. POTENTIAL ANALYSIS. In utilizing potential analysis to arrive at a set of standards for cost analysis and control, a company first attempts to estimate its over-all sales potentialities. Then by apportioning these potentialities among its sales territories it is able to assess the maximum opportunity for each of them. From this assessment it endeavors to devise realistic quotas or goals for each territory. The quotas are predicated in part on the existing opportunity in the territory, on the promotional and sales effort to be exerted, on an appraisal of general economic conditions, and on a realistic evaluation of what the distributors and sales force might be able to sell. Having found the potential and having accepted it as a standard of performance, the company can then measure actual results against the opportunity and projected expenditure of effort. This may be divided among salesmen, dealers, distributors, and even product lines. Deviations from the performance standard may be attributed to the actions of competitors, management, the quality of the selling effort and advertising, unanticipated economic changes, and like causes.

4. BREAK-EVEN ANALYSIS. Here the company endeavors to calculate how many units of its merchandise must be sold to recover the fixed marketing expense. For example, if a certain amount of money is spent on advertising, the gross margin per unit is divided into the cost of the advertising. This will disclose the number of units which must be sold to recover the advertising investment. Similar analyses may be made for funds spent on such matters as research and development, cultivation of a territory, the various aspects of selling, warehousing, transportation, services, and the handling of accounts receivable.

5. RATIO ANALYSIS. By this method the expense charges are taken as ratios to net sales, or balance sheet ratios are taken of assets and liabilities. The company can then compare its performance to the industry's to observe where its ratios diverge from the over-all pattern. If the divergences can be justified the ratios may stand. If they cannot be explained, they require modification.

6. AVERAGES. The use of averages to set a standard is one of the simpler techniques that may be employed. When averages of past performance are used any marked variations from them warrants closer inspection. Averages may be used for sales per salesman, sales per customer, sales per territory, or sales within product lines.

7. SPECIAL INDICES. Finally, it is possible to establish indices of performance. One of these correlates sales to levels of business ac-

tivity. Any deviation from the correlation signifies either increased efficiency or decreased efficiency on the part of management. A complete profit-and-loss statement may be prepared for products, territories, or salesmen by allocating as much as possible of the variable cost to the particular category. This provides a yardstick for measuring actual performance.

These seven individual methods of selecting standards may be combined into groups. For example, a company may use a break-even analysis with any of the other six methods. As standards for distribution cost accounting are still in an experimental stage, companies might explore more than a single method for devising them. If the selected standards predict future performance with any accuracy, they are worth preserving. If they fail to forecast future performance, they require further experimentation. The important objective for any company is to obtain a reliable set of standards, for standards are the basis for ideal measures of performance as well as realistic expectations of what may occur in the future.

Methods of Distribution Cost Analysis

In preparing for distribution cost analysis, the accounting department of a company engages in three activities. It begins by classifying accounts. Then it allocates these accounts according to function and method of distribution. Finally, it estimates the contribution made by the margin to the function or the marketing operation.

Classification. Accounts covering expenses may be classified into two categories, direct and indirect. Salesmen's commissions are direct expenses. The portion of the president's time that is engaged in selling activities represents an indirect expense. Once the expenses have been separated into direct and indirect, they are allocatd among functions and method of distribution. In the case of indirect expenses only the semivariable portions are thus allocated.

The functional method of classifying accounts relates the cost classification to individual assignments of responsibility. For instance, expenses may be allocated to order handling, billing, or a salesman's travel charges. These functional costs should be separated into direct and indirect types since only the direct costs are of concern to cost control. Furthermore, units are selected to evaluate functional activities. These units may consist of pounds, square feet, time, number of calls, or some similar measure. Their respective costs may be ascertained by dividing the total functional cost by the cost of the appropriate unit. Corrective action may be required where unit costs or functional costs fall out of line.

In classifying accounts by the manner in which the distribution effort is applied, the following nine groupings may be germane:

1. Commodity quantitative and qualitative characteristics.
2. Territory-sales unit.
3. Channel of distribution.
4. Method of sales-advertising effort.
5. Foreign, domestic, consumer, industrial.
6. Size of order.
7. Terms of sale.
8. Organization.
9. Salesmen.

A final method of classification amalgamates the foregoing ones. For example, accounts classified as to the manner in which the distribution effort is applied may be subclassified into functional categories. Reciprocally, functional accounts may be subclassified into the manner in which the distribution effort is applied. Moreover, primary accounts may be subclassified into functional accounts.

Basic Documents. Sales invoices contain all necessary basic distribution cost data. These include data on the product, salesman, territory, and customer, all reduced to barest details. These data may be punched on IBM cards and fed to a tape for electronic data processing.

Table 7-2. *Expense of Functional Distribution Sheet*

Functional Expense Breakdown

Natural Expense	Total	Selling	Public relations	Storage	Buying	Delivery
Salesmen's salaries	5,000	5,000	. . .	. . .	. . .	. . .
Advertising	3,000	2,000	1,000	. . .	. . .	. . .
Trucking	1,000	. . .	. . .	. . .	500	500
Rent	8,000	. . .	. . .	3,000	. . .	. . .
Insurance	4,000	. . .	. . .	1,000	. . .	. . .
Total	. . .	7,000	1,000	4,000	500	500

Through the use of expense distribution sheets the expense elements drawn from the invoices may be analyzed. Thus, the direct and indirect aspects of the functional expenses may be broken down and made parts of a functional operating statement. Expenses may be apportioned among customers, product, and channel of distribution so that the resulting contribution of gross margins to profit and overhead may be calculated. Table 7-2 represents a functional expense sheet prepared from an expense distribution sheet.

This sort of information is valuable to management. It provides data upon which a better understanding of distribution costs is developed and supplies a basis for more direct control of costs. The functional operating statement would list these costs in the following manner:

Selling		
Salesmen's salaries	$5,000	
Advertising	2,000	$7,000
Public relations		
Advertising		1,000
Storage		
Rent	3,000	
Insurance	1,000	4,000
Buying		500
Delivery		500
Trucking		$13,000

In the ensuing discussion, we shall be able to observe the structure of customer product allocation sheets and how profit analysis may be derived from their data.

Classification of Accounts

Functional Classification. Although frequently the proportion of direct costs may be significant, the greater portion of a company's distribution and administrative outlays is likely to be indirect. To facilitate both the allocation of these indirect costs and the control of expenses, they are best classified into functional groups. Such groups contain all the expenses incurred for the same activity. Thus, through a single factor, the functional classification of expenses enables the allocation of an entire group of costs.

The basis for classifying expenses in this way is to be found in a company's own marketing and general administrative activities. These classifications ideally should be as detailed as possible and yet as homogeneous as they can with respect to individual functions. The classification of indirect expenses by function resembles the classification of direct expenses by department, which we have already described. Some of the problems it poses are that payments are often made simultaneously for wages, materials, and the equipment necessary to perform various functions, and that some personnel perform more than a single function.

It is usually necessary to apportion many natural expense items among several functional cost groups since they relate to more than one such activity. These items are distributed by means of time study, space measurements, counts, managerial estimates, and other techniques. Table 7-3 illustrates how natural expenses are allocated to functional groups.

After indirect costs have been classified by function, they are allocated on the basis of the utilization of the variable activities that occasion them. The accounting principle applying in such cases it to charge the product or customer—or other segment of sales—with the cost of its share of the variable activity of each functional cost group.

Some functional activities vary because of the characteristics of the product. These are not affected much by the characteristics of the consumer. Other functional activities, conversely, vary because of customer characteristics. For example, in storage and investment the variable activity depends almost exclusively on the bulk, weight, perishability, and inventory value of the product stored, and is hardly affected by the customer who buys it. The credit function, on the other hand, changes with the financial integrity and other credit characteristics of the customer with little regard to the nature of the product for which credit is extended. In other functional cost groups, the relationship between costs and product or customer is not so simple. The shades of combined customer and product responsibility for variable activity are numerous, influencing the amounts of expense within different functional cost groups.

How Distribution Effort Is Applied. Table 7-4, employing the same functional cost groups used in Table 7-3, illustrates the basis for allocating costs to products—and to customers.

Before manufacturers can ascertain their distribution and administrative costs by product, certain data must be obtained. Each factor must be determined separately for each product or group of products

Table 7-3. Classification of Natural-Expense Items Into Functional-Cost Groups [a]

Expense Items	Means by which Natural-Expense Items Are Assigned to Functional-Cost Groups	Function-Cost Groups to which Natural-Expense Items Are Assigned
Sales salaries and expense	Time study	Order routine and promotion
Truck expense	Direct (to cost group)	Handling (or delivery)
Truck wages	Direct (to cost group)	Handling (or delivery)
Truck depreciation	Direct (to cost group)	Handling (or delivery)
Outside trucking	Direct (to cost group)	Handling (or delivery)
Warehouse wages	Time study (or direct to cost group)	Handling, storage, and investment
Office wages	Time study (or direct to cost group)	Order routine, reimbursement, or other functions
Executive salaries	Managerial estimate	All functional groups
Rent	Space measurement	All functional groups
Storage (outside)	Direct (to cost group)	Storage
Warehouse repairs	Managerial estimate	Storage and handling
Warehouse supplies	Managerial estimate	Storage and handling
Insurance:		
Property and equipment	Managerial estimate	All functional groups
Inventory	Direct (to cost group)	Investment
Personnel	Wages	All functional groups
Office expense	Direct (to cost groups and managerial estimate)	Order routine, reimbursement, promotion, or other functions
Utilities	Some direct (to cost groups), others to cost groups via space measurement	All functional groups
Professional services	Managerial estimate	Functions benefited
Taxes, inventory	Direct (to cost group)	Investment
Social security	Add to wages	All functional groups
Bad debts	Direct (to cost group)	Reimbursement

[a] Department of Commerce, *Distribution Cost Analysis*, Economic Series, No. 50, Government Printing Office, Washington, D.C., 1946, p. 17.

Table 7-4. Bases of Manufacturer's Allocation to Commodities and Customers

Bases of Allocation

Functional-Cost Groups	*To commodities*	*To customers*
Investment in finished goods	Average inventory value	(not allocated)
Storage of finished goods	Floor space occupied	(not allocated)
Inventory control, finished goods	Number of invoice lines	(not allocated)
Order assembly (handling)	Number of standard handling units	Number of invoice lines
Packing and shipping	Weight or number of shipping units	Weight or number of shipping units
Transportation	Weight or number of shipping units	Weight or number of shipping units
Selling	Time studies	Number of sales calls
Advertising	Cost of space, etc., of specific product advertising	Cost of space, etc., of specific customer advertising
Order entry	Number of invoice lines	Number of orders
Billing	Number of invoice lines	Number of invoice lines
Credit extension	(not allocated)	Average amount outstanding
Accounts receivable	(not allocated)	Number of invoices posted

whose costs are to be analyzed. In general these data cover the following factors:

1. The average inventory value of finished goods.

2. The amount of storage space occupied by these finished goods inventories.

3. The number of times the commodity is sold, that is, the number of invoice lines.

4. The number of handling units of the product.

5. The weight or number of shipping units sold.

6. The proportion of sales time spent in promoting it.

7. The cost of the space or time in the various media used in advertising it.

These factors determine the shares of the corresponding functional cost groups allocated to the product. For instance, if the average inventory value of product group X is 1 per cent of the total average inventory value for all finished products, group X is charged 1 per cent of the investment cost for the period. If prices have been established, the sum of the shares of the various allocated functional costs, plus any direct costs, is subtracted from the dollar gross margin of the product; the difference represents the relative profitability of the product. Table 7-5 illustrates the results of this procedure.

The manufacturer's bases for allocating the functional cost groups to the customer may be seen in Table 7-4. Here, as in the allocations to product, various data are required and they cover the following elements for both the single customer and classes of customers:

1. The number of invoice lines for all orders for the period.
2. The weight or number of shipping units of merchandise bought by the customer.
3. The number of sales calls made on the customer.
4. The cost of the space or time in various media used to advertise to the specific customer class.
5. The number of orders placed by the customer.
6. The average amount outstanding.
7. The number of invoices posted to accounts receivable.

Table 7-5. Determination of Relative Profitability of a Class of Products

Bases of Allocation

	(1) Total functional cost	(2) Total for firm	(3) Commodity	(4) Commodity's share (3) ÷ (2)	(5) Allocated costs (4) × (1)
Investment	$ 50,000	$500,000	$ 50,000	10%	$ 5,000
Storage	75,000	400,000 sq. ft.	20,000 sq. ft.	5	3,750
Inventory control	25,000	300,000	9,000	3	2,500
Order assembly	100,000	500,000	50,000	10	10,000
Packing and shipping	60,000	500,000	75,000	15	9,000
Transportation	200,000	600,000 tons	125,000 tons	20	40,000
Selling	400,000	10,000 hrs.	2,000 hrs.	20	80,000
Advertising	150,000	. . .	direct	. . .	33,300
Order entry	30,000	400,000	40,000	10	3,000
Billing	50,000	400,000	40,000	10	5,000
Total Costs					$176,550

Sales	$850,000	
Cost of goods sold	632,000	
Gross margin		$218,000
Less: Direct plus allocated distribution costs (from column 5)		176,550
Contribution to profit and overhead		$ 41,450

Table 7-6. Variable Marketing Expenses, Bases of Allocation, Unit Cost, and Costs of Serving One Customer for One Week

Variable Expense	Bases of Allocation	(1) Average Cost per Unit	(2) Number of Units	(3) Allocated Expense (1) × (2)
Delivery	No. of deliveries	$0.17	6	$1.02
Salesmen's salaries and travel	No. of interviews	0.36	2	0.72
Salesmen's telephone calls	No. of calls	0.07	3	0.21
Inside salesmen's salaries	No. of interviews	0.19	0	0.00
Invoice distribution	No. of invoice lines	0.01	20	0.20
Order taking	No. of orders	0.03	2	0.06
Accounts receivable	No. of credit tickets	0.01	8	0.08
Telephone expense	No. of calls	0.01	1	0.01
Office sales expenses	Volume	0.02	0	0.00
Auto depreciation	Volume	0.03	3	0.09
Claims	Volume	0.01	3	0.03
Total expense (A)				$2.78
Gross profit (B)				2.97
Net profit (B − A)				$0.19

Table 7-6 illustrates the results of one manufacturer's allocation of marketing costs to a single customer, together with the classification of expenses and the bases for allocation.

Another way of allocating costs by customers may be seen in Table 7-7. In this example, it may be noted that although sales of $199 and under are made to more than 41 per cent of the company's accounts, these sales result in a net loss to the company. The table shows that more than 35 per cent of the total number of sales calls were made on this group of accounts, but that these calls yielded only 13 per cent of the company's sales. Clearly, corrective action is called for among this class of accounts.

Related Product and Customer Cost Analysis.[3] Most manufacturers prefer a classification that contains both product and customer. This

[3] The method described in this section was adapted from a procedure developed by Wroe Alderson. See Ralph S. Alexander, Frank M. Surface, Robert F. Elder, and W. Alderson, *Marketing,* Ginn, Boston, 1944, Chap. 23.

Table 7-7. Number of Customers, Sales Calls, Sales Volume, Expenses, and Profits by Customer-Volume Groups [a]

Customer-Volume Group Amount of Annual Purchases	Number of Accounts, Per Cent of Total	Number of Calls, Per Cent of Total	Sales, Per Cent of Total	Gross Profit, Per Cent of Sales	Selling Expense, Per Cent of Sales	Operating Profit, Per Cent of Sales
$20,000 and over	0.07%	0.16%	10.91%	15.9%	4.0%	11.9%
$10,000–$20,000	0.07	0.64	2.89	23.6	9.5	14.1
$5,000–$9,999	0.60	3.40	11.71	19.8	10.2	9.6
$4,000–$4,999	0.40	1.54	5.40	18.4	10.2	8.2
$3,000–$3,999	0.40	1.25	3.99	21.8	9.6	12.2
$2,000–$2,999	1.17	3.19	8.47	22.8	10.9	11.9
$1,000–$1,999	3.29	7.21	13.24	23.9	13.4	10.5
$500–$999	7.67	13.40	15.66	25.9	16.8	9.1
$400–$499	3.79	5.09	4.96	29.0	19.3	10.3
$300–$399	5.12	6.27	5.21	31.6	21.9	9.7
$200–$299	9.83	10.75	7.11	31.2	25.3	5.9
$100–$199	16.17	15.65	6.94	30.7	34.3	−3.6
$1–$99	25.64	20.40	3.51	30.9	75.3	−44.4
No sales	25.78	11.05	...	...	[b]	...
Totals or averages	100.00%	100.00%	100.00%	25.1%	18.7%	6.4%

[a] Charles H. Sevin, Department of Commerce, *How Manufacturers Reduce Their Distribution Costs*, Economic Series, No. 72, Government Printing Office, Washington, D.C., 1948, p. 14.
[b] 7.7 per cent of total selling expenses were allocated to "no sales" customers.

is particularly true of cases in which sales of a specific type of product are made only to a certain class of customers. When such classification is possible, it becomes easier for the accounting department of a manufacturer to allocate to customers expenses that might otherwise be attributed to product, and vice versa. Table 7-8 shows the procedure for relating product and customer allocations. The rows on the form signify classes of products, and the columns, the classes of customers. The squares resulting from the cross-classification represent transaction groups, or sales of a specific class of products to a particular class of customers.

One of these forms may be employed for each functional cost group. If the variable activity of the function relates more closely to product characteristics than customer characteristics, the first allocation is made to the product groups. The total of the cost group is distributed as product-group subtotals on the same basis used for the cost group, and the amounts are entered in the appropriate spaces of the right-hand column. These subtotals may then be apportioned among the rows on the same basis used to allocate costs to customers.

Table 7-8. *Form for Relating Commodity and Customer Cost Allocations*

	Customer Classes						Commodity Cost Totals
Commodity Classes	(A) Manufac- turers	(B) Dealers	(C) Jobbers	(D) Main order	(E) Chain stores	(F, G, H, etc.)	
1. Pneumatic passenger tires and casings							
2. Pneumatic truck tires and casings							
3. Tractor tires and casings							
4. Solid tires and casings							
5. Auto accessories							
6. Mechanical rubber goods							
7. Heels and soles							
8. Hard rubber							
9. Footwear							
10. Tiling							
11. Rubber thread							
12. Rubberized fabrics							
13. Sundries							
Customer cost totals							

If the variable activity relates more closely to customer characteristics a corresponding procedure may be followed. Now, the first
allocation is made by customer classes. That is, the total of the
functional cost group is apportioned as customer-class subtotals on
the basis of the allocation chosen, and these are entered on the form's
bottom row. The subtotals are then distributed among the squares
that represent the types of products purchased by the customer.

When all groups have been fully dissected and suitably allocated
on separate forms, a fresh one may be used to compute the totals for
all functional costs. The figures in the corresponding columns of the
several forms are added to obtain the full costs for individual groups
of transactions. These new totals are then added to constitute the
costs by classes of customers. A parallel procedure yields the costs
by groups of products.

Finally, the various dollar gross margins are entered on the fresh,
summary form, and the total allocated costs by transaction groups,
customer classes, and product groups are subtracted from them. This
enables a manufacturer to discover his relatively less profitable products and customers through ranking product groups and customer
classes in order of their marginal revenue excesses over allocated costs.

Allocation to Order-Size Groups. Manufacturers know that different-
sized orders engender wide disparities in distribution costs, administrative costs, and profit margins. But until they know exactly how much
the size of the order affects costs and profits, their sales policies and
discount rates cannot be fixed precisely and are likely to be erroneous.
Through cost analysis they may formulate these policies and discount
structures with confidence that both will contribute to maximum
profits and also conform to the stipulations of the Robinson-Patman
Act.

The detection of variations in cost caused by the size of the order
for an individual product necessitates centering attention on the individual item rather than the order as a whole. The size of the order
may be measured either by the number of units or the dollar value
required per extension of the particular invoice line. The search for
cost variations resulting from the order size of individual customers,
on the other hand, may be pursued through study of the size of the
order; this may be done by checking the dollar value of the order
or the number of invoice lines it contains.

The process of obtaining costs by invoice lines is similar to the
process of ascertaining product costs. The functional classifications
and bases of allocation are much the same. Discernment of costs by

the total groups of order sizes resembles the process of analyzing customer costs, irrespective of whether the order size is determined by the dollar-value or the number-of-invoice-lines approach. Table 7-9 illustrates one manufacturer's choices of functional classification and bases in allocating costs to order-size groups.

Table 7-9. *Functional Classification of Expenses and Bases of Allocation to Order-Size Groups*

Expense	*Basis for Allocation*
1. Selling expense—direct: costs of time spent calling on customers, except sales promotion calls.	Time study by salesmen (for test period, salesmen record time of entering and leaving each store called on).
2. Selling expense—indirect: travel time, time spent on nonproductive calls, miscellaneous working time, and travel expenses.	Number of calls.
3. Routing orders.	Time study (number of orders routed and routing time).
4. Assembling orders and loading trucks	Time study (each order is assembled separately).
5. Packing: container forming, packing, container sealing, weighing, preparing bill of lading, stocking containers.	Time study (packing one order is completed —by one packer—before next order is started).
6. Truck delivery—direct: cost of time spent in customers' store.	Time study (time clock on truck records time stopped at store and time deliveryman return to truck).
7. Truck delivery—indirect: travel time (total time worked less direct time).	Number of deliveries.
8. Freight delivery.	Direct (freight charged direct to order).
9. Billing (cutting orders, pricing, extending and comparing orders and invoices).	Time study.
10. Accounts receivable.	Time study.
11. Other office costs.	Number of orders.
12. Branch rent.	Dollar sales.
13. Branch supervision.	Total direct time of above functions.

Allocation to Territories. Both manufacturers and wholesalers like to analyze distribution and administrative costs by territories. In many respects these are the simplest costs to analyze. If the manufacturer's marketing operations are organized on a territorial basis with the geographic limits of branches and districts clearly defined, a sufficiently detailed breakdown of primary expenses enables the assigning of a large proportion of distribution and administrative costs to the territorial units.

To find the cost of working a particular territory, a company may total the distribution and administrative costs allocated to its customers within that territory. Here again it is necessary for the territories to form distinct geographic units. Then sales volume, margins, and costs may be obtained by totaling the figures for the customers within it. If these customers are all profitable, the territory itself must be profitable. The converse also holds; if the customers are unprofitable, the territory must be, too.

In some instances it may be more satisfactory for a company to assign directly to a territory certain branch and district charges incurred jointly for several sales territories. Moreover, some functional costs that are difficult to allocate to products, or customers, or units of sale may also be charged directly to the sales territory. The best example of this is the assignment of a salesman's salary, commissions, and traveling expenses. If the salesman devotes all his time to the territory, these, of course, are direct expenses. If, however, he specializes by product or customer and divides his time among several territories, his expenses become indirect and must be allocated among the territories covered. This apportionment is achieved either through using the same method employed in allocating selling expenses to customers or use of a time-study survey.

Other indirect selling and administrative expenses, such as the salaries of district and branch managers, are also charged to individual sales territories. To do so, the company divides the total indirect selling and administrative costs of a branch or district by the number of salesmen serving the unit and assigns an equal share to each of them. Or sales or district managers may estimate the indirect cost per salesman on the basis of the relative time and effort put in by each.

Transportation, shipping, and packing costs may be assigned directly to individual sales territories if primary expenses are accounted in broad enough detail. In general, these functional group costs are allocated to the territories on much the same principles used in allocating them among customers. Table 7-10 represents one company's

Table 7-10. *Functional Classification of Expenses and Bases of Allocation to Territories*

Functional Costs	Bases of Allocation to Territories
1. Transportation—factory to branches.	Number of items shipped.
2. Transportation—to wholesalers.	Analysis of actual freight bills for a 3-month test period.
3. Shipping from factory.	Number of items shipped multiplied by shipping time per item.
4. Shipping from branches.	Number of items shipped multiplied by shipping time per item.
5. Billing.	Number of invoice lines.
6. Loss on returned goods.	Direct.
7. Salesmen's salaries and travel expenses.	Direct.
8. Sales personnel expenses: auto insurance and depreciation, social security, premiums, and insurance.	Average number of salesmen.
9. District manager's salary and expenses.	Direct or average number of salesmen.
10. Sales manager's salary and expenses.	Average number of salesmen.
11. Salesmen's training.	Average number of salesmen.
12. Routing and scheduling of salesmen.	Average number of salesmen.
13. Samples and transportation costs on same.	Analysis of actual number of samples sent to each area for a 3-month test period.
14. Circulars and advertising literature to wholesalers and retailers.	Analysis of actual number of each item sent to each area for test period.
15. Broadside printing for wholesalers	Direct to trading area where wholesaler is located.
16. Retail store signs.	Number of signs sent to each area.
17. Direct mail advertising to consumers.	Analysis of actual number mailed to each area.
18. Quotation department.	Number of price-change letters sent to each area (to both salesmen and wholesalers).
19. National advertising media.	Circulation by states for each media: where state is in 2 areas, divided on basis of proportionate number of retail outlets in each area.
20. Advertising overhead.	Total advertising expenses allocated to each area (items 14, 15, 16, 17, and 19).
21. Tabulating department.	Number of invoice lines.
22. Records department.	Average number of salesmen.
23. Marketing overhead.	Total other expenses allocated to area.
24. Product research.	Sales.
25. General administration.	Sales.

Table 7-11. *Profit-and-Loss Statement for Six Zones (Percentages of Net Sales)*

Item	Zone Number					
	1	2	3	4	5	6
Net sales	100.00	100.00	100.00	100.00	100.00	100.00
Cost of sales	60.75	59.44	61.04	57.89	62.28	71.04
Gross profit	39.25	40.56	38.96	42.11	37.72	28.96
Shipping, branch house expense, transportation to branches, transportation to wholesalers, order service.	5.48	6.03	6.11	5.04	4.23	3.02
Loss on returned goods.	0.60	0.66	1.26	0.58	0.23	0.34
Representatives' salary, representatives' expense, representatives' moving expense.	8.30	7.40	7.61	6.26	6.66	5.10
Personnel expense allowance, auto insurance and depreciation, social security, pensions, and insurance.	1.12	0.92	1.04	0.91	0.86	0.72
District managers' salary and expense, executive salary and expense.	1.20	1.19	1.26	1.10	1.02	0.80
Marketing expense.	4.94	3.81	4.45	4.30	4.49	3.43
Total marketing expense	21.64	20.01	21.73	18.19	17.49	13.41
Trading profit.	17.61	20.55	17.23	23.92	20.23	15.55
Administrative and scientific research expense.	8.63	8.63	8.63	8.63	8.63	8.63
Operating profit	8.98	11.92	8.60	15.29	11.60	6.92

procedure for analyzing distribution and administrative costs by territory. Table 7-11 shows another manufacturer's cost analysis on a territorial basis.

Channels of Distribution.[4] The following case history demonstrates how costs were reduced among channels of distribution. After a study of the fixed and variable portions of distribution expenses, the com-

[4] *Ibid.,* pp. 46–48.

pany concerned analyzed sales by its various channels of distribution. It did so by deducting the total variable costs by channel—that is, production plus allocated distributive costs—from these sales.

These figures confirmed what has been suspected for some time, namely, that customers in channel D were, on the whole, unprofitable. But we were not aware of the poor showing of customers in channel C. The facts were that in 1946—a year of very high sales volume—the total sales revenue from channel D was actually less than variable or out-of-pocket cost, leaving nothing for fixed costs or for net profit. Moreover, the results were no better even when we projected these cost trends to a sales volume above that for 1946, while they were even worse at lower levels of volume.

We turned our attention to customers in channel D first. An extensive study, including a similar distribution cost analysis, by customer-volume groups, within this channel, convinced us that there was nothing more we could do to make these customers profitable. Even the larger customers in this channel were unprofitable . . . we decided to eliminate this entire channel of distribution, since it was responsible for an actual out-of-pocket loss at any anticipated level of sales volume. By dropping this channel we figured to save $250,000 in out-of-pocket variable costs, while losing only $200,000 in sales—thereby adding $50,000 to our net profits at 1946 levels of business.

Next, we turned our attention to customers in channel C. We classified them into groups according to the amount of their purchases in 1946, and by allocating the variable costs to each group, we found that the large customers were earning a profit margin over their variable costs. [Table 7-12 contains the results.] This analysis indicated that Class C Customers purchasing under $10,000 were the ones who caused the unfavorable showing for the entire group. They were responsible for an out-of-pocket loss of $58,900. On the other hand, customers in channel C buying over $10,000 in 1946 turned in a profit margin (before nonvariable costs) of $58,680.

The next step was to review with our salesmen every single class C account in the under $10,000 annual-volume group and to cull out all those whose future potential did not promise to make them profitable. This review called for the elimination of about $150,000 in sales and approximately $205,000 in out-of-pocket or variable costs, thereby adding $55,000 to net profits on an annual basis.

These planned changes in our channels of distribution called for an increase in our net profits by eliminating losses. But they would also leave us with the same dollar fixed cost which would be larger relative to a smaller total sales volume. In other words, the elimination of $350,000 of unprofitable sales would leave us with idle manufacturing and distributing capacity.

Therefore, our next step was to plan to utilize this idle capacity by increasing our sales pressure on the profitable accounts in channels A, B, and C. Of course, we realized that this increase in sales could not be accomplished in one year, and it could not be obtained without added out-of-pocket expenditure for sales promotion. Accordingly, in order to increase the number of calls on profitable customers and prospects in our channels of

Table 7-12. Sales, Variable Costs, and Profit Margins by Channels of Distribution

A. Before Changes in Channels, 1946

Channels of Distribution	Sales	Variable Costs [a]	Profit Margin	Per Cent of Sales
A	$ 750,000	$ 400,000	$350,000	47%
B	250,000	100,000	150,000	60
C	300,000	300,000	. . .	. . .
D	200,000	250,000	−50,000	−25 [b]
Total	$1,500,000	$1,050,000	$450,000	30%
Less non-variable expense	. . .		$300,000	. . .
Net profit	. . .		$150,000	10%

B. Estimated Effect of Changes in Channels

Channels of Distribution	Sales	Variable Costs [a]	Net Profit
C	−$150,000 [c]	−$205,000	$55,000
D	−200,000 [c]	−250,000	50,000
A and B	100,000 [d]	85,000	15,000
Total	−$250,000	−$370,000	$120,000

C. After Changes in Channels, 1947

Channels of Distribution	Sales	Variable Costs [a]	Profit Margin	Per Cent of Sales
A	$ 825,000	$415,000	$410,000	50%
B	315,000	130,000	185,000	59
C	120,000	110,000	10,000	8
Total	$1,260,000	$655,000	$605,000	48%
Less non-variable expense	. . .	. . .	$310,000	. . .
Net profit	. . .	. . .	$295,000	23%

[a] Production plus distribution costs. [c] Eliminated.
[b] Loss. [d] Added.

distribution, our plan for the first year called for the retention of two of the salesmen who had been calling on unprofitable customers in channels C and D. We planned to obtain during the first year an increase of $100,000 in sales in channels A and B with a profit margin of $60,000 and added expenditures of $35,000 for sales promotion leaving an increase of $25,000 in net profit.

Our plan of eliminating unprofitable channels of distribution and concentrating on profitable channels, of course, involved much more than has been outlined above. For example, we had to draw up specific plans for dropping certain salesmen and reorganizing remaining salesmen's territories. Similar plans for our office, warehousing, shipping, and delivery operations were also necessary.

As a result of all these changes, we planned there would be an addition of $120,000 in our net profits in the first year [as summarized in section B of Table 7-12]. The results of our actual operations in 1947, of course, varied somewhat from this plan, since there were many other factors operating to influence the results, some favorable, such as the rising price level, and some unfavorable. However the net results [as shown in section C of Table 7-12] were even better than we expected; our net profits were approximately doubled from $150,000 in 1946 to $295,000 in 1947!

Use of Sales Potentials. By using the idea of sales potentials a company obtains an estimate of the maximum opportunity in any area. Once this is known, it may allocate efforts accordingly. For example, more money might be spent for personal selling and advertising in areas having higher potentials than others. Moreover, analysis of sales in relation to the potentialities discloses where the company may not be realizing its share of business and may have to take corrective action. In addition, the consideration of actual sales in relation to the potentiality may make a salesman with a lower dollar volume look superior to a colleague with a higher volume in some

Table 7-13. Sales, Variable Costs, and Profits Margins, by Customer-Volume Groups, Channel C, 1946

Customer-Volume Group, Annual Sales per Customer	Sales	Variable Costs	Profit Margin
$20,000 and over	$ 63,980	$ 23,050	$ 40,930
$10,000 to $20,000	73,600	55,850	17,750
$1,000 to $10,000	131,900	164,000	−32,100 [a]
$1 to $1,000	32,100	58,900	−26,800 [a]
Total	$301,580	$301,900	$ −220 [a]

[a] Loss.

Table 7-14. *Actual Sales in Relation to Potential Sales*

Product, Territory	Market Poten- tial	Actual Volume	Per Cent Poten- tial	Volume Defi- ciency
Product X				
Territory A	$50,000	$25,000	50%	$25,000
Territory B	30,000	20,000	66	10,000
Territory C	20,000	25,000	125	(5,000)
Territory D	15,000	8,000	53	7,000
Product Y				
Territory E	$ 80,000	$75,000	−94%	$ 5,000
Territory F	100,000	80,000	80	20,000
Territory G	25,000	70,000	93	5,000
Territory H	50,000	55,000	110	65,000

other territory. Use of this type of analysis may be applied to product or territory. Table 7-14 illustrates the point.

The figures in the table show that the company is not getting its share of the market for Product X in territories A, B, and D, and Product Y in territories E, F, and G. These weaker spots have thus been isolated as a result of the analysis. The sales manager may then tell salesmen in territory A that his sales are 50 per cent below what is expected of him. The salesman's poor record may be attributable to any number of things—insufficient averages, inefficient application of sales effort, or changing competitive conditions. A review of the number of sales calls and the number of customers may often supply some clue as to the reason for the deficiency.

For Product X in territory D and Product Y in territory H it is apparent that too much sales effort is being exerted in relation to the maximum prospects. This situation may be remedied by transferring some of the sales personnel and general sales effort from these prosperous territories to others that are less successful in fulfilling their promise.

It is important, however, to consider the relative dollar profits in shifting sales efforts. A 10 per cent decline in potential in an area with a $30,000 possibility results, for instance, in a $3000 drop, whereas a 60 per cent drop in a territory having a potential of only $6000 would nevertheless produce a reduction of only $2400.

The effect on net profit of dropping a group of customers may indeed be calculated. The example in Table 7-15 illustrates the effect

Table 7-15. *Effect on Expenses and Profits When Unprofitable Customers Are Dropped*

Expense Classification	(1) Variable Expenses Allocated to 350 Unprofitable Customers	(2) Variable Expenses that Can Be Eliminated	(3) Variable Expenses that Cannot Be Eliminated
Delivery	$5,000	$ 3,800	$1,400
Salesmen's salary and travel	4,300	4,300	. . .
Inside salesmen's salary	1,500	. . .	1,500
Telephone calls	300	300	. . .
Warehousing expense	3,800	2,400	1,400
Office expense	2,800	2,000	800
Auto depreciation	1,200	700	500
Claims	400	400	. . .
Total expense eliminated (A)		$13,900	
Gross margin lost (B)		4,300	
Addition to net profits (A − B)		$ 9,600	

on over-all expenses and profits if a set of approximately 350 unprofitable customers are dropped in one sales district. The affected companies purchase $40,000 worth of merchandise annually, yielding a profit of $4300.

In the table column 2 is sometimes called the *escapable* costs and column 3 the *inescapable* costs. The latter are the costs that cannot be eliminated. The items in column 2, on the other hand, can be eliminated. By eliminating them, $13,900 may be saved. But by the same token their elimination reduces gross margins by $4300. In consequence, the net addition to profit is, as the table indicates, $9600. If the gross margins were more than the savings resulting from reducing the expenses, it would prove more profitable to retain these customers in the short run.

Another use for sales potentials is to estimate the amounts of profit that might have been achieved with an additional amount of sales effort. A sales executive may prefer to fulfill his potential through some alternative means after attempting this kind of calculation. Table 7-16 illustrates the point. In the table, it can be noted that

Table 7-16. **Profit from Additional Sales Effort**

Product, Territory	Potential Volume	Actual Volume	Volume Deficiency	Rate of Gross Profit	Cost Gross	Estimated Additional Direct-Selling Expense to Capture Deficiency in Potential	Estimated Additional Net Gain or (Loss) If Potential Achieved
Product X							
Territory A	$ 50,000	$ 25,000	$25,000	15%	$3,750	$5,000	$(1,250)
Territory B	30,000	20,000	10,000	12	1,200	1,000	200
Territory C	20,000	18,000	2,000	10	200	1,000	1,000
Territory D	15,000	18,000	7,000	11	770	1,000	(230)
Total	$115,000	$ 71,000	$44,000	13.4%	$5,920	$8,000	$ 280
Product Y							
Territory E	$ 80,000	$ 75,000	$ 5,000	12%	$ 600	$ 500	$ 100
Territory F	100,000	80,000	20,000	13	2,600	2,000	600
Territory G	75,000	70,000	5,000	15	750	800	(50)
Territory H	50,000	40,000	10,000	11	1,100	120	(10)
Total	$305,000	$265,000	$40,000	12.6%	$5,050	$3,420	$ 640

added sales efforts for Product X in territories B and C will produce an additional profit for the company. This holds true in territories E and F for Product Y. However, in territories A and D for Product X and territories G and H for Product Y, the projected extension of sales efforts to reach potentials would work to the detriment of the company's balance sheet. In this situation, the sales manager may ask himself how he can trim sales expenses to reduce costs and thereby convert potential losses into profits. This may involve decisions about the substitution of direct mail for personal solicitation, use of the phone in conducting business, and employment of manufacturers' agents in extensive territories. On the other hand, it might pay to intensify the existing sales effort for Product X in territories B and C and for Product Y in territories E and F.

Still another method of analysis based on potentials involves a study of the ratios of sales to expenses and the relation of sales to quotas. The experience of the John Doe Company in Table 7-17 presents this sort of data. From the company's analysis it is evident that Salesman Johnston is the high-volume man. However, he has the lowest operating profit in terms of percentage and the second lowest in terms of dollars. Moreover, Johnston has an unusually high amount of returned merchandise and allowances against his name. This causes a high order-handling cost which is reflected in the allocation of general selling expenses. Johnston also has the highest field-selling expenses suggesting that he might be entertaining too extensively to obtain his volume. His low gross margin suggests that he also may be cutting prices to clinch business.

Smith is a relatively low-volume producer of sales. Yet he shows fewer returns and allowances. His selling expenses are about average. But he does not seem to be exploiting his territory sufficiently since he has obtained only 82 per cent of his quota. Besides, his ratio of sales to total sales is less than the ratio of his potential to company potentialities.

Jones has the second lowest sales volume but shows the highest operating dollar and percentage profit. He has relatively few returns and allowances. His field-selling expenses are low. His selling effort seems to be concentrated on high-margin products. Jones exceeds his quota requirement, and his ratio of sales to total sales exceeds the ratio of his potential to the company's potential.

McCracken surpassed his quota by 8 per cent. His sales, like Jones's, show a better ratio to total sales than his potential in relation to total company potential. O'Leary is under quota but shows a good margin because his selling expense is relatively low. It may

Table 7-17. Statement of Income and Expense by Salesmen, John Doe Company

Item	JOHNSTON Amount	% Net Sales	SMITH Amount	% Net Sales	JONES Amount	% Net Sales	McCRACKEN Amount	% Net Sales	O'LEARY Amount	% Net Sales	TOTALS Amount	% Net Sales
Gross sales	$500,000		$300,000		$200,000		$400,000		$100,000		$1,500,000	
Less:												
Returns	50,000		5,000		5,000		10,000		2,000		72,000	
Allowances	25,000		2,500		5,000		5,000		1,000		38,500	
Freight	12,500		3,000		5,500		5,000		2,000		28,000	
Total Deductions	87,500		10,500		15,500		20,000		5,000		138,500	
Net sales	412,500	100	289,500	100	184,500	100	380,000	100	95,000	100	1,361,500	100
Cost of sales	288,750	70	188,175	65	110,700	60	266,000	70	61,750	65	915,375	67
Gross profit	123,750	30	101,325	35	73,800	40	114,000	30	33,250	35	446,125	33
Field-selling expense	49,500	12	28,950	10	12,950	7	34,200	9	7,600	8	133,165	9
Profit after field-selling expense	74,250	18	72,375	25	60,885	33	79,800	21	25,650	27	312,960	24
Allocated general selling expense	41,250	10	20,265	7	9,225	5	26,600	7	4,750	5	102,090	7
Profit after general selling expense	33,000	8	52,110	18	51,660	28	53,200	14	20,900	22	210,870	17
Share of general expense	8,250	2	5,790	2	3,690	2	7,600	2	1,900	2	27,230	2
Operating profit before income tax	24,750	6	46,320	16	47,970	26	45,600	12	19,000	20	183,640	15
Other data, % of quota	150		82		102		108		80			
Net sales, % of total	30		21		13		27		9		100	
Potential, % of total	20		26		12		20		12		100	

be that O'Leary is not fully covering his territory. Examination of his reports on calls would shed light on the extent of his coverage. Such an examination might show that it may be more effective to alter his territory or reroute him.

Physical Distribution

One of the most promising areas for reduction of distribution costs lies in the analysis of physical distribution. This is one place where a company might be able to take advantage of automation in the warehouse and more efficient modes of transportation. One company compared its average warehousing costs to its costs for storage in each individual warehouse.[5] In some these costs were 68 per cent below the average and in others they were 46 per cent above the average. The company found by investigating the situation that it could eliminate some of these warehouses and accommodate additional volume in others.

Another company discovered that it could reduce the costs of warehousing substantially by using palletized loads and trucks to simplify the handling of merchandise. A third company through the use of a time and motion study was able to estimate the delivery costs of its products. Observing that the cost of delivering a few units was comparatively high, it established minimum loads for each truck, added to the capacity of its trucks, and thereby pared delivery costs.

Reducing Distribution Costs

The direct comments of many companies [6] disclose that the cost of distribution may be reduced in several areas. Among these areas are transportation, warehousing, territorial coverage, order size, packaging, production facilities, labor, product line, training, services, market surveys, and advertising. In essence, they cover just about everything concerned with the production and marketing of goods and services. Besides, there are many techniques and devices that may be used to shave distribution costs appreciably, and these include constant distribution cost analysis, sales analysis, allocation of costs to the selling force, the use of mechanical aids, the attention to costs, the elimination of agents, and the use of the budget. Let us examine some of these.

[5] Author's survey, *op. cit.*
[6] *Ibid.*

Transportation Economies. One way in which companies have reduced transportation costs is through an increase in the hauling
capacities of vehicles. This has called for less frequent delivery.
The concentration of trucks at primary supply points has also helped
to lessen transportation costs both by decreasing the number of deliveries and cutting the costs of maintenance and repair.

The proper routing of trucks so as to minimize backtracking reduces the number of miles traveled. Moreover, where possible, trying
to maintain large loads on trucks both leaving and arriving at the
plant or warehouse enables greater utilization of trucking space.
Thus, a company might use its trucks to deliver finished products
and pick up raw materials or supplies on the same trip.

The use of leased trucks is another method for minimizing transportation costs. Management has the responsibility for maintaining
the trucks at the same or perhaps lower cost than before. Sometimes,
it is possible to find lower-cost carriers than those in current use.
For example, one company learned that it could reduce its costs
drastically by shipping materials from the east coast to the west
coast by boat. The search for better methods of routing traffic and
lowering transportation costs is a constant endeavor among many
companies.

Warehousing. The following methods have been used by companies
to decrease warehousing costs: reworking of warehouse management;
increasing the size of customer storage to permit maximum-sized deliveries; consolidating the stocks of package goods in as few plants
as possible; and intensive studying of the handling of storage.[7]

Branch locations, on the other hand, tend to reduce delivery time
from warehouses to customers. And warehousing costs have been
reduced considerably through the introduction of mechanical and
automatic billing and handling, and also through better cost controls
of the warehousing activities. Many companies have instituted
minimum order sizes or have consolidated orders, thus reducing handling and shipping charges.

Selling Effort. Through both more intensive and more extensive
selling effort several companies said they had been able to reduce
the cost of their sales. This frequently has required the realignment
of sales territories in relation to sales potentials and the establishment of branch offices. In areas in which the full potential was not
being reached, many of these companies began concentrating their

[7] *Ibid.*

efforts in pursuit of additional sales at less cost. Some of them have tried to restrict their distribution to areas near their factories. Others have relocated their plants closer to areas of growing potential volume. Besides undertaking territorial adjustments, many companies have striven to increase sales volume with existing sales forces. Many of them saved on costs by eliminating sales agents.

Labor Cost. Labor is one of the greatest factors in distribution costs. It must be reexamined constantly to see where reduction of inessential costs may be possible. Through cost analysis a company may be able to control such matters as the expenses of salesmen or the cost of freight. It is a general point of any philosophy of economy to stress the need for doing whatever may be accomplished to minimize the costs of distribution.

Budget. The major instrument of cost control is the budget. Through budgets estimates of costs based on reasonable standards are established for the ensuing period. After standards have been developed it is possible to measure performance against them and to act as necessary, as we have seen, to rectify serious discrepancies between actual and planned costs. Most budgets should be reviewed periodically and revised in the light of changing conditions. Budget study also inspires a constant quest for ways to reduce distribution costs without loss of business.

Organization. The over-all organization might be a fruitful area for the lowering of distribution costs. Decentralization of authority has accomplished this result for some companies. Trimming of superfluous staff and office space has achieved it for others. In general, a sound over-all view of the organization necessitates a constant flow of young, wise, competent employees and trainees into its ranks. This also includes the concerted effort to work with and upgrade low-end producers in every phase of the business.

Manufacturing Costs. Distribution costs cannot be considered in isolation from manufacturing costs. One must complement the other. It may be feasible, for instance, to eliminate low-volume plants and thereby lessen the distribution costs of high-volume installations. In the same sense, companies may increase existing plant capacity while using the same sales force. This, too, cuts costs extensively. Other savings may be realized through a more scientific location of manufacturing plants.

Product Quantity and Quality. Both quantity and quality of the product are areas for cost reduction. Items may be added to the product line to reach a more profitable market. Conversely, unprofitable low-volume, low-margin items may be dropped. Sometimes this tactic may consist of adding items of a related nature to the existing items in the line. If the trade demands more versatility products may be added containing greater capacity and higher speeds, and performing more functions to command a higher price in the market place.

Organization

Any deviation from the standards established for marketing costs must be explained either orally or through written reports. Salesmen in the field, as we have noted, are valuable sources of information. They encounter the resistance of customers upon which they must act. If the resistance is provoked by competitive action, this information must be communicated to company headquarters. If it is a matter of general business conditions, this, too, must be relayed to the home office.

Standards are tools to assist the decision-making process. They are not absolute norms of performance. They have to be modified by information acquired in the field. Perhaps salesmen may exaggerate existing conditions. If this be the case, it is important for the marketing research department to have representatives in the field to find out why costs are deviating from the standards. Possibly the fault may lie with the standards by which performance is judged. Both standards and performance need to be reassessed constantly.

In its reports to management the accounting department of a company can perform a useful service. To begin with, it should report only essential information to top management. Too often the financial reports to the chief executives of a company are so complex that it takes a Certified Public Accountant to unravel them. Only information actually required for the making of decisions need be forwarded to top management. Of this information, the accounting staff should star those items demanding immediate attention. Whenever possible graphs and charts should be developed to demonstrate the performance of the marketing department. Performance may be shown as actual performance measured against standards, or against performance records of previous years or of corresponding periods of the past year.

Reporting, furthermore, should occur in all of the company's centers of decision. In highly decentralized companies managers at the decentralized levels need information to be able to make their own decisions more effectively. Good two-way communication is valuable so that management at the decentralized levels may act expeditiously on current market turns. Actually decentralized accounting may be necessary to enable prompt action in the individual, decentralized areas.

Analysis, then, is the precursor to control. Once the numerous factors contributing to cost have been examined microscopically each may be subjected to some measure of control. In the area of distribution this is a boon to a manufacturing company. It permits the enterprise to accomplish one of the prime objectives of any business, namely, to cut its costs. Through distribution cost analysis, especially if the analysis is thorough and shrewd, vital cost reductions may be more than a dream.

Summary

Distribution cost analysis is a technique for assigning both responsibility and accountability. Marketing costs in the broadest context represent all the effort that goes into the product or service other than utility. Two basic types of distribution cost accounting that may be useful in planning are cost control and cost analysis. Cost analysis may be developed from the classification of expenses into functional areas and by the manner in which the distribution effort is applied. Organization for distribution cost analysis should provide the means for rapid and pertinent communication.

Suggested Cases

Ralph L. Westfall and Harper W. Boyd, *Cases in Marketing Management,* Irwin, Homewood, Ill., 1961.

>Ideal Industries—*Manufacturer of Industrial Tools and Electrical Supplies*—Controlling Selling Costs by Product, pp. 504–508.

>Wheeler Tractor Company—*Manufacturer of Garden Tractors*—Keeping Sales Costs under Control, pp. 436–438.

Harry L. Hansen, *Marketing: Text, Cases, and Readings,* rev. ed., Irwin, Homewood, Ill., 1961.

>Oriole Cigar Company, pp. 53–56.

Hector Lazo and Arnold Corbin, *Management in Marketing*, McGraw-Hill, New York, 1961.

Modern Machines, Inc., Reorganization for Marketing, Control of Product Line, Territories, and Advertising by Distribution Cost Analysis, pp. 605–609.

Kenneth R. Davis, *Marketing Management*, Ronald Press, New York, 1961.

Taylor Company, pp. 317–324.

Intercollegiate Case Clearing House, Soldiers Field, Boston 63, Massachusetts.

ICH 3M67—Levi Strauss and Company.

ICH 3M76—Regulus Clock Company (a).

Chapter Eight

Life does not stand still. Neither does the state of business. To meet the conditions that may develop in the future men and companies plan ahead on the basis of current knowledge; and all planning activity, whether for one's personal life, the affairs of state, or the conduct of business, begins with some kind of forecast. The individual or company that does not develop a formal estimate of things to come implies by default that present conditions will continue into the future. This is an unrealistic position to take for nothing in the universe is static. Hence, forecasting is essential to the realization of long-range objectives. The present chapter deals with this important phase of marketing management.

Formal forecasting in a business concern is an attempt to use scientific procedures for projecting future sales and sales potentialities. In a very broad sense there are two types of marketing forecasts,

Forecasting

short-range and long-range. The short-term forecast is expected to help a company adapt to its marketing environment. The long-term forecast aids the company in adjusting to long-range market changes. For the short run, which generally relates to a year or less, forecasting covers the development of production schedules, price and purchasing policies, advertising programs, and similar operational details. In this kind of forecasting a company is concerned only with turning points generated by seasonal variations. Long-range forecasting, on the other hand, is more interested in trends than seasonal patterns of behavior. It may suggest plant expansion or modernization, the improvement of products, or the introduction of new or related ones. The long-range forecast may be concerned with such trends as shifts in consumer requirements based on changing levels of income, altered tastes and buying habits, or a different structure of the market. Such forecasts may cover as few as three years or as many as 25.

Sometimes the two types of forecasting may be combined. Cyclical variations may be employed in conjunction with calculations of trends. Generally, both short-range and long-range forecasts are reviewed periodically, the former semiannually, quarterly, or in some cases, monthly, whereas the latter may be reviewed annually and modified to fit changing conditions.

Management and the Forecast

Donald Cowan has advanced the following ideas about management use of the forecast: [1]

1. The nature of management is to look forward, to forecast. Management has this responsibility and responsibility for the consequences.
2. All kinds of research and fact findings are forecasting, and need to be

---

[1] Donald R. G. Cowan, "Management and Business Forecasting," *Journal of Marketing,* Vol. 15, No. 2, October 1950, p. 218.

welded together or coordinated by management into a logical, forward looking program.

3. The applications of research and forecasting techniques and the development of facts do not take the place of management. Knowledge and
wisdom are not the same thing.

4. The range of chance or error in making decisions is narrowed by facts.

5. Management has an obligation to deal fairly with the business forecaster because he cannot be held responsible for unsound decisions based
on considerations beyond the scope of his work. The effectiveness of his
work may be enhanced by strategic location within the organization.

6. The analyst has the following obligations to management: be objective;
avoid the warping influence of personal speculation based on information
gained in the performance of duty; obtain a wide knowledge and keen appreciation of all factors entering into management's decisions; and probe
the currents of economic affairs.

Company Versus Industry Forecasting

The difference between forecasting at the company level and the
industry or national level is that the company may be able to influence the outcome of its sales effort within territorial limits, whereas a
national forecast may have no such impact at all. If a company, for
example, expects sales to increase in the ensuing year it may decide
to allocate more of its marketing effort to those areas in which the
potential is highest. Conceivably this could increase sales beyond
the normal forecast for these areas. Similar reckoning is not possible
on a national or industry-wide basis.

Forecast, Quotas, and Potential

The three terms *forecast, quotas,* and *potential* give rise to confusion.
All three are similar, yet there are significant differences among them.
A forecast is usually an estimate of sales for the coming year. This
is a total sales figure which may or may not be separated into monthly
or quarterly sales estimates. Most companies do not break down
their sales forecasts on the basis of sales territories. The forecast for
sales territory instead is its quota. This figure may be obtained by
using some of the assumptions governing the sales forecast but modifying them in relation to market conditions in the territory. The
potential is the over-all estimate of how much total business a company might expect from one territory in comparison with another.
Total business may be related to such factors as income and population. Thus, where there is twice as much income and population in
a territory a company may expect twice as much return from the

same amount of marketing effort. This may be a long-run estimate, whereas quotas and forecasts are short-run.

Models for Forecasting

Two types of models may be utilized by a company in its forecasting activities. These are models based on subjective judgment or mathematics. The subjective judgment models include the following approaches: a jury of executive opinion, a sales force composite, and the expectations of customers. The mathematical models fall into several categories. First, there is a general technique applied by a company for its industry or the economy as a whole. This includes a time series and regression analysis. Second, there is a specific technique at the company level consisting of computer programs and market surveys. Finally, there are techniques at the level of the Gross National Product which include GNP accounting approach, Keynesian models, inventory models, and surveys of buying intentions. In the discussion to follow we shall analyze all these models in detail.

Methods of Forecasting

Preparation of Data

Forecasting from raw data tends to distort patterns of the past and to frustrate the projections of data into the future. All time-series data may be decomposed into four elements—seasonal, cyclical, trends, and irregular—and adjusted to account for them.

The seasonal pattern implies some regularity of fluctuation in sales during a year. In spring and fall, for example, the demand for women's clothing may be high, whereas in summer it may be low. Not all industries have regular seasonal patterns, although most of them do. Of those industries whose patterns are regular some have a relatively low amount of fluctuation over any given year. This would apply to food processing, for example, or to the sale of toothbrushes. On the other hand, companies in the appliance business tend to have seasonal variations of wide amplitude. The rate of fluctuation in some concerns may increase while in others it may decrease. The purpose of isolating the seasonality factor from data is to enable a company to measure any general monthly increase in business which does not result from seasonal considerations. For example, if a company's sales jump by $1000 in one particular month, the question is whether the growth represents a normal seasonal change or whether it may be attributed to factors over and above the seasonal pattern.

The cyclical aspect of data usually refers to fluctuations of longer than a year. These fluctuations may or may not be related to the business cycle. The trend element is represented as a rule by a graphic curve or straight line pertaining to future expectations. Trends may be affected by such factors as population and technological change. The irregular aspect of the time-series data embraces whatever else remains—those phenomena not explained by seasonal, cyclical, or trend considerations.

The object of decomposing time-series data is to obtain typical or average information about past periods so that mathematical curves may be devised for them and projected into the future. Armed with this knowledge, a forecaster can study the typical pattern against actual data. He can observe the difference between the adjusted data and actual data, and search for the causes of the discrepancy. Then he may be able to predict whether discrepancies of this type may recur in the future.

Until the development of the computer the adjustment of data was considered a time-consuming chore. Computers have cut this time drastically. There are now two widely used "canned" programs for expediting adjustment. One is the Census II method developed by Julius Shiskin,[2] and the other is the regression technique developed by the Deutsche Bundesbank of Frankfurt-am-Main.[3]

Before either program may be applied, a company has to make certain preliminary adjustments of its own. First, the data should be adjusted for any vacations or shutdowns. This would involve an estimate of what sales would have been had these not occurred. Then an adjustment must be made for the number of trading days in the month. If a company engages in business only five days a week, the same month from year to year will contain a different number of trading days. This difficulty is obviated by dividing current monthly data by the average number of days for the month over, say, the past ten years, a step which actually may be incorporated in the computer program.

The Census II method is essentially a procedure of using a series of

[2] "Electronic Computers and Business Indicators," *Journal of Business*, Vol. 30, No. 4, October 1957, pp. 219–267. For a simpler explanation see: R. L. McLaughlin, *Time Series Forecasting*, American Marketing Association Technique Series, No. 6, 1962.

[3] Deutsche Bundesbank, Frankfurt (Main), *The Practice of Seasonal Adjustment With Regression Equations*, October 1960.

moving averages of months by years, to wit, all the Januaries from 1945 to 1955, and then a series of years by months, such as 1945, 1946, and so forth by January, February, March, and the like. From these averages a method of elementary extremes evolves, eventually yielding a table from which seasonal influences have been expunged. Other tables test the amount of seasonality remaining in the data. The irregular component is then extracted from the data and is used to detect cyclical dominance. This is the length of time necessary for the cyclical effort to overtake the irregular component.

The Regression Program is nothing more than a regression of sales over a period of time utilizing the 12-month moving average as the independent variable. The Bank which developed this program also calculates an area it calls the seasonally adjusted band which varies according to seasonal adjustments of the data.

Subjective Approach

Jury of Executive Opinion. This method of forecasting is simply a technique whereby various executives of a company develop their own forecasts and submit them to top management. Each executive makes a forecast based on a combination of the figures he can assemble plus any subjective judgment he may care to add about factors that may influence future sales. Executives may or may not convene in committee to resolve any differences.

At the Lockheed Corporation members of management assume they are their customers.[4] This forces them to view future sales from the vantage point of the needs and expectations of their customers. Called the "Prudent Manager Forecast," this strategy provides intermediary management with forecasts to be forwarded to the top echelon of the corporation for consolidation with other data to develop a final forecast of sales.

Sales-Force Composite. Salesmen, as we know, are in constant touch with the customers of their company. Through conversations with customers on the state of current and future business they are able to develop some insight into future sales possibilities. Some companies equip each salesman with a record of past sales for his territory. Those data together with his gleanings from customers and other sources enable the salesman to foresee the sales potentialities of his territory. Each salesman turns his estimate over to his district or regional manager, who may temper the forecast in the light of infor-

---

[4] National Industrial Conference Board, *Forecasting Sales,* Studies in Business Policy, No. 106, New York, 1963, p. 16.

mation not accessible to the salesman. These estimates are then sent, region by region, to top sales management. Here the estimates are compiled after further modification on the basis of special information available to the sales manager. Finally, the composite estimate is transmitted to top management where it may undergo additional revision. As a rule, companies engaging in this type of forecasting also make supplementary use of other techniques such as a jury of executive opinion or some of the mathematical procedures.[5]

The major advantage of these two approaches when they are consolidated is that the sales forecast is predicated on the experienced judgment of salesmen in the field and executives at the home office. Many elements that influence the course of sales, of course, are not amenable to quantification. The disadvantage is that salesmen in making their forecasts may be prejudiced by their feelings. An optimistic salesman may exaggerate a favorable outlook. Someone else, however, may fear that if the sales forecast is doubled, he may be forced into the position of having to work harder. This may induce him to discount an upward movement in sales in his forecast.

Besides, utilizing salesmen and executives consumes a considerable amount of time. This time may be invested more profitably in other, more productive endeavors. Finally, neither salesmen nor managers are specialists in forecasting and they may not be capable of interpreting the movement of events analytically.

Consumer Expectations. This approach to forecasting is essentially the same in methodology as the sales-force composite, with one difference. That is the fact that the data are gathered by the company's marketing research department. The department circulates questionnaires and sends out trained interviewers to collect information on expected future sales. It then analyzes these data as they are received and adds other fragments from supplementary sources. In the industrial goods field a consumer forecast tends to be rather accurate. For instance, if the customer chanced to be DuPont, there is considerable likelihood that DuPont has developed a rather sophisticated forecast for the line of products sold by the supplier.

Mathematical Models

General Techniques. As we have noted, there are two kinds of general mathematical techniques involved in composing market forecasts. One deals with time series and the other with regression analysis.

[5] *Ibid.*

1. TIME SERIES. After the seasonal factors have been removed from the data a company may wish to compare the data with what are known as lead, coincidental, and lag indicators. Figure 8-1 describes these indicators graphically.

One of the greatest difficulties in forecasting is to pinpoint the moment at which a trend will reverse itself. If sales are rising, when will they start down, and vice versa? A useful though not infallible technique is the use of leading indicators. These indicators generally turn before sales do. In fact, a leading indicator may turn as many as three months before sales.

Lead, coincidental, and lag indicators have been developed through research conducted by the National Bureau of Economic Research. At the present time these indicators are published monthly in *Business Cycle Developments,* a publication of the Department of Commerce. This publication lists 32 leading indicators. Some of these are the average work week of production employees, value of manufacturers' new orders in durable goods industries, and construction contracts awarded.

Coincidental indicators move with the sales of a company or with the economy. These indicators tend to reinforce current estimates of business conditions. Among them are the unemployment rate, index of industrial production, and sales at retail stores. *Business Cycle Developments* lists a total of 15 of them.

Lag indicators, as their name suggests, turn only after business conditions or sales have turned. These tend to confirm whether the cycle has really reversed itself. There are seven such lag indicators alto-

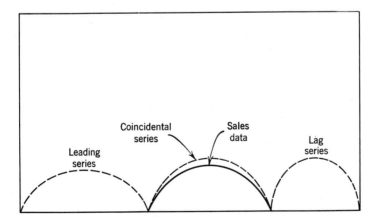

Figure 8-1. Lead, coincidental, and lag indicators.

gether and they include among others the book values of manufacturers' inventories, consumer installment debt, and bank rates on short-term interest rates. None of these indicators may work for a particular company. If they do not work, the company may then experiment to find its own leading and lagging indicators.

Another valuable forecasting tool is the diffusion index. These indices are a group of indicators within a series. For example, all 32 indicators in the lead series may be consolidated into a diffusion index, which measures changes over the previous period for all elements in the series. If, say, as many indicators changed positively as changed negatively from the previous month, one would record a diffusion index of 50 per cent, signifying no appreciable change in business conditions. If, however, there was more positive change than negative change the indicators would be saying that business conditions were improving and the index would rise above 50 per cent. When the index falls below 50 per cent and continues a downward path, one would expect business to recede.

Time-series analysis of data shorn of seasonal factors shows the typical rhythmic pattern of the past. In comparing this pattern with current data one may be able to envisage similar performance in the future. The regularity of these data simplifies their fit into some mathematical curve or line. Nevertheless, time-series analysis does not provide any indication of future changes nor does it reveal how the company might influence the future sales outlook. It is an "other things being equal" approach. Assuming that personnel, resources, and competitive conditions remain the same, the company is able to make a forecast. Unfortunately, these factors cannot be counted on to remain static.

The use of the indicators and the diffusion index has shown some promise for foretelling the future. To date, however, both methods have been slightly less than perfect in indicating the direction of business changes at every turn.

2. REGRESSION ANALYSIS. Regression analysis—or correlation—rests on the principle that a dependent variable like sales is related to an independent variable like income. This relationship may be expressed by the simple linear equation

$$y = a + bx$$

in which y represents the dependent variable, sales; x symbolizes the independent variable, income; a signifies a constant, and b, the slope of the line. By estimating values for a and b and substituting values

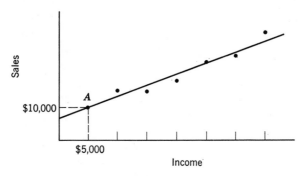

Figure 8-2. Regression relationship.

for x, one may obtain y.[6] Graphically this relationship may be plotted in the manner indicated by Figure 8-2.   In the illustration point A represents the sales—$10,000—that would be realized when income is $5000. Similarly, the other dots on the graph signify other relationships between sales and income.   One may plot a straight-line graph based on the linear equation just cited, use other equations if the relationship appears to be nonlinear, or draw a freehand line as the best choice to fit all the dots.

Regression techniques, however, may use more than a single independent variable.   Frequently a term of error is appended to the end of the equation.   This term would represent the amount of variation unexplained by the independent variables.   The independent variables may also be treated mathematically by some such device as lagging them or using some exponential power of the variable.

In selecting a time period for the regression equation one may compare the data of past years to similar data of recent years.   One may compare, for instance, how forecast data fitted actual data in the 1920's to the fit in the period following the end of the Second World War.   If the independent variables of the past seem to fit well they can be used nowadays for forecasting the future.   If they do not fit effectively then it behooves the forecasters to switch to the more recent data.   As a general rule it is preferable to obtain data for longer periods, specifically data that cover one complete business cycle from peak through trough.

Five things a forecaster might consider in selecting variables include criteria for selection, method of estimation, adjustment for cyclical effects, use of serial correlation, and value of time trend.   The principal

[6] See Appendix for solution of equation.

criterion for the selection of an independent variable is that it relate
to the dependent variable. The problem, however, lies in forecasting
values for the independent variable. Use of a lagged variable eases
the difficulty. Failing this, one must choose the independent variables
that are easiest to forecast.

Changing the number of independent variables may affect the
accuracy of the forecast. Yet this does not mean that the more independent variables used the more accurate will be the forecast. The
accuracy of the forecast may be approximately the same through use
of a regression equation with a fewer number of variables if the "first
difference" method is selected, that is to say, a straight-line projection.
Once chosen, the relevant variables will not change the accuracy of
a forecast. However, the equation should contain as many variables
as necessary to represent a complete function. One may test the
longer equation with many variables and the shorter equation with
fewer variables, noting the difference in the accuracy of the forecast
when the first difference method is used.

One of the obstacles to using a regression equation is the problem of
lack of movement in relation to cyclical conditions. This is a situation that obtains when variables relate to the same unit of time. It
may be overcome by the selection of lagged variables. Instead of
using projected income, for example, one may choose income changes
of the previous period. Different forms of the lagged variable may
be employed, either lagging it to the past period as suggested or
lagging it to a previous cyclical peak.

Some variables related only causally may nevertheless show a close
tie. This tie may result from serial correlation as well as the causal
effect of one upon the other. The use of the first difference method
instead of the variables may be one way of circumventing the difficulty. Or one may incorporate the serial correlation within the regression equation itself. When the dependent variable to be forecast
is sales one may also include last year's sales as one of the independent
variables. In addition, the autoregressive properties—that is, the
serial correlation within the series—of the dependent variable may be
investigated. This becomes quite useful in forecasting on the basis
of lagged variables. Thus, current sales may be a function of the
sales of the previous period and of the change in sales from that period.
When sales are correlated in this manner forecasts tend to be highly
accurate. However, when the length of the time period is extended
this value of the serial correlation diminishes.

The use of a time variable does not indicate any causal connection
between time and the dependent variable. Where there is a statis-

tically significant coefficient for the time variable other causal variables have been excluded. If these causal variables have been identified they may be substituted for the time variable. Otherwise, the time variable may be used with the realization that it is not a causal factor.

In using the coefficient of correlation it should not be assumed that a high degree of correlation signifies causal relationship. A forecast that correlates highly with actual data is not necessarily a good prediction of the future. Ferber has pointed out that in different periods of observation the relationship between the coefficient of correlation and predictive accuracy is negative. This means that a correlation poorly fitting observed data tends to yield more accurate forecasts.[7] Yet it does not follow that the worse the fit the better the predictive tool is. Special factors may intervene in different periods of observation which completely distort the value of the coefficient of correlation as an indicator of predictive accuracy. The basic factors that influence the variable are more important over the long run than the aptness of the fit.

The relative magnitudes of the coefficients of correlation may yield no further information on the size of the residuals or the relative errors of the estimates in the period of observation. Ferber demonstrated as much in forecasts of the savings function. He noted how the same function, fitted to different periods of observation, could have widely varying coefficients of correlation although the residuals for overlapping years in the observation period were identical. He noted further that the accuracy of the prediction for two forms of the same function, each fitted to another period of observation, differed markedly and negatively from the coefficient of correlation. The explanation of both phenomena lay in the differences in amplitude during the period of observation of the variable in question—in this case, savings. When the amplitudes of the dependent variables of two functions differ—whether because of differences in the periods of observation, in the units of measurement, in the variables chosen, or because of distinctions in definitions—no reliance may be placed on the comparison of the coefficients of correlation either for the general adequacy of the functions or their predictive accuracy.

Company-Level Forecasts. At the company level two types of forecasts occur. One of these is based on computer programs, and the other is an outgrowth of market surveys.

---

[7] Robert Ferber, "Sales Forecasting by Correlation Techniques," *Journal of Marketing*, Vol. 23, No. 3, January 1954, pp. 219–232.

1. COMPUTER PROGRAMS. In general, programs for forecasting which involve the utilization of computers have been developed for calculating multiple-regression, simultaneous multiple-regression, and non-linear multiple-regression equations. Multiple-regression equations contain more than one independent variable. Simultaneous multiple-regression equations may be either static or dynamic. A static equation may be expressed in this form: [8]

$$C = .712y + 95.05$$

This represents the relationship between consumption and income, or the consumption function. The business saving function may be expressed by the equation

$$r = .158(c + x) - 34.30$$

In this equation x equals the gross investment. Finally, we may obtain the formula for disposable income which is:

$$y - c + x - r$$

Now it becomes possible to solve for the values of c and r, and to substitute to obtain the value of y.

Nonlinear multiple-regression equations may assume some of the following forms:

$$y = a + b \sin x + Ce^{x2} + dx_1x_2$$

$$y = a + (\sin x)^b$$

$$y = a + \sin (bx)$$

Another procedure used with computers has been the stepwise multiple-regression technique. Under it the variance attributable to each independent variable is evaluated and only those that account for the least degree of variation are selected. The procedure takes this form:

$$\frac{\text{(All the variables)} - \text{(All the variables} - \text{one variable)}}{\text{Variance}}$$

One variable is displaced at a time to note the result when this variable is not part of the total variance.

Computer programs may also be developed in which mathematical curves may be fitted to the sales data. One such method is to take the sales data of the past, predict from it, and observe the variation

[8] Gerhard Tintner, *Econometrics*, Wiley, New York, 1952, pp. 67–68; see pp. 69–75 for a dynamic model.

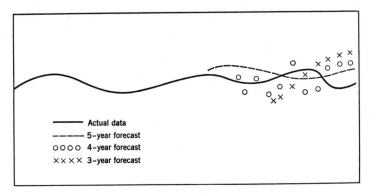

Figure 8-3. Curve fitting.

from both the forecast and the actual data. Figure 8-3 pertains to sales data for ten years. Any number of mathematical formulas may be selected to cover past data. Suppose three were chosen. The analyst would forecast for a five-year period using the three formulas, then forecast for the next four years employing the data of the past six years, and so forth. The computer measures the variance of all these forecasts against the actual data and chooses the one with the least amount of variance. Basically, the computer is a useful mechanism for simulation and experimenting with forecasts.

A technique very much related to the main type of forecast is *exponential smoothing*.[9] This naive forecast assumes that the future will resemble the immediate past with respect to rates of change. The technique presupposes that future sales are governed by sales of the past period plus the forecast for that period adjusted to accommodate any errors in forecasting. The accommodation for error is accomplished by calculating the difference between past forecasts and actual sales. A percentage of the error is used to forecast future sales. Thus, one may use 10 per cent of the error. This is symbolized by the letter *A*. The formula for such exponential smoothing takes the form: expected sales for the coming period equals *A* times realized sales during the last period plus one minus *A* times the expected sales for

[9] See Peter R. Winters, "Forecasting by Exponentially Weighted Moving Averages," *Management Science*, Vol. 6, No. 3, April 1960, pp. 324–342; see also Robert G. Brown, *Statistical Forecasting for Inventory Control*, McGraw-Hill, New York, 1959; for a simpler explanation see N.I.C.B., *op. cit.;* also editorial commentary in Bass et al., *Mathematical Models in Marketing*, Irwin, Homewood, Ill., 1961, pp. 482–491.

the last period. This estimate is adjusted for seasonal and trend factors, but the technique is most successful in industries having only slight seasonal fluctuations.

The problem of forecasting sales of fashion merchandise is the difficulty of predicting the length of the season. The end of a season is fairly well set by such concrete dates as Christmas or Easter. The start of the season is not so precise. Once the latter is known, however, it becomes possible to project sales to the end of the season and estimate profits for the period.

As a beginning, total cumulative monthly sales figures are calculated for past seasons of varying lengths. These are plotted on curves such as those contained in Figure 8-4. The past time periods are then averaged and given a cumulative percentage, as each season has a different duration. Sales are similarly averaged and given a cumulative percentage.

The chart in Figure 8-4 may be used as follows. Suppose that a company estimates that it has traversed 10 per cent of its season. This represents a light period in the total accumulation of sales. Thus, if sales are $8000 in this period, one may forecast a total seasonal sale of $100,000—that is, 8000 divided by .08, the present time period. To obtain the present time period within the season, the current data is plotted against the past average data and the curve that fits best is selected.

Once sales are known it becomes possible to estimate profits for the season. Profits at the end of the season equal the probability of selling during the season multiplied by the profit during the season plus the probability of not selling at the end of the season multiplied by the profit at the end of the season. As the season advances the estimate of sales and of total profit at season's end grows more reliable.[10]

2. MARKET SURVEYS. To forecast future demand numerous types of marketing surveys may be undertaken. A company, for example, might conduct its own survey on consumer responses to new products and new product features. In addition, it might purchase data from various independent marketing research concerns such as the A. C. Nielsen Company or the Marketing Research Corporation of America. These data, regardless of who compiles them, are drawn from sampling

[10] See D. B. Hertz and K. H. Schaffir, "A Forecasting Method for Management of Seasonal Style Inventories," *Operations Research,* Vol. 8, No. 1, January–February 1960, pp. 45–52; see also Bass et al., *op. cit.,* pp. 461–468 for editorial commentary, and N.I.C.B., *op. cit.*

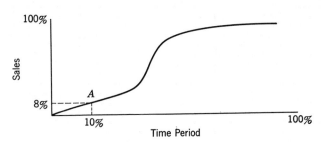

Figure 8-4. Cumulative sales.

procedures, and the samples permit the projection of approximate retail sales.

Or a company might prefer a simple desk analysis to estimate demand. For example, Sylvania estimates television sets by computing the number of first set purchasers. It does so by subtracting the number of homes with one or more sets at the start of the year from those with one or more sets at the close of the year. The difference represents the number of first set installations. The data are obtained from the Advertising Research Foundation.[11] An estimate is also made of the number of nontelevision homes likely to buy sets in the future. This estimate, based on past ones, averages about 18 per cent. The estimate of nontelevision homes is computed by observing the total number of homes listed by the United States Census Bureau and subtracting from them the data on television homes gathered by the Advertising Research Foundation. The 18 per cent is applied to this remainder.

Turning to multiple-set ownership sales are forecast in the following manner: The company learns the number of sets in service at the end of the year through multiplying the number of television homes by the average number of sets per home. Then it subtracts the number of sets in service at the start of the year, which is obtained through the same multiplication process. The remainder equals the number of initial installations. By proceeding one step further and subtracting first-set purchases from the number of sets initially installed, Sylvania is able to estimate sales for multiple ownership.

The rate of wearing out, or replacement, is based on a sample of owners. This is compared with the estimate of the seepage rate obtained from the following calculation: the number of sets which the

[11] N.I.C.B., *op. cit.*

Advertising Research Foundation reports for all homes plus the total number of sets sold to the public during the year, as compiled by the trade association for the electronics industry, less the number of sets the ARF reports in service at the close of the year. One may then select an appropriate seepage rate based on the relationship of the answer to the foregoing formula and to various hypothetical curves.

Other forms of marketing surveys include the use of consumer panels on a continuous basis.[12] The employment of such panels offers a better opportunity to study consumer behavior and thus form a sound basis for forecasting future consumer patterns. This kind of analysis particularly benefits situations in which planning is involved in the purchase. Use of these panels permits a company to undertake analyses that may not be possible under any other means. These analyses would disclose:

1. The role of planning in the purchases of specific types of goods.
2. The importance of planning in actual purchases.
3. Characteristics influencing the fulfillment of plans: length and degree of certainty for the plan; and economic, psychological, and sociological for the purchaser.
4. The effect of changes in family—or company—status on consumer plans and purchases.
5. The predictability of purchases for which no plans were reported on the basis of family—or company—characteristics, financial position, and outlook, as well as changes in the variables.

Purchases may be divided into these categories: *necessity purchases,* those not planned and not postponable; *impulse purchases,* those not planned but postponable; and *purchases planned and fulfilled.*

In a pilot study on planning it was learned from the consumer panels that planning was more concentrated than purchasing. The population groups doing the most purchasing per family were the same ones undertaking the most planning. The purchase of large items was more likely to be planned than the purchase of small ones, and the planning horizon grew with the amount of contemplated expenditures. Actually, the planning horizon varied with the type of product.

The study showed that purchase plans were more likely to be carried out if the approximate time of purchase was known and if the plans were accompanied by a high degree of certainty. Most of the

[12] Robert Ferber, "Sales Forecasting by Sample Surveys," *Journal of Marketing,* Vol. 20, No. 1, July 1955, pp. 1–13.

fulfilled plans were completed no more than a month beyond their scheduled time, when such time was given. Plans whose timing was not known, on the other hand, tended to be fulfilled even sooner than those for which scheduled completion times were given. The degree of fulfillment varied according to the kind of product and the consumer's present and anticipated financial condition. These panel findings have proven highly valuable to companies using them; their major limitation is their high cost.

Total Business Forecast Level. At this level there are four different approaches to forecasting which we shall examine briefly. They are the Gross National Product accounting approach, the Keynesian models, the inventory models, and the survey of buying intentions.

1. GNP ACCOUNTING APPROACH. One manner of estimating the GNP is to use its accounting method. In this regard, the accounts covering income equal the accounts covering expenses or products. The forecast may be pursued by making estimates on a single side or both sides of the accounting ledger and reconciling any differences that may exist. In choosing the product account, for example, one could make projections among the broad categories of consumer goods, durable goods, and goods and services purchased by the government. These categories could then be decomposed into their smallest parts so that each part might be estimated. The added totals would comprise the GNP forecast.

Many companies follow the habit of forecasting the GNP, then the prospects for their industry, and finally, their own expected future sales based on their past percentage of the industry's performance. Often companies that make independent sales forecasts also check their estimates against GNP and industry outlooks.

2. KEYNESIAN MODELS. Perhaps one of the most widely used models for forecasting is the Keynesian model. This model, in line with the economic theory of John Maynard Keynes, assumes that the Gross National Product will grow only if there is an increase in investment. There are basically two types of investment, public and private. Private investment is influenced by expectations of consumer demand, or more precisely by the marginal propensity to consume. This propensity is the rate of consumptive change related to a change in income. The reciprocal of this number subtracted from one is known as the multiplier, the figure by which one would multiply expected investment. This would yield the total investment addition to the new GNP over the previous one. Adding this investment to the GNP supplies the new forecast.

3. INVENTORY MODELS.   These models presuppose that inventory is a function of demand.   That is to say, a small increase in demand requires a great increase in inventory.   Figure 8-5 illustrates a characteristic inventory cycle.   It demonstrates that inventory accumulates very slowly at first as demand grows.   At this point, inventory is still being liquidated.   Finally, as inventory is fully exhausted demand requires more production.   The inventory produced to accommodate this demand creates a greater increase in the economy and therefore in demand.   However, inventory has begun to expand even beyond the requirements of demand.   This precipitates a drop in inventory at a precipitous rate.

Through the help of computers companies have been able to minimize this overproduction.   This has resulted in inventory cycles of lower amplitude but greater frequency.   For a time, it was thought that recent recessions had been caused by matters of inventory.   Investigation by the President's Council of Economic Advisers has dispelled this fear.   Changes in demand seem to have been more pertinent to recessive onslaughts than changes in inventory.

4. SURVEY OF BUYING INTENTIONS.   Probably the best known non-continuous survey is the one conducted by the Federal Reserve Board in association with the Survey Research Center at the University of Michigan.   This survey asks the consumer about intentions to buy specific kinds of goods, expectations of business conditions, and the general state of his financial liquidity.   The survey has not been successful, however, in predicting actual expenditures as compared to expectations.   It has not been able to forecast when a change would occur nor how great the change would be.

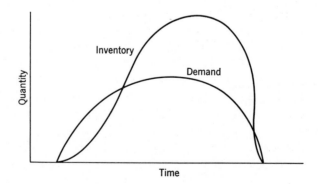

Figure 8-5. Inventory cycle.

Yet this does not mean that such data is useless. When consumer survey data is cross-tabulated by income, liquid assets, existence of personal debt, individual financial situation, living in small towns or open country, and age groups under 45, there seems to be a greater portion of people who fulfill their planned expectations.[13]

Other factors in a consumer survey which suggest whether an individual will fulfill his intentions include price expectations, regional differences, and occupational differences.[14] If data on consumer attitudes are taken as a measure of willingness to buy and are adjusted for factors that affect buying ability, a better forecast can result from these surveys of consumer intentions.[15]

Moreover, where the purpose is to classify the independent variables into those directly related to the product and those indirectly related to it, forecasting seems to be improved.[16] When a product is not purchased often the direct method may be used. Otherwise, the indirect method applies. Thus, an analysis of income changes indicating future purchases of meat exemplifies the indirect method. With this information it becomes possible to establish a regression of the independent variables and the dependent variable. The time lapse between the collection of data and the actual forecast may be greater for items requiring a longer period of planning and having a lower frequency of purchase than for items with a short period of planning and a high purchase frequency. It seems preferable, besides, to study consumers intensively in a relatively narrow area than to survey them extensively over a much wider area.

Evaluation of Forecasting

The evaluation of forecasts, in general, poses two main problems.[17] One deals with determining the accuracy of the forecast and the other with determining its economic usefulness. Three principles have

[13] Jean Namias, "Intentions to Purchase Compared with Actual Purchases of Household Durables," *Journal of Marketing,* Vol. 24, No. 1, July 1959, pp. 26–30.
[14] Jean Namias, "Intentions to Purchase Related to Consumer Characteristics," *Journal of Marketing,* Vol. 25, No. 1, July 1960, pp. 32–36.
[15] Stephen Paranka, "Marketing Predictions from Consumer Attitudinal Data," *Journal of Marketing,* Vol. 25, No. 1, July 1960, pp. 46–51.
[16] Ferber, "Sales Forecasting by Sample Surveys," *loc. cit.*
[17] James H. Lorie, "Two Important Problems in Sales Forecasting," *Journal of Business,* July 1957, pp. 172–179.

proven quite useful in solving these problems. First, forecasts should be written in clear, unambiguous language and should discuss exactly the statistics being forecast. Second, when choosing among simple statistical models, the guiding principle must be to select the one that accounts for the most variability in the series to be forecast. Finally, a forecast is judged to be superior if the consequences of decisions based on it turn out to be more profitable than decisions based on other estimates. This may be called the *pragmatic* approach to forecasting. A logical or rational approach attempts to evaluate forecasts from *a priori* and *ex-post* points of view.

A Priori and Ex-Post Evaluations

A Priori. This is essentially a statistical method of evaluation based on variance analysis. The statistical procedure endeavors to determine the range of error in repeated samplings. It tries, for example, to answer the question: if one were to continue to sample data what would be the chances of coming up with an answer within a certain range? Or in 95 cases out of 100 what is the range of error which might be anticipated? [18]

Ex-Post. Evaluation of this kind is an assessment of the method itself. Forecast errors may be weighed on the basis of complete or comparative accuracy. The objective of absolute evaluation is to ascertain the extent to which forecasts deviate from actual values and whether the errors which do occur are consistent in any one particular respect. These are the biases in the forecasts.

Deviation of the forecast from the actual data may be measured by summing the difference between the actual and forecasted amounts, dividing it by the actual, and then dividing the result by the number of forecasts. One may investigate deviations with respect to sign and look for patterns among them. If the points fall above the line the forecast has been overestimated or overoptimistic. If they fall below the line the forecast has been underestimated or overpessimistic. (See Figure 8-6.)

An alternative method consists of calculating the error of the ith variable and then developing a yardstick for predictive accuracy. In this case, the error of the ith variable consists of realization of that

[18] Robert Ferber and P. J. Verdoorn, *Research Methods in Economics and Business,* Macmillan, New York, 1962, pp. 470–473.

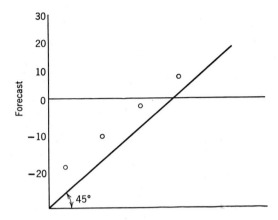

Figure 8-6. Comparison of forecast with realization.

variable in time t, less the expectation of the variable in that time, or as the formula expresses it

$$u_{i,t} = A_{i,t} - E_{i,F}$$

The subsequent measure of predictive accuracy would be represented by the formula:

$$u^1 = \frac{u_{i,t} \quad \text{(Error)}}{SA_i \quad \text{(Root mean square of actual period to period change)}}$$

One can determine whether the results of many observations of the equation yields a normal distribution. If the mean differs significantly from zero, bias is indicated. If the variance exceeds unity, growing dispersion of the forecast may be in the offing. For the forecast of a number of variables there is the standardized root mean square residual which is the root mean square of the values observed for each of the variables. It may be expressed in this way:

$$u_t = \sqrt{\frac{1}{n} \Sigma u_{i,t}}$$

If a forecast misses the actual value by a certain percentage, or even predicts the actual value accurately, there remains the question, can this same forecast be accomplished by a simpler method such as the naive, or exponential smoothing, approach? As we have said earlier in the chapter, the naive forecast states that the future will change very much like the recent past. This kind of forecast does

Table 8-1. Realization Measures

(A) Per Cent Change Unadjusted Series		Per Cent Realization		
		(B) Seasonal forecast	(C) Actual forecast	(D) Optimal forecast
October	18.3%	11.2%	−5.6%	−1.3%
November	39.9	14.4	−3.3	1.9
December	25.8	−7.8	−2.4	−2.2
January	11.3	18.7	9.8	2.6
February	−4.3	6.5	6.9	−0.5
March	8.8	7.5	8.3	1.2
April	9.2	7.7	7.7	−1.6
Averages for 7 forecasts	±16.87%	±10.5%	±6.3%	±1.6%

not predict turning points. It merely says that what has been going on in the past will continue in the future. The question persists: how much better is one's forecast than the naive forecast?

One method of evaluating the ability of a forecast to predict turning points is to compare it to a naive forecast of such points. One may count the number of times that the forecast correctly anticipates a reversal of the current trend and correctly anticipates the turning point. These predictions may then be compared with the naive model.[19] One procedure postulates that by using the naive forecast which assumes there is no turning point one might err through maintaining that a turning point does in fact occur during a 12-month period. If a forecast were made in each month this would account for 78 errors over a period of one year.

Another technique using the comparative or relative approach is suggested by McLaughlin [20] and illustrated in Table 8-1.

In Table 8-1, column A contains the results of a forecast predicting the same change for each month as the previous one—that is, the naive forecast. Column B represents the ratio of the figure achieved to the seasonally adjusted realization. This should be an improvement over the naive forecast. Column C demonstrates the forecast

[19] See Arthur M. Okun, "On the Appraisal of Cylical Turning Point Predictors," *Journal of Business*, April 1960, pp. 101–120.
[20] Robert L. McLaughlin, "Computer Technique for Time Series Forecasting," *Proceedings of the Forty-Fifth Conference of the AMA,* June 20–22, 1962, American Marketing Association, Chicago, pp. 239–247.

in ratio to the actual realization. This average should surpass both A and B. Column D is the optimal forecast, an estimate of the effect of change if the irregular element were lacking. This is really the ratio of the trend cycle to the seasonally adjusted data.

McLaughlin then tries to fix an average for a forecast. In baseball parlance, he says that batting between .300 and .400 may be considered as doing well. He calls this the *standard realization percentage* and obtains it by the following computation:

$$SR\% = .1 \left(\frac{\text{Seasonal forecast R\%} - \text{Actual forecast R\%}}{\text{Seasonal forecast R\%} - \text{Optimal forecast R\%}} \right) + .3$$

Substituting the averages from Table 8-1 we get:

$$SR\% = .1 \left(\frac{10.5 - 6.3}{10.5 - 1.6} \right) + 3$$

$$= .1 \left(\frac{4.2}{8.9} \right) + 3$$

$$= .347$$

Organization of Forecasting

Forecasting responsibility is about equally divided between the accounting and marketing departments of a company. Traditionally, forecasting was a function of the accounting department which drew up the budget. Later it was found that the sales department was also attempting to estimate its sales for the days to come; thus, the sales department got into the forecasting business. Yet both accounting and sales managers were preoccupied with other responsibilities and were unable to give adequate time to forecasting. Hence, forecasting became the responsibility of the marketing research department. Nowadays within most marketing research departments there are one or more individuals saddled with the assignment of forecasting sales. In some companies, like the Ford Motor Company, a forecast is made by both the sales department and the economics department for each division of the company. In addition, a major forecast is made for the entire corporation.

Survey on Responsibility

The primary responsibility for the sales forecast most frequently falls on a marketing executive. In a survey conducted by the American Management Association at the organization's sales-forecasting conference in the spring of 1956, two-thirds of the companies responding said that control of this function belonged in the marketing department.[21]   In about half these companies the marketing research department participated in development of the sales forecast.[22] Nearly half said their production departments also participated. Other departments involved included finance (39 per cent), advertising and promotion (slightly over 25 per cent), and a scattering of engineering, purchasing, economic research, and planning participants.   Manufacturers of consumer goods drew their advertising and promotion departments into forecasting more frequently than other companies.

Participants and Use.   There is no relationship between those who use the forecast and those who participate in its construction.   Usage of the forecast for the following purposes was reported in the survey:

	Per Cent of Companies
Sales	97
Production planning	89
Budget preparation	86
Earnings forecast	76
Equipment and facilities planning	68
Setting sales quotas	63
Manpower planning	57
Raw materials stockpiling	54
Promotion planning	43
Other	8

On the average, the survey showed, three departments participated in composing the forecast.   In a few companies only one department was involved, and in some as many as six or seven.   Not long ago only half the country's companies placed primary responsibility for the forecast on one individual or on one department.   Now more than 80 per cent of them do so.[23]

Shift.   Crawford has noted a tendency to move forecasting from a marketing research group under the sales department to a commercial research department attached to a higher level of company ac-

[21] *Sales Forecasting: Uses, Techniques, and Trends,* American Management Association, Chicago, 1956, p. 145 ff.
[22] *Ibid.,* p. 146.
[23] *Ibid.,* p. 147.

tivity, such as the office of the executive vice president.[24] This reflects the coordination of sales forecasting with planning which is a top-management responsibility. Crawford suggested further that instead of a commercial research department reporting to the executive vice president, what might be needed is an operation-planning-and-research department with production-planning and sales-planning subdivisions. He found no companies that had evolved such a form but believed it to be a logical outgrowth of the emphasis on implementing forecasts with planning. In many companies, however, objections have been raised to elevating the planning function to higher management levels. The contention is that planning must be tied closely to daily operations. Even so, as we have seen in this chapter, it takes a view from the corporate summit to grasp the broad opportunities lying ahead, and forecasting certainly belongs somewhere near the top of the marketing ladder if a company is to plan judiciously to make the most of future conditions.

Summary

A sales forecast is the basis for any short- or long-range planning activity of the firm. After data is seasonally adjusted one may use either the subjective approach or mathematical models. The subjective approach includes the jury of executive opinion, the sales-force composite method, and consumers' expectations. Mathematical models may be divided into those techniques that may be used at a general level, those used at the company level, and those used at the national level. Of those techniques that are used at both the company and national levels we have time-series and regression analysis.

Various techniques have been developed at the company level with the advent of the computer. Also market surveys are useful in forecasting at the company level. At the total economy level there is the accounting approach, Keynesian model, inventory models, and the survey of buying intentions. Forecasts may be evaluated by using the *a priori* technique and the *ex-post* method. Forecasting is becoming more and more the responsibility of the marketing department.

Suggested Cases

Ralph L. Westfall and Harper W. Boyd, *Cases in Marketing Management*, Irwin, Homewood, Ill., 1961.

Controls Company of America—*Manufacturer of Control Components*

[24] C. M. Crawford, *Sales Forecasting: Methods of Selected Firms*, University of Illinois Press, Urbana, 1955, pp. 55–57.

for Electrical Appliances—Forecasting by Use of Salesmen's Estimates, pp. 121–123.

Bordo, Inc.—*Major Appliance Manufacturer*—Long-Range Forecasting and Planning, pp. 117–120.

Hector Lazo and Arnold Corbin, *Management in Marketing*, McGraw-Hill, New York, 1961.

Universal Paint Company, Sales Forecasting, Disagreement Among Top Management, Sales, Advertising, and Marketing Research, pp. 398–400.

Kenneth R. Davis, *Marketing Management*, Ronald Press, New York, 1961.

Gately Company, pp. 239–248.

Vaga Company, pp. 248–250.

Appendix

Solving Linear Regression

Let us assume that x is the month under investigation and y is the income reported. For the first month we see in Table A-1 the income listed is $3 million.

Since we wish to solve the equation $y = a + bx$, and we have the necessary data of x and y, we must solve now for the coefficients a and b. To do this we use the normal equation.

$$(1) \quad \Sigma(y) = na + b\Sigma(x)$$

$$(2) \quad \Sigma(xy) = a\Sigma(x) + b\Sigma(x)^2$$

Table A-I

x	y	xy	x^2
1	3	3	1
2	4	8	4
3	6	18	9
4	5	20	16
5	10	50	25
6	9	54	36
7	10	70	49
8	12	96	64
9	11	99	81
Total 45	70	418	285

Substituting in the above equation we have the following simultaneous equation:

$$(1) \quad 70 = 9(a) + 45(b)$$

$$(2) \quad 418 = 45(a) + 285(b)$$

Multiplying Equation 1 by 5 cancels the *a* coefficient and obtains the following:

$$418 = 45 + 285(b)$$

$$\underline{350 = 45 + 225(b)}$$

$$68 = \qquad 60(b)$$

$$b = 1.13$$

Inserting the value of 1.13 for *b* in the original equation $y = a + bx$ we get:

$$70 = 9(a) + 50.85$$

$$a = 2.12$$

Substituting the values of *a* and *b* in the equation $y = a + bx$ we get:

$$y = 2.12 + 1.13x$$

In order to obtain the values of *y* we must multiply the corresponding value of *x* by the coefficient *b* (1.13) and add this to the coefficient *a* (2.12). Thus for an *x* value of 2, *y* will equal 4.38. Plotting the *y* values on graph paper against the *x* values will yield a straight line.

Chapter Nine

Following the end of the Second World War, a new staff function has infiltrated the management of business organizations—operations research. Although there have been many definitions of this function agreement seems to be lacking on what actually constitutes it. One set of writers, Churchman, Ackoff, and Arnoff, has defined operations research as the application of scientific principles, techniques, and tools to the operation of a system in order to control the system through supplying the best possible solutions to its problems. In their view, the procedure includes six phases: formulating the prob-

Operations Research
and Electronic Data Processing
in Marketing Management

lem, constructing a mathematical model to represent the system under study, deriving a solution from the model, testing the solution and the model, establishing controls over the solution, and putting the solution to work. P. P. Morse, on the other hand, has defined operations research as a scientific method for providing executives with a quantitative basis for making decisions. A third definition, offered by the Arthur D. Little organization of business consultants puts it this way:

First the analysis undertaken and the results obtained were quantitative. Furthermore, the results were capable of being verified by experimental methods, and the analysis included the establishment of two types of experiments, informational and critical. The primary goal of the analysis was the understanding of the operation although that understanding, once achieved, ultimately provided a basis for action. The results were not restricted to the specific questions asked, but the model developed became one component of a more general model of the client company's whole operation.

In actual practice, operations research is characterized by the use of teams of specialists who work on a particular problem. Members of a team may be physical or social scientists, or management functionaries. These men formulate the problem. In so doing they are concerned not only with the immediate situation, but also with all the interrelated aspects of the problem as they affect the operation of the company. This is called a *systems approach*. Once the team has satisfactorily defined the problem and its relationship to company operations, it is in a position to develop a model. The model may be based on theories developed in the mathematical, physical, or social sciences. Two models have been most useful in solving business problems. They are probability theory and linear programming. After development of the model, figures are inserted into it and its effectiveness in predicting reality is observed.

299

Models

A model is a simplified way of describing reality. It represents a situation in the real, workaday world. It attempts to reduce reality to symbolic form from which it seeks to build up to the actual situation. The mathematical theory may be physical, such as a model airplane or a wind tunnel which simulates currents of wind, or it may be conceptual, such as the theory of gravity or the theory of relativity. Either concrete or abstract, it serves the same purpose of simplifying actuality.

The theory of competition is a simplified model of a situation in the market place. It makes assumptions about buyers and sellers, rationality of behavior, and homogeneity of goods sold. The model suggests that more goods will be purchased at lower prices than at higher prices and that each successive higher price will draw additional supplies of products to the market. Moreover, it notes the equilibrium point in the price of an item where supply is exactly equal to demand. When supply exceeds demand, prices tend to fall thus attracting additional buyers. As the buyers begin to outnumber the supplies available and prices head for a rise, new suppliers enter the market to pull the price down again.

Modifying the Model. The attributes of this model also describe imperfect competition. However, the model is modified to account for the homogeneity of the products sold and the number of suppliers selling them. A primitive economy, such as Robinson Crusoe's, may be reduced to a model of how man satisfies his wants in it. To this may be added more complex elements until the modified model approximates the sophisticated market economy dominating today's civilized society. Figure 9-1 [1] illustrates such a modification in which elements are discarded if unsuitable until the right model emerges. In the illustration, data are used to form an initial model of the real world. From a test of the model new data derive which do not yield a satisfactory evaluation. The model is supplanted by a second one involving still newer data which also do not work out satisfactorily and hence make a third model necessary. This time the data produced by the model suffice, the evaluation of them is satisfactory, and the model helps us to understand and interpret the real world.

Viewed mathematically, we let E represent the effectiveness of the

[1] Irwin D. Bross, *Design for Decision,* Macmillan, New York, 1953.

Symbolic World

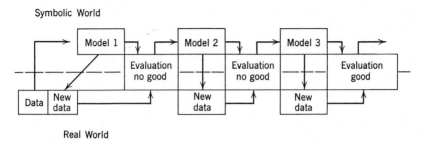

Real World

Figure 9-1

model and X_1 the aspects of the system—that is, the variables—which can be controlled by decisions of management. The uncontrollable aspects of the system are symbolized by Y_j. In constructing the model, the attempt is made to formulate one or more equations in the form

$$E = f(X_iY_j)$$

This equation states that the effectiveness of the model is a function of both the controllable and uncontrollable variables confronting management. The finding of a solution consists of determining the values of X_i for which the effectiveness of the model is greatest.

Types of Models. In operations research at least three types of models have been used: the deterministic model, the stochastic model, and the game model. In the *deterministic model* all variables are under the control of management; chance plays a small role. The effect of any given action can be determined with a reasonable amount of accuracy. These models may be used to maximize such things as objectives, profits, or rate of return. Some of the problems may be solved through the use of linear programming.

A *stochastic model* may be defined as one based on the probability of an event's occurring. It may be used in assessing future eventualities when important variables are not under management's control. The values in the model are subject to random variations and the outcomes of the related actions fluctuate accordingly. This model is employed to obtain the best results from a series of possible outcomes. It is of great use in analyzing advertising problems that involve mass behavior under unpredictable circumstances.

The *game model* is selected when the result of an action depends on the behavior of several opponents. It is not necessarily the objective of this model to maximize the outcome of one's own course of action, but rather to minimize the advantages of one's opponents. Let us examine these three models in order.

Deterministic Model

One mathematical technique widely applicable to the solution of many industrial problems is linear programming. This is an effort to distribute resources as efficiently as possible subject to existing restrictions. Linear programming assumes that linear relationships exist. If a person ships 50 tons of merchandise twice as far, for example, he pays twice the cost. Moreover, linear programming assumes that one resource may be substituted for another at a constant rate. The uses to which these resources are put, however, are governed by specific limitations.

At the present time two models appear to be the most popular for linear programming. These are the *simplex technique* and the *transportation model*. Each of them permits a dual solution—the maximizing of one item simultaneously with the minimizing of another, as in the case of maximizing profits while minimizing costs. Under the simplex model, for which computer programs have been worked out, the effort is made to maximize or minimize a combination of resources within the limits of the restrictions.[2] The transportation model endeavors in the most economical manner to allocate costs of shipments to various destinations from several sources.[3] The duality in both models consists of attempting to maximize one parameter while minimizing the other. The diet problem exemplifies this: the dieter seeks to increase the nutritious value of the diet while trying to reduce its cost.[4] Although linear programming tends to deal with static situations there have been attempts to add the influence of time to it through dynamic programming.[5]

Linear programming has been used also in nonlinear situations that involve risk.[6] For instance, an illustration of the application of the simplex technique may be found in the appendix to this chapter.

---

[2] For an excellent discussion of the Simplex technique see Dakota Ulrich Greenwald, *Linear Programming,* Ronald Press, New York, 1957.

[3] A very simple explanation may be found: Alexander Henderson and Robert Schlaifer, "Mathematical Programming Better Information for Better Decision Making," *Harvard Business Review,* May–June 1954, pp. 73–100.

[4] See Robert Dorfman, Paul A. Samuelson, and Robert M. Solow, *Linear Programming and Economic Analysis,* McGraw-Hill, New York, 1958, pp. 39–63.

[5] *Ibid.,* Chap. 11.

[6] See Earl O. Heady and Wilfred Candler, *Linear Programming Methods,* Iowa State College Press, Ames, 1958, Chap. 17.

Another example of its application is the selection of media for an advertiser, which may be accomplished in this manner: [7] Certain facts about the media available for advertising are stored in a computer. These facts may include the cost per unit and the discount rate for use of the advertising unit. A unit consists of the kind of space or time available for a single insertion of a particular type of advertisement in a newspaper or magazine, or for a single commercial message on radio or television. The computer also stores audience sizes and profile data on such matters as the age, sex, and income of the devotees of each vehicle. Finally, it stores information on the kinds of units available in each medium, when they are available, and what the audience overlap might be among the media.

Having this assorted information on file, the computer operator can feed into the machine the media requirements for any advertising campaign. These data include the profile characteristics of the intended audience for the advertisements, the budget to be allocated, and the numerical "guestimates" of the value of exposure in one vehicle compared with another. These "guestimates" might involve, for example, a rating of the value of a full-page, four-color advertisement in *Life* compared to a half-page, black-and-white one in *Reader's Digest*, or with a 60-second prime-time spot on network television, and so forth, without regard for the respective costs or likely powers of attracting attention. The attention factor is fed into the computer separately along with judgments about the relative values of initial versus repeated exposure. Contractual restrictions also go into the machine; if, for example, the advertiser contracts to spend 40 per cent of his budget in television, the machine acknowledges this decision. Finally, the advertiser's biases are reduced to numbers and fed into the machine.

Mixing this plethora of information together at furious speed the computer describes how many units should be bought in various media vehicles to get the maximum advertising exposure permissible at minimal cost within the limits imposed on the program.

Several other business problems have been attacked through the deterministic model, that is, through linear programming, and these are some of the kinds of problems that have been solved through it.

1. Determining the most profitable product mix to be obtained from existing facilities.

---

[7] John C. Maloney, "The Use of Computers in Marketing and Advertising Today," a speech presented at the Advertising Club of New York, April 1962, Research Dept. of Leo Burnett Co.

2. Determining which parts to make and which to buy to obtain a maximum profit margin.

3. Establishing the best location of warehouses to minimize transportation costs.

4. Planning profits on a fiscal-year basis to maximize the profit margin from net investment in plant facilities and equipment, cash on hand, and inventory.

5. Supplying a fluctuating sales demand at the least inventory cost to maintain a fixed level of production and stabilized employment.

6. Allocating production releases among several plants to maximize profits on the basis of manufacturing and distribution costs.

7. Determining equitable salaries and sales-incentive compensation.

8. Determining a feed mix that satisfies the nutritional requirements and minimizes the cost of raising livestock.

9. Programming a chemical distilling operation, including the processing of purchased material, to obtain highest manufacturing margin within the sales demand.

10. Planning the most profitable match of sales requirements to plant capacity to obtain a fair share of the market.

Stochastic Model

One company facing a gradual decline in frequency of purchase among its customers sought to increase business from individual customers by a factor of two through the institution of a promotional effort. The company knew, however, that it would have to concentrate on those customers who bought most frequently, or whose ordering characteristic was highest, if the investment in promotional activity was to pay off. The company knew that the ordering characteristics among customers was a negative exponential. From this it was possible to estimate maximum business from the customers for any level of promotional effort. But it lacked any economical method of measuring the orders placed by its customers, however much it desired as close an estimate as obtainable of each customer's ordering characteristics. Of course, it could examine the number of orders placed by each customer over as long a period as possible. But this was certain to be cumbersome and time consuming. Instead the company hit upon a simple method to be substituted for the more complex statistical techniques employed for singling out customers for promotional attention. This newer method was to select the average number of orders a customer had placed monthly over a 12-month interval, and to apply promotional pressure among those whose averages were highest.

This approach to allocating promotional sales time was found to improve the relative efficiency of the promotional sales force to more than 90 per cent.[8] That is, it raised to that level the ratio of business obtained to the total attainable under ideal conditions for that amount of sales effort. The new approach, moreover, cut in half the inefficiency of the previous use of promotional effort. The company has extended it to all its sales endeavors and has estimated that annual sales have moved into the multimillion-dollar class with correspondingly large increases in profits.

Another use of the stochastic model deals with queueing theory. This theory pertains to waiting lines wherever they exist, and they exist wherever there is a service facility and individuals or activities that must be serviced over a period of time. For example, there may be a waiting line for the barber, for a table in a restaurant, for planes landing, for ships arriving in the harbor, for cars approaching a toll gate, or patrons waiting in the checkout line at a supermarket. Each person in one of these lines does a certain amount of waiting and requires a certain amount of time for servicing. Depending on the efficiency of the service facility, the line may grow or it may be able to move new customers as quickly as they arrive.

Two probability techniques may be used to estimate arrivals and servicing. One is to assume that both arrivals and servicing are distributed randomly and that the rate at which individuals approach the servicing point tends to approximate a *poisson* distribution. The other is to use the *Monte Carlo* method in which various rates of arrival are taken at random and different answers are developed for each presupposed rate. This latter method may be called the experimental method; the *poisson* method is discussed in the appendix.

Decision Making. The making of decisions is fraught with risk and uncertainty. Both may result from the assignment of a probability to the outcome of an event. This assignment may involve either a frequency distribution or a subjective probability estimate. In the former, if a consumer survey finds that 38 per cent prefer a particular brand, one might ask the probability of coming up with the same results in taking 100 samples. If the sample were selected in a ran-

---

[8] John F. Magee, "The Effect of Promotional Effort on Sales," *Journal of the Operations Research Society of America,* Vol. 1, No. 1, November 1952, pp. 64–74; "Application of Operations Research to Marketing and Related Management Problems," *Journal of Marketing,* Vol. 18, April 1954, pp. 361–369.

dom manner, one might say that in 68 times out of 100 the value would fall within a 10 per cent zone of error. That is, the true value would lie somewhere between 33 per cent and 43 per cent. In assuming this to be the case one risks the chance of not hitting the right answer through 68 trials. But one might desire greater assurance of obtaining the exact figure. For example, one might wish to be certain 95 times out of 100 of the universe value, plus or minus a margin of error. Thus, the risk of not getting the true value would be 5 out of 100 or 5 per cent. The greater the number of observations is, the slighter the risk. Since an increased number of observations costs more money the decision maker must select a balance between risk and monetary expenditure. His decision results from the information he is seeking. If he is estimating average income he may wish to be more precise than if he wants to find out what most people like in a new product, or whether they even want it.

In the case of a subjective probability one may assign a probability to an event or several events and calculate the likelihood of the outcome. This method presupposes that the individual bases his subjective assignment of probability on experience. The technique has been applied to the evaluation of optional marketing research procedures and distribution problems in the baking industry.[9] It is especially designed for a one-time decision in contrast to a frequency probability.

Game Model

Game theory is characterized by the number of persons involved and by the payoff.[10] In the instance of a single person playing a solitary game, the individual vies against the odds. Game theory does not apply in this situation. In two-person games, which are the most frequent type, two contestants participate, one opposed to the other. The literature is scant on a three-person game.

[9] See Frank M. Bass, "Decision Model for Marketing Research Expenditures," *Institute for Quantitative Research in Economics and Management,* Institute Paper 19, January 1962, School of Industrial Management, Purdue University; also, Robert D. Buzzell and Charles C. Slater, "Decision Theory and Marketing Management," *Journal of Marketing,* Vol. 26, No. 3, July 1962, pp. 7–16.

[10] See R. D. Luce and H. Raiffa, *Games and Decisions,* Wiley, New York, 1957; also Robert Schlaifer, *Probability and Statistics for Business Decisions: An Introduction to Managerial Economics Under Uncertainty,* McGraw-Hill, New York, 1959; John Davis Williams, *The Compleat Strategist,* McGraw-Hill, New York, 1954.

As to payoff, there is the payoff associated with a zero-sum game and one associated with a nonzero-sum game. In the former the winnings of one player are the losses of the other. Thus, in a two-handed card game, one person wins and the other loses. In a non-zero game a real or hypothetical third person appears. In this game the gains do not counter the losses. Criteria for decision become necessary. Maximums may be minimized, minimums maximized, averages chosen, and the like.[11] After the problem has been determined and picked game theory may help to evaluate the choices, particularly those dealing with uncertainty. Here the criteria for decision come into play.

Game theory is a useful way of exercising the thinking process. One may modify one's strategy without showing one's hand. In game theory, one has an additional tool for thinking about duopoly, price competition, and similar matters.[12] Some of its ideas relate to ideas in statistical decision theory and psychology. Besides, through game theory decisions may be quantified if considered from another point of view. Thus, in considering an additional line of goods the prospective purchaser could check costs and decide the payoff in terms of competitors' actions. By the use of game theory, moreover, individuals can develop logical thinking in creating fundamental concepts.

Operations Research and Marketing

OR and Marketing Research [13]

Operations research in marketing, marketing research, and statistical analysis all endeavor to assist in the solution of management problems, but each of them differs in emphasis. The elements of solving any problem are facts, findings, and recommendations. Marketing research, as we have seen, concentrates on the collection of facts through surveys or other mechanisms. Statistics aid in deriving logical findings from the facts. The analysis of findings include, in the case of marketing, estimates of market potentialities and measurement of the results of selling efforts. In operations research the interest cen-

---

[11] See Luce and Raiffa, *op. cit.;* see example in chapter on advertising.

[12] See Martin Shubik, *Strategy and Market Structure: Competition, Oligopoly, and the Theory of Games,* Wiley, New York, 1959.

[13] *Cost and Profit Outlook,* Vol. VI, No. 12, December 1953, Alderson and Sessions, Marketing and Management Counsel, Philadelphia.

ters on recommendations. This interest is governed by a conception of the problem and the form the recommendation should take.

A question about efficiency or productivity in some operating system may be a problem for the operations research expert. An acceptable solution may take the form of a rule of action for getting the best results. The goal is the same as in conventional economics but the approach differs. Operations research in marketing, which might also be called operational economics, pursues numerical results which can be useful in the situation at hand. The methods it employs in finding these numbers are drawn from many branches of science and mathematics. Yet the resulting rule of action often can be stated and applied as simply as the ordinary rule of thumb which it replaces.

Reducing Uncertainty. An executive responsible for decision may be beset with uncertainty over the course of action to follow. To solve a problem is to reduce uncertainty to the point at which a choice can be made. There are at least four areas of uncertainty which are readily distinguishable in management problems. These pertain to allocation of effort, control and coordination, information and contact, and competitive strategy and value theory.

Programming Marketing Activities. The allocation of marketing effort is the same as the selection of a program. Like any other economic activity marketing can be described in terms of inputs and outputs. The inputs are the marketing operations including selling, advertising, and sales promotion. The outputs are the projected sales of the company's products for the next operating period as set forth in a sales budget or a schedule of market forecasts.

Operational analysis has made headway in other phases of marketing than personal selling, advertising, or sales promotion. Requirements of the number and size of trucks for a delivery operation, for example, have been ascertained by balancing the cost of movement over the road against the cost of waiting time. Similarly, the principles of layout for display in retail stores are predicated on weighing the traffic generated by one product against its response to the pull of other products.

Much of the economic discussion centers on the optimum allocation of effort or resources. For this purpose the analytical tool favored by economists is marginal-productivity analysis. This means that resources should be used until the last dollar spent on each is equally productive. In marketing excellent results may be obtained in cases through use of this method in conjunction with multiple-correlation analysis.

Control and Coordination

Another sort of problem for the operations research analyst requires him to find an appropriate formula for optimizing marketing activities. He offers analytical help to management in minimizing costs, maximizing results, or identifying the best possible pattern of activities in a complex procedure. This phase of operational analysis is called control and communication theory. In one version it has been given the name *cybernetics* which freely translated means "steermanship." [14]

A central principle of control is called negative feedback. That is to say, when an operation penetrates areas beyond the region of control, information is fed back to management through appropriate channels so that corrective action may be instituted. Human systems of communication and control are no less vulnerable to distortion than mechanical systems. The message may be obscured by noise or interference. There is frequent danger of overloading the channel, or the channel may fail because it is not a closed circuit. Moreover, the feedback may produce overcompensation so that the system oscillates farther and farther out of control.

Coordinated Models. An elementary model of coordination consists of two participants whose actions are conditioned in some manner by a feedback of information on the respective actions of each other. The study of such models may be expanded step by step to encompass larger coordinated systems. The model has already been employed in studies of inventory problems. It may also be used in the coordination of any sequence of steps or in the balancing of production and selling activities. Once the parameters of control have been established through operations research, electronic devices and other means of facilitating coordination may be designed.

Organizational Improvement. Still another study of this kind is directed toward improving organizational structure so as to enable more effective coordination. One technique of operations research is the operational experiment. This sets up a probability model with a structure resembling an actual or potential situation which may be put through an operating cycle. In a waiting line of units to be serviced, for example, this makes possible simulation of the arrival of units on a random basis by pulling numbers from a random table. How well a standard of service can be maintained may thus be esti-

---

[14] Wroe Alderson, *Marketing Behavior and Executive Action,* Irwin, Homewood, Ill., 1957, p. 408.

mated. Because of the relatively low cost of obtaining data through
these so-called Monte Carlo methods, optional patterns of operation
can be solved on paper before any plan is put to a final test of action.

OR in Marketing [15]

In the following case history of an operations research project, we
may observe the method of organization, the definition of the problem, its solution, and the shortcomings of utilizing quantitative techniques exclusively.

The Sun Oil Company, which had been the only company to market
a single grade of gasoline, recognized that octane requirements for
automobiles were changing. It felt that future requirements would
be more variable than current ones. Hence the company assigned
an operations research team composed of social scientists, physical
scientists, and operating and administrative personnel to attack the
problem. After exploring various courses of action for the company
to pursue, the group decided to concentrate on a gasoline pump that
would be able to supply various grades of octane with the turn of
a dial. It then became necessary for company engineers to design
a suitable pump and the right concentrate for it. The next step involved development of refinery techniques to manufacture the concentrate.

Having solved these technical problems, the operations research
force turned its attention to how the motoring public would react to
an entirely new concept in gasoline retailing. Since this "custom
blending" system was so different from familiar retailing procedures,
the group decided it could evaluate consumer and competitive response
only through actual performance tests at service stations.

For two-and-a-half years the preliminary, pretest work was carried on in utmost secrecy. Only top management and the members
of the operations research team knew of the proposed change in marketing policy. Against the advantages of securing its plans from
competitors, however, the company faced two disadvantages. It lost
the help that might have been obtained from employees not on the
operations research team as well as from market information.

The first of these became evident when the new pump was demonstrated to members of the marketing staff. It was apparent to the
marketing officials that the pricing mechanism of the pump was not
sufficiently flexible to cope with all possible pricing situations. To

[15] James S. Cross, "Operations Research in Solving a Marketing Problem,"
Journal of Marketing, Vol. 25, No. 3, January 1961, pp. 3–34.

correct this deficiency the price computer was redesigned. However, it was the second disadvantage, the lack of knowledge of how the system would work in the market place, that persuaded the company to remove the cloak of secrecy and undertake a pilot test.

Sun Oil's southeastern region, embracing Florida and part of southern Georgia, was selected as the test site for dual reasons. First, it was an isolated area for the company; there was little advertising "spill over" from other Sun Oil marketing regions. Second, the resort character of the area would expose the new concept, Custom Blending, to a diverse group of motorists and thus obtain the reactions of consumers driving a wide range of automobiles.

The first phase of the experiment began in February 1956, in Orlando, Florida, and was extended to the rest of the region the following June. Competitive reactions were soon apparent. Within a short time competitors began offering three grades of gasoline. Others stepped up their second grades to "super premium" quality and price. Consumer reaction was highly favorable. Paired stations were pinpointed to permit comparisons with competitors' filling stations and also Sun's own stations *without* Custom Blending. By observing traffic through these paired stations, Sun found that Custom Blending increased both the volume of sales and the promotion of sales to high-priced, high-octane requirement autos at those stations possessing the new pumps.

Generalizations. This case study demonstrates an important difference between a purely mathematical operations research approach and one more concerned with a dynamic marketing situation. With a mathematical model experiments may be performed without altering the model or the environment it represents. However, when an experiment is performed on a system that operates in a social setting, both the system and the environment are usually responsive to outside influences, no matter how much care is exercised to keep the experiment pure.

In the case of Custom Blending two things happened. Competitors altered their marketing strategy, as we have noted. By selling three grades of gasoline they changed the rules of the game. In addition, they increased marketing pressure in advertising, promotion, and station building. Nevertheless, careful examination of very small markets showed that the effect of a changed environment could be discounted substantially.

Evaluation. The final task of the operations research team was to weigh each of the possible policies—Custom Blending, the two-grade system, and the three-grade system. It accomplished this task by constructing a model to evaluate the rate of return on investment for a fixed-sales volume for each policy. The problem was stated this way: consider three different courses to Sun's traditional single-grade fuel system—Custom Blending, the two-grade system, and the three-grade system. For each system at what point in sales volume would additional revenue equal additional costs? At what point would sales volume yield 10 per cent, 15 per cent, or 20 per cent on the investment before taxes?

Measurements were made on an incremental basis. That is, the costs, investments, and revenues for each system were compared with the dollar sales that would have been generated by Sun's traditional single-grade system as it would have operated in the year of experimentation. Only the incremental amounts were reported.

Detailed estimates of the capital requirements and operating costs for each of the systems were acquired and substituted in the model. The marketing and manufacturing assumptions were varied in order to determine the effects of different sets of operating conditions. For example, separate computations were made for a two-fuel system, one assuming a 3-cent differential and the other a 4-cent differential. Similarly, the expected results of a three-grade system were calculated with varying differentials for each grade. For Custom Blending, estimates of profitability were made for a range of octane-concentrate ratios.

The final report did not specify the best solution to the problem. Rather it presented management with the return on investment for each possible course of action. These returns covered a variety of sales volumes and sets of operating conditions. Management decided in favor of Custom Blending.

Final Considerations. During the work on the project, several pertinent operations research factors came to light. Some of those worth noting are the following:

1. It is not always possible to construct a mathematical model that represents the system under study.

2. At almost every point conflicts of interest arise among functional units of a system. These should not be suppressed, but rather balanced to achieve an optimum solution for the entire system.

3. It may not be possible to supply an optimum solution because one or more of the system's essential variables may not be susceptible to objective evaluation. Under these circumstances a plausible range of values may be postulated with possible values specified within this

framework. The decision maker may then exercise subjective judgment about the value most probably to effect a solution.

4. Provision must be made for possible changes that may emerge from experimentation in the market place.

5. The advantages and disadvantages of a high degree of security should be weighed thoroughly.

6. Final decisions should be made by management, not by the operations research team.

Electronic Data Processing

In 1955 the capital investment in electronic data-processing machines installed or to be delivered in the next two years exceeded $1 billion. This enormous investment became obsolete in most cases by 1960 and in its entirety by 1962. In consequence, a 20 per cent annual return on invested capital, or $200 million a year, was needed just to break even on obsolescence.[16] The value of computers sold or rented in 1957 totaled $350 million—four times as great as the figure for 1956 and ten times as great as the 1955 sum.[17] In 1960 the potential market for computers was 1200 units. By 1965, this was expected to reach 1500.

A computer is a person, or more generally a machine, capable of ingesting information—that is, problems and data—performing reasonable operations on the information, and producing answers. Reasonable operations are logical and mathematical. The computer is characterized by its memory which may consist of a magnetic core, drum, or disc. It takes information, operates on it, and does so reasonably, yielding logical solutions to problems.[18]

Most computers consist of an input system, an operation system, a control system, a storage unit, and an output unit. The input unit converts instructions into the language of the computer, but problems have already arisen over the rate at which computers can accept input information. The operation system is an arithmetic unit based on the binary system. Data appear on magnetic spots, the machine recognizing their presence or absence. It notes both states equally

---

[16] B. F. Butler, "Computers in Business and Industrial Systems," *Eastern Joint Computer Conference and Proceedings,* Nov. 7–9, 1955, Boston, Mass.

[17] "Brain Boom," *Wall Street Journal,* Aug. 15, 1957, p. 1.

[18] Edmund Callis Berkeley and Lawrence Wainwright, *Computers: Their Operation and Their Applications,* Reinhold, New York, Chapman and Hall, London, 1956, p. 3.

well. The arithmetic operations resulting from the computer are addition, subtraction, multiplication, division, the taking of square roots, and the like. It can also transact more advanced mathematical operations such as raising to a power, finding the derivative, and integrating. The control system supplies instructions to the machine. These may be logical operations which include comparing, selecting, sorting, matching, and determining the next instruction to be performed. The instructions may be wired into a specialized machine, or they may be programmed on a general-purpose machine. The storage unit is the computer's memory. The output represents the result of the operation.

Types of Computers. Computers fall into two types, digital and analog. The digital computer uses a series of separate and distinct digits, letters, characters, yesses and noes. Its output appears in exact numbers. A date stamp exemplifies this kind of computer.

The analog computer may be defined as a calculating machine which represents quantities through such things as a measurement along a scale, an angle of rotation, voltage, or a magnetic flue. The speedometer in an automobile symbolizes an analog computer. It tells how fast the automobile is moving. A thermometer is another example of an analog computer. Information in both of these relate to magnitude, divulged either by position or voltage.

Two schools of thought exist on the degree of specialization computers should have. One school believes in the specialized unit, the other in the general-purpose machine. Proponents of the specialized computer contend that it is more economical to acquire machines that perform special functions, such as accounting, billing, and the handling of inventory, than to employ a general computer.[19] The general-purpose machine, however, is more flexible. The choice of machine really depends on the work load and accessibility, for the problem is essentially one of a single general machine in a centralized location or many specialized machines in decentralized locations.

Installing a Computer. Prior to the purchase of a computer it behooves a company to conduct a feasibility study.[20] Mathematicians and programmers need not necessarily compose the study group. It

[19] Arguments for this point of view are advanced by Kenneth E. Iverson, "The Role of Special Purpose Equipment," *Proceedings of the Automatic Data Processing Conference,* Sept. 8–9, 1955, Division of Research, Graduate School of Business Administration, Harvard University, Boston, 1956, p. 97 ff.
[20] See Joseph Pelej, "A Practical Program of Study," *Electronics Data Processing in Industry,* American Management Association, Chicago, p. 551 ff.

has been found that it is easier for an individual who understands the complexities of management to be trained in computer technology rather than the other way around. In this respect a company's marketing department is a good source of potential computer expertise because of the number of its personnel trained in quantitative reasoning.

The study group must ask itself what kinds of problems can be solved by computers. It must consider the volume of work and where this work is processed, the exceptions to the routine, the need for rapid access, and the scheduling of the sequence of work. It may perhaps be even necessary to overhaul the whole system of record keeping so that data may be handled in a centralized location. This requires a systems study.[21] When its investigation has been completed, the study group should invite the various manufacturers of electronic data-processing machinery to present their proposals for solving the problems faced by the group's employer.

What a Computer Can Do

The most common application of computer technique is to accounting and bookkeeping. Here the outputs of the computer are easily verified and the volume of the routine can profit from its speed. One company that has used computers for purposes other than pure accounting has been General Electric. At its plant in Appliance Park in Louisville, Kentucky, General Electric used its computer to gather marketing information on district sales and inventory reports.[22] Later, it kept information on weekly and monthly sales to dealers and industry. Short-term and long-term forecasting were also programmed on the computer which provided data on cyclical variations, monthly seasonal variations, and irregular or random variations. Finally, the computer was used to simulate the company's distribution system.

Other companies have had similarly favorable experiences with computers. Inland Steel wanted to set up differential equations covering the behavior of materials. The computer required some 3600 calculations. The computer accomplished the job in eight hours. Commonwealth Edison Company of Chicago has been using a computer for operations research to program the best possible method

---

[21] See Richard F. Neuschel, *Streamlining Business Procedures,* McGraw-Hill, New York, 1950.
[22] From talk given by J. T. Burges, *A Marketing Information System,* delivered to the Iowa Chapter of the American Marketing Association Seminar on Long-Range Planning, April 10, 1959.

for purchasing coal.   The machine evaluates the quality, sources, transportation costs, and prices of available coal to determine the quantities and kinds to be purchased and the power stations to which they should be delivered.   The company's savings have run into several thousands of dollars a year.

Sears, Roebuck and Company uses a computer for handling payroll, for market and sales information, and for comparing inventory performance of a group of sales departments in one area to similar groups in other areas.   Thus, the shoe department in Rhode Island can be compared to the shoe department in Texas.   Abbott Laboratories employs a computer to obtain weekly inventory reports on its pharmaceutical products.   The company planned to extend its computer activity to the control of branch inventories by speeding the turnover of stocks and deliveries to warehouses.

In Purchasing and Inventory Control.[23]   In the important areas of purchasing and inventory control, computers have been employed to determine the order quantity, the reorder point, lead time, and safety stock.   These machines are also able to write orders, follow up on open orders, check and verify invoices, and distribute material charges.

In Retailing.[24]   The demands of fashion may be met by anticipating changes at the start of the season through use of a computer program. The computer has been utilized to compare sales to inventory.   Markdowns of merchandise have been minimized by computer instructions, for it is timing that causes cost reductions.   The computer may also program a balanced assortment of merchandise; and for branches and chains it has solved problems of both assortment and merchandise handling.

In Life Insurance.[25]   In the vast complex of life insurance, the computer has been programmed to prepare involved policy proposals. This has freed salesmen to apportion more of their workaday time to personal selling effort.   The machine has taken over the drudgery and left the man unfettered to engage in the creative work of selling.

In Marketing and Advertising.[26]   Perhaps one of the largest consumers of computer technology is the A. C. Nielsen Company, which

[23] See Stuart F. Heinritz, *Purchasing Principles and Applications,* Prentice-Hall, Englewood Cliffs, N.J., 1959, pp 328–337.
[24] See Bernard W. Smith and Herman Radolf, "How Machines Improve Merchandising," *Journal of Retailing,* Vol. 35, No. 1, Spring 1959, pp. 45–50.
[25] Edwin P. Gunn, "Calculator Ends Salesmen's Headaches—Gives Them a New Sales Tool," *American Business,* March 1959, pp. 27–28.
[26] *Ibid.*

utilizes computers for recording inventory movements and radio and television listening habits. Other companies have been greatly influenced in marketing forecasts by the availability of computer technology. One popular computer approach to these trend analyses stems from a method developed by the United States Census Bureau. Through the method and appropriate computer facilities, a company may reduce weekly or monthly changes into the following basic components:

(a) *The basic sales trend for the product:* a fairly straight line showing the over-all, long-term rate of growth or decline in product sales.

(b) *The effects of economic cycles:* a gently curving line showing month-to-month or year-to-year influences of economic recessions and recoveries on the product's sales.

(c) *The effects of seasonal sales patterns:* a uniquely shaped sales line which repeats itself during each year for which sales are traced.

(d) *The effects of irregular occurrences:* a jagged line showing the fairly randomly distributed effects of strikes, floods, competitors' promotions, or other irregularly occurring impacts on product sales.[27]

Both the sales response model and the Markov process, which were described in the chapter on advertising, may be handled by computer. Using one of these methods, many sales organizations have estimated the potentialities of their sales territories. Such regional estimates may have been taken as a basis for salesmen's compensation plans, the planning of branch office locations, or other purposes. These regional budgetary allocations have been achieved through utilization of a computer which follows three basic steps:

(a) Past sales are correlated with a wide variety of marketing data for each region. General market data are largely available for this purpose from the Census Bureau, the annual *Sales Management Survey of Buying Power,* or from local authorities. These correlations usually reflect certain regional characteristics which relate closely to sales for any one product.

(b) Once the sales-related marketing factors are determined, their intercorrelations are studied and "beta weights" are assigned to reflect the relative importance of each factor as a determinant of sales.

---

[27] See R. L. McLaughlin, "The Use of Computers as an Aid to Forecasting," *Effective Marketing Coordination,* edited by G. L. Baker, Jr., American Marketing Association, Chicago, 1961, pp. 537–553; Julius Shiskin and Harry Eisenpress, "Seasonal Adjustments by Electronic Computer Methods," *Journal of the American Statistical Association,* December 1957, pp. 415–438.

(*c*) With the proper market factors isolated and weighted, a sales "par" is estimated for each region through use of the "beta weight" formula. Actual sales are then plotted against the sales "par" to find the "under par" regions which might be expected to profit from extra advertising weight.

The use of a system such as this presupposes that no unusual factors influence the sales potentiality of any one region. Moreover, the assumption that the below par areas will benefit from advertising bears further investigation.[28] Similarly, computers may be used for allocating advertising budgets on a seasonal scale. The analysis of seasonal variation has proved valuable in this respect, especially when the information supplied by the computer is coupled with computer estimates of the lead time necessary for various types of advertising to take effect.

The computer, besides, has often played its role in reducing the guesswork involved in determining the consumer groups at which advertising should be aimed. It helps to define the audience profile in terms of assumptions about the importance of delivering advertising messages to opinion leaders for some products and to opinion followers for others. It aids in distinguishing heavy buyers from light buyers, former buyers or users (if these may be different people) from present buyers or users. It identifies the significant groups and describes them with refined tabulations, and it cross-tabulates product familiarity, trial, use, and frequency of use with age, sex, income, and other demographic data.

Having been used to profile the audience, the computer may also be drawn into selection of media. Here there are two approaches. In one, the computer is used to choose media through *linear programming,* and we saw how this was accomplished earlier in the chapter under the heading of the "deterministic model." The alternative approach for deciding media involves *simulation.* In this approach, whose main proponent is the Simulmatics Corporation, somewhat different information is stored in the computer at the start of the process. The storage unit in this case contains descriptions of hundreds of hypothetical consumers who fit the standard demographic characteristics. Each of these mythical individuals is also described according to postulated habits of magazine reading, television watching, radio listening, and so forth. These people might also be described in terms of ownership, purchase, or usage habits in relation

---

[28] Jay M. Gould, "The Science of Setting Sales Quotas," *Sales Management Survey of Buying Power,* May 1957, pp. 44–51.

to the advertised product. Together these spurious consumers are considered a representative sample of all members of the United States' consuming public.

With this information in the computer, a tentative media plan developed in the conventional manner is fed into the machine. This input characterizes the tentative plan as so many units of one cost and type in one vehicle and so many in another. The output estimates the reach and frequency of the advertising exposures which will result from the media plan, broken down by various consumer types. A typical media-mix report of the Simulmatics Corporation will contain as many as 100 tables which clients contend bear on their questions.

Use of this approach requires essentially the same kind of assumptions demanded by the linear-programming method. The advertiser must have faith in the reliability and relevance of the innumerable estimates and pieces of information either stored in the computer or fed into it. If the answer supplied by the computer is not favorable enough, he can continuously vary the inputs until he achieves a satisfactory result.

The computer even has a role in the selection of advertising themes. At the outset, it is provided with a set of numerical instructions for making the necessary calculation. These instructions, often put into the machine in the form of magnetic tapes, are usually called *multiple-regression-analysis programs* in studies of this kind. With the program in the machine, data on consumer attitudes toward the product are fed into it together with data for some criterion. One criterion used was in the form of information on the known usage and non-usage of the advertised brand and on consumer statements of whether they would or would not buy the brand the next time. The computer output estimates the relationship between each consumer attitude and the criterion. It further estimates the relation of each consumer attitude to every other attitude studied. Thus, the advertiser receives from it some guidelines on:

Which attitudes suggest different selling themes. (For example, do attitudes about high price and low price go together as might be expected? Or does high priced mean expensive, whereas low priced means low quality?)

Which attitudes cluster together in the consumer's mind to suggest single selling themes. (Does quality equal durability, for instance, or are modern design and quality synonymous?)

Which themes relate to apparent interest in buying the product.

(Do individuals who buy or express an interest in buying have different attitudes from other consumers toward product durability and services facilities?)

Which themes show promise as "reason why" supports. (That is, which themes correlate with the attitudes that separate interested from noninterested consumers, even though they may not discriminate between these consumer types?)

Finally, which themes show the greatest relative degree of correlation with purchase or interest in purchase.

This sort of information permits an advertiser to rank themes according to value if he can assume that the correlation between attitude and purchase reflects the extent to which the former leads to the latter rather than vice versa; that no attitude or group of attitudes is underestimated because of faulty attitude scales; that each theme can be rendered satisfactorily in advertisements; that no theme leads to an illegal or invalid advertising claim; and that no important theme is omitted in the input of attitude data. Needless to say, these assumptions do not hold invariably for all attitudes studied or all themes suggested by the computer.

Additionally, the computer has been used to help determine the best manner to *render* advertising themes. In this respect, it analyzes the data obtained in advertising research laboratories. The process begins, as in other instances, with the storage of appropriate data in the machine. The inputs consist of numerical descriptions of various advertisements on the basis of how they have been executed. In a recent study conducted jointly by the DuPont company, the Advertising Research Foundation, and the H. R. B. Singer Company, these descriptions covered by codes the size, use of color, amount of illustration, and other physical characteristics of various advertisements. Moreover, some estimate of the advertisement's effectiveness must be fed into the computer, whether this take the form of laboratory measures of the advertisement's visual dominance or readership scores obtained after publication.

From such studies, an advertiser obtains an estimate of the relative influences of different creative approaches. A number of advertisements have been devised on the basis of such studies which suggest the optimum weight for such factors as picture size, color use, and headline length. These ads resulting from formulas have scored well when evaluated by the same standards of effectiveness as used in the development of the formula. One must assume, of course, that the measures of advertising effectiveness employed in the study are valid

—that the highest possible visual dominance or readership score is worthwhile and important. One must also assume that the creative characteristics are aptly described by the "input number system."

Computers have been used, furthermore, for helping to pretest finished or semifinished advertisements before their insertion into media. Here the role of the computer is either to assist in analysis of data or in the development of research that leads to standardizing pretest methods. Nevertheless, this pretest work may be done equally well without a computer.

Computers have not been used very often for posttests of advertising. And when they have been utilized for studying the impact of campaigns already completed, their results have not been impressive. Yet their employment in posttesting activities enables refinements of experimental test-market methods which would not have been considered without the availability of the machine. This was the case in a Department of Agriculture study of various promotional themes for apples grown in the state of Washington. For such studies the program stores in the computer instructions for analysis of variance or covariance procedures. The Department of Agriculture used both analyses plus multiple-regression analysis. Studies of this sort are usually elaborately designed and controlled, using different advertising weights, different themes, or different media-mix patterns in various test markets. In each test market sales are measured very carefully.

The computer inputs consist of sales data identified by the market from which they come. These identifications are made in terms of the type, weight, or both, of advertising in the market for the sales period covered, the type, amount, or both, of other sales promotional efforts on behalf of the product in the same market during the period, and sales figures for related or competing brands or products in the same market for the period. This information makes it possible to classify the effects of various factors—to see how they vary with sales of the advertised product and covary with advertising and sales of the product.

Thus, depending on the specific considerations of any single study, the computer output provides estimates of the following factors: the relative influence on sales of advertising compared with no advertising; the influence of one campaign over another, in which differences arise from various media combinations or campaign themes; the impact of varying amounts or types of advertising on the product's brand share; the effect of advertising in comparison with other sales influences such as instore promotions or display space for the product; and the relative "carry over" effects of different campaigns —that is, whether the campaign's sales influence lasts or fades rapidly.

Studies of this kind offer very great promise for the solving of advertising problems on a long-term basis. They avoid many of the pitfalls of the usual other-things-being-equal assumption made by advertisers in tackling their problems. But even these studies which have such elaborate controls and methods for "partialing out," or taking account of, nonadvertising influences require certain assumptions; they must not be taken at face value. Assumptions must be made that the sales data are influenced only by the amount, type, or both, of the advertising used, or by factors which exert self-canceling influences on sales attributed to varying amounts or types of advertising, or by factors remaining constant in the experiment, or by factors "partialed out" in the analysis. The assumption must also be made that the statistical method itself imposes no bias. In these procedures statisticians sometimes encounter what they deem a "confounding problem." This occurs when one sales influence is so inextricably linked with another that it becomes difficult to know which is the most important.

The very nature of things may be changed by attempts to measure them carefully. For example, assumptions may dictate that in studying the effects of advertising on apples one must make certain that the sales of apples are not hampered by some stores running out of stock during the test. Thus, sales personnel are assigned to maintain the displays properly. This, however, introduces artificiality; apple displays are not ordinarily maintained so meticulously. One final assumption is therefore required: an assumption about the effect of advertising on sales if displays are as fully maintained under normal as under study conditions.

What Computers Cannot Do

For routine, number-processing problems where results may be easily verified, computers have no peer; a company only needs enough work for them to make them pay their way. For the more complex problems, they offer the advantage of great computational speed and thereby allow the use of more intricate and precise analytical procedures than do adding machines and slide rules. Nevertheless, it is not true that a guess can become a hard fact simply by putting it into numerical form and running it through a computer. The computer requires facts if it is to provide a logical, plausible solution to the problem it is called on to consider. But this is not its only limitation.

Human Error. The computer operator is also a limiting factor. Although computers are supposed to provide speed and reduction of the chances of human error, they do, in fact, increase the likelihood of error. They make it possible to commit five times as many mistakes in half the time. For example, the first member of an operations research team, who might be a psychologist, might translate the advertising problem into a theory of how consumer behavior is influenced by advertising. A second member, who might be a mathematician, might translate this theory into a mathematical model—a formula of how the problem should work itself out if the psychologist were right about its basic nature. A third member, a computer programmer, converts the model into a computer program, a set of instructions for the machine in "computer language." Thus, all the pertinent facts about the problem are reduced to holes in a tape or on a punch card for processing by the mere pushing of a button. The computer then turns the mass of data into a complex pattern of electrical impulses and prints out an answer which is relayed to the advertiser after retranslation into language he can understand. The chance of human error lurks at every step in the process.

Too often each specialist on the operations research team is interested only in his own field of competence. The psychologist is concerned only with psychology, much like the advertising artist whose prime interest is in art for art's sake. He may not care about advertising as a marketing tool; to him it is only a device for testing psychological notions. The mathematician may be fascinated by the precision of his methods but neither aware of nor interested in the *reason* for solving the problem. Computer men are neither advertising nor marketing experts. Most of them have a lot to learn about advertising and marketing problems. As they learn, they will discover that computer methods good enough for inventory control are inadequate for setting advertising budgets. Until they master the requirements of these more complicated problems, they will continue to invite error.

Cautions. When computers are used for advertising, "the proof is in the eating" for the simplest or most routine applications. If the computer were used only to automate an old procedure, its results could be compared to those of the old procedure. But since the computer generates a new approach for the solving of problems, its output must be accepted or rejected by judgment as heretofore. It is no easier to prove that a media plan selected through linear programming is any better or worse than any other media plan.

Only the obvious errors can be observed easily. If a computer plan calls for 85 insertions a year in *Life* or 15 in *Reader's Digest* something is manifestly amiss. The model builder must be told to inform the computer programmer that *Life* publishes only 51 issues a year and *Reader's Digest* only a dozen. If judgment indicates that the media plan looks unrealistic from some other point of view, the model or the program must be changed again, adding and subtracting assumptions and biases to taste. But this must be done on the basis of judgment, on the basis of faith in one assumption in preference to another.

When working with computers, a company must not let the apparent purity of numbers obscure the weaknesses of the underlying assumptions. The assumptions must be brought into the open and compared with judgments that may or may not fit into a computer. And there is no reason to give computer technology the benefit of the doubt in these comparisons.

The Future of Operations Research

Operations research in one sense may be said to be the continuation of the scientific management movement into the area of business. Just as the scientific management movement found its most immediate application in the field of production, so has operations research. Yet some of the problems of operations research teams are common to manufacturing and marketing, whereas others are peculiar only to marketing.

Communication. One of the greatest problems facing operations research teams is communicating to management. This applies to production management as well as to marketing management. Frequently, as we have observed, the teams are composed of men who are well versed in the physical sciences but whose understanding of the social or business problems facing the company is scant. Some teams produce formulas that portend to solve problems when in reality they have only scratched the surface. Other teams endeavor to communicate in terms of formulas so sophisticated that they prove incomprehensible to management.

Nomographs. Following the development of the Dodge Romig tables [29] it became possible to achieve wide acceptance for quality control. Today a foreman with less than high-school education may

[29] E. L. Grant, *Statistical Quality Control*, McGraw-Hill, New York, 1946.

conduct quality-control tests and interpret their results through these tables. Similar tables may be constructed to fit other formulas. Another aid of comparable value is the nomograph. Through nomographs one may find a graphic solution to an equation, and they have already been developed for quantity purchasing and inventory control. Others may prefer to obtain the answers to equations from the charts. This, too, is a simplified method of interpreting the data contained in formulas.

The use of formulas through tables, nomographs, or charts should eliminate the necessity for middle management personnel to solve these equations. This liberates them to devise new formulas or revise old ones and also makes them available for more creative work at higher policy levels. Where the company has a computer, tables, nomographs, and charts are really unnecessary; the computer can produce the answers required. Frequently, however, it is valuable to supplement the machine with these other devices, especially when there is a premium on computer time. In sum, these aids may be useful to both large and small companies.

Paucity of Theory. Another problem in the application of operations research to marketing is the scantiness of analytical theory. Marketing has reached the stage at which there is a willingness to submit its problems to analytical solutions although concern remains over the descriptive aspects. Solution of these problems calls for a comprehensive theory of marketing. Suggestions for such a theory will be found in Chapter 11.

Many leaders in marketing management do not possess the sophisticated mathematical background necessary to handle several of the problems that would be classified as operations research. This results in part from their lack of education and experience in analytic areas. Many marketing problems still defy analysis. Intelligent judgment and intuition remain the only means for making decisions in many phases of marketing.

Actually, even the best use of analytical techniques does not guarantee the unqualified success of a marketing project. This has been seen in the case of the Edsel. Despite employment of excellent tools to develop and sell the product, it proved a dismal failure. In contrast, there are many success stories in the food and drug industries where scientific procedures have been followed. In the views of many, marketing remains more in the realm of art than of science.

Routinization. One reason for the rapid application of scientific method to production has been the constant effort toward greater routinization. There are also some areas in marketing in which routinization has progressed rapidly. Physical distribution is one. Yet one may truly question the desirability of too much routinization in the total marketing process. Marketing has a long way to go, for example, before it can routinize the methods of selling women's hats. It must, moreover, be cautious of creating too much routinization at the consuming level, for this would tend to violate individual freedom of choice and fashion a nation of stereotypes.

One more problem remains: quantifying many of the variables in marketing. How should one measure the satisfaction obtained from the purchase of a product or a service? What is the exact influence of a particular advertisement on an individual's purchase? How does one square verbal acceptance of a product with its actual purchase? How is sales resistance measured? Operations research and electronic data processing certainly have their places in the management of marketing, as we have seen in this chapter, but it is clear that problems of this kind as well as many others defy quantification and instead require intelligent judgment by management for the correct making of decisions.

Summary

Although there is no generally accepted definition of operations research, there seems to be agreement that specialists are involved in a group effort to solve problems. Operations research attempts to simplify reality by the creation of models. There are three types of models: deterministic, stochastic, and game models.

An example of a deterministic model would be linear programming. Stochastic models involve the application of the principle of probability. Examples of stochastic models that may be used in marketing are those used for promotional effort, queueing models, and decision-making models. Game theoretic models may be used where one is dealing with opponents.

The application of operations research techniques in marketing may help to reduce uncertainty and assist in the programming of marketing activities. Operations research is useful in the control and coordination of marketing systems. Operations research techniques were used in a Custom Blending experiment of the Sun Oil Company. This study points out the values and limitations of quantitative analysis.

Computers are being used for many of the models created through operations research. A computer is organized with an input system, operation system, control system, storage, and output. There are two types of computers: digital and analog.

In installing a computer it is important that a feasibility study be made. Computers have been able to solve many problems of a routine nature in business. It is only recently that they have been used in the broad areas of unprogrammed decisions. Some examples of computer use are in purchasing and inventory control, retailing, and life insurance. In the broad area of marketing and advertising the computer has been used for forecasting, establishing advertising budgets, determination of a media plan, selection of advertising themes, executing advertising, and measuring effectiveness of advertising.

Computers do not make facts out of numerical guesses. Computers increase the chance for human error. Computer experts are accustomed to simpler problems. It is difficult to prove the computer method of solving the problem superior to other methods. The computer results are only as good as the assumptions that are made.

Operations research is just a continuation of the scientific management movement. One of the problems of operations research is to communicate the results in a form understandable to management.

One technique that may speed up the use of the formulas developed through model building is the use of nomographs. More basic theory in marketing is needed if operations research is to contribute to model building in the future.

Scientific techniques today are not adequate enough to solve existing marketing problems. Scientific method is more appropriate where marketing activity is amenable to greater routinization. There is still the problem of quantifying many of the variables used in marketing so that they may be tied into formulas.

Suggested Cases

Intercollegiate Case Clearing House, Soldiers Field, Boston 63, Massachusetts.
    ICH 3M38—Rayco Manufacturing Company, Inc.
    ICH 2C2—Bay State of Races Product Company.

Appendix

Queueing Theory

The *poisson* approach holds that units arrive and servicing takes place at a random rate of time. If the mean arrival time is greater than the mean service time the waiting line will increase indefinitely. Waiting lines are not abolished unless both arrivals and service operation are regularized and not random. A central problem of waiting-line theory is the relationship between the mean length of the waiting line and degree of randomness of arrival and disposal. One may determine the optimum waiting time against the increased cost of servicing.

The chance of a waiting line of length n for a single service station may be expressed as:

$$P_n = \left(\frac{A}{S}\right)^n \left(1 - \frac{A}{S}\right) \quad \text{if } \frac{A}{S} < 1$$

P_n = probability of having n units in the waiting line

n = number of units in waiting line

A = mean arrival time

S = mean service rate (assumed larger than A)

$\dfrac{A}{S}$ = traffic intensity

The probability of two in a waiting line with a mean arrival rate of 5 minutes and a mean service time of 10 minutes would be:

$$P_2 = \left(\frac{5}{10}\right)^2 \left(1 - \frac{5}{10}\right)$$

$$P_2 = .125$$

This means that about 12½ per cent of the time one might expect two individuals to be waiting in a line with a mean arrival of 5 minutes and a mean service rate of 10 minutes.

Using the same mean arrival and servicing times, the probability of three in the waiting line would be 6.2 per cent. Continuing on to higher numbers in the line we steadily reduce the probabilities of those in the waiting line to a mean arrival of 5 and a service rate of 10. If we were to decrease the servicing time or increase the rate of arrival the probability would decrease as long as the other variables remained constant. For example, if the mean arrival time is one and servicing time is 10 minutes, the probability of a waiting line of two is .9 per cent. Thus, as the ratio of arrival time to service time comes close to one the probability of a waiting line decreases. Therefore, increasing the service facility decreases the waiting time more rapidly.

The mean length of the waiting line is [1]

$$M = \frac{A/S}{1 - (A/S)} \quad \text{where } \frac{A}{S} < 1$$

[1] See C. West Churchman, Russell L. Ackoff, and E. Leonard Arnoff, *Introduction to Operations Research*, Wiley, New York, 1957. See p. 397 for derivation of formula.

We may expect the following queue lengths with the following traffic intensities:

With traffic intensity	A/S	½	¾	⅞	¹⁵⁄₁₆
Expected queue length	n	1	3	7	15

Linear Programming

Let us assume that a company wishes to know the number of units of product X and product Y to be sold given certain conditions. The company knows that it earns a certain profit on product X and a certain profit on product Y. Thus, if it makes \$9 per unit on product X and \$7 per unit for product Y, we may state this in the form of an equation.

$$(1.1) \quad 9X + 7Y = Z$$

This equation states that \$9 times the number of units of X to be sold plus \$7 times the number of units of Y to be sold equals the profit to be maximized. In linear programming this is called the *objective function*. Since a company cannot sell negative quantities of X and Y, we may state this as follows:

$$(1.2) \quad X \geqq 0, \; Y \geqq 0$$

These two inequations state that the amounts of X and Y that can be sold may be equal to or greater than zero. This is one *restriction* in our problem.

The company has a certain amount of warehouse space to take care of its sales operations. The amount of sales that a warehouse can handle is restricted by its capacity. The company also has a certain amount of time that a salesman needs to sell product X and product Y. The amount of X and Y that may be sold is limited by the amount of selling time the salesman has. The company also knows how much it wishes to spend on advertising product X and product Y. The amount spent on advertising, however, cannot exceed the total budget for advertising. Warehousing, space, selling time, and advertising dollars are our *activities* or processes. Each of these activities are restricted by space, time, and dollars to be allocated. We shall assume that there is a linear function in the use of space, time, and advertising dollars. Thus, a doubling of sales of products X and Y will cause a proportionate increase in the utilization of space, time, and dollars.

In the case of warehousing for every unit of X sold 10 feet of warehousing space is needed. The 10 is usually called a *coefficient* or process vector. Product Y needs 5 feet of warehousing space. The total amount of warehousing space available is 50 feet. We may now state this in the form of an inequation:

$$(1.3) \quad 10X + 5Y \leqq 50$$

This inequation states that 10 times the amount of X to be sold plus 5 times the amount of Y to be sold may be less than or equal to the 50 feet of warehousing space available.

Salesmen need six hours to sell product X and six hours to sell product Y. However, they do not work over 36 hours per week. We obtain the following inequation:

$$(1.4) \quad 6X + 6Y \leqq 36$$

This inequation states that six times the amount of X to be sold plus six times the amount of Y to be sold may be less than or equal to the total time available to salesmen—36 hours.

From previous sales tests we know that we must spend $4.50 of advertising to sell one unit of product X and $18 of advertising to sell one unit of Y. The total amount that we may spend on advertising may be equal to but not exceed the budget for advertising, which is $81:

$$(1.5) \quad 4.5X + 18Y \leqq 81$$

This inequation states that the $4.50 to be spent on product X plus the $18 to be spent on product Y may be equal to or less than the total budget for advertising, $81.

Any solution which will take into consideration all the foregoing restrictions would be called a *feasible* program. We are concerned with *maximization* or an optimum program.

Geometric Solution

All of our activities of warehousing, sales time, and advertising may be stated as linear equations with equalities. This is possible because we state that our answer may be equal to or less than a certain boundary which is the equality. Thus, inequation 1.3 may be stated as:

$$(1.6) \quad 10X + 5Y = 50$$

Let us plot this line. First let us have X equal to zero. This would make Y equal to 10. Next let us make Y equal to a zero, which would make X equal to 5. We may plot this in Figure A-1. All other values of X and Y will fall on line AB. Since inequation 1.3 states that our solution may be equal to or less than 50, the answer may lie on line AB. However, inequality 1.2 tells us that both X and Y must be greater than zero. This means that our solution must lie at the boundaries or within triangle ABC.

We now proceed to inequation 1.4 and make an equation of it:

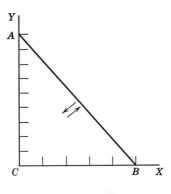

$$(1.7) \quad 6X + 6Y = 36$$

We proceed in the same manner as for equation 1.6 and obtain the second line on Figure A-2. Line DE is formed by this equation. Any point on this line will satisfy this equation. From our inequation we note that our answer cannot be greater than line DE (that is to the right). Therefore,

Figure A-1

the answer may not lie above line segment DF. However, our inequation for line AB states that our answer cannot be to the right of this line. Therefore, the answer may not be to the right of line segment FB. We have already stated that our answer must be greater than zero. Therefore, our answer may lie on the boundaries or within polygon $CDFB$.

We now make an equation of inequation 1.5.

$$(1.8) \quad 4.5X + 18Y = 81$$

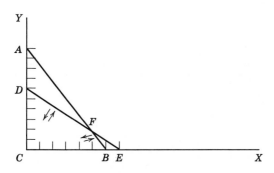

Figure A-2

We plot this equation as we have the others on Figure A-3. The line formed by this equation is HI. We see from this restriction that the answer must lie on the boundary or within polygon $CHGFB$.

In Figure A-4 we shall experiment to determine where we may have the greatest profit. Our profit is stated by equation 1.1: $9X + 7Y = Z$. One may experiment by substituting values for X and Y to see which combination of values will give the maximum profit. One could also select a maximum profit figure and manipulate the values of X and Y to fit it. However, when this is done the values for X and Y must be on the line or within the space described by the convex polygon. Otherwise the values exceed the restrictions placed on them. Let us first try a line within the polygon formed by $X = 2$, $Y = 3$.

$$(1.9) \quad (9)(2) + (7)(3) = 39$$

Let us now plot the equation $9X + 7Y = 39$. When X equals zero Y equals $5\frac{4}{7}$. When Y equals zero, X equals $4\frac{1}{3}$. This is shown by line I on Figure A-4. This is a feasible solution. Let us see if we can improve the profit. We shall allow zero units of X and 4.5 units of Y. This gives us the following equation:

$$(1.10) \quad (9)(0) + (7)(4.5) = 31.5$$

This equation is shown by line II. It does not give as much profit as 1.8.

Let us substitute 4 units of X and 2 units of Y. This gives the equation:

$$(1.11) \quad (9)(4) + (7)(2) = 50$$

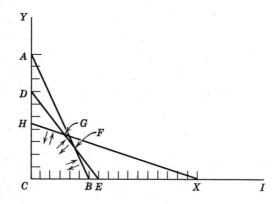

Figure A-3

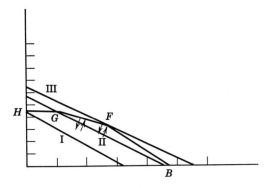

Figure A-4

We call this line III. This line gives the maximum profit. It is tangent to the polygon at point *F*. One of the rules of linear programming is that the maximum or minimum of the objective function is to be found at the corner point of a convex polygon.[2] We may proceed to develop a line to the right of line III. This line, however, would not satisfy the restrictions in our problems.

Changing Restrictions

It is possible to have a different maximum when we change the restrictions in our problem. Suppose we allocate more funds for advertising, what would happen to the amount of profit that we may earn? Let us assume that all the other restrictions remain the same, but that we double the allocation for advertising. The advertising formula now becomes:

$$(2.1) \quad 4.5X + 18Y = 162$$

Figure A-5 shows the new polygon *ABCD*. Checking the corners of the polygon we find that the most profitable combination is at point *B*, with 3.75 units of *Y* and 3.5 units of *X* at a profit of $57.75.

We may ask ourselves if the additional $7.75 more profit justifies the additional advertising expenditure of $81. If we are not satisfied we may want to increase some other restrictions. For example, we may decide to build a new warehouse, thus increasing available warehouse space. We may also add manpower to the sales force, thus

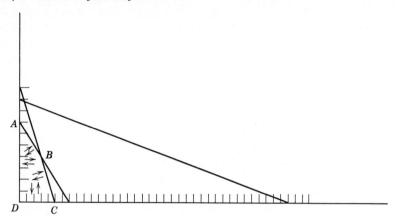

Figure A-5

increasing the available time to sell. We may do this as long as the relationships are linear.

Many linear programming problems have more than two choice variables. In this case we may not use the same two-dimensional space illustrated in our graphs. We may get three-, four-, or even one-hundred-dimensional space. This is very difficult to visualize and impossible to plot.

Chapter Ten

"No man is an island entirely of itself," the poet has written, and no phase of human activity may be truly said to stand alone. In an orbit so complex as modern society every movement is connected to a score of others with even the flick of an eyelash likely to set other events in motion. This is a world of components, all contributing to the whole, each thoroughly enmeshed with many others, each dependent on its related brethren, which, in turn, depend on it. What

The Role of the Behavioral Sciences

is said of the animate is equally valid for the inanimate; the forces of business cannot thrive alone. They flourish in mutual reliance on one another and on forces presumably beyond the borders of the business community.

Because of this, the management of a marketing program requires all the help other resources can supply to render the best possible decisions on the problems confronting it. One rich storehouse is the academic disciplines called the behavioral sciences. These contain a vast collection of generalizations and descriptive data of distinct relevance to the marketing situation. In many instances behavioral scientists have immersed themselves in marketing problems. In many more they have shunned the requests for their help. As a matter of fact, they have disdained the whole field of marketing and looked on the discipline with snobbish contempt. For this reason those desirous of developing a science of marketing and improving the effectiveness of the marketing task must largely undertake their own investigations into the achievements of the behaviorist to extract the practical applications of his theoretical constructs.

Most aspects of marketing management need the findings of the behavioral sciences. For example, the behavioral sciences may help encourage heightened effort among marketing department personnel. They are useful in making decisions on the marketing mix. Pricing, to cite an instance, is not only a quantitative matter, it is also a part of the total image the consumer forms of the product itself. To determine the nature of this image and generalize it to a concept of utility, the marketing manager must avail himself of the tools of the behavioral sciences. Perhaps the circumstances surrounding the decision to purchase constitute one of the most crucial areas of marketing. If marketing management has more exact information on this topic, it is better able to market its products effectively.

What will it take to persuade the consumer to buy the marketing manager's product? What do consumers infer from a company's advertisements? What do the advertisements mean to them? Are these the same meanings the advertiser seeks to convey? Here, too, the behavioral sciences supply enlightenment on the techniques of effective communication. Probably one of the great challenges of marketing is discovering the latent needs of the consumer so that products may be created to satisfy these needs. Discovering these needs requires some rather special tools of the behavioral sciences. In the course of this chapter we shall discuss the importance of the behavioral sciences in dealing with the consumer. We shall cite recent examples of applying these sciences to marketing problems and shall present some generalizations from them that may have relevance to marketing management.

Importance of Behavioral Sciences in Marketing

The behavioral sciences deal with the individual in isolation and in groups. The academic disciplines forming this group of sciences include anthropology, economics, geography, history, jurisprudence, political science, psychology, social psychology, and sociology. We shall limit ourselves in this chapter to the contributions to marketing of only four of these: anthropology, psychology, social psychology, and sociology.

Marketing is a phenomenon of group behavior.[1] The market analyst formulates most of his problems in terms of group behavior. The actual activity of marketing consists of the exchange taking place between consuming groups over an interval of time. These groups are really temporary associations for the negotiation of major transactions. The groups must be recognized as organized behavior systems.

In addition to these groups which are marked by a consciousness of membership, there are interactive groups in which individuals are bound together by function in the performance of a task, even though they have no awareness of group membership. A "trade channel" exemplifies such a group. The channel may exist only in the mind of the manufacturer who is using it to reach the consumer. The companies constituting a trading center also exemplify an interactive marketing group. In addition, there is a loosely bound entity like the national market for a specific class of products.

This functional concept includes both groups and organized behavior systems. A system is a set of elements tending toward some point of balance or equilibrium. Included in it are the instruments

---

[1] Wroe Alderson, *Marketing Behavior and Executive Action*, Irwin, Homewood, Ill., 1957, p. 13.

and resources involved in its operation. An organized behavior system consists of a group and the environment in which it moves and has its existence.

Individual and Group. A group may be defined as two or more individuals whose common thread is the expectation of something positive to emerge from their association. On becoming a member of a group each individual assumes a role. Thus, he has expectations within the group and the other members of the group have expectations of him. Within any group each member strives for status. An individual, for example, may seek status within the sales department of a company. The department may be endeavoring to realize its full opportunity within the company. And the company, in turn, may be functioning as a component of a system of production and distribution, supplying consumers with a certain class of product. The system that coordinates groups in an established pattern of behavior may be called an *ecological system*. Since marketing involves the activities of organized behavior systems, the behavioral sciences play an important part in every phase of the process.

The Consumer and the Behavioral Sciences

The goal of all productive activity is consumption. But how does this consumption occur? What are the forces affecting it? May a company and its consumers communicate with each other on this matter, and how do both do so? What are the unknown factors in consumer behavior? If a consumer indicates a reason for the purchase of an item, is this reason bonafide? Which tools of the behavioral sciences best help management to answer these questions and make shrewder decisions? This section will attempt to consider some of these problems.

The Choice Problem

Classical economic theory preached that consumer choice was rational. It held that the consumer was so well informed that he was able to evaluate the possibilities and make a choice that provided maximum utility. This theory might have served in a frictionless, atomistic society. For our civilization, however, both the premises of rationality and full information must be modified.

The psychologist says that the reason an individual purchases an item is to satisfy some need or combination of needs. These needs create tensions which are relieved by the purchase. One list of needs includes the following: [2]

A. Physiological tension—hunger—thirst—sex
B. Social:
    1. Affectional needs—harmonious relations with others
    2. Ego bolstering needs—gain prestige—domination
    3. Ego defensive needs—protect personality—avoid ridicule
    4. Gregariousness
    5. Dependency

Learning and Cognition. Most individuals are moved by more than one need. When they are moved by something such as a need we say that they are motivated. In addition to a list of needs as the basis for motivation, individuals require cognition and learning. Cognition is a mental faculty, consisting of perception, memory, judging, and thinking. Learning is the change in behavior occasioned by external stimuli. Identical behavior does not imply identical motivation.

Judging a brand is an example of cognition. Through memory there is awareness of brand differentiation. This is composed of signs or symbols. These signs have certain expectancies, such as color of ranges, spots, color packages, and the like. Different objects have different expectancies depending on the strength of the needs. There may be differences in products and gradients in generalizations. Instrumental costs, for example, such as going downtown or squeezing oranges may have positive or negative values.

Learning takes place when the original need is gratified through attainment of what psychologists call the *goal object.* When attainment produces gratification, reinforcement occurs. As the same behavior is repeated through reinforcement, learning eventuates. With continued reinforcement comes less need for decision making. The making of decisions becomes automatic, habitual.

Group Influence on Personal Behavior. Social psychologists point out the effect of the group on an individual's behavior. Customs and traditions in this respect play an important part in the government of behavior. For instance, in New York City housewives are positive that white eggs are better than brown eggs. In Boston, on the other hand, they are equally certain that the brown egg is superior. Thus, it is evident that the consumer does not make a purchase on the basis

[2] James A. Bayton, "Motivation, Recognition Learning—Basic Factors in Consumer Behavior," *Journal of Marketing,* Vol. 2, No. 3, January 1958, p. 282.

of maximized utility. The conditioning factors are his needs, the group, and the culture in which he lives.

Through advertising the consumer is informed of some of the available choices. Some advertising may be misleading, however. Then again the consumer may not see all the advertisements, or if the product is not advertised he may not know all the prices and qualities available. We may assume, of course, that he acts in an "intendedly" rational manner. Although he may not maximize the utility of his purchase, he may be satisfied with less than full utility. This depends on his personality, surrounding group influences, and the cultural setting.

Recent Applications of Behavioral Sciences to Marketing

In the past several years the behavioral sciences have been applied in wide measure to motivation research and the closely related areas of scaling, imagery, use and purchase decisions, family members' influence on buying decisions, family life-cycle impact, behavior research and market experimentation, use of social class, and vector analysis. Of these phenomena, motivation research has attracted the most public attention.

Motivation Research

Motivation research is not an area. It is not another field of research like copy, media, or market research. It is *another frame of reference* for the investigation of the same problems traditionally studied by these other areas.[3] It provides information which complements and extends their findings. It does not eliminate or replace these other areas or their activities. Motivation research is not primarily distinguished by the problems it investigates. Neither is it distinguished by its techniques of data collection nor by the quantitative or qualitative nature of the results it reports. It is characterized expressly by the frame of reference it uses in thinking about man's mind.

The motivation researcher starts with a problem. His first step is the development of a theory [4]—that is, a tentative or assumed explana-

---

[3] M. J. Helfgett, Director of Research, Ogilvy, Benson, and Mather, Inc., "How to Develop a Motivation Research Project," American Management Association, Luncheon, New York, Oct. 10, 1955, mimeographed.

[4] The term *theory* as used here is synonymous with *hypothesis*.

tion of the problem. The concepts that may be useful in the development of a theory are those developed through the social sciences. The most useful ones are those that relate to the specific problem. There is no intrinsic superiority of one scientific concept to another. Each is an available tool for thinking, and there is an open choice of them. Despite the lack of intrinsic superiority of any single concept, dynamic personality models have been the most fruitful.

Uses. The recent change-over in the style of Chrysler products was partly the result of a motivation study conducted some years ago. Socony Vacuum Oil Company changed its name to Socony Mobil Oil Company only after it spent $5000 to test customers' reactions to the proposed change and found the results satisfying. Philip Morris Ltd. undertook extensive psychological studies on consumer reaction to color combinations and masculine versus feminine associations in cigarettes before proceeding with a massive two-year project that produced its new Marlboro and the red, white, and gold Philip Morris package.

One manufacturer of luggage advertised that its new fiberglass suitcases could survive even a drop from an airplane. When motivation research showed that its advertising evoked unpleasant thoughts of plane crashes instead of a desire for its products among prospective purchasers, it promptly changed its tack. Perplexed because its cameras were losing out to lower-quality competitors even when price was not a factor, Bell and Howell learned that the average weekend cameraman was basically afraid that its model looked too professional or contained too many gadgets. In consequence, the company designed a simplified, more marketable unit. The Corning Glass Works discovered that the reluctance of industrial customers to use its Pyrex glass piping resulted from deeply ingrained feelings about the fragility of glass even though the customers knew that Pyrex piping would not break. The company attacked the fear head-on in an advertising campaign and promptly boosted sales.

The Institute of Motivational Research convinced General Mills that cooking was not just a chore to most housewives but an important symbol of their status in the family and an outlet for creativeness. As a result the company began telling the housewife what she and Bisquick could do together instead of what Bisquick could do for her. Moreover, it modified some of its prepared cake mixes so that the housewife had to add an egg making her feel more creative.

A number of coffee drinkers resented the attacks of Sanka's producers on the sleep-destroying evils of ordinary coffee. They considered it an insult to their favorite beverage. Hence, the company switched to another theme. "Now you can drink all the coffee you want," its new slogan read.

The sales gains in the prune and tea industries may be attributed in part to motivation research. These industries were advised that consumers associated their products with sickness and weakliness, and were persuaded to stress the vigor and masculinity of these foods. And one motivation research company uncovered 13 reasons why people smoke. These included that smoking is a "satisfying ritual," that it signifies "conformity," and that it is "proof of daring." [5]

Tools. Several types of tools are used in motivation research, among them seven types of projective techniques: Rorschach tests, thematic apperception tests, picture frustration, word association, sentence completion, using third person, and house-tree-person (HTP) tests. We shall examine each of these briefly.

1. RORSCHACH TEST. One group of tools used in motivation research stems from the theories evolved by Sigmund Freud. Freud observed that an individual inclined to see the world as he wished to see it rather than as it actually was. Thus, a person projected his personality and feelings in interpreting the real world around him. The indirect technique used to study a person's behavior is composed of projective devices. Rorschach applied the technique in the form of ink blots. He placed a drop of wet ink on a sheet of paper and folded the paper so that the ink formed a configuration. He then requested mental patients to relate what they saw in the blots. From their remarks Rorschach was able to classify their mental disturbances. Psychologists now dispute the utility of the Rorschach test. However, its basic idea has been developed into a thematic apperception test which has been employed in motivation research in order to sell products to normal consumers.

2. THEMATIC APPERCEPTION TEST. This test was originally devised to deal with mental patients. Such patients were shown a series of pictures and asked to tell a story about them. Their responses provided significant clues to their ailments. In motivation research, however, the normal consumer is generally shown a picture relating to a particular subject area. For example, one picture showed a man seated behind a steering wheel with the speedometer reading 70 miles per hour. The consumer was asked to explain what was happening: what the circumstances were which led to the situation and what the outcome might be. The replies indicated that individuals liked speed

[5] Above examples taken from *Newsweek,* Oct. 10, 1955, pp. 89–91.

but feared for their safety. Advertisers took heed of these feelings and sought to assure prospects for new cars that speed could be combined with built-in security.

3. PICTURE FRUSTRATION. Closely related to the thematic apperception test is the picture frustration test. This is a cartoon situation in which a balloon appears above the head of one of the characters in the cartoon. The individual being tested by this method may be asked to tell what the other characters in the cartoon are saying. In one cartoon, for example, a woman is talking to another in a living room and is commenting: "My Johnny likes to drink milk because 'Hoppy' says that it is good for him." Responses to this cartoon [6] indicated that some mothers would give their children anything as long as they drank their milk. Other responses maintained that mother was the boss in the house and would determine what the children would drink.

Picture techniques of any kind should be used with caution. The changing of any feature of a picture can alter the responses. Furthermore, faces should contain general features so that a person being tested can project himself into the situation. Although picture techniques may yield more information than open-end questions, they have to be validated statistically as in any other sample study.

4. WORD ASSOCIATION. In word association the consumer is told that he is about to be given a word and is to mention the first word it brings to mind. For example, if the given word is "black," the response might be "white." Some researchers like to obtain a second word or a third word associated with the original one. With this technique an interviewer must note the timing of the response. Unless it is virtually instant, say, within three seconds, the response its meaningless. Some blockage has prevented a true response, and this must be guarded against in the interest of obtaining valid results from the test.

5. SENTENCE COMPLETION. In this kind of test the person being tested is given an incomplete sentence and is asked to finish it. For example, "People smoke cigarettes because _____." Story completion is also used and it involves the same technique.

6. USING THIRD PERSON. Mason Haire used a different technique in a survey on instant coffee.[7] Consumers were given two grocery lists. One contained instant coffee and the other ground coffee; otherwise the lists were composed of identical items. Persons questioned were

[6] Study conducted by writer.

[7] Mason Haire, "Projective Techniques in Marketing Research," *Journal of Marketing,* Vol. 14, No. 5, April 1950, pp. 649–656.

asked to describe the type of individual using each list. From the replies, it was found that women who purchased instant coffee were thought to be lazy. This technique may be applied from somewhat different approaches. For example, consumers might be asked, "What do you think of a person who buys instant coffee?" Now the consumer is able to disclose his true attitude indirectly rather than directly. Either way, the third person is the key to the response.

7. HTP TEST. Still another technique is the house-tree-person test. An individual is instructed to draw a house, then a tree, and finally a person. This technique has been used among psychotic individuals and found to have been of value in discovering their personalities. A modification of this test has consisted of requesting an individual to draw a picture of an automatic washing machine and then a picture of a person who would use it.

All seven projective devices have limited value because of the difficulty of interpreting their findings. A good depth interview can elicit much of the same information without use of these devices. In field work, however, it is easier to teach a crew to use the devices than to interview consumers in depth. Generally, it takes a person trained in the behavioral sciences—that is, a social worker—to evince skill in depth interviewing. The skilled interviewer's method is to reach for the information sought through informal conversation on an uninstructed basis. Certain key words and phrases are used to penetrate the individual's mind—for example, "what do you mean?" and "tell me a little more."

Nose Counters Versus Head Shrinkers.[8] The debate between quantitative research and motivation research has been dubbed the battle of the "nose counters against the head shrinkers." This may be called more properly the quantitative versus the qualitative approach. Alfred Politz represents the former point of view and the late Ernest Dichter the latter.

Politz is critical of the small samples used by Dichter and his disci-

[8] See "The New Debate: Does the Consumer Know His Own Mind," *Newsweek,* Oct. 10, 1955, pp. 89–93; Alfred Politz, "Product Changes and Consumer Reactions," speech before the Fourth Annual Conference of Consumer Behavior, Sept. 16, 1955, University of Michigan, Ann Arbor, mimeographed; Lester Frankel, "The Role of Statistical Techniques in Consumer Motivation Research," speech before the New York Chapter, American Marketing Association, Oct. 29, 1955, mimeographed; Ernest Dichter, "Scientifically Predicting and Understanding Human Behavior," *Consumer Behavior and Motivation,* edited by Robert H. Cole; *Marketing Symposium,* October 1955, Bureau of Business Management, College of Commerce and Business Administration, University of Illinois, Urbana, pp. 26–41.

ples in motivation research. He contends that it is not possible to psychoanalyze an individual in the time allotted to a single interview. Politz is also critical of the lack of standardized interpretations of the same interview by different psychologists and psychiatrists. Furthermore, he holds that it is difficult to quantify these data.

Dichter, on the other hand, maintained that the nose-counting survey did not reveal the basic attitudes and motivations of the individual. The early study of portable television sets, to which reference was made in a previous chapter, justifies Dichter's contention. It will be recalled that the study found no market interest in portable television. Yet one company ignored the results of the poll and proceeded with plans for a portable set with the astonishing result that its effort brought an immediate success.

Motivation Research in Industry. A questionnaire sent to a number of companies some years back inquired about their use of motivation research.[9] The responses ranged the entire gamut from complete interest to utter disdain. The broad general objective of those who employed motivation research was to develop hypotheses for subsequent verification by quantitative research. Other uses to which motivation research was put included the development of advertising themes and the creation of product features related to consumer needs. Companies expressing negative reactions toward motivation research said they considered it much too intangible.

Scaling

A scale is a series of interrelated questions regarding an attitude. The attitude may be any of several such as an attitude toward war, authoritarianism, a company, a product, masculinity, status, or just about anything else. The questions in a scale are so designed that they all relate to a single attitude. Thus, it becomes possible to quantify many qualitative attributes through use of a scale.[10] Many scaling techniques are available, including the Thurstone scale, the Lickert scale, Lazarsfeld's latent analysis, Osgood's semantic differential, and the Guttman scale.[11] Green, moreover, discussed six major scaling methods: judgment, summated ratings, scalogram analysis,

---

[9] Author's survey, *op. cit.*

[10] Bert Green, "Attitude Measurement," in C. A. Murchison (Ed.), *Handbook on Social Psychology,* Addison-Wesley, Reading, Mass., 1954, pp. 335–369.

[11] Samuel A. Stouffer, Louis Guttman, Edward A. Suchman, Paul F. Lazarsfeld, Shirley A. Star, and John A. Clausen, *Measurement and Prediction, the American Soldier,* Princeton University Press, 1950; T. W. Adorno, Else Frenkel-Brunswik, Daniel J. Levinson, and R. Nevitt Sanford, *The Authoritarian Personality,* Harper, New York, 1950.

unfolding, latent structure analysis, and rating.[12] In judgment the scale is developed from judges' ratings of items. Summated ratings, scalogram analysis, unfolding, and latent structure analysis develop scales from the data given by respondents, and hence may be called response methods. The final of the six methods mentioned by Green, ratings, uses judges to evaluate the individuals.

Scaling in Marketing. Elizabeth A. Richards[13] has described a technique for determining the segments of a market based on attitudes deduced from the Guttman scale.[14] The procedure she described employed the Guttman scale along with the zero point developed by Suchman.[15] From this the attitude toward two products could be compared based on their relative positions to the zero point. Thus, if product A, located at the zero point, drew a 25 per cent favorable attitude and product B, also located at the zero point, obtained a 45 per cent favorable attitude, these proportions might very well be used to determine the desirability of marketing the product with the highest score.

The Guttman scale has also been used to measure learning, which has been defined in various ways including a sequence of repetition, response, motivation, and interference. Questions were designed for each of these categories and were used to compare media and competing brands. For example, the questions on repetition took this form:

I. Repetition
    A. Have you noted any Lucky Strike advertisements in newspapers, radio, television, other?
        1. Frequently.
        2. Some.
        3. None at all.
    B. How strongly do you feel about the above question?
        1. Very strongly.
        2. Fairly strongly.
        3. Not at all strongly.

[12] *Ibid.*
[13] "Predicting Consumer Behavior by Attitude Scaling Devices," *Proceedings*, American Marketing Association, June 1959, pp. 223–235; see also Elizabeth A. Richards, "A Commercial Application of Guttman Attitude Scaling Techniques," *Journal of Marketing*, Vol. 22, No. 2, October 1957, pp. 166–173.
[14] For scoring procedure see Louis Guttman, "The Cornell Technique for Scale and Intensity Analysis," *Educational and Psychological Measurement*, 1947, 7:247–280; Robert Ford, "A Rapid Scoring Procedure for Scaling Attitude Questions," *Public Opinion Quarterly*, Vol. 14, No. 3, Fall 1950, pp. 507–532.
[15] Stouffer et al., *op. cit.*

In comparing brands, it was found, as we noted in an earlier chapter, that the brand receiving the highest percentage of favorable responses, employing the zero-point method, turned out to be the largest seller for the year.

In addition, several different scales have been used to classify consumers as to whether they might qualify as leaders in the purchase of automatic washing machines. After these leaders were singled out a series of intensive depth interviews and projective devices were administered to them. It was found that the group composed of housewives was not characterized by income level but rather by its attitude toward the home. Specifically, these women preferred doing things around the house to working in a career capacity.

Scaling has also been used extensively in cross-tabulation of the characteristics of fertilizer dealers and users. Some of the scales used were progressivism, traditionalism, knowledge scale, and scientific agriculture.[16] These scale items were cross-tabulated with many other variables such as the type of business. Other applications of scale analysis to marketing research include a study of food preferences,[17] a quantification of brand, product, and company image through use of the semantic differential,[18] and a study of consumer personalities attracted to different product images.[19]

Advantages. The major advantage of scaling is its capacity to quantify qualitative matters. The scale may be used in a projective manner to array such devices as thematic apperception.[20] A scale

[16] George M. Beal, Joe M. Bohlen, and John Harp, "The Role of the Retail Dealer in the Adoption of Commercial Fertilizer by the Ultimate Consumers," *Rural Sociology, Report No. 2,* Iowa State College Agricultural Experiment Station in Cooperation with Tennessee Valley Authority Division of Agricultural Relations, Agricultural Economics Portion, Department of Economics and Sociology, Iowa State College, November 1958; see also Richard Dean Warren, "A Dealer Education Program Based on Fertilizer and Agricultural Chemicals Merchandising Research," master's thesis, Iowa State University, Ames, Iowa, 1960.

[17] Francis J. Pilgrim and Joseph M. Kamen, "Patterns of Food Preferences through Factor Analysis," *Journal of Marketing,* Vol. 24, No. 2, October 1959, pp. 68–72.

[18] William A. Mindak, "Fitting the Semantic Differential to the Marketing Problem," *Journal of Marketing,* Vol. 25, No. 4, April 1961, pp. 28–33; for an article which describes a technique similar to the semantic differential see Irving Crespi, "Use of Scaling Technique in Surveys," *Journal of Marketing,* Vol. 25, No. 5, July 1961, pp. 69–72.

[19] Ralph L. Westfall, "Psychological Factors in Predicting Product Choice," *Journal of Marketing,* Vol. 26, No. 2, April 1962, pp. 34–40.

[20] Frank Auld, Jr., Leonard D. Eron, and Julius Laffal, "Application of Guttman's

offers quantitative proof of some relationship among all the questions bearing on one particular attitude. It also provides assurance that the questions have a common meaning for all individuals participating in the test.

In addition, the latent content of a response may be distinguished from its manifest content through use of a scale. The manifest reply is what is actually asserted. It might be made to please the interviewer. The latent reply is the meaning behind the manifest answer. In marketing, for example, a direct question to children on whether band-aids make good toys would probably elicit a negative response. Yet a series of questions pertaining to play habits might disclose a favorable attitude toward using band-aids as toys.

The scale may be used, moreover, as a predicting tool. Meehl claimed that he was better able to predict the behavior of psychotic individuals by the use of scales than through the depth interview or some other projective device.[21] Whether this kind of predictability is applicable to marketing research is as yet unknown.

Disadvantages. In a discussion of scaling one psychologist maintained that the predictability of scale scores was not very satisfactory and wondered how sociometric scores might work out in measuring an individual's overt behavior. Some work has been undertaken to relate sociometric scores to scale scores,[22] but it is not sufficient to warrant hypotheses.

Another source of criticism has arisen from the problem of defining a "unidimensional" universe.[23] Some writers believe that unidimensionality includes many dimensions. They hold that scales have not been able to indicate the relative intensity of a series of attitudes. This is a challenging area for research as some attitudes may be more important than others. Perhaps paired comparisons will be employed together with scales of attitudes as a solution to this problem.

Lazarsfeld has said that a scale does not evoke as satisfactory information as an open-end interview for an attitude of short duration. But when the attitude has a longer duration use of a scale is preferable

Scaling Method to the T. A. T.," *Educational and Psychological Measurements,* Vol. 15, No. 4, Winter 1955, pp. 422–435.

[21] Paul E. Meehl, *Clinical vs. Statistic Prediction,* University of Minnesota Press, 1954.

[22] See chapter on sociometric techniques in scaling, M. W. Riley, J. W. Riley, Jr., J. Toby et al., *Sociological Studies in Scale Analysis,* Rutgers University Press, 1954.

[23] See Leon Festinger and Daniel Katz, *Research Methods in the Behavioral Sciences,* Dryden Press, New York, 1953.

to use of the interview.[24] A final criticism of scaling is the large amount of manipulation necessary to achieve a scale, although this has been solved in part by application of computer technology.

Imagery

Product Image. One area in which the behavioral sciences have contributed substantially to marketing is in understanding human perceptions about a company and its products. An individual's perception is conditioned by his needs, and he tends to see the things he wants to see. This has been shown through the use of projective devices employed to ascertain consumer motivation. In the case of products individuals tend to visualize them as symbols. They conceive of them on the basis of size, shape, color of the product or its package, and the name of the product itself. Large sizes may denote economy. Small sizes may suggest convenience of storage. Round shapes may connote femininity and square ones masculinity. Bright colors like red may attract. Light colors may signify aloofness and sophistication. Names of products may conjure up the names of movie stars, other products, or the satisfaction to be derived from them.

Company Image. The company image may prove an influence on the consumer, who may view the concern as friendly, or as having a high quality of products, or as being friendly to its employees, or as being able to render good service, or as old and reliable. All these elements contributing to an individual's image of a company and its product affect the disposition to purchase. The actual facts of the situation are less important to the consumer than is what he feels and believes will inspire his purchase of the product.

In a study conducted in 1955, it was found that most consumers in a small community bought their meat from a local grocer who, in turn, purchased it from local farmers.[25] As he had no standard grading system the meat the grocer sold was of a variable quality. A chain competitor across the street sold United States government choice grade meat but nevertheless had lower sales despite the superior quality of his product. That the consumer passed up this meat for the lower-quality product indicated that other symbols

---

[24] Paul F. Lazarsfeld, "The Controversy over Detailed Interviewing," *The Public Opinion Quarterly*, Vol. 8, No. 1, Spring 1944, pp. 38–60.
[25] Martin Zober, "Some Projective Techniques in Marketing Research," *Journal of Marketing*, Vol. 20, No. 3, January 1956, p. 282.

were at play. Some of these included local ownership, self-service, and locally originated advertising instead of boiler-plate from a distant home office. These factors were brought to the attention of the chain store, which promptly undertook a heavy advertising campaign that stressed government inspected choice beef. Its advertising format was developed expressly for the town. In a few months the chain branch's sales began to increase and they have maintained the higher level since.

Many public utilities have been concerned with the image of bigness. Is bigness good or bad? Studies on the subject show that people do not fear bigness as much as they did in the past. This may be due to the fact that large concerns are handling their bigness through good public relations. They are telling members of the community what they are doing for them beyond selling products.

Because the image held by an individual of a brand or a company stems from the individual's needs, the J. Walter Thompson Company submitted the problem to the members of its consumer panel.[26] Some of the needs expressed by these persons included association (liking to be with people), dominance (wanting to lead, supervise, influence, and control others), analysis (needing to understand people and accomplish something of great significance), change (wanting to do new and different things, wanting to experience variety and novelty), and heterosexuality (attitudes toward sex). A definite relationship was found to exist between the product purchased and these articulated needs. In a study of one product, moreover, it was discovered that nonusers tended to be conservative, compliant, and self-depreciating. This kind of information helps a company to plan its appeal both to customers and noncustomers.

Rating. Another fruitful technique for measuring the image of a consumer product is the rating scale.[27] This is formed by selecting a sample appeal from various advertisements. Each appeal—word or idea—is typed on a card. The consumer is then shown a graphic scale used to measure intensity and is asked to rate each word or idea in terms of how it does or does not apply, in his opinion, to what he expects of the best possible product. In so doing he presents his image of the product. He next rates each word or idea on the

[26] Arthur Koponen, "Psychological Response Patterns of Consumers," *Marketing's Role in Scientific Management,* edited by Robert Clewett, American Marketing Association, Chicago, 1957, pp. 319–334.

[27] Charles E. Swanson, "Branded and Company Images Changed by Advertising," *ibid.*

basis of a brand or product in current use to provide an image of it. Now the consumer is exposed to advertising or actual experience with the brand; this is its advertised image. Finally, the consumer rates each word or idea according to its application to the ideal product. This yields the ideal product image after exposure to advertising or hard experience with it. It thus becomes possible to study one or more of these images—the image of an ideal product, the image of a brand or product in use, the advertised image of a brand, or the image of an ideal brand or product after it has been exposed to advertising—to observe changes in consumer imagery as a result of advertising and to develop future advertising appeals based on the ideal image of the product itself.

Use and Purchase Decisions

The behavioral sciences may also help the marketing man to distinguish between the use of the product and the purchase decision. Men buy a great deal of perfume for ladies. Yet the lady uses the perfume. Women, conversely, buy pipes for men. What is the interaction between the decision to buy and the decision to use. How does the person who will use the product convey his need to the individual who purchases it? How really important is this communication of need in relation to the forces actually engulfing the purchase decision? What about the surrounding mood and atmosphere? What symbols influence the decision to purchase? The answers to these questions may be obtained by drawing on the behavioral sciences.

Family Members' Influence

Although most purchases are made by women, many years ago *Time* magazine directed its advertising toward a male audience. Its theory was that the magazine would attempt to reach the source of family power behind the actual purchaser. Sometimes other members of the family provide the directive purchasing force. For instance, from responses to a picture frustration test it was learned that children influenced some mothers on the brand of milk they drank, whereas other mothers indicated they made the decision on the brand to be purchased.[28] This illustrates that not all advertising aimed at children will produce influences over the buying decisions

[28] Unpublished report by writer for client.

of parents. The effectiveness of such advertising depends on who rules the roost.

In this regard, we might comment in passing about the influence of parents over the thinking of children. Some years ago children were permitted in an experiment to buy anything they wished in a grocery store. Instead of filling their baskets with candy, cake, and ice cream, they bought pretty much the same sort of products their parents would have purchased. Children, it would seem, are strongly influenced by their parents in their ideas of what is right and what is wrong.

As children grow older, however, the influence of their peers, particularly during adolescence, may be considerably greater than the influence of their elders. The teenage group, for example, may show its defiance of parental authority by the clothes it wears, the records to which it listens, and the books it reads. Adults are even more prone to the views of peers in their own purchases. This has been demonstrated clearly in the purchase of air conditioners in suburban communities. After one family bought an air conditioner, neighboring families also acquired air conditioners. To remain on an equal footing with one's peers has necessitated "keeping up with the Joneses."

Adults want to be individualistic. But they do not want to differ from the crowd in the clothing they choose, the houses in which they live, or the automobile they drive. To do otherwise would be to invite the disdain of the community. Hence they conform. The average community is based on conformity with few individuals daring to exceed the range of the acceptable.

P. D. Converse has found that the gender of the purchaser depends on the economic bracket in which the family falls and also whether the family is a rural or urban one.[29] In higher-income groups men incline to shop for their own clothing. In middle- and low-income groups husband and wife shop jointly for clothing. If a family resides on a farm, the chances are that the farmer will do most of the household's buying. Generally, he shops at the same time that he sells his produce or conducts business transactions. In cities most of the shopping is undertaken by women. Even though more and more men have begun to shop for groceries where grocery stores and supermarkets remain open in the evening, women still predominate.

Ferber has studied the relative influence of husbands and wives

[29] Paul D. Converse and Harvey W. Huegy, *The Elements of Marketing,* 3rd ed., Prentice-Hall, Englewood Cliffs, N.J., 1946, pp. 31–32.

in purchasing by inviting both to rate their spouses on the other's impact in buying a list of items.[30]   He stated that the reliability of ratings of the relative influences of different family members or of different sexes was highly limited.   Not only did the ratings of the same individual by two or more members of the family bear slight relationship to one another, but also the numerical values of the ratings and their distribution differed according to whether the husband or the wife was responding.   Family members generally tend to deprecate their own influence relative to the influence ascribed to them by other members of the family.   As a rule, Ferber found, wives seem to be more uniform in their ratings than husbands.

The ratings point in a general way to which family members or sex wields the lion's share of influence over the purchase of an item. Yet the usefulness of ratings for planning marketing campaigns is limited by their variability.   Moreover, the basic reliability of these ratings remains in doubt.   There is not much evidence of how far the responses agree with actual behavior.   Ferber suggested that better results should be obtained by other approaches, such as by indirect questioning and the case history method.

Roles of Spouses.   An experiment explaining the roles of husband and wife in decision making was conducted at Iowa State University.[31] The object of this experiment was to ascertain how much influence each spouse wielded in the decision-making process and to learn whether each could predict his or her actions.   Analysis of the influence was restricted to three variables: the total number of actions performed by each spouse; those actions that consisted of giving ideas and suggestions; and those that contributed to the functioning of the group.   The measure of self-prediction was the question posed before and after the experimental session against what actually occurred.

The study disclosed that the husband did most of the talking and had the greatest influence on the decision.   The wife was the peacemaker.   In most cases, however, neither husband nor wife could predict the roles each would play in making the decision, even after the completion of the experimental session.

[30] Robert Ferber, "On the Reliability of Purchase Influence Studies," *Journal of Marketing,* Vol. 19, No. 3, January 1955, pp. 225–232.
[31] William F. Kenkel and Dean K. Hoffman, "Real and Conceived Roles in Family Decision Making," *Marriage and the Family,* Vol. 17, No. 4, November 1956, pp. 311–316; William F. Kenkel, "Influence Differentiation in Family Decision Making," *Sociology and Social Research,* September–October 1957, Vol. 42, No. 1, pp. 18–25.

The experiment showed the difficulty of obtaining information about the respective roles of husband and wife in decision making. Perhaps depth interviewing might have been more fruitful on specific purchase situations to determine the respective influences of husband and wife. Decision making varies with convenience items as compared with shopping for specialty goods. Certain items necessitate more deliberation and planning than others.

Interaction of Spouses. In an effort to determine the interaction of husband and wife through depth interviews, it was noted that the housewife was the principal purchasing agent of the family, albeit influenced by other members of her household.[32] She normally wishes to buy things which will please the members of the family provided this does not conflict with her own views of what is right, proper, healthy, and esthetic. Through their behavior, however, the other family members exert pressure to cajole her to buy the things that satisfy their own desires. That both influences are often exercised subconsciously and manifested in camouflaged form does not reduce their importance.

In shopping for major products such as appliances or automobiles, the wife rarely acts alone. These products are purchased jointly. The interviews suggested that answers on major purchase decisions tended to be governed by the buyers' notions of the right and conventional things to do. For example, the husband was often credited for judgment on mechanical details and operation of equipment, although further searching indicated but little basis in fact for this at times and observed that it was asserted largely because it represented the respondent's view of the proper masculine role. The amount of cooperation taking place between husband and wife is also an outgrowth of their social and economic status.[33] Among lower-income families the purchase of an automobile is a combined decision, whereas the upper-class husband makes the decision alone. Yet this is not necessarily the pattern for other economic decisions.

There is greater autonomy in the spending of money and handling of bills at the top and bottom of the economic hierarchy than among the middle class. At the bottom most of the available income is spent on necessities. At the top there is less disposition to debate expenditures because there is enough economic leeway. What is broadly

---

[32] *Basic Research Report on Consumer Behavior,* published by Alderson and Sessions, Philadelphia, April 1957, mimeographed, pp. 602–605.

[33] "Family Buying Decisions: Who Makes Them, Who Influences Them," *Printer's Ink,* Sept. 19, 1958, p. 21 ff.

defined as the middle class may be expected to show the greatest cooperation in making economic decisions because of aspirations to advance its status. Among these middle-class families, particularly the intellectual and professional classes with moderate rather than high incomes, there is a particularly high frequency of cooperation in making buying decisions because of the need to weigh alternatives.

Conflicting values of husband and wife also influence the purchase decision.[34] While husbands are usually the first to mention buying a new car for the family, wives may often try to talk them out of it. Wives generally place less value on having a new car than do their husbands. As a result they may argue against buying a new model, or failing that, may persuade their husbands to buy a lower-priced one. This resistance reflects a difference between husband and wife over the scale of values rather than opposition to a new automobile on the basis of safety or some other inherent characteristic. Furnishing the home, saving money, providing for the children are objectives in the hierarchy of values usually regarded more highly by the wife than by the husband.

Yet when the make-model preferences of husbands and wives are compared with purchases, the husband usually wins. The family usually buys the car he prefers or that he and his wife agree is best. One-third of the nation's families purchase makes that neither the husband nor the wife prefers. This may result from lack of knowledge of trading in for a new model; the family may be compelled by the trade-in allowance to buy a lower-priced car. The lower valuation placed by women on cars suggests, moreover, that they would lean toward the lower-priced makes.

Communication also plays a central role in husband and wife decision making.[35] This communication is affected by the following factors: [36]

The more rigid the roles of the husband and wife, the less is the communication.

The greater the couple's aspirations are for themselves and their children, the more communication.

The stronger the ties are of parent to siblings, involving the individual in a separate network of obligations and rights, the greater the likelihood that

[34] *Ibid.*

[35] *Ibid.* "The view of marriage as personal companionship, fulfilling the personality needs of the spouse . . . the greater the demand for joint participation and personal communication."

[36] *Ibid.*

some services are taken over by the relatives, which weakens the intensity of communication between the husband and wife.

The more frequently couples continue to live in the neighborhood or small town of their birth the weaker is the communication. Conversely, migration from such stable friends and surroundings throws the spouses upon each other.

A marriage that is characterized both by satisfactory adjustment and some, though not excessive, differences in orientation of the spouses will exhibit more communication than if only one of the two conditions were present.

The more equalitarian the husband and wife are the more communication.

The less rigidly the husband and wife define their obligations to the household, the more communication.

If childhood education produces mistrust between the sexes, the communication will be impaired.

Lack of complexity of personality—less education, less exposure to differences, less participation in a great variety of social relationships—would tend to lower the need and the capacity for communication.

The presence of an excessive sense of guilt will create fear of self-disclosure and reduce communication.

Family Coordination and Efficiency.[37] Alderson has classified families on the bases of compatibility and degree of coordination. By compatibility he means both sexual and social compatibility. He defines coordination as the husband having a steady job and a well-managed household. Using these two terms, he classifies families into those that are neither compatible nor well coordinated and those that are both compatible and coordinated. The uncoordinated compatible family is largely permissive. It may be spending beyond its income and not managing well. The coordinated incompatible family might be well managed but its conjugal relations might be poor. One reason for this may be the attachment of either or both of the marriage partners to their parents. Alderson suggested that about half of the nation's families were both compatible and well coordinated, about 35 per cent coordinated but incompatible, 10 per cent uncoordinated but compatible, and 5 per cent uncoordinated and incompatible.

Although this is one parameter that the marketing man should investigate in developing his marketing appeals and new products, there may be other equally if not more important factors than degrees of compatibility and coordination. Some of these factors may include the social stratum of the family, the occupational status of the wage earner, the current phase of the family life cycle, degrees of authori-

[37] Wroe Alderson, *Marketing Behavior and Executive Action,* Irwin, Homewood, Ill., 1957, pp. 175–179.

tarianism versus democracy in the family, family size, and national and racial origins of the family.

Family Life Cycle [38]

In developing a strategy of market segmentation, the concept of the family life cycle may prove helpful. Once data are available on the various stages of the family life cycle a company may be able to develop its strategy of pricing, product development, personal selling, advertising, and channels of distribution. In general, the family life cycle reveals the existence of market opportunity. The company has to match this opportunity with effort. For example, it has been demonstrated that women in the 30–45 age group of housewives are more efficient shoppers as a rule than others. To this group price appeal may have more significance than product differentiation Among newlyweds, conversely, the image of product differentiation may be more important than price. Since housewives under 35 remembered the new product, Pream, it may be assumed that women in this group may be particularly amenable to new products. Advertising appeals to housewives in the 20–35 age bracket, it may be said, will bring richer rewards than advertising appeals to other age groups.

Product use varies according to the stage in the family life cycle. For instance, packaged soaps and detergents are purchased more heavily by families with children than those without. Advertising appeals, therefore, may include children and the satisfaction of children's needs. Soap manufacturers should bear in mind the problems of maintaining clean clothes among active youngsters and of minimizing the mother's efforts. The highest purchase rate for shampoos, on the other hand, is found among families with daughters in the 15–24 age bracket. This is the teenage market. Population forecasts indicate this segment of the market will become much more prominent in the future than it was in the past or is at present. Both product development and advertising programs must recognize the existence of this enormous potentiality.

Products may be designed to account for differences in taste. Children under six prefer bland cereals, whereas those in the six to twelve group, where consumption is high, lean to the presweetened, expanded, and exploded types. Wheat flakes and shredded cereals have

[38] See Lincoln H. Clark (Ed.), *Consumer Behavior*, Vol. II, New York University Press, 1955.

become more popular among these children. The wheat cereals and corn flakes come into their own among the 13- to 20-year-olds.

Ownership of housing and durables also changes with the phases of the life cycle. Home ownership in 1954 was highest among older married couples with no children under 19 years of age. On the other hand, ownership of one or more automobiles was greatest among young married couples whose youngest child was at least six years old. This latter group also represented the largest number of television-set owners.

Moreover, income varies with stages on the family life cycle. In 1953 it was observed that additional income from a wife's working was found predominantly among young childless couples. Older married couples without children under 18 received the highest percentage of income from dividends, interest, trust funds, and royalties. Studies in both Great Britain and the United States have shown that the largest family incomes appeared in the 35–44 age bracket. The largest percentage of low-income families was noted among those 65 years of age and over. Saving was highest in the 55–64 group, and in 1949 it was reported that persons with college educations among the 35–54 group had the biggest incomes.

Implications for Marketing. The implications of these data for marketing management should be rather evident. They guide marketing men to important decisions of strategy. They more or less pinpoint the targets for certain kinds of marketing programs and emphasize where efforts should be made. The data may be accumulated through marketing research or special tabulations of census information, or they may be compiled from special studies conducted by the government or private organizations. Marketing men must then tabulate and cross-tabulate the data on the basis of the relevant lessons of the family life cycle so that they may be able to aim their operations as effectively as possible to account for income, occupation, education, age of family members, and product and advertising proclivities.

Behavior Research and Market Experimentation [39]

The term *behavior research* describes an important addition to the tools for predicting the effects of marketing decisions on consumer behavior. This method is typified by direct experimentation. The conference room that houses the consumer clinic is the market re-

[39] *Basic Research Report on Consumer Behavior, op. cit.*

searcher's laboratory. There the market situation is simulated as closely as possible, and the responses of a consumer sample to contemplated business decisions are carefully studied. Several groups, for example, may be offered the same product at different prices, or they may be asked to read magazines with alternative advertisements and make a purchase decision. The subjects may be given money in advance to spend according to their inclinations. Some of it they may choose to invest on the products being tested, thereby increasing the commonality of behavior in these feigned exercises and behavior in a real shopping situation. Thus, there are two principal features of behavior research: recreation of the market environment in the laboratory with variation permitted only in the feature, price, product line, or promotion techniques under investigation, and observation of the reactions of consumers involved in the experiment.

Use of Panels. Through interviews of members of the consumer panel, information is collected every two weeks on prepurchase matters such as requirements for items desired, prepurchase planning and discussion, influences of advertising and other market information, and anticipated difficulties, if any, in finding the items. Other data are gathered at the same interval on the course of the shopping trip— where the shopper went, what she saw, and her reasons for buying or not buying. Finally, data are accumulated on postpurchase matters such as use of the items, postpurchase satisfaction, and rationalization of the decisions as to which items were to have been purchased.

Use of Games. Games have also been used to simulate purchasing activity.[40] In one case respondents were given a set of ten envelopes which contained small slips of paper, each numbered, and were instructed to search for the highest possible number. The incentive was to find the number while opening only a few envelopes. Each consumer played the game ten times, that is, each was given ten different sets of envelopes. At first most women opened as many as five envelopes before they settled on what they considered to be the highest number. By the second or third go around, they opened only one envelope. The results almost paralleled the shopping trip results gathered from the same women. These results demonstrated that more than 80 per cent of their purchases were made by these panel members at the first store visited. The points or tokens forfeited in the game for opening another envelope compared with the effort of walking an extra block or dragging the children to another store.

[40] *Ibid.*

A second game was played with geometric figures. It had many of the same components of the number game but included additional elements. Women were given a geometric figure of a certain size, shape, and color, and were instructed to search a series of envelopes for another figure which matched the sample as closely as possible. A penalty of 100 points was levied for opening additional envelopes. The more closely the panel member was able to match the sample the higher was her score. Here, too, the results illustrated that the women tended to rely on one particular envelope to find the appropriate geometric match. This was equivalent to buying at the first store visited without incurring the costs of going on.

A third game, the shopping game, exhibited the same behavior as actual shopping reports. Women in real life and in the shopping game both built up strong preferences and usually bought at the first store; if they could not find what they wanted in the first store, they visited one or two more but rarely went to more than four or five. In other words, their orbit of acceptable stores was very small. The game further showed an interaction of three variables—number of merchandise line, depth of assortment, and width of price line.

Social Class

While the size of each social class is not constant from one community to the next, as a rule 3 per cent or less of any society constitutes its upper class. In contrast, about 12 per cent accounts for the upper-middle class, with about 65 per cent concentrated in the lower-middle and upper-lower classes. Approximately 20 per cent compose the lower-lower class.[41] The two highest rungs on the socioeconomic ladder, the upper-middle and upper classes, form what is referred to as the class market. The lower-middle and upper-lower classes compose the mass market. The lower-lower class presents a special problem of merchandising and marketing, and is quite different in many respects from the other groups. These classes are only slightly related to family incomes, especially since a long period of high wages has boosted the factory worker's and working-class incomes to surprisingly high levels. Nevertheless, the $8000-a-year laundry-truck driver has a way of life much different from the $8000 teacher or professional man.

[41] Burleigh B. Gardner, "Social Status and Consumer Behavior," in Lincoln H. Clark (Ed.), *Consumer Behavior,* Vol. II, New York University Press, 1955, pp. 58–60.

Class and Communication. A problem of social-class influence on consumption lies in the area of communications or media. Among magazine audiences, for example, some fit into a fairly restricted pattern while others range widely. *The New Yorker* is essentially a magazine for members of the upper-middle class or for ambitious people seeking intellectual sophistication. At the other extreme are the romance fiction magazines which draw wide readership among upper-lower class groups. In terms of total reading habits there is an obvious falling off in amounts of reading done by the lower-lower class. However, many magazines essentially purveying middle-class standards are seen to have tremendous followings from the upper-middle to the upper-lower classes.

Class and Home Furnishings. In the home many items of furnishings are particularly subject to the pressures of social standards. The living room is primarily the housewife's concern, and she is consciously or unconsciously affected by the impression it creates. From past experience, as a rule, she has developed standards of taste and of personal liking in style of furniture, patterns of rugs, and designs of wallpaper. Since she shares these standards with her friends, what she likes will be approved by them, and she will approach anything new or different with trepidation. That is why the so-called "borax" styling continues to flourish in spite of availability of "better designs." One of the dilemmas of the furniture buyer or dress buyer of upper-middle-class background is that too often the design he and his wife would choose would not sell in the lower-middle and upper-lower-class market; he is therefore constantly obliged to spend his working day buying designs he personally finds distasteful.

Classifying the Class System. Warner has described a six-class system.[42] It contains the upper-upper, or old families; lower-upper, or newly arrived families; upper-middle, mostly the professional and successful businessmen; lower-middle, or white-collar salaried class; upper-lower, or the wage-earner, skilled-worker group; and lower-lower, or the unskilled-labor group. To classify an individual's position in a practical way, Warner devised the following kind of rating index based not on amount of income but rather on type of income, occupation, and house, and place of residence.[43]

[42] Pierre D. Martineau, "The Pattern of Social Classes," *Marketing's Role in Scientific Management,* edited by Robert L. Clewett, American Marketing Association, Chicago, 1957, pp. 233–249.
[43] *Ibid.*

Middle Class	*Lower Status*
1. Pointed to the future.	1. Pointed to the present and past.
2. His viewpoint embraces a long expanse of time.	2. Lives and thinks in a short expanse of time.
3. More urban identification.	3. More rural identification.
4. Stresses rationality.	4. Nonrational essentially.
5. Has a well-structured sense of the universe.	5. Vague and unclear.
6. Horizons vastly extended or not limited.	6. Horizons sharply defined and limited.
7. Greater sense of choicemaking.	7. Limited sense of choicemaking.
8. Self-confident, willing to take risks.	8. Very much concerned with security and insecurity.
9. Immaterial and abstract in his thinking.	9. Concrete and perceptive in his thinking.
10. Sees himself tied to national happenings.	10. World revolves around his family.

The *Chicago Tribune* found the following consumer types to exist in the upper-middle and lower-lower classes.[44]

Consumer Type	Upper Middle, Per Cent	Lower Lower, Per Cent
Friendly	28	50
Impersonal	72	50
Sale minded	76	33
Not sale minded	25	67
Downtown centered	28	83
Local centered	72	17
Other directed	84	25
Inner directed	16	75
Economy minded	76	0
Not economy minded	24	100
Vicarious shopper	76	25
Not vicarious shopper	24	75
Impulsive	20	75
Not impulsive	80	75

[44] *Ibid.*

Significance of Social Stratification. Of what significance, then, is this concept of social stratification? First, it presents a basis for product differentiation and market segmentation. Products and services have to be tailored for segmented social classes. Moreover, the types of advertising appeals to the different classes will have to vary, appealing in each case to another set of need patterns. There are social-class distinctions as to where an individual shops, which influence channels of distribution. And finally social class will indicate the nature of the response to price changes. Among thrifty or economy-minded classes the response is likely to be quicker than otherwise.

Vector Analysis

Kurt Lewin has suggested still another valuable approach to the study of behavior.[45] Lewin said that a person engaged in shopping encounters numerous forces—or *vectors of influence*—that determine where and what items will be purchased. If an individual were about to embark on a grocery-shopping trip, the first choice would be the place of shopping. The forces shaping the choice might be familiarity with the stock of a particular store, ease of moving through the aisles, wide selection of merchandise, fresh meat and produce, friendly clerks, and ease of checking out. Some negative factors drawing the shopper away from her first choice might include the prices noticed in competing stores, availability of more items and easier parking at a second store, and a more sophisticated atmosphere. In a classical economic sense the consumer is evaluating the utilities to be gained from shopping in various stores. The utilities are evaluated against the disadvantages, and where the net utility is greater the consumer is likely to shop.

The same process can be extrapolated for selection of the goods the shopper purchases. Here the impacts of advertising, shelf position, size of container, color of package, and need for the product as expressed by some family member will govern the purchase of a particular item.

Warren Bilkey has developed a quantitative technique to find these relative forces.[46] Bilkey asked a consumer to evaluate his own psychic tensions on a scale similar to a thermometer with numerical gradations from zero to 100. One hundred represented extreme feelings whereas

[45] K. Lewin, "Forces Behind Food Habits and Methods of Change," *National Research Council Bulletin,* No. 108, 1943, pp. 35–65.
[46] Warren J. Bilkey, "Psychic Tensions and Purchasing Behavior," *Journal of Social Psychology,* Vol. 41, May 1955, pp. 247–258.

zero represented none at all about a purchase decision. These tensions were studied over a period of time for many items. Measures were made, for example, of the tensions accompanying the purchase of a rug or the yearning for an automobile. These were weighed over a period of time against resistance to the purchase. Moreover, positive correlations were found between average net valences for food and average monthly expenditures. This shows that it is possible for consumers to describe their feelings which, in turn, determine purchase behavior.

Generalizations of Social Science to Marketing

Contributions of Sociology

The sociologist undertakes to isolate, define, and describe human behavior as it occurs in groups and social settings. He seeks to formulate valid laws and generalizations about human nature, social interaction, social organization, and culture. Sociological contributions to marketing are most apparent in the modern institutional approach, which sees economic processes as part of an organic whole of society. Through such an approach marketing activities are not viewed as the individualistic acts of atomistic man, but as *functions* which operate through various marketing structures forming part of the total social organization.

Sociologists view marketing processes as the *activities* of groups of people—buyers, sellers, and marketing functionaries—who are motivated by group pressures as much as by individual preferences.[47] Sociology recognizes the influence of culture, custom, heritage, and mores in shaping the final outcome. Specifically, sociology has made numerous contributions to the study of population. It has added to knowledge of consumer motivation, particularly in its researches on class, voluntary association, leisure-time activities, and the measurement of attitudes. It has enlightened us on human ecology—the study of spatial and temporal adaptations of human beings, their distribution, and their institutions—and it has elucidated collective behavior, measurement, and scaling. Some ideas such as Reilly's Law were anticipated in the earlier sociological writings on human ecology. The concept of the life cycle was also developed by sociologists.

[47] Christen T. Jonassen, "Contributions of Sociology to Marketing," *Journal of Marketing,* Vol. 24, No. 2, October 1959, pp. 29–35.

Bartels points out similarities and dissimilarities between the sociologist and the marketing expert.[48] He defines the individual occupied with the scientific aspects of marketing as a *marketologist*. Both sociologists and marketologists, he holds, are social scientists. Their common goal is to understand the behavior of people and institutions in their diverse activities. The contrasts between these two are of three kinds: the subject or substance of their respective interests, their concepts and nomenclature, and their techniques and methodologies.

The sociologist is interested in the discovery of primary knowledge. The marketologist, on the other hand, is more concerned with mechanisms and processes in the behavior of people and the functioning of institutions *in the market*. He is also interested in the laws and generalizations that relate products, institutions, and people *in their distributive roles*.

The sociologist expresses his ideas in such terms as population, class, status mores, motivation, collective behavior, culture, custom, heritage, human sociology, folkways, interacting groups, and groups in a community. The marketologist thinks and talks of such concepts as distributive institutions, commodities, operating margins and mark-ups, services, competitive practices, distribution channels, markets and trading areas, trade gravitation, rates of turnover, quotas, potentials, and budgets, calculated risk, grades and standards, and price and competition.

Sociologists have made notable contributions of technique and methodology to instruments and scales for measuring attitudes; to systematization of analysis of spatial and temporal factors in human institutions; to mathematical models for describing retail gravitation, theory of intervening opportunities, and message diffusion; to research design; to use of control groups; to study of paths of diffusion; and to mapping of social data. Marketologists have refined these techniques: analysis of financial statements, especially for purposes of credit; analysis of internal data relating to inventory control, cost analysis, and operating profit; predicting and setting potentials and quotas; and measurement of radio-listening habits.

Yet there are several areas in which sociologists and marketologists might undertake common investigations. These include identification of market strata, delineation of market areas, study of the population structure, and the appraisal of marketing and other business institu-

[48] Robert Bartels, "Sociologists and Marketologists," *Journal of Marketing*, Vol. 24, No. 2, October 1959, pp. 37–40.

tions as social institutions. In addition, they may find a common interest in considering business practices as mores of the society, in the social control of business, in social growth and change, in the regarding of marketing practices as motivational influences, in the origins of cultural trends and their impact on marketing, and in comparative marketing systems.

Then there are the areas in which sociological concepts may not be relevant to marketologists. These are primarily the classification of marketing institutions as business and not as social institutions, the interpretation of distribution as a specialized economic function, the classifying of products to ensure efficient distribution, and the designation of functions that constitute the operational mechanisms of marketing. They also include the classification of the consumer from a distributive standpoint; the determination of marketing policies, pricing, branding, standardizing, and agency relationships; the estimating of the value added by marketing to the Gross National Product; the analysis of institutional operating costs and margins; studies of the various scales of institutional operation, of flow of products through channels, and of funds, payments, and obligations; and finally, institutional operating techniques.

Contributions of Anthropology [49]

Anthropology is ordinarily defined as the study of man. The field is usually divided into four subfields: archaeology, cultural anthropology, linguistics, and physical anthropology. Archaeology deals with the historical reconstruction of cultures that no longer exist. Cultural anthropology examines the behaviors of man including social, linguistic, technical, and familiar behaviors; it is often defined as the study of man and his words. Linguistics cover the comparative study of the structure, interrelationships, and development of languages. Physical anthropology is concerned with human biology and the development of the human organism, with special interest in racial differences. When anthropology is employed in marketing, the reference is usually to cultural anthropology. The differences among anthropology, sociology, and psychology are that sociology addresses itself to the social system, psychology explores the personality, and anthropology investigates the culture.

[49] Charles Winick, "Anthropology's Contributions to Marketing," *Journal of Marketing,* Vol. 25, No. 5, July 1961, pp. 53–60.

The anthropologist is trained to sympathize with groups other than his own and to "tune in" on their cultural patterns. Because his schooling exposes him to a wide variety of cultures, he can view a situation globally and place it in a larger context. His preparation makes him sensitive to cross-cultural differences which may be of crucial importance in different situations because his entire training is aimed at awareness of such situations.

Anthropological knowledge has been applied to marketing in three kinds of situations: specific knowledge, awareness of a culture's themes, and sensitivity to taboos. Anthropologists have made specific studies of various aspects of our culture. For example, a study on the symbolic meaning of heat was influential in introducing central heating to one part of the country. Specific knowledge on fashion has been useful in the design of clothing. Knowledge of such subgroups as Negroes, Puerto Ricans, and Jews has been advantageous in developing new products and advertising themes. Knowledge of the meaning of symbols has similarly aided in the refinement of package symbols and advertising.

Through his awareness of a culture's themes, the anthropologist has shed valuable light on the practice of gift giving. This knowledge aided one company in directing its merchandising, packaging, and advertising formats to the gift theme. Anthropologists, moreover, have discouraged another manufacturer from aiming his advertisements for the purchase of men's shirts at women. They found that men resented the extent to which women had been borrowing and buying men's clothes. Another study suggested that shoes should be designed and advertised in relation to the various stages of growth in the individual. For the four-to-six set advertising material was included on how children might be taught to tie their own shoes, as this is the age at which they learn the operation. For adolescents the wearing of high heels opens up new vistas. For older persons shoes are designed as stylishly as any model for younger adults so as not to attach a visible stigma of "old people's shoes" to them.

With respect to sensitivity to taboos, it was learned that different colors assume different meanings. Blue is for mourning in Iran, green is a nationalistic shade in Egypt and Syria, white signifies mourning in Japan, brown and gray are disapproved in Nicaragua, and purple is associated with death throughout Latin America.

A situation confronting the United States in the 1960's is the changing cultures of underdeveloped countries around the world. Anthropologists have offered many valuable insights into the problems of cultural change.[50]   Changes in consumption which may be introduced include the elements of sustenance for life itself although hungry people may very well reject unfamiliar food.   They also involve sensory changes up to a point, such as sweets, cigarettes, alcohol, gum—and Coca-Cola.   Moreover, some goods become interpreted as symbols of display, and certain tools, weapons, utensils, and other practical articles are welcomed for their inherent values.   The final items are more readily introduced if they relate to something the people already have.   Ord-Brown uses the term "target" for certain types of goods which are especially desired for display or usefulness, such as sunglasses, watches, and bicycles, but which do not necessarily lead to broad change.[51]

Beyond the point of consumption change is very different.   These changes relate to cultural patterns in the following ways: first, an increase in purchasing power does not truly engender a rise in the standard of living.   Besides, where purchasing power is lacking, it is not necessarily coveted.   Second, if the desire for goods is far-reaching it involves changing the pattern of life, and people are reluctant to change their ways even though we may see merit in their doing so.   These changes may require crucial adjustments of values for people who inhabit underdeveloped countries.   Third, major change is facilitated when people asked to undertake it have a sense of participation in the lives and values of others whose cultures already embody the changes; they must admire and trust these others.

Hoyt points out that the order of major change involves any number of combinations of the three considerations.   The third one is the most fundamental in present-day society.   The first two can get started without the third but cannot realize any fruition without it.   Conversely, if the third one takes hold, the other two can follow more readily.

Anthropology's Marketing Findings.   In some primitive economies the act of exchange is considered a form of gift giving.   In other economies it is considered a status symbol.   The practice of potlatch among certain Indian tribes involves the giving of greater amounts of goods in exchange for goods received in order to gain status.   This sometimes leads to giving away all of one's personal possessions.

---

[50] Elizabeth E. Hoyt, "Some Lapses in the Theory of Economic-Cultural Change, with Special Application to the Present," mimeographed report, Iowa State University, 1959.

[51] *Ibid.*

Among certain tribes in Africa, exchange with other tribes is associated with taboos and evil spirits. To ward these off trade is conducted with intervening tribes which are capable of banishing the evil spirits.

Recently a group of scholars studying the early exchange found that essentially it assumed a form quite different from that known as the market economy.[52] This interchange consisted of reciprocity, redistribution, and exchange.[53] Under reciprocity the amount put into and received from the economy in each case was not determined by buying, bargaining, or selling, but by custom. In such a system the allocations of work and product related closely to such social structures and institutions as kinship, caste, rank, and status.

Under redistribution the product was brought to a central place, sometimes physically but other times only in the sense of control or possession, where it was redistributed according to established convention. Each individual took a predetermined amount of goods. There was no buying, selling, or pricing. The shares were set by custom. Under exchange, essentially the market system we know, bidding took place with the buyer seeking the lowest price and the supplier the highest one.

The authors of this study pointed out that it was possible for all three types of interchange to exist simultaneously. It was not necessary for one to evolve into another. In our own society, for example, we find illustrations of these systems. In the family exchange takes place through reciprocity. Under social security in which unemployment benefits, old-age assistance, and aid to dependent children occur, we observe elements of a system of redistribution.

Instead of an order in which prices were determined by supply and demand, the early economies contained systems of equivalencies. Certain fixed ratios were established for the exchange of goods— irrespective of fluctuations in supply and demand. Traders acting as middlemen exacted fixed commissions for performing their duties and trade took place without a formal market place. Instead there were *ports of trade.*

Finally, the methods of social group work apply directly to the management of personnel in any company, and indirectly to relations

[52] Karl Polanyi, Conrad M. Arensberg, and Harry W. Pearson, *Trade and Market in the Early Empires: Economies in History and Theory,* Free Press and Falcon's Wing Press, Glencoe, Ill., 1957.
[53] *Ibid.*

with consumers, stockholders, suppliers, and distributors. The general goal of all social group work is to effect changes or adaptations in the attitudes, relationships, and social behavior of an individual so that he will achieve a greater sense of adequacy and social adjustment.[54] This production of change to engender personal adequacy and social adjustment may be a management goal for assisting the individual to perform up to maximum capacity.

Thus, we see the many ways in which the behavioral sciences—principally anthropology, sociology, and psychology—serve the interests of scientific marketing management. They make it easier for the marketing man to plan a campaign accurately aimed at the appropriate market to the ultimate ends of expanding sales and enhancing his company profits.

Summary

Marketing is a phenomenon of group behavior. Central to all marketing planning is the role of the consumer. To understand the consumer, marketing management must be aware of his needs. Motivation research has provided the marketing research department with some useful tools to gather qualitative information and develop hypotheses. A new device that has attempted to quantify qualitative information has been the device of scaling. This technique offers interesting possibilities for research.

Marketing management has been concerned with the problems of imagery associated with products and the company. It has also been concerned with the varying influences on purchase decisions. Varying influences exist among men, women, and children in the family. A concept that may be useful in examining family purchasing behavior is the degree of coordination and efficiency achieved by a family. The family life cycle is another way that marketing management may think of market segmentation. The social class may be looked on as another segment of the market.

It may be possible to simulate purchase conditions and conduct experiments with individuals without actually making any purchases. A technique of analysis that seems promising is the use of vector forces that may affect consumer behavior.

The disciplines of sociology, anthropology, and social group work offer some interesting insights into market behavior. These tools require further investigation as to their applicability in the solution of marketing problems and in the development of theories on the various phases of marketing.

[54] Helen Northen, "Interrelated Functions of the Social Group Worker," *Social Work Journal of the National Association of Social Workers*, Vol. 2, No. 2, April 1957, p. 64.

Suggested Cases

Ralph L. Westfall and Harper W. Boyd, *Cases in Marketing Management*, Irwin, Homewood, Ill., 1961.

   Shaefner Company—*Manufacturer of Equipment for Electronics Industry*—Influence of Company Image on Objective, pp. 71–76.

Milton P. Brown, Wilbur B. England, and John B. Matthews, Jr., *Problems in Marketing*, 3rd ed., McGraw-Hill, New York, 1961.

   National Biscuit Company, pp. 36–38.

   Stuffer Company, pp. 47–55.

Harry L. Hansen, *Marketing: Text, Cases, and Readings*, rev. ed., Irwin, Homewood, Ill., 1961.

   Pan-American Coffee Bureau, pp. 142–152.

Intercollegiate Case Clearing House, Soldiers Field, Boston 63, Massachusetts.

   ICH 3M89—H. C. Bleeker.

   ICH 3M93—Consumer Attitudes Toward Irradiated Products (b).

Chapter Eleven

The term *theory* has been described in poetic manner by one writer
as a net cast to catch the world—to rationalize, to explain, to master
it. The human role in this process is to weave the net ever finer.[1]
Philosophically a theory is considered a set of statements that could
prove false. Essentially, no statements may be proven true; state-

---

[1] Karl R. Popper, *The Logic of Scientific Discovery*, Hutchinson, London, 1959,
p. 59.

Marketing Theory

ments are only capable of being falsified. Although some statements may not be testable they are still stimuli to scientific investigation because they may suggest a problem. The problem is the starting point in any theory.

The mere existence of a theory does not necessarily imply an explanation of causation. All that a theory does is to acknowledge a relationship. Some relationships are explained more easily by theories than others. To maintain an inquiring attitude an individual must not presume that A causes B, but that the outcome of B is very much related to A. Subsequent research may actually suggest better ways to explain the outcome of B through C, D, or E. In other words, the explanations of outcome must be capable of falsification if a true spirit of scientific inquiry is to prevail; statements must be falsifiable.

A theory is said to be empirical or falsifiable if it divides all possible statements into two distinct classes: first, all those basic statements with which it is inconsistent, or which it rules out or prohibits—these are the potential falsifiers of the theory; and second, those basic statements that it does not contradict, or which it permits. A theory is falsifiable if there are enough potential falsifiers at hand. If a potential falsifying statement occurs only once or rarely, the theory is not falsified. The falsification must recur frequently or constantly for the theory to prove untenable. This recurrence leads to an hypothesis which upon corroboration becomes a falsifying hypothesis. If this hypothesis is supported by evidence, it is clear that a new theory is needed.

A theory is stated in the form of a universal or all-encompassing statement. Universal statements may be universal theories, such as natural laws, or they may pertain to single statements or groups of single statements. Every application of science is based on inference from an hypothesis, which is universal—that is, on the deduction of singular predictions. To give a causal explanation of an event means to deduce a statement that describes the original conditions. This deduction is predicated on the use of one or more universal laws or on singular statements. For example, take the following hypothesis: When the price of a commodity is greater than its marginal utility to the consumer, the product will not be sold. In this case, the singular statement might refer to a specific price of $10,000. Put universally, the law might state that for every price P there is such a utility U that the consumer may not buy the product if P exceeds U. The initial condition is a certain price P and a specific utility U. From the universal statement coupled with the initial condition the singular statement is deduced—namely, the consumer will not buy. This is known as a *singular prediction effect.*

In the foregoing illustration the rule replaces the principle of causation. Nevertheless, the search for universal laws and for a coherent theoretical system is not to be abandoned, nor is the effort to explain causally any kind of event to be discontinued. Moreover, the universal statement must be capable of falsification. To the illustration must be admitted those propositions that say the product will be sold when the price exceeds its marginal utility to the consumer. If there is a sufficient number of recurring instances in which falsification appears, it may be necessary to modify the law.

Models

Every system of concepts that satisfies a system of axioms may be called a model of the axiom system. The axiom, or theoretical, system must be sufficiently clear and definite to permit the easy recognition of every new assumption for what it is: a modification and therefore a revision of the system. A theoretical system follows these rules: it must be free from contradictions—that is, not every arbitrary statement may be deduced from it; it must not be independent or contain any axioms deducible from its own axioms; the axioms should suffice for the deduction of all statements belonging to the theory; the axioms should be necessary axioms containing no superfluous assumptions.

The model contains the following characteristics: [2] first, it should simplify the facts so that they become amenable to manipulation and analysis. This may mean, however, that the greater the simplification is the farther the model may be from reality. Yet simplified models may be developed to approximate reality to a considerable

[2] W. J. Baumol, "On the Role of Marketing Theory," *Journal of Marketing,* Vol. 21, No. 4, April 1957, p. 416.

extent. Second, the model should relate to the important facts in the situation. Facts become important through the nature of the problem under investigation. Caution must be exercised, however, lest one model be applied to all kinds of problem situations. Models must vary according to the kind of problem confronting the decision maker. And in certain circumstances situations become so complicated that the model tends to misrepresent reality. Finally, any conclusions drawn from the model should hold up even when the assumptions on which the model is based are changed. It was observed in one study of cost that the optimum price did not change under a variety of assumptions about cost. However, any inaccuracies in the model's assumptions will be reflected in the conclusions.

Empirical and Theoretical Laws [3]

One may distinguish between empirical and theoretical laws. Reilly's Law of Retail Gravitation is a good example of an empirical law. It says, as we have seen, that the attraction of two trading areas varies directly with population and inversely with the square of the distance. These conclusions were reached by Reilly after an empirical study of charge accounts in department stores.

A theoretical law, in contrast, may be exemplified by a manufacturer's definition of a trading area based on hypothetical assumptions. For example, a trading area may be determined by the cost of transportation to a particular market. The periphery of the area might be described as a hyperbola. At this point two manufacturers may compete on an equal basis. Beyond it the higher cost of transportation for one of them gives an advantage to the other. All this may be expressed in a theoretical law in which letters are substituted for the two companies and the relationship of the markets to the transportation rate structure is presented.

Empirical conclusions describe situations. They do not explain how things work. It may not be possible to predict from them what will eventuate under changed conditions until the results of the changes have been observed. Theoretical laws, on the other hand, clarify the structure of the situation and illuminate its inner workings.

Empirical laws are closely related to facts. They state the facts, whereas theoretical laws describe a model which attempts to approximate the facts. An empirical law may be right or wrong. A theoretical law, which abstracts from reality, can only present a wrong picture

[3] *Ibid.,* pp. 415–416.

of the world because it omits certain aspects of the problem under investigation. Theoretical laws may not be derived directly from experience. An hypothesis may be formulated instead and then stated in the form of a theoretical law.

In Popper's view, bold ideas, unjustified anticipation, and speculative thought are the only means for interpreting nature, and they must be risked to master it. Individuals who are unwilling to expose their ideas to risk cease to participate in the game of science. Even the careful and severe testing of ideas by experience is inspired by other ideas, for experimentation is nothing more than planned action in which each step is guided by theory.[4]

Science and Theory

Science does not have to be looked on as a body of knowledge. It is rather a system of hypotheses. It is a system of guesses and anticipations which cannot be justified but which may be used again and again as long as they can stand up to testing. The scientist is never able to assert that his hypotheses are true or even probable. All he can say is that they are testable.

A distinguishing characteristic of empirical statements is their susceptibility to revision. They can be criticized and superseded by superior ones. Therefore, an observer must note the manner in which choices are made among conflicting statements. If one demands strict proof—or disproof—in the empirical sciences, one will not gain from experience nor learn when one is wrong. In the empirical sciences method is the preeminent consideration: what counts is how the individual deals with them, what he does with them, and what he does to them. Empiricism requires complete flexibility, the ability to sway with the wind of new fact and to shift course, modify, revise, or devise in the light of new conditions.

In principle, "the game of science," as Popper called it, never ends. The individual who decides that scientific statements can be regarded as fully verified calling for no further testing retires from the playing field.[5] But once an hypothesis has been proposed, tested, and proven its mettle, it may not be allowed to drop out without reason. This may include its replacement by another hypothesis which is more testable or the falsification of one of its consequences.

[4] Popper, *op. cit.*, p 280.
[5] *Ibid.*, p. 53.

The supreme rule of scientific methodology is that other rules of scientific procedure must not protect any statement against falsification. Rules must be constructed with the aim of ensuring the applicability of the falsifiability test. Any theory not to be subjected to further testing is no longer falsifiable. It is this systematic connection between rules which makes it possible to speak of a theory of method. The logic of scientific knowledge may be described, therefore, as a theory of theories.

Is Marketing a Science?

Bartels has suggested that although marketing is not a science at the present time it has the potentiality for becoming one.[6] This potentiality may be realized by borrowing from the disciplines of the social sciences, as we noted in the previous chapter. He contends that the science of marketing may consist of any number of theories, each supplying an explanation of some aspect of the science. Some theories may be narrow and simple, dealing with perhaps a technical phase of the subject. Others may be more encompassing, embracing topics of broader scope and import. As theory, they all possess a conceptual pattern and go beyond merely compiling and classifying observations described as self-evident facts. Individual perception of the related attributes of marketing phenomena precedes the classification and conceptualization of facts. Both classification and conceptualization, however, are likely to appear obvious to many and to be taken for granted. Thus, "channels" of distribution, "convenience" goods, "agent" middlemen, "rational" buying motives, and price "schedules" are clearly conceptions; they are all ideas, not material facts.

By relating the pertinent aspects of several concepts it may prove possible to formulate a statement of marketing principles. The following principle may be suggested for determining a channel of distribution: the channel tends to be relatively longer for goods of low unit value, small size, general consumption, and staple nature, which are not bought frequently and habitually by large numbers of consumers. Furthermore, the distance goods travel to market is a direct function of the difference between prices in two markets and the costs of transportation to both. The study of any aspect of marketing which proceeds from conceptual premises and is generalized in the form of basic principles, if carried to a sufficient stage of development,

[6] Robert D. W. Bartels, "Can Marketing Be a Science?" *Journal of Marketing,* Vol. 15, No. 3, January 1951, pp. 319–328.

would constitute a theory. The consistent integration of these broad theories would, in turn, create a science of marketing.

In contrast to Bartels, Hutchinson maintained not only that marketing was not a science, but also that it could never become one.[7] It was his view that marketing was very much like medicine and engineering. In both these professional fields the natural sciences were drawn upon for the solution of problems. The physician merely *applied* such sciences as biology, physiology, chemistry, physics, psychology, and many more. Engineers *applied* some of these same sciences, notably chemistry, physics, and psychology. They themselves were no more scientists than marketing men could be, although they might draw on the social sciences to solve their problems. Vaile similarly suggested that a comprehensive theory of marketing was not possible, but acknowledged that marketing men had to work with the social sciences to solve certain marketing problems.[8]

Despite their disagreements over marketing's capability of becoming a science, both Bartels and Hutchinson agreed that the source of useful generalizations was the social sciences. Science, as we have noted, is a method applied to theory. And as in theory the starting point of any science is a problem. From the problem hypotheses emerge; from hypotheses universal statements capable of falsification develop, and from universal statements there come individual statements which relate to the universal ones. Presently, we shall return to the problem approach, but for a moment let us review some principles of marketing.

Principles of Marketing

Marketing principles, as Bartels has pointed out, have developed slowly for three reasons.[9] First, marketing was considered as an activity of institutions on a par with the mechanisms which performed a function. Whatever yielded improvements in operating techniques and developed rules of action was regarded as most important. Second, the need for better rules of action required an elaborate description of the marketing process. Emphasis was therefore placed on description which often did not strike beyond the bounds of summariz-

[7] Kenneth D. Hutchinson, "Marketing a Science: An Appraisal," Part 1, *Journal of Marketing,* Vol. 16, No. 3, January 1952, pp. 286–293.

[8] Roland S. Vaile, "Towards a Theory of Marketing—A Comment," *Journal of Marketing,* Vol. 13, No. 4, April 1949, p. 520.

[9] Robert D. W. Bartels, "Marketing Principles," *Journal of Marketing,* Vol. 9, No. 2, October 1944, pp. 151–157.

ing individual cases observed, failing to venture into the area of generalization. Third, writers on marketing have not always been aware of the assumptions supporting their logic. They were generally more concerned, as a group, with the practical than the theoretical aspects of the subject. Hence, let us continue by classifying the principles of marketing, as Bartels has.

Classifying Marketing Principles

Principles of marketing fall into five classifications each of which we shall survey briefly. They are operational principles, principles involving institutional relationships, principles relating to the marketing task, hypothetical principles, and truisms.

Operational Principles. Operational principles pertain to business conduct. They are accepted as laws or rules to be employed in the operation of a marketing institution. We see them in the leasing of departments in a department store when skill, specialized knowledge, and risks are necessary in the handling of a particular type of product. We see them also in good lighting; this creates a pleasing atmosphere for trading; it facilitates the examination of merchandise, enhances its appearance, and gives an impression of modernity and prosperity. We further observe these principles in the establishment of a pricing policy. A store cannot base its pricing policy on the gross margin of any one profitable item. Its policy must be a composite, reflecting the nature of the demand for all the goods it carries, the accessibility of merchandise, the practices of its competitors, and the cost and ease of handling items.

Principles Involving Institutional Relationships. These particular principles relate to the combination of institutions in marketing channels and to the competitive forces among the establishments. Examples of these institutional relationships may be observed in the variance of outlets through which goods are distributed, the variance being occasioned by the buying habits of consumers. They may be noted, furthermore, in sellers' markets where competition among middlemen for goods leads to specialization and in buyers' markets where the reverse tendency prevails. Or they may be seen when conditions demand modification of the existing marketing structure; in such cases the change may consist of either altering current practices or developing new ones.

Principles Relating to the Marketing Task. These principles apply to the relationship of marketing to more general social and economic phenomena. Because personal service and convenience, for example, are generally more important to consumers than mechanical performance, the use of mechanical and automatic labor-saving devices is less wide-spread in distribution than in production. Moreover, the enjoyment of the fruits of mass production cannot be fully realized without the smooth operation of a vast and complex system of distribution. Finally, as a family's income increases, the proportions allocated to food and housing decrease while the percentages apportioned to buying clothing and miscellaneous items sharply rise.

Hypothetical Principles. Principles that break away from bases of observation and statistical verification to project generalizations from assumptions may be said to be hypothetical. They set up hypothetical situations from speculations rather than concrete situations from hard fact. For example, as long as tastes continue to vary it will be impossible to standardize consumer goods the same way as paving blocks or steel rails. As long as the process of exchange is obstructed by some obstacle, marketing has to find some way to circumvent or overcome the barrier. And as long as consumers demand and expect to obtain commodities instantly when they decide to buy or discover a need for them, merchants will incur the cost of foresight and risk, which is made part of the total distribution cost.

Truisms. These are principles so apparent as to be obvious. Their statement is valuable mainly for the attention it calls to matter-of-fact situations. For example, every middleman exists because of a demand for his service. Or the growth of any marketing structure is evolutionary, not revolutionary. Or the demand for certain qualities of raw materials leads to the development of standards. All these principles are indeed self-evident. No apter designation can be made of them than to call them truisms.

Development of Principles

To develop the foregoing principles more generally Bartels has suggested that they be treated in terms of five categories: markets, marketing functions, institutions, distributive channels, and operating costs. Let us have a cursory look at each of these. To them may be added the principles necessary in selling, advertising, product development, and pricing, which have been discussed elsewhere in this book.

First, in determining the principles of markets, Bartels would investigate whether the existence of the market hinged on the existence of demand and supply. A market is seldom an automatic, perfectly balanced transaction. To the contrary, many efforts are made to equate commodities with anticipated demand, and demand is adjusted to make the commodities available acceptable to it. However, the relationships among the elements of exchange may be expressed through any number of other principles, of which this is only one.

Second, in developing the principles of marketing functions, it is necessary to consider the claim that there is only a single list of such functions. Indeed more information is needed on the relationship of the marketing task as circumstances change to the functions involved.

Third, existing marketing institutions have come to be logically and popularly classified. The history of each type is known. The relations, however, between historical, economic, social, geographic, and other conditions, and these institutions have not been fully studied.

Fourth, the passage of various commodities through their channels has been traced, and the merits of different combinations of institutions as channels have been discussed at length. Nevertheless, need remains for an organized presentation of the conditions and policies that result in the establishment of diverse channels of distribution.

Finally, the economic principle of overhead, or operating, costs applies in the field of distribution, Bartels believed, because the factors of production are combined in ways that are unexplained in traditional economic tracts. Although statistics offer inconclusive evidence of trends and tendencies in distribution costs, they do represent the character of those costs and make numerous relationships among costs and circumstances discernible. Moreover, the tie between distribution costs and policies of market selectivity may be expressed more generally than it is at present. All in all, these principles suitably applied should lead to a more efficient marketing program.

The Problem Approach

A problem has been defined as a condition that prevents the reaching of a goal.[10] The goal of marketing may be considered from a *micro* point of view—that is, maximizing the company's profits—or from a *macro* point of view—that is, maximizing utility of the product or service to the consumer. In seeking to attain its goal, a company may wish to develop standards for measuring its success in pursuit

[10] Harry L. Hansen, "The Use of Generalizations in the Analysis of Marketing Problems," *Marketing Concepts in Changing Times,* edited by Richard M. Hill, American Marketing Association, Chicago, 1960, p. 168.

of the goal. In developing concepts of marketing administration relating to its goal, the company may employ the following mixes: a marketing mix, an administrative mix, and a "frustration" mix.[11]

The marketing mix, to refresh our memories of earlier observations, may consist of market research, product including packaging and inventories, distribution channels, advertising, sales promotion, personal selling, pricing, discounts, and the sum of these, the marketing mix itself. The administrative mix, as we have seen, includes determination of objectives and plans, organizing, motivating, coordinating, measuring, and controlling, as well as the administrative mix itself. The "frustration" mix consists of time, search, value or utility, probability, communication, persuasion, and the frustration mix itself. All marketing decisions, it should be noted, are pervaded by time.

The search of consumers for sellers, and, conversely, the search of sellers for buyers is a fundamental aspect of marketing. Search for opposites is also to be found in all administrative functions. Value or utility, the weighing of costs and gains, is common to functions in both the administrative and frustration mixes. Probability reflects the fact that the marketing administrator is operating in an uncertain world. Communication embraces the measures unique to the inner workings of a marketing organization spread through space and time and also the exchange of information between buyers and sellers. Persuasion alludes to the crux of the exchange of any good or service either within the marketing organization or between the marketing organization and a buyer.

Solving Problems [12]

To solve a problem first requires an understanding of it. To begin with, what is the unknown? What are the data? What is the condition and can it possibly be satisfied? Does the condition suffice to determine the unknown? Or does it not suffice? Is the condition redundant or contradictory? The various parts of the condition must be separated and written down if possible.

Once this has been done, the connection between the data and the unknown must be found. If an immediate connection cannot be detected, it may become necessary to examine auxiliary problems. Eventually a plan of solution appears. Has the problem been seen before? Has it perhaps been seen in a slightly different form? Might

---

[11] *Ibid.,* p. 175.
[12] G. Polya, *How To Solve It,* 2nd ed., Doubleday, New York, 1957, p. xvi.

there be a related problem? In any event, one looks at the unknown and tries to recall a familiar problem having the same or some similar unknown. Here is a related problem which has been solved before. Can it, its results, or its methods be used? Or does it require some auxiliary element to make its use possible? Can the problem be restated or put in some quite different manner?

If the proposed problem cannot be solved, perhaps some related problem might be solved first—some problem that is more accessible, more general, more special, or merely analogous. Possibly a part of the problem might be solved and the remainder dropped. To what extent, then, has the unknown been determined, and can it vary? Is there something useful to be derived from the data, or are there other data suitable to determine the unknown? Can the unknown, the data, or both be changed so that a newer unknown and newer data might draw closer to each other? Furthermore, have all the data and the whole condition been used, and have all the essential aspects of the problem been taken into account?

Now the plan is ready for execution. Every step is checked. Is the step the correct one to make, and can its correctness be proven? Finally, a solution to the problem is obtained. When this is achieved, it is time to examine the solution closely. It is time to check the result and the method that led to it. Some final questions remain for the individual to ponder. Could he have derived the same result through some different approach? Could he have seen the result at a glance? Could he use the result, or the method, for solving some other problem?

Some Marketing Problem Areas

Various problems at the *macro* level were suggested by Alderson and Cox.[13] We shall outline seven of them: price discrimination, spatial aspects of marketing, temporal aspects, economic entities, limited alternatives, attitudes and motivation, and market organization.

Price Discrimination. Differences in prices paid by competing buyers for goods purchased from the same supplier or in the prices received from a single buyer raise critical problems of managerial and public policy. This seems to be twentieth century's version of a hoary problem—the problem of the just or fair price. Apparently there

---

[13] Wroe Alderson and Reavis Cox, "Towards a Theory of Marketing," *Journal of Marketing,* Vol. 13, No. 2, October 1948, pp. 139–142.

is a feeling that policy decisions rest on the acceptance of mere conventions as objective facts. Thus, the conventional, narrow definition of price as a ratio between quantities of money and quantities of goods dominates in situations where only a broader definition in terms of completely negotiated sales transactions can be valid.

Spatial Aspects of Marketing. Marketing men often help merchants determine how large a trading area is served by a particular store or by a cluster of stores. Neither the marketing man nor the analyst of land utilization, however, has received much assistance from the general economist. Because of his theories of pure rent and his tendency to assume the existence of spatial distribution in marketing activities, the general economist has not been able to explain this distribution in a manner that shows how the forces of supply and demand can be brought to bear on prices.

Temporal Aspects. Economic theory has often evaded problems raised by time. It has engaged in the analysis of instantaneous relationships instead of utilizing period analysis. This procedure has reduced the economy to a timeless phenomenon in a universe in which noneconomic problems become more amenable to analysis.

Economic Entities. Essentially we think of such economic entities as the company, the market, and the economy. Perhaps it might prove more fruitful to think of marketing channels. It might also be beneficial in this respect to pursue the cooperative efforts of companies rather than only their competitive struggles.

Limited Alternatives. Economic theory is constructed on the premise that businessmen try to maximize results. Little weight is given to the discontinuity of decisions, which are made in "lumps" or "bundles," as it were, and to the making of real choices among specific options, which are quite limited in number and scope. Marketing men know these facts, yet have done little toward formulating alternative courses based on their knowledge of the limitations under which managers and consumers function.

Attitudes and Motivation. Every theory of management as well as every theory of economic behavior must rest on a concept of human motivations and attitudes. Students of marketing working together with those in the behavioral sciences may develop applicable generalizations in this area.

Market Organization. The economist tends to regard the market as an existing entity. He does not give much thought to the fact that someone has to exert continuous effort to keep it operating. The intricate organization required to inform potential buyers and sellers, the bringing them together in the actual negotiation of a transaction, the completing of negotiated transactions all necessitate the human touch. None of these activities is self-generated. It takes a high degree of organization to maintain them.

So much for the problems posed by Alderson and Cox. Bartels suggested that society had to undergo a transformation evolving the institution of marketing before it could use marketing as an instrument of ethical or social responsibility.[14] Some of the developments he believed had to take place included consumer orientation, expanded markets through demand creation, profit motivation, and standardization and uniformity. Briefly, Bartels held that until a viewpoint of production *for the market* were obtained, the significance of the market would not be recognized. This need for consumer orientation was imperative, in his opinion, even though the market economy historically developed with production surpluses.

Bartels further conceived of markets not as created by supply but as capable of expansion through the creation of demand. For him the effect of following tradition rather than promoting innovation in marketing operations produced unimaginativeness and hopelessness for gaining a higher standard of living. In addition, he felt that profit motivation could counteract indifference and inertia. Modern marketing cannot evolve, that is to say, where business prefers the low-volume turnover with high mark-ups to higher profits resulting from lower mark-ups but large volume. Finally, companies had to accept standardization and uniformity in marketing practices. The notion of real or fancied individualism in the market place, held by distributors and consumers, prevents the use of techniques based on mass consumption, mass distribution, and mass production, which are all inherent in modern marketing.

Society's Ends. Besides commenting on these necessary developments for an effective marketing operation, Bartels reviewed some of the ends society attained through marketing. These were:

1. Supplying men's physical needs.
2. Providing for a high degree of specialization of labor in society.
3. Achieving a great diversity of products available for consumption.

[14] Robert D. W. Bartels, "Marketing as a Social and Political Tool," *Marketing: A Maturing Discipline,* Proceedings of the Winter Conference of the AMA, Dec. 28–30, 1960, edited by Martin Bell, American Marketing Association, Chicago, 1961, pp. 210–216.

4. Accelerating the rate of acquisition. This has been done largely through credit.

5. Defining a concept of fairness in society.

6. Shifting responsibilities for consumer decision-making to technical specialists. The maintenance of supplies available for consumption has been shifted to retailers and wholesalers.

7. Creating uniform living standards through the mass market.

8. Achieving cultural integration among nations as the institution of marketing is introduced. Marketing is a means by which social values are taught to peoples with differing social structures, values, and customs. For example, the Swiss Migres chain of food stores has recently authorized the use of its name, trademarked merchandise, and operating methods in Spain to aid the development of voluntary chains there and to extend consumer protection. Likewise, the opening of American-type, consumer-loan companies in Latin American and European cities will teach the commercialization of confidence, the impersonalization of borrowing, and the superiority of legal commercial practices to unregulated and illegal forms of lending.

9. Expressing society's changing sense of values. The values in our society are not fixed. Having elevated materialism somewhat, we have through the medium of marketing emphasized appeals which the world regards as superficial, wasteful, and decadent.

Three Problem Areas. Three problem areas were designated by Cox before the American Marketing Association in 1960.[15] The first of these was the history of marketing. Very little is known about the forces that have wrought institutional change in the economy. The second area is the institutional approach to marketing and the third is the concept of marketing itself.

In the institutional approach to marketing there arise the problems of statistical definition employed by the Census of Business and the efforts to find relevant explanations of the data contained in the statistics. Cox posed several questions for consideration. Why, for example, were there so many business enterprises? Why in a period considered one of consolidation of small companies into larger ones had the number of small companies grown? An hypothesis is suggested that there might be a relationship between the size of the business population and the size of the human population as well as between the business population and the size of the Gross National Product measured in stable numbers. Furthermore, how close was society to maturity in terms of marketing entities? What was the significance of the decreasing number of small independent grocery stores? Was there an over-all stability of the business population?

What actually determined the number, variety, and distribution by size of the economy's establishments? And what determined the number of companies that specialized in one aspect of marketing or another? How did the numbers vary in different economies, and why? Was the hypothesis of too much effort being devoted to marketing in underdeveloped economies tenable? Why did small-scale retailing persist?

As to the concept of marketing, Cox noted that there were several different definitions current. One kind of definition viewed marketing as the performance of business activities that directed the flow of goods and services from producer to consumer or user. Another set of definitions stressed the institutional approach to marketing. A third sort of definition derived from institutional economics or sociology, considering marketing as a social institution. Despite the varied definitions, there remained several questions to be answered properly. How, for instance, did marketing in the United States differ from marketing elsewhere? Was marketing needed in all societies? What type of marketing activity occurred in organized commodity exchanges?

Optimum Level of Material Goods. Another rich province for exploration was mapped by Hollander.[16] He raised the question of how much material goods might be too much for the consumer. Might there be such a thing as total saturation of the market with material goods? In an economy of limited resources there could be the necessity for employing rationing devices. How did the initiative shift in such cases from seller to buyer, and as a result, what organizational changes ensued? As markets changed, what institutions and arrangements persisted, and for how long? These questions and many like them could easily stimulate rewarding investigation leading to the development of valuable marketing hypotheses.

Sources for a Theory of Marketing

Several distinct domains supply materials for theoretical development in marketing management and the contributions of these sources are highly welcomed by students of marketing theory. In the next few pages we shall examine some of these contributions and note the

[16] Stanley C. Hollander, "Adjusting Marketing Theory to a World of Abundance," *Marketing Concepts in Changing Times,* edited by Richard Hill, American Marketing Association, Chicago, 1960, pp. 152–162.

sources from which they emanate. The four principal ones are economic theory, systematic studies of group behavior, ecological studies, and marketing literature.[17]

Economic Theory

Marketing theorists inherit several valuable ideas from institutional economics. Of these one of the most promising approaches to a theory of marketing derives from a study of group behavior. From the sociologists the institutionalists have received the concept of patterns of group behavior. Both the retailing and wholesaling institutions may be considered such patterns whose behavior revolves about some physical facility such as a store or warehouse. Either of these facilities or others like them can be singled out and isolated for counting or measurement.

Institutional economics has also bequeathed to marketing men Commons' proposition for dividing transactions into routine and fully negotiated ones.[18] From this division a marketing theorist may obtain a clue to developing a meaningful analysis of how buyers and sellers change their methods of doing business and of the significance of these changes for the cost of marketing. Moreover, Von Neumann and Morgenstern took the fully negotiated transaction as their point of departure in developing a new mathematical approach to the analysis of market behavior.[19] Starting with an exhaustive study of the negotiated transaction they presented a fresh attack on such problems as efficiency in distribution and monopolistic restriction. Finally, game theory has come to represent the pinnacle of economists' efforts to develop decision theory which is of inestimable value to marketing managers.[20]

Classical Approach. The pioneer work of Clark in the first quarter of this century on overhead costs is a source from which definitions of cost and the relationships between cost and price may emerge as significant contributions to a theory of marketing.[21] Since market-

[17] Alderson and Cox, *op. cit.,* pp. 142–148.

[18] John R. Commons, *Institutional Economics,* Macmillan, New York, 1934.

[19] John Von Neumann and Oskar Morgenstern, *Theory of Games and Economic Behavior,* Princeton University Press, Princeton, N.J., 1944.

[20] For excellent discussion of decision theory and extensive bibliography see Ward Edwards, "The Theory of Decision Making," *Psychological Bulletin,* Vol. 51, No. 4, July 1954, pp. 380–411.

[21] J. M. Clark, *Studies in the Economics of Overhead Costs,* University of Chicago Press, Chicago, 1923.

ing is of necessity involved with competition and price, modern price theory with its stresses on different sorts of competitive situations may very well add to marketing theory. The ideas of Chamberlin,[22] Robinson,[23] and Triffin,[24] as well as the views of such men as Bain,[25] on the subject of nonperfect competition pose a vital challenge to marketing theorists. Furthermore, product differentiation in what Triffin considers heterogeneous competition may replace monopolistic competition. Companies producing standardized items may be able to achieve a competitive status through differentiation of product. These companies may find it possible to allocate their savings in production to advertising and thereby broaden their market.

Differentiation, as we have seen in earlier chapters, is a function of the market carried out primarily through channels of distribution. It is intimately related to the problem of efficiency in marketing. Chamberlin recognized the utility of time and place, along with all specialized services, as aspects of product differentiation but he did not treat the matter at any length. For marketing theory a critical problem is the point in the distribution flow at which differentiation does or should occur. As a general maxim it seems clear that this point should be avoided as long as possible in order to get the most benefit out of that part of the distribution job which can enjoy the economies of minimum differentiation.

In studying sales costs, economic theorists have assumed that the effect of competition in imperfect markets has been to raise these costs. This assumption has to be tested against an analysis that starts from the negotiated transaction as the normal state of things but recognizes the numerous ways of achieving relative economy through routine transactions. For one class of products advertising may help to perform the routinizing of transactions achieved by others through commodity exchanges. Theorists and others concerned with marketing problems should remember that specialization and routinization provide the original basis for increasing efficiency in both production and distribution.

[22] Edward H. Chamberlin, *The Theory of Monopolistic Competition: A Re-Orientation of the Theory of Value,* 1st ed., Harvard University Press, Cambridge, Mass., 1933.

[23] Joan Robinson, *The Economics of Imperfect Competition,* Macmillan, London, 1933.

[24] Robert Triffin, *Monopolistic Competition and General Equilibrium Theory,* Harvard University Press, Cambridge, Mass., 1940.

[25] Joe S. Bain, *Pricing, Distribution and Employment,* rev. ed., Holt, New York, 1953.

One question relating to the heterogeneous competition prevailing in the economy is whether a theory of competition may be developed to serve public needs in such matters as the regulation of marketing policy. Adhering to the views of Clark and Triffin, a revision of competitive theory would have to consider overhead costs and differentiated market position in a heterogeneous economy. The theories of these two economists indicate the need for an analysis of the process of price negotiation and of the conditions for balancing economic forces through bargaining in the market place. In a mass-production economy the central consideration in negotiation, as a rule, is the attempt to balance access to markets through diversified channels against the need for sufficient volume to reach the break-even point in product costs. But such automatic functioning of the market mechanism, as Keynes suggested, may not be taken for granted.[26]

In still another area, no research has formed a better basis for the analysis of the economics of trading areas, or the economic regions within a national economy, or the various sections of a metropolitan community than Ohlin's study of interregional trade.[27] This work undertaken more than 30 years ago is still without peers in its field. It is a major source of theoretical contributions for the marketing theorist steeped in trade among regions.

Finally, in the classical sense, there has been an increasing awareness among scholars of the inefficiency of what economists, in a loose use of language, have long called the "theory of the firm." In an exact sense in both the United States and England, a *firm* applies only to a partnership as distinguished from a corporation, and it has no legal entity apart from the members who form it. A theory of the "firm" therefore would literally preclude the vast number of corporations owned by stockholders which form so vital a part of the economy. The term *company* covers the whole range of business enterprise—individual proprietorship, partnership, and corporation.

In any event, Bowen suggested that the variables of the "firm" be classified according to the level of explanation desired.[28] First, he wished to know the overt company actions which might be explained by the environment. Next, he raised questions about what were the environmental conditions that affected the company. Finally, he

---

[26] J. M. Keynes, *The General Theory of Employment, Interest and Money,* Harcourt, Brace, New York, 1936.

[27] Bertil Ohlin, *Interregional and International Trade,* Harvard University Press, Cambridge, Mass., 1935.

[28] Howard Bowen, *The Business Enterprise, The Subject for Research,* Pamphlet 11, Social Science Research Council, New York, May 1955, p. 29.

sought to find out the internal conditions that influenced the company.

A company's environmental and internal influences may be discerned by studying its physical, biological, psychological, sociological, political, and historical characteristics. Simon suggested that the "theory of the firm" dealt with two factors: [29] first, an explanation of the motives that induce groups to participate as customers, employees, or owners, that is, to assume their *roles* in the company; and second, an explanation of the behavior of the full-time participants, that is, the employees and executives during the period in which they actually take part. Katona proposed that a theory of business action distinguish between what was given and what was precipitated.[30] The former would consist of enabling conditions such as financial assets and socio-cultural norms. The precipitating circumstances would consist simply of stimuli. Katona held that not enough emphasis had been placed on the norms and rules of thumb prevailing in the company, the industry, or the society; on the company's goals and motives, and their changes; or on the expectations that changed simultaneously among groups of people.

Economics and Social Science. The assertion has been made that there is no such thing as economics, only social science applied to economic problems.[31] Indeed, there may be no such thing as social science, but only general science applied to the problems of society. Boulding, in making these contentions, defined the setting of economics as a theory of the individual and a theory of interaction. He tried to introduce the balance sheet as the central concept in explaining the behavior of all economic organisms. The older theory of maximizing profits, he held, was clearly a special case of the more general theory of preference. It was valid only when markets for the individual were perfect. Consumption, and therefore production and income, were seen by him as quantities to be minimized rather than maximized in the interests of maximum enjoyment.

Systematic Studies of Group Behavior

Social scientists have developed many concepts in anthropology, sociology, and social psychology which may aid in the formulation of marketing theories. Lundberg's measurable patterns and clusters

[29] *Ibid.*
[30] *Ibid.*
[31] Kenneth E. Boulding, *A Reconstruction of Economics,* Wiley, New York, 1950.

of communication demonstrate what may be done with ideas borrowed directly from sociology.[32] Essentially, his theory showed the role of leaders in influencing communication. His study proffered a promising device for analyzing the economic significance of such entities as cities, towns, trading centers, trading areas, and individual retailers together with their customers and sources of supply. It further enabled the analysis of advertising media and the people they reached, as well as studies of the many other patterns of communication through which human wants were translated into economic demand, information was circulated among buyers and sellers, and transactions were negotiated and put into effect.

Boulding speculated on the limitations of the principle of maximization of returns as a foundation for a theory of individual business enterprise.[33] He proposed instead that a principle of organizational preservation might prove more productive. Alderson, moreover, pointed out that organizations acted as if they had a will to survive.[34] This drive, he noted, arose from the individual's struggle for socioeconomic status.

Vector Forces. Among psychologists, the topological concepts developed years ago by Lewin[35] and Leeper[36] opened the door to a more knowledgeable understanding of human motivation. Lewin, in particular, tried to explain social behavior through vector forces. In industrial relations, Mayo[37] and Bakke[38] developed promising concepts and procedures for inquiring into the behavior of human beings

[32] George A. Lundberg, *Marketing and Social Organization,* Curtis, Philadelphia, 1945; George A. Lundberg and Mary Steele, "Social Attraction Patterns in a Village," *Sociometry,* Vol. I, January–April 1928, pp. 375–419.

[33] Kenneth E. Boulding, "Samuelson's Foundations: The Rate of Mathematics in Economics," *Journal of Political Economy,* Vol. LVI, No. 3, June 1948, pp. 187–199.

[34] Wroe Alderson, *Marketing Behavior and Executive Action,* Irwin, Homewood, Ill., 1957.

[35] Kurt Lewin, "The Conceptual Representation and the Measurement of Psychological Forces," *Contributions to Psychological Theory,* Vol. 1, No. 5, Duke University Press, Durham, N.C., 1938; Kurt Lewin, *Principles of Topological Psychology,* McGraw-Hill, New York, 1936.

[36] Robert W. Leeper, *Lewin's Topological and Vector's Psychology: A Digest and a Critique,* University of Oregon Press, Eugene, 1943.

[37] Elton Mayo, *Human Problems of Industrial Civilization,* 2nd ed., Harvard University, Division of Research, Boston, 1946.

[38] E. W. Bakke, *Mutual Survival: The Goal of Unions and Management,* Yale University Labor and Management Center, New Haven, 1946.

as employers, employees, and members of trade unions. In addition, students of public opinion and consumer attitudes, among them Cantril,[39] have advanced many suggestions for the construction of questionnaires and interviewing procedures to be used in marketing research.

Ecological Studies

The researches into broad problems of human geography, population, traffic, and city planning have offered many enrichments to marketing theory. Haig's essay of the 1920's on the economic functions of the metropolis [40] and Mayer's classification and analysis of the growth patterns shown by secondary shopping centers in Chicago [41] represent important contributions to marketing theory from the efforts of city planners. Reilly's Law of Retail Gravitation also constitutes an ecological contribution to marketing theory.[42] This law, as we saw in an earlier chapter, was modified by Converse [43] and later by Welch.[44] As we have noted, it has been employed with some minor changes by the McGraw-Hill Publishing Company to develop trading areas throughout the United States.[45] Also in this bailiwick, Stewart has applied concepts much like those he used as a physicist and astronomer to the distribution of population and the influences that individuals and clusters of people exert on each other at a distance.[46]

[39] Hadley Cantril et al., *Gauging Public Opinion*, Princeton University Press, Princeton, N.J., 1940.

[40] Robert Murray Haig, "Toward an Understanding of the Metropolis," *Quarterly Journal of Economics*, Vol. 40, February and May 1926, pp. 179–208 and 402–434.

[41] Harold M. Mayer, "Patterns and Recent Trends of Chicago's Outlying Business Centers," *Journal of Land and Public Utility Economics*, Vol. 18, No. 1, February 1942, pp. 4–16.

[42] William J. Reilly, *Methods for the Study of Retail Relationships*, University of Texas, Austin, 1929.

[43] Paul D. Converse, *A Study of Retail Trade Areas in East Central Illinois*, Bureau of Economic and Business Research, University of Illinois, Urbana, Business Studies No. 2, 1943.

[44] James W. Rouse, "Estimating Productivity for Planned Regional Shopping Centers," *Urban Land News and Trends in City Development*, Vol. 12, No. 10, Urban Land Institute, November 1953.

[45] Frank Strohkarck and Katherine Phelps, "The Mechanics of Constructing a Market Area Map," *Journal of Marketing*, Vol. 12, No. 4, April 1948, pp. 493–496.

[46] John Q. Stewart, "Concerning Social Physics," *Scientific American*, May 1948,

His method, which he summed up under the heading "social physics," may yet lead to the clearest insight and the most precise measurement attained of the forces that determine how people form into markets and exert influence on one another. This may eventually provide a method for reducing to quantitative measurement the sociologist's concepts of patterns of social communication or influence.

Marketing Literature

Copeland was the first writer to classify commodities on the basis of the shopping methods of the consumers who bought them—convenience, specialty, and shopping goods.[47]   Among early writers who have been influential in defining and describing the function of marketing have been Shaw,[48] Cherington,[49] Clark,[50] and more recently, McGarry.[51]   Moreover, Grether has used the concept of interregional trade as a source for building a theory of marketing, and has worked with theoretical ideas of price discrimination and price structures.[52]

Other contributions to theory to be found in the marketing literature include Phillips' attempt to use the ideas and principles of value developed by neoclassical and monopolistic competition economists as part of a body of marketing principles.[53]   Bartels has attempted to cull from the literature all principles or theories.[54]   Breyer struggled with problems of space and time in marketing, with the concept of marketing as a social institution, and with the influence of changes in costs imposed at one level of the channel on costs incurred at other

pp. 20–23; John Q. Stewart, "Empirical Mathematical Rules Concerning the Distribution and Equilibrium of Population," *Geographical Review,* Vol. 37, No. 3, July 1947, pp. 461–485.

[47] Melvin T. Copeland, "Relation of Consumers' Buying Habits to Marketing Methods," *Harvard Business Review,* April 1923, pp. 282–289.

[48] A. W. Shaw, "Some Problems in Market Distribution," *Quarterly Journal of Economics,* August 1912, pp. 703–765.

[49] Paul T. Cherington, *The Elements of Marketing,* 1st ed., Macmillan, New York, 1920.

[50] Fred E. Clark, *Principles of Marketing,* 1st ed., Macmillan, New York, 1922.

[51] Edmund D. McGarry, *The Functions of Marketing,* manuscript.

[52] E. T. Grether, "Geographical Price Policies in the Grocery Trade, 1941," *Journal of Marketing,* Vol. 8, No. 4, April 1944, pp. 417–422; E. T. Grether, *Price Control Under Fair Trade Legislation,* Oxford University Press, New York, 1939.

[53] Charles F. Phillips, *Marketing,* Houghton Mifflin, Boston, 1938.

[54] Robert D. W. Bartels, "Marketing Principles," *Journal of Marketing,* Vol. 2, No. 2, October 1944, pp. 151–517.

levels.[55] Paver,[56] Pelz,[57] and others used traffic flows and movements of pedestrians to indicate the structure of markets and trading areas. Cassady has analyzed price discrimination and its legal significance and has also worked on the problem of decentralizing retail trade in large cities.[58] Vaile [59] and Borden [60] have provided noteworthy studies of the economic effects of advertising. This has been supplemented by Ricketts' work on procedures for evaluating the business effects of advertising.[61]

Thus, we have seen a rundown of some of the major sources of materials for a theory of marketing. In these diverse concepts and principles lodge the seeds for developing a theoretical system applicable to marketing operations. Many scholars through recourse to these sources have struggled to evolve a viable marketing theory and we shall end this chapter by noting some of the more pertinent approaches.

Some Suggested Approaches to Theory

Shaw

To A. W. Shaw the study of the activities of marketing was the application of motion to matter. These activities pervaded every phase of business. From this notion Shaw developed a concept of marketing functions. In general students of marketing concurred

[55] Ralph F. Breyer, *Bulk and Package Handling Costs*, American Management Association, New York, 1944; Ralph F. Breyer, *The Marketing Institution*, McGraw-Hill, New York, 1934.

[56] John Paver and Miller McClintock, *Traffic and Trade*, McGraw-Hill, New York, 1935.

[57] Traffic Audit Bureau, *Methods for the Evaluation of Outdoor Advertising*, Traffic Audit Bureau, New York, 1946. This study was done under the direction of Victor H. Pelz.

[58] Ralph Cassady, Jr., "Some Economic Aspects of Price Discrimination Under Non-Perfect Market Conditions," and "Techniques and Purposes of Price Discrimination," *Journal of Marketing*, Vol. 11, No. 1, July 1946, pp. 7–20, and No. 2, October 1946, pp. 135–150. Ralph Cassady, Jr., and William K. Bowden, "Shifting Retail Trade within the Los Angeles Metropolitan Market," *Journal of Marketing*, Vol. 8, No. 4, April 1944, pp. 398–404.

[59] Ronald S. Vaile, *Economics of Advertising*, Ronald Press, New York, 1927.

[60] Neil H. Borden, *The Economic Effects of Advertising*, Irwin, Homewood, Ill., 1942.

[61] William B. Ricketts, *Testing and Measuring Advertising Effectiveness*, manuscript.

with him on the existence of transactional functions of buying and selling and physical functions of transportation and storage. They have disagreed to some extent over facilitating functions but have accepted the concept as an integral part of distribution cost accounting. Shaw's functional concept has also been a tool in the development of a science of marketing. Indeed the functions of marketing may be regarded as its atomic structure. Like matter the functions are indestructible but they may appear in many different guises.

Alderson

Perhaps the most prolific writer on the subject of marketing theory has been Wroe Alderson.[62] It was he who substituted the term *sorting* for allocation in the definition of economics. The economist is interested in the most efficient allocation of scarce resources to attain a particular end. Alderson maintained that the science of marketing was the study of the process of *double sorting* in the application of marketing effort to marketing opportunity. This meant having the right assortments of goods available for consumers at each level of distribution. By market opportunity Alderson had reference to the market potentiality, and by effort he meant the dollars spent to make the most of the opportunity.

From production Alderson borrowed the term *routine* and fused it with strategic transactions. He observed that the greater the number of routine transactions, the lower the cost of each of them became. He then added the routine transaction to his definition of marketing theory, augmenting it in the following manner: The science of marketing, he said, was the study of the conditions under which the double sorting in the application of effort to opportunity resulted in the maximum routinization of transactions. The theory was then rephrased in functional form to encompass the new term *expectations*. Thus, marketing science became the study of the conditions under which double sorting in the application of effort to opportunity could result in the maximum fulfillment of expectations.

Alderson also emphasized the problem-solving nature of marketing. The object of solving problems in marketing was to reduce uncertainty. In addition, he called attention to the organic construction of the market itself.

---

[62] Alderson's ideas are expressed in the article cited previously and also in his most recent book, *Marketing Behavior and Executive Action*, Irwin, Homewood, Ill., 1957.

Together with Reavis Cox, Alderson stressed the central role of group behavior in marketing activity. Alderson, in particular, underscored the role of the group in searching for status. He pointed out, moreover, the power relations among groups, such as one seeking to dominate the others, and observed that group behavior pervaded the operation of a company itself, the competitive environment in which it flourished, and the consuming public with which it dealt. In this respect, the channel of distribution could be regarded as a group and the market as a group of interacting individuals or companies. Group behavior consequently influenced decisions on pricing, product development, advertising, and personal selling effort. Furthermore, group behavior was controlled both by the government and by the moral and ethical standards of a society. These standards and controls ultimately influenced the decision making of individuals.

Verdoorn

In the model of P. J. Verdoorn for marketing theory the cost of the correct mix of pricing, quality of product, sales promotion, and the choice of a distributive channel all may be suitably allocated.[63] Verdoorn's analysis showed the minimum cost at which a specified quantity could be sold at a designated price. He plotted the minimum cost-curve mix that would yield the largest profit. Superimposed on the cost calculation, however, was a set of boundary conditions—share of the market and maintenance of liquidity. Within these bounds a company could select the mix that would maximize its profits.

Verdoorn recognized the need for supplemental theories to determine the efficiency of each of the instruments—pricing, product, channels, and advertising—as a tool for fashioning a link in the marketing chain. He also acknowledged the need for additional theories to ascertain the interdependence of the various instruments' efficiencies, and the interaction of the specific character and general situation of a company with the efficiency of its marketing instruments.

Shepherd

Geoffrey Shepherd attempted to establish an ideal model for the over-all evaluation of marketing activity.[64] His basic question was

[63] P. J. Verdoorn, "Marketing from the Producer's Point of View," *Journal of Marketing,* Vol. 20, No. 3, January 1956, pp. 221–235.
[64] Geoffrey Shepherd, "The Analytical Problem Approach to Marketing," *Journal of Marketing,* Vol. 20, No. 2, October 1955, pp. 171–173.

how well was the marketing job being done and how could it be improved. He developed what he regarded as an analytic technique to answer the question.

Under ideal conditions of atomistic competition, he held, a uniform price prevailed and could be extended in *time, place,* and *form.* This price was then constant, plus or minus storage costs over time, transportation costs over distance, and grade or other cost differentials of form.[65] Market imperfections could be measured in relation to the perfection of the model in the interest of getting the goods to the consumer at a minimum cost through existing technology. In agricultural marketing Shepherd divided his concept into three parts: consumer demands, the price system reflecting the demands back to the producers, and the transfer of goods from the producer to the consumer at the lowest cost.

In applying the analytic concept to consumer durables, one may question whether consumer preferences are reflected back to the producers; this is a matter of form. Does the "price surface" over a market area—a matter of place—correspond to the "cost of transportation surface?" Do consumers and producers benefit from price stabilization of automobiles? This is a matter of time. Where the answers to the questions are negative, it becomes necessary to dig for explanations.

Form. Continuing with the automobile illustration, let us examine form utility. Consumers' tastes in automobiles vary. First, there is the group that prefers to own automobiles and the group that does not. The former group constitutes the market. Of this group, some would rather buy new cars whereas others would lean to used ones. Of those interested in a new car, some would choose a Plymouth, others a Ford, still others a Cadillac, and so forth. Of the Plymouth partisans, some would prefer a two-door model. Of these, some would like red paint. Of the red paint devotees, some might want green upholstery. This dichotomy proceeds until the car has everything the consumer wants. For the manufacturer to achieve proper utility of form he must have perfect communication with the consumer to perceive his needs and desires.

How may imperfections in form be measured? They may be detected through checking the forecast of automobiles expected to be sold against the actual sales of cars. One reason for excess inventory may be that too many of the wrong style of car reached the market.

[65] For a discussion on the space and time aspects in marketing see Ralph W. Breyer, *The Marketing Institution,* McGraw-Hill, New York, 1934.

Form relates not only to the physical vehicle itself but also to the consumer's image of the manufacturer, the product, and the salesman. These images are inspired by advertising, by talking with friends and relatives, and by conversing with the salesman. The cost of the physical conversion of form may be obtained by calculating the costs of converting the raw materials into the finished automobile and adding to these costs a reasonable return on investment. If to these the costs of psychic conversion of form through advertising, packaging, personal selling effort, and the maintenance of dealerships are appended, a more inclusive form conversion cost results. The question is how do these costs compare with the selling price? If the ratio of the total cost to the selling price varies over a period of time there is an obvious imperfection in form.

Time. When supply and demand are constant and a product is brought to market, the difference in its price from one day to the next represents the carrying charge of keeping the product in storage. This is the time factor, or the transaction cost over an interval of time. In the case of an automobile, assuming a constant supply of vehicles and a steady demand for them, any cost added to the form cost constitutes the storage carrying cost. Any cost in excess of these two—form and storage—indicates a market imperfection. When supply is greater than demand, a carrying charge over a period of time arises, but the increment in the price of the product should not exceed this interest on the storage.

Place. Place signifies the cost of transporting a product from its manufacturer to the market. If perfect information and a free flow of supply and demand are assumed, the differences in price from one place to another result from the transportation cost. For example, the influence of place on the price of automobiles may be observed by taking the selling price of vehicles at Detroit, where they are manufactured, and adding to it the transportation costs to the various markets where they are sold. In the automobile industry supply is controlled. If supply is enough to meet demand and an increment is added for the interest on the storage, the only other supplement to price would be to cover transportation. Market imperfection results when the additional price is more than the transportation cost.

The foregoing model offers many eclectic possibilities. For example, the problem of channel costs might be included under time. In channel costs, the transaction costs are measured. These comprise a whole spate of costs including the cost of storage and handling, selling and advertising, and other factors related to wholesaling and retailing, as well as a reasonable return on investment.

In addition to the presence of form, time, and place utility in the product itself, there is the principle of massed reserves in the channels of distribution. This is a division of labor carried out where a few wholesale institutions contain large reserves rather than each retailer stocking complete supplies.[66] The practice of postponement is a concomitant of this principle. Postponement suggests that other things being equal marketing costs may be reduced by deferring, as we have already observed, the commitment of a unit of material to a specific use as long as possible. For example, a ton of iron should be kept in the form and at the place in which it gives its owner the widest possible choice of how it may be utilized. This would explain any variation in costs through time.

Carlston

The final approach we shall consider is the marketing management theory proposed by Carlston.[67] To begin with, Carlston established the province of marketing as the actions of business organizations and consumers in their joint adaptation to the market environment. These actions occurred in transactions and related activities. The objectives of both the organizations and the consumers were to realize their respective values. From this beginning Carlston proceeded to develop nine propositions to expand his basic point of view. The first proposition said that the creation of any science was the statement of its area of concern or its boundaries. One had to know not only the discipline of marketing but also all the disciplines germane to it.

The second proposition stated that marketing theory had to stand above business organizations and consumers, viewing both from a perspective in which they were observed interacting in a market environment. Although concerned with organizational theory and consumer motivation, marketing theory had to establish a vantage point from which to survey its whole province in order to reach full flowering. Since the science of marketing was concerned with the adaptation of the business organization to its environment, there had to be an understanding of decision making in the marketing actions of the

[66] Reavis Cox and Charles S. Goodman, "Marketing Housebuilding Materials," *Journal of Marketing*, Vol. 21, No. 1, July 1956, pp. 36–61.

[67] Kenneth S. Carlston, "The Province and Function of Marketing Theory," *Marketing a Maturing Discipline: Proceedings of the Winter Conference of the AMA,* edited by Martin L. Bell, American Marketing Association, Chicago, Dec. 28–30, 1960, pp. 134–410.

business organization. The making of decisions by top management involved leadership, administration, and control.

In behavioral terms, action in an individual could be said to include three phases: the creative or exploratory phase, the performance phase, and the control or appraisal and regulative phase. The creation of future action was institutionalized in the business organization in the leadership phase of management and the performance of action in the administrative phase. Leadership created ideas for action; administration determined the action's physical content. And control both reflected upon and regulated action.

Carlston's third proposition held that an organization's marketing decisions embodied the same decision-making patterns as dominated top management's procedures for governing the affairs of the business as a whole—namely, leadership, administration, and control. His fourth, fifth, and sixth propositions dealt with each of these patterns on an individual basis.

The fourth proposition maintained that marketing was concerned with the exercise of leadership in a business organization's adaptation to the market environment. Marketing leadership theory never accepted the *is* of organizational behavior as the final criterion of rightness and validity, but always tested the *is* for future suitability. Leadership ensured the gearing of the organization to allow the participation of consumers in decision making so that they might realize the values they cherished both currently and in the future.

The fifth proposition dealt with adapting the organization's administration to market environment. Whereas leadership theory found its mooring in the future, marketing administration theory found its base in the present. The theory of marketing administration was interested in those principles and propositions deriving from the behavior of business organizations as they *in fact* adapted to the market environment. The planning stage was now at end. Plans were jelled or frozen. This was it!

Advertising and sales theory were both part of marketing administration theory. Although both were concerned with communication, they were also intent upon developing a body of principles and propositions bearing on effective communication *from* consumers *to* the business organization. Moreover, they were concerned with departures from the communicated image or message of "value-realization," with the actual transaction and associated activities, and with ensuring the occurrence of consumer behavior. Such a body of principles and such a channel of communication from consumers to the organization is part of the theory of control in advertising.

The sixth proposition held that marketing was concerned with the performance of control as a business organization adapted to the market environment. Control was concerned with appraisal of past action to ascertain whether goals had been reached, and reached economically, and whether experience demanded that goals of means be shaped anew. It was one of the functions of the theory of marketing control to supply a scientific basis for originating and evaluating marketing legislation. Thus, leadership dealt with the future, administration with the present, and control with the past.

The seventh proposition specified that marketing theory was concerned with the realization of values by consumers through participating in the system of action with a business organization. This they did through a transaction and related events. The most important single criterion of management success was the extent to which a company's resources were so coordinated that they invited consumer participation.

The eighth Carlston proposition maintained that the function of marketing theory was the determination of the conditions whereunder a fixed quantity of energy in the business organization could provide the consumer with an opportunity to achieve a realization of value. In the use of a business organization's resources, the concept of efficiency was an area for marketing theory. It had to tell which conditions produced a difference between what was accomplished and what might have been accomplished with a given quantity of resources. Accomplishment represented the degree to which the overriding goal of the business organization had been attained.

The final proposition asserted that the eight previous principles and hypotheses not only provided a standpoint from which to bring into perspective and order the hierarchy of relationships among the several parts of marketing theory, but also facilitated inquiry into those social sciences that could contribute to the growth of marketing theory. Among such sciences were anthropology, management theory, psychology, public administration, and sociology.

It is clear from all this that theory is of vital importance to marketing management, especially if marketing management is to have a scientific rationale. The main challenge for marketing men in this area is to build their theories on established principles drawing on the spade work of the theorists who have come before them. The foundations have been well laid, as we have seen; many scholars have already spun workable theories that are relevant to marketing operations. Whether these suffice or there is room for further development and refinement will be decided by future generations of marketing men. It has been the purport of this chapter to show what has been done. The rest is up to the marketing profession.

Summary

The basic characteristic of a theory is that its statements may be falsified. Theories may be expressed in the form of universal statements. Individual statements may be derived from the theory. These statements may be set up in axiomatic form and thus a model is created. The difference between an empirical and theoretical law is that the theoretical law tells the structure of things under unchanging conditions.

Science is a systematic theoretical explanation of a phenomena. In some aspects of marketing theories have been developed to explain phenomena in a scientific way.

Bartels has classified the principles of marketing into five categories: (1) operational principles; (2) principles involving institutional relationship; (3) principles relating to the marketing task; (4) hypothetical principles; and (5) truism.

A problem is a condition which prevents attaining a goal. Some of the problems of marketing administration are the market mix, the administrative mix, and the frustration mix. Problem solving involves: first, understanding the problem; second, devising a plan; third, carrying out the plan; and fourth, looking back and evaluating.

Some marketing problems related to price discrimination, spatial aspects of marketing, temporal aspects of marketing, economic entities, limitation of alternatives, attitudes and motivation, and development of market organization. Other problems relate to the optimal amount of goods for consumption, marketing as a tool of social responsibility, and the ends of our society promoted through marketing.

The sources that are useful in developing a theory of marketing may be classified as economic, group behavior, ecological, and the marketing literature. Suggestions for a theory of marketing have been made by A. W. Shaw, Alderson, Verdoorn, Shepherd, and Carlston.

Suggested Cases

Ralph L. Westfall and Harper W. Boyd, *Cases in Marketing Management*, Irwin, Homewood, Ill., 1961.

The Eversharp Pen Company—*Pen Manufacturer*—Reappraisal of Marketing Program, pp. 530–534.

The Dow Chemical Company—*Antifreeze Manufacturer*—Revolutionary Marketing Program under Changing Conditions, pp. 535–542.

Milton P. Brown, Wilbur B. England, and John B. Matthews, Jr., *Problems in Marketing*, 3rd ed., McGraw-Hill, New York, 1961.

Indian Head Mills, Inc., pp. 766–788.

Ludlow Corporation, pp. 789–804.

Chapter Twelve

When a housewife bakes a cake she arrays her ingredients before her and carefully mixes them into a batter. When a symphony orchestra prepares a concert its conductor blends the various instrumental parts into a well-balanced musical whole. When a building contractor erects a house he instructs his helpers to follow a unifying plan in which assorted materials all fall into their proper places. In each of these instances, as in any endeavor of the human hand or human mind, raw materials or ideas are organized into a cohesive structure. In principle they are all the same. They differ only in kind and scale. The housewife can complete her organization of materials alone. The conductor and the contractor both need organizations composed of colleagues or subordinates to carry out their organizing activities. Marketing is no exception. It, too, requires the organization of all of its elements and the establishment of a marketing body headed by a qualified marketing executive so that the marketing process may function smoothly, efficiently, and effec-

Organization

tively to strengthen the position of the company in its business or industrial community.

Over the years much thought has been expended on the problems of organization. This has dealt with both the principles underlying organization and the mechanics of the organizations to be formed. In this chapter we shall consider several aspects of organization and the workings of organizations from principles to practice. We shall begin with a study of some of the propositions that may be derived for marketing management from the existing literature on the subject of organization. Then we shall turn to the actual practices of marketing organization as they occur at present and as they are expected to evolve in the future.

Propositions about Organization Behavior

In their study of organizations, March and Simon grouped propositions of organization behavior into three kinds.[1] First, there were those propositions that assumed that members of organizations—and employees in particular—were primarily passive instruments. They were capable of performing work and accepting directions, but not able to initiate action or exert influence in any significant way. Second, there were propositions that assumed that members brought attitudes, values, and goals to their organizations. They had to be motivated or induced to participate in the system of organization behavior. Between their personal goals and organizational goals the chasm was deep. Actual or potential conflicts over these goals gave central importance to power phenomena, attitudes, and morale in the explanation of organizational behavior. Third, there were propo-

---

[1] James G. March and Herbert A. Simon, *Organizations,* Wiley, New York, 1958, p. 6.

sitions assuming that members of organizations were makers of decisions and solvers of problems. In consequence, perception and thought processes became central to the explanation of behavior in organizations.

To March and Simon there was nothing contradictory among these three sets of assumptions. Human beings were all these things, and perhaps more. An adequate theory of human behavior in organizations had to account for the instrumental, motivational, attitudinal, and rational aspects of behavior. Indeed no substantial body of writings about organizations has single-mindedly and consistently adopted one of these viewpoints. All three of them, in fact, are emphasized in the literature on organization.

The model of the employee as an instrument permeates the writings of the scientific management movement. In the last several decades the second set of propositions which stress attitudes and motivations has gained more prominence in research into bureaucracy, human relations, leadership and supervision, and power phenomena. The third set stressing the rational aspects of organizational behavior has appeared less frequently than the other two. Yet it represents the work of economists and others on the planning process and of psychologists on communication by an organization and on the solving of problems.

Classical Administrative Theory

The origin of the classical administrative theory—that is, that employees are passive instruments—stems from the works of Taylor, Gulich, and Urwick. Taylor stressed time and methods study [2] Men were viewed as adjuncts to machines. Management was concerned with individual capacity, speed, and durability. Gulich and Urwick, on the other hand, were interested in the grand organization problems of departmental division of work and coordination.[3]

Through the application of time and motion study to sales effort, billing procedures, order handling, warehousing, and transportation, Taylor has had a pronounced influence on marketing. Information gathered through time and motion analysis has been used as a basis for cost data, development of standards of performance, and the introduction of automation. Taylor's concept of durability was concerned essentially with fatigue and incentives. It was assumed in

[2] F. W. Taylor, *The Principles of Scientific Management,* Harper, New York, 1911.
[3] Luther Gulick and L. Urwick, *Papers on Scientific Administration,* Institute for Public Administration, New York, 1937.

marketing that the major means of motivating men to put forth their greatest effort was monetary reward. In many companies this has taken the form of motivating salesmen through strong financial incentives. But as we have seen executives can be motivated by other things than financial inducements.

According to Gulich and Urwick one had to define the purpose of the organization and then determine the set of tasks needed to accomplish the purpose. Tasks included productive activities, service activities, and activities of coordination. The challenge for administration was to fill the jobs in larger and larger administrative units eventually arriving at the top level. In the organization process Gulich and Urwick viewed each department as a collection of tasks to be allocated and performed by the department's employees. It was the opinion of Gulich and Urwick that as the basic concept of organization grew it became possible to achieve more specialization of functions. Thus, in marketing the general task of selling became fractionated into personal selling, advertising, marketing research, and product development. This gave rise to the need for the coordinating post of the marketing manager.

Specialization precipitated another problem—the proper classification of activities. This problem was basic. One had to pay close attention to functions and processes. Although these might be well defined and highly routine the occasion for the performance of any particular one of them might depend on environmental stimuli, instructions and information, or any one of a number of things. Thus, one might question whether the separation of the marketing department into the functional divisions mentioned was really the most sensible procedure. Might it not be preferable to denote specialization on the basis of the decision-making process, such as pricing, product, advertising, personal selling, and channels of distribution? As to the environmental stimuli, they might be tradition, the changing competitive situation, personalities in the company, economic and political changes, or the changing nature of the company itself.

Classical theory of organization regards personnel as a fixed entity rather than as a variable. It defines the job of the salesman, for example, and fits an individual into it. There is no consideration of the personality of the individual and how it may modify the job description. Furthermore, classical theory holds that once the objectives of a company are known it is a relatively simple matter to define the means for reaching those ends. Thus, with the end of the marketing department taken to be the actuation of the consumer the means for accomplishing this objective are assumed to be simple. However, the end of the marketing department is only a means for the company to attain its own ends, which may be the maximization of long-run profits. Correspondingly, the means leading to the marketing department's goals become ends in themselves. Let us apply these theoretical considerations to marketing management and the selection of a marketing executive.

Classical Theory and Marketing Management. Too many executives have tended to oversimplify the basic implications of the marketing concept. For an executive to say that a company employs this concept and relates its thinking to consumer needs, or for a company suddenly to consider itself *customer-oriented* is likely to create marketing overemphasis now as financial overemphasis was created in the past.[4] Many company directors, members of executive committees, and presidents lack experience in marketing because they have risen through the ranks of production, finance, and other divisions of the concern. These men may not be able to supply proper guidance to the marketing program, yet such direction is imperative. Moreover, there may be errors in promoting individuals. Some companies follow the policy of promoting from within. This may prove dangerous in a quickly competitive field, as the following example suggests:

A large industrial chemical company formed a new consumer division charged with the responsibilities of packaging basic chemicals, developing a consumer line, and launching new products as consumer goods. Quite obviously this posed a complex marketing problem.

However, only three men out of the entire head-office staff had the necessary experience to fulfill their particular jobs. The five product managers came out of the field sales force, basically with a background of selling bulk chemicals to other manufacturers; and the sales promotion managers came from either the laboratory or the industrial sales force.

The sales manager himself came from one of the industrial divisions where for 15 years he had been the sales manager directing six men selling to 56 large users who bought on an annual contract basis. He was an excellent personal salesman, a loyal company man, but (a) had never directed a sales force of any size, and (b) had no experience with wholesalers or retailers in any field. His principal qualification was years of successfully writing multimillion-dollar carload orders personally.[5]

In many instances, sales management is an obvious recruiting ground for the new coordinating job. However, success as a sales manager does not guarantee success as a director of marketing. One basic

---

[4] Arthur P. Felton, "Making the Marketing Concept Work," *Harvard Business Review,* Vol. 37, No. 4, July–August 1959, pp. 55–65.
[5] *Ibid.*

qualification for good sales management is the ability to plan, and to organize, select, and lead other salesmen. The duties of a modern and advanced director of marketing, as we have observed, require him to be much broader than the successful sales manager. He has to qualify in the following respects:

He must think in corporate terms rather than dollar or unit sales.

Not only must he have a higher degree of analytical ability than that normally required (or even advisable) in sales management; but, most importantly, he must have the ability to define problems for research and then capably analyze results and develop the indicated plans and policies.

He must have a high degree of capability and experience in planning and organization to be able to integrate and coordinate the many other marketing functions that must be performed in today's competitive situation.

He must be able to get the best out of his director of marketing research as well as his advertising, sales promotion, and product managers.

He must, in addition to all this, be a man who can sit down with the production director, the personnel director, the treasurer, the lawyer, the president, and in many cases, the board of directors, and put the interests of the corporation first, while representing the broad marketing aspects of the business. In many cases, because of the particular personality, breadth of technical know how, and ability to effect integrated operations required of the director of marketing, the aggressive, dynamic "leader of the groups" type of sales manager completely falls apart when promoted to the position.[6]

The personality characteristics of individual division managers may actually impede the development of an integrated marketing operation. In several cases, a man who might be a vice president in charge of a division was formerly the owner, operator, or manager of a smaller independent company. He probably became the owner or manager of this smaller enterprise because of his individual productivity, forceful driving personality, and fiercely independent spirit. He is an entrepreneur at heart who does not find it easy to fit into a corporate set-up. He is not the corporate type. He cannot handle a complex marketing program.

When dissimilar companies with such individualistic managers merge or are purchased, problems of this kind often increase by the square of two. Top management of the headquarters company has so little knowledge of its subsidiaries in the field that it is incapable of helping when its individual divisions encounter trouble. This situation is most likely to occur when a small businessman sells out to a corporation at about the time he runs into problems in trying to manage his own enterprise. By his determination to maintain auton-

[6] *Ibid.*

omy he continues to keep the parent company at arm's length while he ostensibly runs his own show. But when a recession in sales strikes, he is incapable of coping with it. More unfortunately, the parent company is also incapable of handling the situation because it has not had a real opportunity to learn the business of its subsidiary.

First and foremost, the organizational plan for a marketing department or division of a company requires a basic concept. A violation of good organizational principles rather than a lack of ability or product is often the principal cause for the failure of a marketing operation. As a management consulting concern pointed out in one of its brochures:

> The current shift from a Sales Management to a Marketing Management concept increases substantially the number and complexity of the problems and decisions facing the division's Chief Executive. He is, more than ever before, a key member of the Top Management Group, and he must be capable of thinking, planning, and administration of the highest order. For that reason, it is imperative that the Vice President-Marketing's job be analyzed meticulously, and that his basic function, his major responsibilities, and key duties be stated in the most precise terms. When this is done, he is in position to delegate the component responsibilities and authorities specifically, and to follow through regularly and efficiently to insure their effective performance by his subordinates.
>
> Such a position analysis must be carried out in greater depth than is usually the case for a conventional job description. . . .[7]

Often final responsibilities must be assigned in the light of the character of the total operation and modified by the experience and personality of the executives available. The personality and experience of the team members must complement and balance each other. Top management must clearly resolve whether the director of marketing is to be completely responsible for all the necessary marketing functions, including sales, or whether he should be, in fact, a director of marketing services or of marketing planning. In many companies the integration of the marketing effort is effectuated by the president or the owner. In others it is carried out by the executive vice president or the vice president in charge of sales. In the latter cases the director of marketing may be a staff post and as such is responsible for all marketing functions except sales. Sales fall on the shoulders of another executive who directs the sales force and supervises sales training, sales analysis, and product servicing. In a multidivisional company the director of marketing may be even further removed

[7] Barrington Associates, Inc., *The Kind of Executive Needed for the Position of Vice President—Marketing,* New York, 1957, p. 1.

from the intimate direction of such functions as marketing research, advertising, sales promotion, and so forth. Here he functions primarily as an over-all marketing coordinator and as a consultant to the president of the company.

It is important, however, to define clearly the basic responsibilities of the marketing director. This has a strong bearing on the background and personality of the man selected for the position. For instance, one very large, multidivisional corporation was looking for its third marketing director in five years. One reason that neither of the first two directors was able to handle the job was the lack of definition of duties and responsibilities. Both were, however, held responsible for serving as adviser and coordinator to the president of the corporation, for advising 13 divisions, and for participating in a loosely defined manner in the marketing phases of the company's acquisition program.

On many occasions the previous marketing directors were summoned on a "panic button" basis to solve detailed sales promotion problems for strongly autonomous divisions in a wide arc of varied industrial activity. That each of these men was not able to function effectively in any one area was hardly surprising.

In trying to develop more exact personnel specifications for a new marketing director, two of the corporation's top officials continued to hold widely divergent views as to the job requirements. One was seeking a candidate with stature in the industry, sales experience, and skill in public speaking. The other official placed more emphasis on analytical ability, marketing research competence, and a broad range of experience in consumer and industrial goods industries. The most difficult problem for this corporation to resolve was the realization that no single individual could fit both sets of specifications.[8]

Size, Complexity, and Responsibility. From the nature of the company itself arise additional factors that bear on the definition of responsibilities. Two of the important ones are the size of the concern —that is, whether it is large or medium-sized—and its number of divisions. In a large company the top marketing man is more likely to be a coordinator, planner, and a "corporate thinker." He therefore needs great skills in administration and over-all planning. In the various marketing functions he requires only enough experience to give adequate direction to his various department heads and to evaluate their performances. In the smaller company, in contrast, the marketing executive actually has to *perform* a wide variety of market-

[8] Felton, *op. cit.*

ing functions himself. Since he has a more intimate connection with the daily work, he is expected to possess greater experience in specific marketing skills.

In the multidivisional corporation the basic requirements for the marketing director place the main emphasis on long-range planning skill, competence in coordination, and human relations. In a personal letter to an executive recruiting agency, the board chairman of a large, multidivisional corporation explained his requirements for a brand-gauged director of marketing in the following manner:

Our chief requirement is for a man with sufficient knowledge of the principles of marketing research, merchandising, advertising, sales, etc., to be able to help set objectives and evaluate the work of his own department heads as well as those in each of our divisions. Even more important is the ability to exercise across-the-board coordination and quality control while at the same time aggressively represent marketing interests at our top management level and to put it bluntly, sell the marketing concept to our divisional presidents.[9]

To avoid trouble every company should take a careful look at the job requirement. It should develop a complete job description with clearly delineated duties and responsibilities and then draw up a man specification before rushing out to hire or promote someone for the post. Typical samples of what might be done may be seen from the following job descriptions for three types of marketing directors drawn from as many professional sources.

1. DIRECTOR OF MARKETING

The basic function of the position is to: plan and manage all aspects of the marketing program; maintain and equip a well-trained organization to carry out the program; and direct all marketing operations so as to attain stated objectives within company policy and budgets.

Major Responsibilities:
1. Sales Planning and Policy
2. Sales Organization, Training and Compensation
3. Sales Forecasts, Quotas, Budgets and Controls
4. Selling Operations
5. Industry and Customer Relations
6. Pricing
7. Advertising, Sales Promotion, Publicity and Public Relations
8. Product and Market Research and Development
9. Sales Operations Research
10. Employee Relations.[10]

---

[9] *Ibid.*
[10] Barrington Associates, Inc., *op. cit.,* p. 2.

2. DIRECTOR OF MARKETING SERVICES—MARKETING PLANNING

Basic function . . . responsible for administering, coordinating, and controlling all aspects of the total marketing program for his assigned product lines and for assisting the sales organization in successful implementation of the program. . . .

Specific Responsibilities:

1. To develop and recommend for approval to the Vice President . . . complete marketing program pertaining to his assigned product lines, including a factual analysis of the markets, an enumeration of problems and opportunities [in] specific marketing objectives, advertising and promotion plans, packaging and some brands, selling methods, forecasts of sales, cost of sales, and profits for at least the ensuing year.

2. To direct the Product Managers in conducting similar marketing planning activities for the assigned products.

3. To organize and [chair] planning meetings of representatives from Research and Development and from Production, together with the Product Managers, for purpose of expediting the development and production of present products as well as the coordinated development of new and improved products.

4. To represent his assigned product lines in the product-planning sessions of the Executive Product Committee. . . .

5. To work with Research and Development and with Production in the development of improved products by interpreting the needs and preferences of the market.

6. To work with Finance and Accounting in providing recommended budget estimates and accounting controls necessary to determine the profitability of present products and methods of marketing, as well as to measure current marketing performance in relation to objectives.

7. To work with the General Sales Manager and the Regional Sales Managers in the development of all aspects of marketing planning. . . .[11]

3. VICE PRESIDENT OF MARKETING

As vice president of marketing, the successful candidate will report directly to the president. Primary responsibility is the coordination in a staff capacity of all sales and related activities among 12 autonomous manufacturing and sales divisions. The vice president of marketing may have acquired a broad knowledge of sales methods and market research as a top staff man in a company producing both consumer and industrial goods, or as a management consultant. He must be able to recognize and cure duplication of sales or allied efforts between divisions without creating friction. He must act as the profit center conscience of the entire company's distribution system. He must be highly creative and have the ability to use all the knowledge gleaned from divisional sales personnel to benefit the company's over-all planning and scheduling.[12]

[11] From a report prepared by Bruce Payne & Associates, Inc., Westport, Conn., 1958.

[12] Ward Howell, "Marketing Managers Wanted: Big Rewards, Key Responsibilities for Right Man," *Printer's Ink,* March 21, 1958, p. 61.

Balance of Talent.   The next task after drawing up specifications for the kind of man wanted for the top marketing job is to fill the blocks on a preliminary organization chart with men possessing an appropriate combination of executive ability, technical competence, and personality.   The final definition of duties and responsibilities must wait upon the selection of the men so that the written descriptions will constitute a realistic blending of personalities and capabilities with the duties and responsibilities to be assumed.

One error to be avoided is staffing from the bottom up.   In this type of situation the company develops a new organization chart and fills in all or most of the positions before it hires a director of marketing, or it fills the jobs in a department before hiring the department head.   Trouble eventuates when the new top man finds his subordinates incompatible, or his previously hired department does not contain the right balance of ability and personality.

Often a corporation comprising a range of companies can improve its marketing efficiency by organizing its subsidiaries into logical industrial groups and by adding or dropping companies within each group.   As an example of grouping and realignment one nationally prominent corporation purchased 12 companies between 1938 and 1955.   The individual companies were engaged in such widely diversified ventures as the manufacture of automatic processing machinery, atomic energy research, industrial OEM components in electronic instruments, parts for automobiles, and consumer goods sold through hardware, sporting goods, and grocery stores.   A careful analysis of the groups of companies showed that they could be combined logically to benefit from common research and manufacturing or marketing efforts—or both.   The corporation consequently formed a research and development group, a recreational industry group, a machinery automation group, and an industrial electronics group.   Subsequently the corporation divested itself of divisions that did not contribute to or benefit from a common research, manufacturing, or marketing program.   It also purchased companies that would complement and round out the operation in each industry group.[13]

In recreation and machinery automation, in particular, the greatest emphasis was placed on developing new products either through acquisition or through research and development.   These products had common channels of distribution and also lent themselves to benefiting from a common advertising campaign to achieve maximum

[13] *Ibid.*

marketing efficiency. The moves made in the first year of this stream-lining process improved operating efficiency and were quickly reflected in better net profits and higher earnings per share.

Actually, one of the most effective methods of strengthening cor-porate control over independent divisions, as well as improving market efficiency, is through development of a carefully designed advertising and public-relations program. In such cases a corporation finds it economically advisable to establish a strong "corporate character" among various publics so that its name or insignia becomes a market-ing tool for its individual subsidiaries. Frequently, when properly promoted, the corporation name or insignia becomes so much of a competitive advantage that even the hard-bitten former owner or manager rushes to tie in with it.

Attitudes, Values, Goals

March and Simon held that the influence over an individual's moti-vation to produce was a function of the influence over the evocation of courses of action for him, the consequences of those courses, and the values attached by him to those consequences.[14] Each of these was partly under the control of the organization and partly determined by extraorganizational factors. The actual amount of organizational control depended, in turn, partly on supervisory practices and partly on economic conditions; the former represented the behavior of the organization and the latter, factors beyond the organization's control.

As long as the satisfactions derived from the organization were greater than the pain suffered or the effort exerted the individual would remain in the organization, March and Simon postulated.[15] This was the hedonistic principle. The satisfactions derived by the individual were related not only to the organization but also to such extraorganizational factors as status in the community, economic conditions, and the like. Satisfactions and participation went hand in hand. As satisfactions increased so did participation. Conversely, as satisfaction diminished participation dropped off. The theory of organization participation was a theory of organization equilibrium.

Within the organization conflict was apt to develop for the indi-vidual. Conflict fitted two types.[16] First, there was essentially intra-individual conflict in which organization members themselves had

[14] March and Simon, *op. cit.*, p. 82.
[15] *Ibid.*, p. 83.
[16] *Ibid.*, p. 135.

difficulty in making a choice. Second, there was interindividual conflict in which members of the organization had mutually inconsistent choices. These conflicts could arise from the incomparability of alternatives, from their unacceptability, or from uncertainty about their consequences. Both organizational environment and the characteristic of the organization were sources of these sorts of conflicts. The problem for organization was to create a body in which individuals could obtain maximum expression without conflict and in which the organization itself could realize optimum satisfaction of its demands.

It is simple to put a statement of objectives on paper and draw up organization charts. Yet it is important to discover the *role* performed by the individual in carrying out his duties.[17] The lines on the organization chart do not always convey a true image. In actual operations they may be crossed, with direct communication existing between separate levels. Although there are written objectives in most organization, other "unwritten" ones also deserve attention. Goal achievement, for example, is an important area for study. Furthermore, the size of an organization presents a problem of communication. Larger organizations require leaving the making of decisions to their higher echelons. Because of these various factors it is important that the member of an organizational structure have a perception of the structure. He sees his own role more sharply when he perceives the organizational goals. Behavior, said Boulding, is molded by the role played by individuals simply because people want to do the expected thing.[18] Finally, successful leadership consists of behavior or acts performed by persons commanding some measure of influence to stimulate actions by others in the direction desired.

Attitudes, Values, Goals, and Marketing Management.[19] Sometimes men cannot accomplish their professional objectives because of clashes of personality. This occurs when the introvert or nonconformist is so right on so many matters that he stirs up antagonism and resentment among other department heads. It also happens when an executive dedicates himself exclusively to what he thinks is his own personal advancement. The tactics of this kind of executive are often subtle. He gives lip service to the group effort in meetings and conferences and then proceeds to undercut his associates. Many such situations

---

[17] Carrol L. Shartle, "Organization Structure," *Current Trends in Industrial Psychology,* University of Pittsburgh Press, 1949.
[18] Kenneth E. Boulding, "A Look at the Corporation," *The Lamp & 75th Anniversary of Jersey Standard* (Booklet), Standard Oil Co., 1957, p. 6.
[19] Felton, *op. cit.*

are inherited by the director of marketing. He must solve the problem by providing for the development of a mutually cooperative attitude and for the coaching of his subordinates in teamwork. Often this ability counts for 80 per cent of a marketing director's value to his employer.

There are also companies dominated by "one man" autocrats. Although these men have been outmoded, by and large, by fully and professionally developed techniques of integrated marketing, they still exist, as the following example indicates.

A large and well-known cosmetic company called in one of the leading management consulting firms at the insistence of its bank. It received a thorough analysis and a new, well-designed marketing organization, complete with advertising manager, brand manager, marketing research department, merchandising department, marketing administration section, and a reorganized sales force. Professionally competent marketing men with specialized qualifications were added, some of the least competent incumbents were let go, and other old-time employees were reassigned duties and responsibilities under the new organization chart—in short, a virtually perfect textbook solution.

Only one thing was missing—a proper state of mind on the part of the president. He still made all the decisions; he still second-guessed the professional; he still was out of touch with the current marketing problems. As a result at the end of two years the company was still functioning in the same manner that it had for the previous 20 years. The entire marketing group, which by and large represented at least average if not above average individual competence, was never allowed to function in a professional manner.[20]

It should be obvious, moreover, that in many companies the board of directors needs the revitalization supplied by mature, topflight, marketing-oriented directors. These men may be directors or top-level executives of other successful noncompeting corporations, retired executives with broad marketing experience, professors in business schools, or consultants. Recently companies have begun to pay substantial fees to obtain the active participation of men who act as director-consultants. Smith-Corona Marchant, for example, has an interesting board of directors, to judge from the following report:

At Smith-Corona Marchant, a unique and close-working relationship opens up direct channels of communication between the president, the board, and staff executives. It puts the president's directors' knowledge and experience at the disposal of the operating executive. Moreover, the vice president in charge of marketing can call on a director without going

[20] *Ibid.*

through the president or the board chairman. This organizational structure paves the way for support of marketing objectives and the marketing concept at the top level.

Dr. Litchfield recruited several outside men for the board, including Clarence Francis, formerly chairman of the General Foods Corporation. The board was then organized into eight working committees to parallel the major fields of operation. Each committee works directly with the vice president in its designated field.

The chairman of the board marketing committee is Clarence Francis. The vice president in charge of marketing is not a director but is the sixth member and secretary of the committee. The marketing committee convenes periodically, and makes objective appraisals of marketing, sales, advertising, and promotional plans. The final approval for the marketing program must come from the operating committee headed by the president. Any major step is thus reviewed and coordinated with the corporate long-range plan at one of the weekly meetings.[21]

The marketing function is clearly well-integrated at the topmost level. The marketing and operating committee of the company provides control as well as consultation on all marketing decisions.

The chief officer and the key executives of a company, on the other hand, have to initiate their own self-improvement program. All presidents of companies including some excellent ones are not born with an innate appreciation and understanding of an integrated marketing operation. How can they compensate for this? Consider these suggestions:

One effective tool is the long-range corporate plan. Perhaps the greatest benefit to a company developing such a plan is the *education* the executives get from the fact-finding and analysis requisite for the development of the plan. This research includes studying future growth characteristics of the country in general and technical and economic growth trends in the specific industry, as well as in related firms.

An evaluation of competitive trends to determine what niche the company should carve out for itself over the next five to ten years is also a part of the background work. This study is normally followed by detailed yearly sales forecasts for current products. Then specific plans for new product additions, diversification, and mergers are incorporated. And finally, this future planning is tied in with similar planning by the production, personnel, research, and financial departments to form a carefully integrated and coordinated, but flexible, long-range plan.[22]

Executive exposure to this kind of analysis and planning aids in the development of a state of mind that insists on planned, coordinated

[21] *Ibid.*
[22] *Ibid.*

efforts in the marketing areas. Such a plan is only the *foundation* for the proper corporate attitude. While a long-range plan will give direction in broad terms, executive officers must be imbued with an understanding of the problems confronted by the integrated marketing operation and the reasons that marketing functions are performed as they are. The company president needs to be a "marketing man," but top management has to have enough comprehension of the marketing aspects of a business to achieve an effective establishment of objectives, their attainment, and a measurement of results. Implied in all this is a knowledge of product planning, advertising, merchandising, selling, distribution channels, servicing, and a score of other carefully integrated functions. To achieve it requires "an education course for top-echelon corporate managers, specifically designed to offer instruction in the broad aspects of integrated marketing closely tied to long-range corporate planning." (Courses for junior executives should also be developed as they are indicated.) [23]

Certainly the experience of the advance management programs conducted by several business schools shows that mature executives can absorb a vast amount of information and ideas in short, concentrated courses. Moreover, executives attending these courses believe that they benefit as much from the associations with fellow executives as from the course fare itself.

There is still considerable merit in considering the personality requirements for a director of marketing despite the derision of the "organization man." A new director of marketing, especially if he fills a newly created post, faces many problems in human relations. In any company he has to contend with a spate of diverse situations. He is certain to be resented by any unsuccessful internal candidates for the job and may experience difficulty in winning their cooperation. He will be viewed with suspicion and apprehension by divisions and department heads who will instinctively fear any dilution of their highly cherished prerogatives. He may be considered an intruder if selected from the outside, particularly if his peers have arrived at their positions through a long-standing company policy of promotion from within and they form a tightly knit group. The ability of the new executive to handle these problems may be more of a key to his success than his professional competence and experience.

The marketing director must be sufficiently aggressive to hold up his end of the corporate give-and-take in addition to making certain that the jobs within his division get done on time. At the same time

[23] *Ibid.*

he needs sufficient personal flexibility to relate successfully to these very same associates. In the smaller company, a man with the capacity to make quick decisions based on undocumented *pros* and *cons* is the superior choice. In the larger company containing more staff assistance and readily available facts, the need calls for a more analytical, more moderate personality, a man who will weigh the *pros* and *cons* more thoroughly and then *communicate* his decisions through the organization.

In a multiplant company with many offices, integration of all efforts after a decision has been reached becomes a high-level exercise in executive ability, particularly if profits are to be maximized. "Bull-in-the-china-shop" tactics can prove disastrous. Each individual must tailor his conduct to the rest of the top executive team for a harmonious performance. Unprofessional as it may seem human factors often govern the effectiveness of teamwork.

Decision Makers and Problem Solvers

The propositions governing decision making, according to March and Simon, dealt with decisions that were routinized and those that were not. Routinized decisions were made on continually recurring problems. These could be production-line decisions, decisions on how to process paper procedures, or decisions on a more sophisticated level, such as the ordering of inventory. Nonroutinized decision necessitated more solving of problems than the routinized kind. Decisions of a nonroutinized nature demanded a search for the most desirable choice among multiple possibilities. They covered such matters as whether to embark on a new product or invest in a new plant. Many decisions in this category could become routinized through the establishment of a model or a program. This has been the experience with problems dealing with location of a warehouse, transportation from several plants to a number of warehouses, and inventory control.

To facilitate routinized decisions requires the development of a model. The problem of perfecting a model might be simplified, March and Simon observed, by incorporating the following features: criteria of performance, alternatives, repertoires of action, restricted situations and consequences, semi-independence of action program, and a model-building staff function.[24]

1. CRITERIA OF PERFORMANCE. To begin with, satisfaction replaced

[24] March and Simon, *op. cit.*

optimization. It was not necessary to attain an optimum level of profits from each product, each territory, each salesman. A satisfactory level considerably below the optimum level might very well suffice. The satisfactory level might consist of "being in control" as was noted in Chapter 1 of this book. For the company as a whole, the satisfactory level might be nothing more than survival. Nevertheless, additional descriptive data about the company were needed to permit a finer understanding of its behavior. With these data it might become possible to establish criteria for a more adequate "theory of the firm." For pricing, for example, meeting competition, beating competition, or outpricing competition might be effective criteria for satisfactory performance. For the product, these criteria might consist of product quality, rate of obsolescence, relative profits from the product and the product line, or the image created by the product. For advertising, the criteria might be the amount of communication measured by readership or by the imagery surrounding the product and the company. For channels of distribution, they might comprise the rate of flow through the channels, the cost through various other channels, and the cooperation through these other channels. For personal selling, they might be the relationship of sales to the potential or the quota, the development of new accounts, or the services provided.

2. ALTERNATIVES. Alternatives to actions and the consequences of actions were found through search. In this quest the past experience and its consequences for the company and for its competitors might be noted and an alternative not previously tried by the company or its competitors developed, and its consequences anticipated. The choice of the alternative was based on the criteria for satisfactory levels of performance, the resources at the command of the company, and the amount of control the company exercises over its environment.

3. REPERTOIRES OF ACTION. Organizations and individuals both developed such programs. In recurrent situations these served as optional courses. As was indicated in Chapter 1 this might be pursued through a simulation project on a computer or through the assignment of subjective probabilities to the outcomes of the courses proposed. This would assume that a complete strategy were worked out for each course.

4. RESTRICTED SITUATIONS AND CONSEQUENCES. Each specific action dealt with a restricted range of situations and consequences. The situations related to the environment in which the company was acting.

The range of consequences was a result of the impact of the parameters of the environment on the course of action to be taken.

5. SEMI-INDEPENDENCE OF ACTION PROGRAM. Each action program was semi-independent of the others. Each could be executed semi-independently since all were coupled together only loosely. Thus, decisions on pricing, product, advertising, channels, and personal selling might all be independent; still they might be joined together in a coordinated program.

6. MODEL-BUILDING STAFF FUNCTION. The job of setting up the models for the company was to be largely a staff function. The staff men were to be in a position to provide the line men in the organization with repertoires of action for all conceivable circumstances.

Decision Making, Problem Solving, and Marketing Management. Management at top level is in a position to influence the entire pattern of a company's decision-making process. It may encourage more effective operation by having its executives think in terms of future plans, both of a short-range and long-range character. In addition, top management may request subordinate executives to establish some system of uniform control.

Under this practice, each division of a company develops its own long-range plans as part of the corporate long-term project already discussed. This is a model of the future. The additional benefit of individual divisions' developing their own long-range plans is that top management in a diversified corporation can be more completely informed through its review of the details of these plans about present and future industry trends and each division's unique corporate problems. For closer control, if this is desired, top management may require an annual marketing plan for each product line. A plan of this kind is predicated on extensive research and analysis, as we have seen; it is complete with monthly forecasts, it defines the marketing strategy, and it contains an implementation on a month-by-month basis. The simple act of sending a copy of this plan to headquarters plus monthly or quarterly progress reports gives top management a good look at current information.

A uniform control system affords the means of determining goals and limitations as well as supplying proper yardsticks for measuring the progress toward these goals. Such a system represents more than the standardized balance sheets and profit-and-loss statements usually prepared by the financial department. The control system should result in clear, concise charts of report forms which not only provide facts and figures but also show them in relation to past records and in comparison with forecasts. This enables top management to see problems developing before they reach the danger point rather than after. To permit necessary action in time a reporting system has to be developed to give corporate headquarters current information on exactly what is happening from an operating standpoint in each subsidiary division. This kind of financial reporting can be set up automatically and painlessly by extracting the information from each division's own operating figures which it should have for its own use, anyway. Thus, management may be adequately informed as to the exact efficiency of a division without appearing to hover over the division manager or encroach on his prerogatives. An excellent publication providing both the philosophy and several examples of such a control system is the pamphlet *How the DuPont Organization Appraises Its Performance.*[25]

Present and Future Marketing Organizations

" 'The time has come,' the Walrus said, 'to talk of many things; of shoes—and ships—and sealing-wax—of cabbages—and kings.' " [26] Thus, we come to a discussion of the crux of marketing management where theory and practice meet, where all the points developed in the course of these pages converge in the marketing organization of the present and the shape it is to take in the future. Here the challenge awaits, the opportunity to test in the crucible of everyday experience how well the lessons have been learned. It is here in the marketing organization that the marketing manager undergoes baptism by fire. What form has this organization on which the success of a comprehensive marketing operation hinges? To the answers to this question we address the remaining portion of this chapter.

Present

In a survey conducted not long ago business organizations were classified into two sorts: those whose functional specialization was general and those whose functional specialization was specific.[27] The former kind of organizations generally lacked a marketing research department and occasionally had no advertising department. Re-

[25] American Management Association, Financial Management Series, No. 94, New York, 1950.
[26] Lewis Carroll, *Through the Looking Glass.*
[27] Author's survey, *op. cit.*

search and advertising in these companies were pursued ordinarily in conjunction with other functions. The percentage of total company employees in the marketing department, however, was greater among concerns of general specialization than concerns of specific specialization. Moreover, there was no consistent pattern of organization related to type of industry, and this applied equally to the general and specific classes of functional specialization.

Fewer than half the companies surveyed had their marketing departments organized on a pure type of product, functional, or territorial basis. The majority organized their marketing departments on a hybrid scale combining various groupings of product, function, territory, process, and customer. The pure organization might be all product, all functional, or all territorial. Common among the product type was the use of division of product chiefs. These men might be responsible for a single product or for a group of products. Authority was generally vested in a higher centralized executive who might be the head marketing executive, the sales manager, a vice president, an executive vice president, or the president himself. Division or product managers had decentralized authority in their respective areas. They were thus completely accountable for the sales and profit performances of their products.

As practiced by a company in the petroleum industry, the managers of the company's trademarked products as well as its unbranded products that moved in bulk all reported to the chief executive in charge of marketing. Each of the product managers supervised clearly defined divisions with the authority to carry out their varied responsibilities. For advertising and selling, however, they joined in an Advertising and Sales Promotion Committee composed of themselves, the vice president and general sales manager, and the sales and advertising manager.

The functional type of pure organization was headed up as a rule by a sales manager or a chief executive in charge of marketing. As epitomized by a company in the heating industry a sales manager directed the entire marketing operation. His department determined the advertising program without consultation, collaboration, or interference. In a newsprint, pulp, and building paper company, the sales manager reported to the vice president in charge of marketing. The salesmen all reported directly to the sales manager.

In the pure territorial type of organization, authority rested in the territory. The territorial monarch reported to an executive in charge of marketing or of sales, or directly to the company president. In one company in the canned food product industry, the regional sales managers reported to the sales manager. The local representatives reported to the regional sales managers. In another case in the same industry branch sales managers reported to district sales managers who, in turn, reported to the company's executive vice president.

Thus, the pure types of organizations. Let us turn now to the hybrids. A common type of hybrid was the combination of the functional and territorial organization. In the baking industry one company had two functional activities—physical distribution and selling—whose heads reported to the vice president for sales. The men in charge of them were the distribution manager and the sales manager. An assistant sales manager reported to the sales manager. Reporting to the assistant sales manager were the branch managers who formed the territorial part of the organization. Thus, there was functional specialization at the top and territorial division down the line.

Another hybrid type consisted of a combination of product, customer, process, and functional. In a company manufacturing receiving and picture tubes, the line function was performed by a product manager called the equipment sales manager and two customer managers called a distribution sales manager and a goverment sales manager. All three reported to the vice president in charge of sales. The service and staff functions also reported to the same vice president but their activities were functional and process. The manager of market administration engaged largely in a process activity—administering and coordinating. The functional activity was carried out by the advertising manager.

Other hybrid combinations included functional and product; territorial, process, and functional; territorial and product, and functional, territorial, and product.

Most of the surveyed companies with a greater amount of specific functional specialization had larger sales volumes and a greater number of employees.[28] However, as noted previously, fewer workers proportionally were engaged in the marketing activities of these companies than in concerns of general functional specialization. Altogether there were more companies of specific than of general functional specialization.

Among the companies of specific functional specialization only a small number had a pure functional type of organization. The others represented some hybrid variant. The combination of territorial and functional seemed most evident. In one company engaged in the

[28] Author's survey, *op. cit.*

manufacture of watches and jewelry, a functional vice president of marketing reported to the president. A functional sales manager reported to the marketing vice president, whereas territorial or district sales managers reported to the sales manager. Staff functional specialists included a marketing research manager and an advertising manager who both reported to the marketing vice president.

Geographic, Product, and Customer Organizations.[29] A company with national distribution in many parts of the country would covet some kind of geographic organization. In many cases customers vary from region to region. And as more and more customers are gained there may be some disposition to extend the organization geographically. Organization by geographic division is an effort to cut the job of administration and selling to more realistic size. Thus, more authority is granted to subordinates in the field. At first the geographic regions may be large. Later they may be compressed for more intensive selling effort. Geographic organization has five advantages: sales problems may be handled by supervisors in the decentralized areas; there is better supervision of salesmen in the field; there should be better service to the customer; local markets may be cultivated more intensively; retaliation to competition may be speedier. Against these are two disadvantages: the expense of administration increases and the problem of coordinating regional offices becomes much more complex, which may lead to conflicting policies.

In a product organization each product manager utilizes a pool of staff consultants or these consultants are under his jurisdiction. The advantage of this kind of organization is the higher degree of specialization it permits in selling and marketing by product. This is particularly beneficial for a company with many products or a company seeking to reach different markets with different products. The major difficulty of employing this method is its high cost. Ordinarily a company would have to have a separate sales and administrative organization for each product or product line. Some customers may also dislike having more than one salesman from the same company call on them.

In a customer organization the attempt is made to divide the sales force according to the different types of customers. For example, paper towels may be sold to retail stores, to factories, and to institutions. But different channels of distribution may require different kinds of selling effort. It is not likely that selling a chain store would

[29] Richard R. Still and Edward W. Cundiff, *Sales Management,* Prentice-Hall, Englewood Cliffs, N.J., 1958, pp. 47–52.

occasion the same technique as selling an independent wholesaler or an institutional consumer. Different types of training programs are therefore needed to sell to different types of customers.

The Changing Role [30]

Change and growth have come about in the marketing organization in three distinct ways. First, there has been the "breaking out" of functions that were previously nonexistent or that were combined with other responsibilities. Then, there has been the "slotting in" of new functions designed to coordinate the expanding responsibilities. Finally, there has been the closer integration of marketing with other business functions.

Breaking Out. The breaking out of new functions is the major method for expanding marketing, going far beyond the mere addition of supplementary personnel. It is the assignment of specialists to perform specialized functions in the marketing department. In breaking out, a company often engages trained marketing specialists and uses them for existing tasks. Once breaking out has occurred the new force grows rapidly. The presence of the specialist seems to incur pressure for new facilities, new methods, and new personnel, as well as for more advance planning of manpower. But there looms a danger if breaking out moves too hastily. To avert the threat of overexpansion the company should have enough work for its new specialists to keep them fully occupied. If it cannot do so, the company may find it preferable to call on professional consultants.

The following conditions are recommended for breaking out: It should occur as soon as several subfunctions can be combined on a logical basis. For example, until marketing research is regarded as a necessary function encompassing all or most of its separate responsibilities, breaking it out should not even be considered. Next, early action seems preferable. If this is taken it becomes possible to hire young men to grow with the job. Third, functions must not be broken out before they justify a full-time job. There is a tendency, especially among medium-sized companies, to break out functions prematurely. Finally, it should be borne in mind that breaking out both aggravates and restrains the danger of empire building.

Research is the function moving fastest toward an expanded concept of marketing. Eventually product development, corporate long-

[30] Henry Bund and James W. Carroll, "The Changing Role of the Marketing Function," *Journal of Marketing,* Vol. 21, No. 3, January 1957, p. 273 ff.

range planning, and other functions may overtake it. For the time being, however, it is in the forefront because of these factors. First, there is pressure from top management for a firmer basis for making forecasts, and planning has grown, even when forecasting has been separated from marketing research or sales; in the future the specialists in marketing research may concentrate on sampling, operations research, or projective techniques.[31]   Second, the steady expansion of budgeting has generated a demand for facts to replace hunch and guesswork.

In many companies the training of marketing manpower is still handled by the personnel department. Only recently has this responsibility been transferred to the marketing department where it really belongs. At the present time the same type of manpower development is being applied to staff members as well as to salesmen and supervisors in the field. This may have to be modified to include more emphasis on analytical thinking. Every day the instruments and channels used for sales training are being improved.

Slotting In. Both cost control and profit analysis are likely to advance the status of marketing. Through them a new dimension is added to the objectives of operations. Exclusive preoccupation with sales figures is obsolete. Most sales managers are now guided by the profitability of individual items and the sales operation itself. The new control and administrative function gives the marketing executive the pertinent facts directly. This enables him to modify the sales operation, the entire product mix, and methods of producing and warehousing. Moreover, marketing is tied into longer-range profit planning in the belief that almost any business can soundly anticipate total sales volume, costs, and earnings. Marketing, in other words, can capitalize on the growing acceptance of the comptroller function.

Closer Integration. Most marketing managers have held their posts for a relatively short time, having only recently moved up from a sales managerial rank to their current jobs. The transition from a sales position to a broader marketing view has been beset by three difficulties. To begin with, it takes time to develop an integrated operation. Three years may be said to be the absolute minimum required to achieve the first stage of an integrated operation.[32]   Most companies

[31] See Donald R. Longman, "The Role of the Marketing Staff," *Journal of Marketing,* Vol. 26, No. 3, July 1962, pp. 29–33.
[32] Bund and Carroll, *op. cit.*

allow five to seven years to develop a working one. Next, there is a problem of personnel. Not enough candidates for these jobs are available. Emphases on recruiting, training, and developing manpower for the new marketing function reflects the concern of top management and marketing management for this shortage. Finally, the individuals in staff positions must be thoroughly familiar with the company's total operation. Line personnel who have spent considerable time in actual selling make excellent material for staff positions because they have acquired a first-hand knowledge and "feel" of the company's marketing policies. However, some personnel cannot be transferred to these staff jobs because of over-all company policy, morale, or some other human consideration. To obviate this problem other members of the management team must accept the fact of broadened marketing responsibility. Unless and until the rest of the business organization is willing to accept a full-fledged marketing team and work with it, there is no point to building one.

Departmental Approach [33]

Many manufacturers and distributors for purposes of effective management have found it desirable to divide their operations on the basis of the types of customers they serve. Often this may result in a two-department system, with one department concentrating, for example, primarily on customers who sell to ultimate consumers and the other dealing directly with the final consumer. From a marketing point of view this makes good sense for there is a considerable difference in the buying motives of the two groups. A successful departmentalization of this kind can be achieved only through a careful analysis of the individual company, the industry of which it forms a part, company personnel, the product line, and the market or markets being served. The specific objective of the first phase of such departmentalization is finding or determining a suitable basis for it. Customer type is one of these. Some manufacturers may discover that their products are being used industrially not by one, but by a number of industries. It may pay for them to organize their marketing activities in a way that provides special attention to the markets created by these various industries. Under other circumstances customer types may best be established on a geographic scale or some other sort of differentiation.

[33] Wendell R. Smith, "The Departmental Approach to Marketing Management," *Iowa Business Digest,* Vol. 24, No. 5, May 1953, p. 1 ff.

A second basis for departmentalization is the selling techniques and kinds of promotion to which a company's product respond most readily. Within a line of products, a retailer, wholesaler, or manufacturer may find one group whose buyers are primarily interested in the availability of technical service. Other products in the line may respond principally to negotiation and considerations of price. Still other products, such as home appliances, may sell best through demonstration. And there are products that should be grouped together because people buy them on impulse or through convenience; effective display and point-of-sale promotional material often stimulate the sale of such products. From a marketing point of view the ideal system of departmentalization collects in one department all those products that elicit a common response to the same type of sales approach.

A third basis for departmentalization is the use to which the buyer puts the product. This approach is most useful at the retail level of distribution. It results in consolidating those products that consumers normally use in association with one another.

Once the basis for departmentalization has been determined additional steps must be taken to see that departmentalization works. It is often desirable, for example, to place those products assigned to a particular department in a single location in a store or plant. Physical departmentalization of this kind often reduces the cost of handling besides emphasizing the management approach in use. Moreover, the accounting system should reflect the effort by making it possible to determine expenses, profits, and other measures of performance on a departmentalized basis. Then, too, both responsibility and authority for the various departments must be assigned to the appropriate personnel.

Through departmentalization management is often able to maintain a greater degree of control over the various aspects of the business. At the retail level this is almost certain to result in improved store layout and a better display of merchandise. Sales attention naturally gravitates toward products that respond to similar techniques. Thus, sales people are able to analyze the nature of their customer's requirements and choose sales presentations that are best suited to product and customer type. Departmentalization, in addition, often infuses new life into nonpersonal selling adjuncts such as advertising. It also supplies a more practical basis for establishing prices and price policies. Another of its advantages is that it sharpens product-line and inventory policies by suggesting an approach for proper merchandise control. Normally it leads to better employee relations and improved morale, and it provides a realistic method for assigning responsibility and conferring authority among members of an employment group. Finally, departmentalization heightens the marketing orientation of management from top to bottom.

Decentralization [34]

Decentralization of the marketing organization achieves importance when the post of chief marketing executive is an advisory and staff function, and marketing decisions are made at the divisional level. All through the business community there has been a marked tendency to pass decision making down the line to the locus of action. Marketing has been affected by the same trend. In large corporations greater autonomy for product departments or company divisions seems to be the wave of the future, if it is not already here. Already essentially independent operating divisions, which can call on corporate staff facilities for assistance, have been established in many large companies. The next marketing step is to set up separate product departments with at least skeleton marketing facilities. With marketing functions thus decentralized to the divisional level—and even the product departmental level—the top marketing staff officials become consultants, advisors, and coordinators whose ideas are adapted to each product line.

Line organization may also be decentralized. The district manager is usually the pivot. A manufacturer of office equipment explained that it had moved toward decentralization in its sales and service organizations by giving its regional managers much of the authority previously exercised by the home office staff. Since doing so, it had gradually extended their authority and urged them to confer increasing amounts of authority, in turn, on their branch managers. The company reported that the decentralization program had worked exceptionally well.[35]

The need for additional staff, however, is an invariable consequence of decentralization. District managers and others who assume responsibility must be trained and developed more fully. Furthermore, the home office must furnish more information. Some companies have even assigned marketing specialists to district offices. Others have assigned product specialists to regional sales offices to cope with the demand for specialized knowledge.

[34] Bund and Carroll, *op. cit.*
[35] *Ibid.*

The optimum extent of decentralization is limited by this need to expand and by the duplication of staff. In some companies this had led to pulling back duplicated responsibilities to the divisional or even the corporate headquarters office. There is concern also that too much decentralization can create confusion in corporate policy. In one instance, for example, decentralization of advertising led to a variety of advertising approaches. The same confusion, it is feared, might snarl organization lines, especially where district personnel communicate directly with their production counterparts and by-pass immediate supervisors. This may expedite intracompany dealings but it leads to contradictory actions. Many of these problems can be solved by "centralization with delegated responsibility" and "centralized control over any decentralization effort." RCA has been able to achieve effective control of decentralized activities by combining regular operational review meetings with a series of status and trend charts and graphs which highlight current problems and provide the basis for group discussion and management decisions.[36]

Top management thus has a wide latitude of choices for devising its organization for marketing management. No doubt individual tailoring to fit the particular company's needs will yield the best results. The main objective is to develop a marketing management organization capable of enhancing any company's *raison d'etre*—greater volume, better margins, bigger profits.

Summary

The literature on organization relates to three bodies of theory. One deals with the measurement of efficiency through time and methods study and defines organization tasks and the method of coordinating them. A second concerns the attitudes, values, and goals of the individuals in the organization. The third pertains to the organization as being composed of decision makers and problem solvers. Marketing management and the marketing literature reflect all three phases of organization theory.

Marketing organizations may be classified into those having general functional specialization and those having specific functional specialization. Of these groups we find pure types of product, functional, territorial, and consumer organizations, and also hybrid organizations. The changing marketing function is characterized by the "breaking-out" and "slotting-in" of new functions. A company should constantly keep in mind whether it is possible to departmentalize a particular function or process. Where the corporate

[36] J. R. Curley, "A Tool for Management Control," *Harvard Business Review,* Vol. 29, No. 2, March 1951, p. 45.

marketing director function is an advisory and staff position, and marketing decisions are made at the division level, the principle of decentralization assumes importance.

Suggested Cases

Ralph L. Westfall and Harper W. Boyd, *Cases in Marketing Management,* Irwin, Homewood, Ill., 1961.

Union Carbide Plastics Company—*Plastic Manufacturer*—Reorganization of Marketing Department, pp. 347–350.

Rheem Manufacturing Company—*Manufacturer of Wide Line of Industrial and Consumer Products*—Organization of Marketing Department in Multi-Product Firm, pp. 338–343.

Hector Lazo and Arnold Corbin, *Management in Marketing,* McGraw-Hill, New York, 1961.

Blair Beauty Preparations, Reorganization of Marketing, pp. 133–136.

Electronics Inc., Marketing Reorganization for Better Integration of New Divisions, pp. 136–138.

Supreme Foods Company, Organizational Conflicts Arising from Integration of Acquisitions and Adoptions of the Marketing Concepts, pp. 620–622.

Intercollegiate Case Clearing House, Soldiers Field, Boston 63, Massachusetts.

ICH 3M115—Dennison Manufacturing Company.

Chapter Thirteen

The Economist and Competition

Laws Relating to Competition   *Sherman Act · Extension of Anti-Trust Legislation · Mergers*   MERGERS AND LEGISLATION · RELEVANT MARKET *Robinson-Patman Act*   FUNCTIONAL DISCOUNTS · QUANTITY AND VOLUME DISCOUNTS · DEFENSES · QUANTITY LIMITS PROVISO · TERRITORIAL PRICE DISCRIMINATION · BROKERAGE · PROPORTIONALLY EQUAL ARRANGEMENTS · BUYER'S LIABILITY · MEETING COMPETITION IN GOOD FAITH   *Refusals to Deal · Exclusive Dealings · Resale Price Maintenance*

Summary

Suggested Cases

In a utopian society where men are motivated by ideals and actions are dedicated to the general welfare laws are seldom necessary. The visionaries composing the society impose their own restraints on the conduct of affairs by their zealous concern for the interests of their fellowmen. Under no circumstance would any individual exploit another lest he betray the principles by which he exists. Indeed his conscience as well as his code would be compromised by the mere suggestion that he take advantage of somebody else.

Alas, men do not live by Sir Thomas More's dreams. The real world is far from utopian. Avarice and selfish interests are more prevalent than altruism. The hard facts of life and its keenly competitive spirit impel men to enact laws, for law keeps men and organizations in line and redresses the balance when human or corporate actions threaten to upset it and jeopardizes the common good.

To protect the interests of all the members of American society two kinds of laws thwart irregularities in marketing operations. One of these guards against predatory tactics of companies that attempt to

Anti-Trust Laws
and Marketing

stifle competition. Laws of this sort seek to prevent the enormous power of large corporate entities from devouring the private property of smaller competitors. They try to establish a standard of conduct or fair play to maintain a healthy state of rivalry. We see them epitomized in the Sherman Anti-Trust Act, the Clayton Anti-Trust Act, and the Robinson-Patman Act. The second type of laws strives to protect the health and general welfare of the American public. We see this represented in the Pure Food and Drug Act. In this final chapter we shall explore the various laws enacted by the American government to prevent marketing operations from running wild. Having studied the sinews of marketing management and seen how scientific method may be applied to its development and practice, let us conclude our survey with an analysis of government restraints on power in the market place. First, however, let us consider briefly the kind of competition to which our discussion will pertain.

The Economist and Competition

The problem of understanding competition has been intensified by the economist's general failure to tell jurists exactly what competition is and to distinguish between monopoly and monopolization. The classical economist assumes that competition involves a series of small companies in which no one of them has the power to control supply—and hence, price. The company is presumed to be acting in a rational manner to maximize its profits and to publicize complete information. The products of all the companies are assumed to be homogeneous. The analysis of cost curves shows that as a company grows larger a point of diminishing returns is reached, after which costs increase. This is viewed as being harmful to the public—particularly to the consumer because it results in higher prices.

The neoclassical economist recognizes that each company may have a monopolistic factor in its location, service, or product differentiation.

437

He uses the term *imperfect competition* as being closer to reality. To him, the analysis of cost curves indicates that the monopolist will sell products at the point at which profits are maximized or at which the marginal costs equal the marginal revenues. The oligopolistic company will not sell at a price above rival companies because it knows that it would lose business to them. Neither will it cut prices because this would force the industry to follow suit, thereby reducing profits. However, the analysis of oligopoly is not of much use to the jurist when he is trying to prove monopolization. The jurist is seeking out the predatory activities which tend to drive other companies out of business.

What it boils down to is that the government tries to protect business through its anti-trust laws. If the condition is the one described by the classical and neoclassical economist and the government is seeking to protect the idea of "imperfect competition," the conditions of competition must be understood. Clark has laid down rules for what he calls *workable competition*, which have appeared in a relatively recent report of the Attorney General.[1]

The market area for workable competition includes substitute products in rival industries. Thus, two or more products, or two or more areas, should be combined into one if an appreciable fall in the price of one product or in one area diverts a relatively large number of purchasers from other products or areas. For this purpose an area may be international, national, regional, or local. Several factors bear on the identification of workable competition and in substance they are:

1. THE ISSUE OF RELATIVE SIZE. The number of effective competitive sellers in a market can be considered only in relation to a particular market. Effective competition in an economic sense requires a degree of self-interested, independent rivalry in any market in which no company or group of companies acts in concert to create a monopoly. That is, no single company or group of companies could hold for long the power to choose its level of profits by giving less and charging more or to block the entry into the market of additional sources of supply.

2. OPPORTUNITY FOR ENTRY. The entry and withdrawal of companies, whether new ones or existing ones from other market areas, other industries, or other stages of production and marketing, is the market mechanism for achieving economic results. The cost conditions

---

[1] *Report of the Attorney General's National Committee to Study the Anti-Trust Laws,* March 31, 1955, pp. 322–342.

for a new entry should not be excessively higher, at least after a reasonable period of initial development, than cost conditions for companies in the industry. In some cases, in fact, the new entries may start with a cost advantage because of the use of new techniques.

3. INDEPENDENCE OF RIVALS. A primary condition of workable competition in an economic sense is a genuine independence of business units in an industry so that each company may pursue its own advantage.

4. PREDATORY PRECLUSIVE PRACTICES. No predatory preclusive tactics can be tolerated. Their natural effect would enable the company using them to eliminate rivals irrespective of the latters' efficiency, or at least place them under severe handicaps totally unrelated to their efficiency.

5. RATE OF GROWTH OF INDUSTRY OR MARKET. The speed of an industry's growth is not a direct economic indicator of its internal state of competition. An industry actually may be in decline and yet have an active, effective competitive spirit.

6. MARKET INCENTIVES AND COMPETITIVE MOVES. Competition may be effective or ineffective in relation to how the market is organized and behaves, and according to the incentives available for independent competitive actions. These include the hope of gain for the individual seller and the risk of loss.

7. PRODUCT DIFFERENTIATION AND PRODUCT HOMOGENEITY. An important factor in determining the boundaries of a market is a knowledge of buyers of competitive products or services. If other conditions are equal, the more homogeneous the product of rival sellers, the more easily buyers could switch from the output of one manufacturer to the output of another. Therefore, the wider the market is, the greater the competition in it.

8. MEETING OR MATCHING RIVAL PRICES. In effective competition, the rivals attempt to meet an inducement any one of them may offer, or at least present some equivalent to it. Effective competition also includes the freedom to undercut the prices of rivals.

9. EXCESS CAPACITY. In a period of generally good business, the existence of unused capacity, which could be utilized at or near prevailing costs, may help to demonstrate the presence of monopoly or competition.

10. PRICE DISCRIMINATION. Price discrimination in an economic sense occurs whenever there are price differences for the same product or service sold by a single seller, which are not accounted for by differences in cost or by changes in the level of demand. It also occurs when two or more buyers of the same product or service are charged

the same price despite the difference in the cost of selling in each case. To know when there is such price discrimination among two or more buyers, one has to know both the price and the cost applicable to each type of transaction at issue.

Laws Relating to Competition

Sherman Act

The United States government enacted the Sherman Anti-Trust Act in 1890. The first law of the land passed to prevent predatory conduct in the business community, it owed its origins indirectly to the medieval law of *engrossing*. This was the amassing of large quantities of goods so that the seller could control the price. The Sherman Act emanated from English common law which prohibited restraint of trade and conspiracy. Although the English laws did not prevent monopoly, they forestalled certain predatory practices. In particular, the English laws forbade the seller of a business to enter into competition with the person to whom he sold his enterprise.

The core of anti-trust legislation in this country since 1890 has been the first two sections of the Sherman Act—"an act to protect trade and commerce against unlawful restraints and monopolies," as it was called. These sections read, in part:

Sec. 1. Every contract, combination in the form of trust or otherwise, or conspiracy, in restraint of trade or commerce among the several States, or with foreign nations; is hereby declared to be illegal. . . .

Sec. 2. Every person who shall monopolize, or attempt to monopolize, or combine or conspire with any person or persons, to monopolize any part of the trade or commerce among the several States, or with foreign nations, shall be deemed guilty of a misdemeanor. . . .

Both sections included fines for violation of up to $5000—amended to $50,000 in 1955—and prison terms up to one year. Section 4 of the Act empowered the Attorney General to bring civil proceedings in the federal courts to curb violations. Section 7 permitted persons injured by violations to sue for treble the amount of damages suffered plus a reasonable attorney's fee. Section 8 specified that the term *person* included "corporations and associations." [2]

In 1911 in the Standard Oil decision the philosophy of the Sherman

---

[2] 26 Stat. 209, Chap. 647; U.S.C.A. 1.

Act was declared to be "the rule of reason." [3] This doctrine required the courts to examine the circumstances surrounding the formation of a combination as well as the pattern of its business behavior. The rule of reason attempted to discover an *intent* to monopolize through the exercise of excessive power. Intent was to be demonstrated by a company's actions; power referred to the control which, barring interference, had been or would be exercised. It included the joint suppression of rivalry and the exclusion or threatened exclusion of competitors through unfair methods.

There has been some feeling that this rule of reason has been modified by per se rulings of the courts. That is, the courts have not applied a standard of reasonableness but have said that price-fixing arrangements per se were illegal. Jurists maintain that this has created a double standard of jurisprudence, the rule of reason and the per se rulings. Use of either standard seems to have varied with political administrations. During the Eisenhower regime, for example, the emphasis was on the "rule of reason" which required a higher measure of proof.

Extension of Anti-Trust Legislation

In 1914, Congress passed two laws to extend the Sherman Act, and President Wilson promptly signed them. These were the Federal Trade Commission Act and the Clayton Anti-Trust Act. The first of these acts created a Federal Trade Commission to replace the Bureau of Corporations, which had been a part of the Department of Commerce since 1903. The Commission was empowered to take over the economic investigative activities performed until that time by the Bureau. The chief provision of the Federal Trade Commission Act was its Section 5, which read at the time of passage:

> The commission is hereby empowered and directed to prevent persons, partnerships, or corporations, except banks, and common carriers subject to the Acts to regulate commerce, from using unfair methods of competition in commerce.[4]

Subsequent amendments first excluded livestock and meat companies from its protection, and then airlines. In 1938, the prohibition of "unfair methods of competition" was amended to include "unfair

---

[3] Standard Oil Company of New Jersey vs. United States (1911).
[4] Sept. 26, 1914, 38 Stat. 717, as amended by Wheeler-Lea Act, March 21, 1938, 52 Stat. 111; U.S.C. 15: 41–58.

or deceptive acts or practices." Thus, the unfair practices to be prevented grew from those that injured competitors to those that injured customers. Section 5 applies nowadays to acts that are unfair ethically and those that are unfair because they are monopolistic. Agreements in restraint of trade may be prosecuted by the Department of Justice either as unfair competition under the Federal Trade Commission Act or under anti-trust provisions of Section 1 of the Sherman Act.

The Clayton Act, in addition to containing procedural provisions and exemptions, forbade certain anticompetitive practices. It gave the Federal Trade Commission equal power with the Department of Justice to enforce its provisions, whereupon the Commission assumed primary jurisdiction in such cases. Section 2 of the Act prohibited price discrimination between purchasers "where the effect of such discrimination may be to . . . lessen competition [substantially] or tend to create a monopoly in any line of commerce." The Act provided, however, for defenses based on quantity sold, cost of selling or transportation, and price cuts designed to meet competition "in good faith." [5] These allowances, of course, weakened the prohibitions of the Act.

In 1936, Section 2 of the Clayton Act was amended by the Robinson-Patman Act. This grew out of an extensive investigation of chain stores, which disclosed that their competitive advantage resulted from mass purchase of goods. The new legislation:

(1) Added to substantial lessening of competition a criterion of unlawfulness easier to prove: that the discrimination "injure, destroy, or prevent competition with any person who either grants or knowingly receives the benefit of such discrimination, or with customers of either of them";

(2) Tightened the justification of price differences "on account of" quantity sold or that made "only due allowance for difference in the cost of selling or transportation" to a requirement that they "make only due allowance for differences in cost of manufacture, sale, or delivery resulting from the differing methods or quantities";

(3) In determining whether a price difference was lawful put the burden of proof on the person charged;

(4) Denied the defense that the discount had been given to meet competition in good faith if the price set was lower than the competitor's.[6]

[5] 38 Stat. 730; I.S.U.S.C. 12 ff.; Public No. 212, 63rd Congress (1914).
[6] 49 Stat. 1527, 1526, 1528.

Other aspects of the Robinson-Patman Act dealt with brokerage, advertising allowances, liability of a purchaser who knew he had received a price advantage, and a new right of the Federal Trade Commission, as yet to be exercised, to fix maximum quantity discounts if necessary to prevent monopoly. Section 3 of the Clayton Act was amended to make it illegal to "tie in" contracts, that is, to refuse to sell or lease one product unless another were taken with it. It also now forbade exclusive dealing arrangements if the effect might be a substantial lessening of competition or a tendency toward monopoly.

Section 7, as amended, prohibited the purchase of stock by one corporation in another if the result would reduce the competition between the two considerably or tend toward monopoly. Evasion became possible through purchase of assets rather than stock or by purchasing all the stock of the smaller concern and dissolving it before the Commission could take action. The Celler-Kefauver amendment of 1950 strengthened this section to prohibit mergers through purchase of either stock or assets if the mergers tended "in any line of commerce in any section of the country" to reduce competition or create a monopoly.

Section 8 now outlaws interlocking directorates between corporations when either has a net worth of over $1 million and elimination of competition between the two would violate any of the anti-trust laws.

Mergers

Mergers concern marketing men from two points of view. First, the merger implements a company's product line or expands its distributive facilities. Second, it has an effect on public policy as it pertains to competition. The expansion of a company's product line through merger with another company may smooth out seasonal fluctuations by the addition of supplementary products. It may also make it possible to market the acquired line of merchandise without any marked addition of distribution cost. The increase of distribution facilities as a result of merger may lower costs of production when the company is manufacturing at scale.

As a matter of public policy mergers may constitute a form of monopoly power. Studies by the Federal Trade Commission illustrate the extent of mergers in the American economy. From 1919 to 1956 the following industries showed great increases in concentration in proportion to the size of the entire industry: food and allied products, textiles and apparel, paper and related products, printing and publishing, leather products, metals and metal products, nonelectrical machinery, electrical machinery, transportation equipment, lumber and furniture, and stone, clay, and glass products. In terms of assets, single companies owning more than 50 per cent of the total resources of their industries were found in linoleum, tin cans and other tinware, and aluminum.[7] Situations in which two or more companies controlled more than 80 per cent of the assets in their industries were found in the same areas. In these industries three companies dominated more than 90 per cent of the assets. Most of the mergers between 1940 and 1947, the Commission found, were horizontal mergers, that is, mergers of companies in direct competition with each other. Second came the conglomerate merger—the merger of unrelated companies. Third were the vertical mergers.[8] These were mergers with companies that could be a source of supply or distribution.[9]

Mergers and Legislation. The Sherman Act was not very effective in reducing or eliminating monopolistic mergers. Between 1890 and the end of 1903, only 23 public cases were prosecuted under it.[10] The number involving mergers was even smaller. From 1895 to 1927 the United States Supreme Court handed down only 14 decisions involving combination and these decisions were not all calculated to limit the growth of substantial market power.[11] In spite of its owning 95 per cent of the nation's shoe machinery, the United Shoe Machinery Company was not found to be in violation of the law.[12] Nor was United States Steel found guilty of violating the law in 1920; size alone was not enough of a basis for prosecution.[13] The majority opinion held that the government had not proved that predatory tactics were being pursued by the steel company at the time of the litigation. In the words of Justice McKenna, "our consideration should be of, not what the corporation had power to do or did, but what it has now power to do and is doing. . . ."[14] It was Justice McKenna's con-

---

[7] Federal Trade Commission, *Report on Corporate Mergers and Acquisitions,* 33 (1955); Federal Trade Commission, *New Summary,* Feb. 18, 1957, compiled from Moody, Standard Corporation Records, etc., and *Business Concentration and Price Policy,* 175 (1955).

[8] Federal Trade Commission, 1949, *The Concentration of Productive Facilities, 1947.*

[9] Federal Trade Commission, *Report on Corporate Mergers and Acquisitions,* 1950.

[10] Hans B. Thorelli, *The Federal Antitrust Policy,* 590, 1955.

[11] John Kramer, "The Antitrust Division and the Supreme Court," 1890–1953, 40, *Virginia Law Review,* 533 (1954).

[12] United States vs. Winslow (227 U.S. 202) (1913).

[13] United States vs. United States Steel Corp. (251 U.S. 417) (1920).

[14] *Ibid.*

tention that the Federal Trade Commission had not offered this type of evidence. In a dissenting opinion Justice Day wrote "But when that intent and the consequent dangerous probability exist, this statute [Sherman Act] like many others and like common law in some cases, directs itself against the dangerous probability as well as the completed result." [15]

The Clayton Act required a lower standard of proof. Its Section 7 was incorporated to nip the use of power in its incipience. The Act, as we noted a while ago, prohibits the acquisition of stock in another corporation if this may lessen competition and tend toward monopoly. The key words are *may* and *tend*. Section 7 did not require proof of monopoly or of injury to competition. Intention was enough grounds for prosecution. Since the Act did not mention the purchase of assets of competing organizations this was the loophole seized by many companies.[16] To plug the loophole, Congress passed the Celler Antimerger Act in 1950.[17]

The Celler Act made three major changes in Section 7. First, it broadened the domain of the section to encompass corporations acquiring not only the "whole or any part" of the stock of another company, but also the "whole or any part" of its assets. Second, it eliminated the illegality test which determined whether the effect of acquisitions "may be" to substantially reduce competition between the acquiring and acquired corporations. Finally, Congress removed the prior test—that is, whether the acquisition might restrain commerce "in any community"—and substituted the wider concept of whether "in any line of commerce in any section of the country" the acquisition might substantially affect competition or promote monopoly.

The intent of this most recent Act was to reach mergers beyond the periphery of the Sherman Act. Thus, a Senate report asserted that the purpose was to cope with monopolistic tendencies in their incipience well before they attained such effects as to justify a Sherman Act proceeding. The report stated further that the intent of the Act was to have "broad application to acquisitions that are economically significant." [18]

Although it is theoretically possible to prosecute a company only on the basis of potential injury to competition, one study has pointed out that most of the cases prosecuted by the Federal Trade Commission

[15] *Ibid.*
[16] See *Report of the Federal Trade Commission on the Present Trend of Corporate Mergers and Acquisitions* (1947).
[17] Public Law 899, 1950.
[18] Sen. Rep. 1775, 81st Congress, 2nd Session (1950).

and the Department of Justice have charged substantial injury to both competition and to potential competition.[19] The courts have called injury to potential competition a "reasonable probability" that a merger would substantially lessen competition. In a ruling handed down by Judge Weinfeld the circumstances of reasonable probability were presented as follows: [20]

When a merger substantially increases concentration, eliminates a significant factor in competition, eliminates a major source of supply, or establishes a relationship among buyers and sellers which deprives rivals of a fair opportunity to compete, such as making competitors dependent on one of their number for supplies, a reasonable probability exists that competition will be substantially reduced.

The *Attorney General's Report* listed the long-range competitive consequences that might injure potential competition.[21] First, there were the changes in the opportunity for sellers to make independent decisions about products, prices, advertising sales methods, channels of sales, classes of customers, and business activities in which they would engage. Second, there were changes in the opportunity for buyers to shop freely for products, prices, channels of purchases, and classes of suppliers, and to select the business activities in which they would engage. These changes might occur individually or concurrently. An acquisition which markedly reduced the incentives for sellers or potential sellers to enter new markets and improve their products or services, widen their distribution, lower their prices, or pass cost savings on to customers might substantially narrow competition. Similarly, an acquisition which largely reduced the incentives for buyers or potential buyers to seek what they needed at the lowest prices, to shop various sources until they had made satisfactory arrangements, and to sell and resell in their own ways might thwart competition substantially or encourage monopoly.

Relevant Market. In expanding his company's marketing activities through merger, a marketing manager may be concerned with the product and the geographic areas in which he may compete without

---

[19] J. W. Markham, "Merger Policy under the New Section 7: A Six Year Appraisal," *Virginia Law Review*, May 1957, pp. 512–521.

[20] *U.S. vs. Bethlehem Steel Corporation and Youngstown Sheet and Tube Company*, CCH 69, 189 (D.C.S., New York, November 1958).

[21] Stanley N. Barnes and S. Chesterfield Oppenheim, *The Attorney General's National Committee to Study the Anti-Trust Laws*, Government Printing Office, Washington 25, D.C., March 31, 1955, p. 127.

countervening the law. In examining court decisions on the relevant geographic market, Markham found that 16 of 28 public complaints and the one private suit on threats to competition all involved national markets.[22] The remaining 12 related to regional or local markets, or classes of customers that the trade press or simply the logic of the facts identified as "the market." Books on the paper industry and paper trade journals, for example, have recognized the "west coast paper market" as a relevant market area.[23] Each urban area has been similarly identified as a "milk market."[24] Competition among hotel chains for conventions and patronage of travelers obviously occurs in the cities where the hotels are located.[25] We can infer with reason that farm journals primarily direct their advertising to farmers.[26] The high costs of transport fairly well protects lake sand producers from outside competition.[27] And customers ordinarily do not think of near or distant cities as competitive sources for their purchases of flour-base mixes.[28] In one of the cases studied by Markham the market was national for manufacturing and local for retailing.[29]

In the Bethlehem Steel case, the court held that the company dominated two areas and Youngstown Sheet and Tube a third, although the two corporations operated in different markets.[30] Their tripartite division of areas through merger, said the court, was an "obvious gerrymandering of the country to meet the exigencies of the case." Any area in which the court felt that the impact of the merger would be significant was a market area with which the court was concerned. It would make its determination on the basis of past sales and potential future sales where buyers could reasonably turn to them as alternative sources of supply.

Court interpretations of the product market have varied from narrow to broad in merger cases. The broad view may be seen in the Brown case.[31] Thinking of market segmentation, the company main-

[22] Markham, *op. cit.*
[23] Crown Zellerbach Corp., FTC, Dkt. 6180.
[24] National Dairy Products Corp., FTC, Dkt. 6651.
[25] Hilton Hotels Corp. and Statler Hotels Del. Corp., Dept. of Justice, Dkt. 1889–55.
[26] Farm Journal, FTC, Dkt. 6388.
[27] Erie Sand and Gravel Co., FTC, Dkt. 6670.
[28] Pillsbury Mills, FTC, Dkt. 6000.
[29] U.S. vs. Brown Shoe Company et al., CCH 69, 532 (C.C.E. Mo., November 1959).
[30] U.S. vs. Bethlehem Corp. and Youngstown Sheet and Tube Co., *op. cit.*
[31] U.S. vs. Brown Shoe Co. et al., *op. cit.*

tained there were separate markets for shoes: for men, women, and children. This claim was rejected by the court because the buying behavior of the consumers showed that shoes were interchangeable. In the Columbia Pictures case,[32] the court held that the line of commerce was not "feature films," as the government had contended, but the programming of materials of all sorts—live shows, videotaped telecasts, short cartoons, and the like. Perhaps the broadest view of the market was taken in the DuPont Cellophane case.[33] Here the court held that all flexible wrapping materials competed in the same market.

In contrast with the DuPont case, a narrow view of the market was taken in the Crown Zellerbach case.[34] Here the examiner concerned himself with wrapping paper—wrapping, bag, and sack. The company wanted all paper to be included, taking in all states west of the Mississippi. The court rejected both requests commenting that the papers were a distinct product line with similar end uses and that the western states were separated from the rest of the market by transportation costs.

In the Brillo case, the court held that the common product of the merged corporations was industrial steel wool, constituting a separate product sold in its own market distinct from other abrasives.[35] The test was the existence of peculiar characteristics and uses. To determine these, the manner of marketing the product, its physical nature, prices, and other factors had to be considered.

A narrow view was also expressed in the Transamerica case.[36] The Federal Reserve Board received an injunction in the lower courts to restrain the company from acquiring stocks in other banks. The higher court reversed this decision contending that the line of commerce was local; as a result no competition could be lessened geographically. In the Affiliated Music case the lower court and court of appeals found that the performance rights to gospel music constituted a distinct market subject to monopolization.[37] In International Boxing, the court ruled that professional championship bouts were a product distinct from nonchampionship fights and hence formed

[32] U.S. vs. Columbia Pictures Corp. et al., CCH 69, 766 (D.S.S., N.Y., July 1960).

[33] U.S. vs. E. I. DuPont de Nemours & Co., 76 S. Ct. 944 (June 1956).

[34] Crown Zellerbach Corp., FTC, Dkt. 6180, CCH 26, 923 (December 1957).

[35] Brillo Manufacturing Co., FTC, Dkt. 6557, CCH 27, 243 (May 1958).

[36] Transamerica Corp. vs. Board of Gov. of Federal Reserve System 206F, 2d 16.3 (CCa 3, July 1955).

[37] Affiliated Music Enterprises Inc. vs. SEASAC, Inc., CCH 69, 376 (CA-2, June 1959).

a separate market.[38] In the *Kansas City Star* case the court held that newspapers did not compete with radio or television.[39] And in the Guerlain case, the court contended that branded perfumes composed a distinct market.[40]

In Markham's study it was noted that in most cases the merger gave the acquiring company at least 25 per cent of the defined market.[41] Since share of the market has been an important measure of growth in a market area, a marketing manager may be concerned over any share that tends to threaten competition. The following cases illustrate court attitude on market share.

In the Crown Zellerbach case the court ruled that 60 per cent of the paper market was a dominant share.[42] The Commission ordered the company to dispose of the firm it had acquired in order to restore competition. In the United Fruit case, the court said that a 60 per cent share of the banana business throttled competition.[43] The case was settled by a consent decree. United would create its own competitor. In the Alcoa case, despite the reduction of the company's share of the market from 90 per cent to 50 per cent, the court called Alcoa an illegal monopoly because of its power to exclude competitors.[44] In the United Shoe Machinery case, the court maintained that the company's 75 to 85 per cent of the market for shoe machinery was sufficient to constitute illegal monopolization, unless that company's dominant position arose innocently from such things as superiority of its products, economies of scale, or research and natural advantages rather than from barriers erected by deliberate and avoidable business policies.[45]

In the Reynolds case the Federal Trade Commission ruled that an increase in the share of the market resulting from a merger was not in itself enough to find or to deny a probable lessening of competition as required in Section 7 of the Clayton Act.[46] Other matters had to

[38] U.S. vs. International Boxing Club of New York, Inc. et al., CCH 68, 649 (DCS, N.Y., March 1957); International Boxing Club of N.Y. et al. vs. United States, 79 S. Ct. 245 (January 1959).
[39] The Kansas City Star Co. vs. United States, 240 F. 2d 643, CCH 8 (June 1957).
[40] U.S. vs. Guerlain, Inc., U.S. vs. Parfum Corday, Inc., United States vs. Lanvin Parfums, Inc., CCH 68, 771 (DCS N.Y., July 1957).
[41] Markham, *op. cit.*
[42] Crown Zellerbach Corp., *op. cit.*
[43] United Fruit Co., CCH 68, 941 (D.C.E., La., February 1958).
[44] Aluminum Co. of America et al., CCH 68, 755 (D.C.S., N.Y., June 1957).
[45] United Shoe Machinery Corp. vs. United States, 74 (S. Ct. 499, May 1954).
[46] Reynolds Metal Co., FTC, Dkt. 7009 (CCH 27, 857, March 1959).

be investigated, such as the general competitive situation, the number of competitors, and the degree of concentration in the industry. In this respect the Commission found Spalding innocent of endangering competition.[47] Through merger the sporting goods manufacturer had increased its share of the market from 15 per cent to 25 per cent. The hearing examiner of the Commission held that this did not impair competition because there were 12 strong competitors in the industry, one with a 19 per cent share of the market. Moreover, this was an industry of easy entry.

Stigler suggested the use of the following standards regarding share of output to determine whether competition had been violated.[48] First, there should be a presumption that every company with less than 5 to 10 per cent of an industry's output following a merger may engage in that merger. Within this range, the larger the industry is, the lower the percentage. Second, every merger by a company possessing a fifth or more of an industry's output after the merger had occurred may be presumed to have violated the statute. Third, in the area between these limits the merger may be investigated by enforcement agencies if the aggregate annual sales of the merged companies exceed some absolute legal ceiling after merger. The legal limit should be judged by the conditions set forth above. Finally, when a company having a fifth or more of its industry's output acquires more than 5 to 10 per cent of the capacity of industries to which it sells, it may be presumed to have violated the law.

Robinson-Patman Act

Functional Discounts. Under Section 2 of the original Clayton Act functional discounts were considered a possible source of price discrimination. In the Mennen case the character of the selling rather than the character of the buying determined who should receive the functional discount.[49] In the Van Camp case functional discounts were acceptable where there were differences in quantity.[50] As a result of these rulings functional discounts became immune from prosecution under the Clayton Act.

Actually damage from functional discounts may affect competition at three different levels. To begin with, functional discounts may be

---

[47] Re A. G. Spalding & Bros., Inc., FTC, Dkt. 6478 (CCH 27, 868, March 1959).
[48] George J. Stigler, "Mergers and Preventive Antitrust Policy," *University of Pennsylvania Law Review,* November 1955, pp. 176–184.
[49] Mennen Co. vs. Federal Trade Commission, 258 Fed. 774 2d Cir. 1923.
[50] Van Camp and Sons vs. American Can Co., 2870 S. 245, 1929.

discriminatory against competitors in the primary line. Moreover, two or more classes of distributors may receive different functional discounts when competing for the same customers. Finally, customers of one class may be in competition with customers of another class, such as retailers buying from wholesalers and those buying direct from manufacturers.

The Robinson-Patman Act which gave teeth to the Clayton Act not only protects the vigor of competition but also preserves it against injury by sellers or favored customers, such as functional discounts may precipitate. Discriminations are illegal if they prevent or impair competition. The problem of applying the law has been relatively simple in ascertaining whether the same discount has been given to equivalent marketing intermediaries. However, difficulties arise when manufacturers use several channels of distribution or when sales are made to vertically integrated buyers who purchase in large quantities. Among such buyers there are differences in the functions performed in the marketing process. From a horizontal point of view distributors may differ in the number of functions they perform, their coverage of the market, and their type of customers. In some cases manufacturers may classify their customers in more than one category. Sometimes, moreover, manufacturers have used two price lists when selling; failing to sell on the basis of one list, they switch to the other. And sometimes discounts are awarded on the basis of buying power.

Five types of problems arise in functional discount cases.[51] First, incorrect customer classification may occur, thus giving ineligible companies the discount. Second, companies have divided functions. Third, manufacturers may provide more than one rate of discount for customers in the same class. These have been called multiple-discount customers. Fourth, competition develops among functional classes. And fifth, there may be classifications of favored and disfavored customers for discount purposes.

Quantity and Volume Discounts. Quantity discounts are received for purchasing large quantities at one time. Volume discounts are obtained for cumulative purchases of large quantities over a period of time. From 1936 to 1957, in the first 21 years of the Robinson-Patman Act, the Federal Trade Commission issued orders in 49 cases involving quantity and volume discounts. Most of the cases involved volume discounts.[52] The reasons that the Commission has paid more

---

[51] Corwin D. Edwards, *The Price Discrimination Law,* Brookings Institution, Washington, D.C., 1959, pp. 294–299.
[52] *Ibid.*

attention to volume than quantity discounts are the provisions of the Act, the relative ease of justifying quantity discounts by cost, and the incentive for suppliers to grant price concessions to large volume buyers. Edwards has reported that it has been difficult, moreover, to find a basis of legality for decisions in quantity-discount cases.[53]

Volume discounts have been condemned by the Commission on two grounds. The discount schedules themselves were unlawful and they were not uniformly applied. In the latter respect discounts were based in one case on purchases from a single source, whereas purchases were made from all sources. In another instance discounts were based not only on the volume of purchases but also on the purchases of the buyer's own customers from the manufacturer or distributor. There has been a woeful lack of recognition of the buying functions performed by the integrated wholesaler-retailer. Thus, there is no payment for execution of the wholesaling role. This has tended to curb experimentation designed to establish new purchasing techniques amid the channels of distribution.

The volume discounts have varied in complexity. In a simple situation a single discount was given to buyers who purchased more than a certain amount in a specific period. In more complex cases different volume discount schedules applied to as many as 11 distinct volume brackets. As a rule, the more elaborate the discount structure, the more varied were the ways in which injury to competition might arise.

Volume or quantity discounts are both unlawful if there is a reasonable probability that their effect on competition will be deleterious. The law recognizes three types of damage: a tendency to monopoly, a substantial lessening of competition, and injury destruction, or prevention of competition through collusion with those who receive preferential treatment. These types of damage may occur either on the seller's side, the primary line of commerce, or the buyer's side, the secondary line of commerce, giving rise to six possibilities of jeopardy. The tendency to monopoly means that if the process is not halted a monopoly will probably result. Substantial lessening of competition and reducing the degree of competitive protection enjoyed by the consumer, the supplier, or both, have been called the broad type of injury. The third kind of damage, involving injury, destruction, or prevention of competition through collusion with participants, relates to groups of companies affected competitively, rather than to the whole market. It has been called the narrow type of

[53] *Ibid.*

injury. In the primary line of commerce the distinction between narrow and broad forms of injury has been obscure. In the secondary line the meaning of the narrow concept of injury is clearer. It refers to the inability of less favored buyers to compete with the more favored. The broad type of injury in the secondary line, on the other hand, would harm the ultimate consumer.

Defenses. To companies and individuals prosecuted for granting functional discounts, two defenses are available. One is the defense of cost, and the other is the defense of meeting competition in good faith. The cost defense must show that distribution costs justify the lower functional discount. In all the cases reviewed by Edwards, the Federal Trade Commission rejected the cost defense because of the inadequacy of the data or because the distribution cost system had not been used before.[54] Meeting competition in good faith may be used when a company reduces its price to combat the low price of its competitors. In the Standard Oil case, the Commission argued that the company had maintained its functional discount system prior to the change in the competitive situation. The Supreme Court, however, accepted the company's contention that it had met competition in good faith.[55]

The same types of defenses apply to charges of quantity discounts and volume discounts. In most cases where cost was claimed as a defense both the Commission and the courts have rejected the figures presented. Either the basis for the presentation of the distribution costs was weak or the figures had been compiled after proceedings had been initiated against a particular company. In only a few of these cases was there any effort to justify the action on the ground that it had been taken in good faith to meet the low prices of a competitor.

Quantity Limits Proviso. A quantity limits proviso of the Robinson-Patman Act states that there may be a tendency toward monopoly if discounts are granted on the basis of cost savings beyond a certain quantity limit. Section 2(a) of the Act which says that price differentials may not exceed due cost savings flowing from economical "methods or quantities" of sale or delivery is followed by a qualification. This further proviso authorizes the Federal Trade Commission to "fix and establish quantity limits . . . as to particular commodities or classes of commodities, where it finds that available purchasers

[54] *Ibid.*
[55] *Ibid.*

in greater quantities are so few as to render differentials on account thereof unjustly discriminatory or promotive of monopoly in any line of commerce; and the foregoing shall then not be construed to permit differentials based on differences in quantities greater than those so fixed and established."

The quantity limits proviso authorizes the Federal Trade Commission to impose a ceiling on cost savings resulting from economical quantities, though not methods. Beyond this level these savings may no longer be reflected lawfully in lower prices. This provision had been dormant for 15 years. It was finally put to use by the Federal Trade Commission against the B. F. Goodrich Company in 1951, and was subsequently reviewed by the courts.[56] On December 31, 1951, the Commission ruled that on and after April 7, 1952, "the quantity limit as to replacement tires and tubes made of natural or synthetic rubber for use on motor vehicles as a class of commodity [would be] 20,000 pounds ordered at one time for delivery at one time." In support of the rule, the Commission found that available purchasers "in the greater quantities of annual dollar volumes of $600,000 or more" were so few that they rendered the differentials "unjustly discriminatory and promotive of monopoly" in the lines of commerce in which buyers and sellers were engaged.[57]

The case reached the Court of Appeals on July 16, 1953.[58] The court held that the complaints alleged a kind of damage from application of the Commission rule which, if proved, would justify injunctive relief. It remanded the case to the District Court for consideration on merits. On September 7, 1955, the District Court issued a summary judgment against the rule.[59] This was upheld by the Circuit Court of Appeals for the District of Columbia on February 28, 1957.[60] The matter was not appealed to the Supreme Court. The Court of Appeals said that the Commission "chose to make a finding concerning the paucity of available purchasers in quantities greater than a certain annual dollar volume, and then fixed a quantity limit in terms of a carload. Even though the Commission's accompanying statement may indicate its belief that available buyers in quantities greater than a carload are so few as to give it authority under the

---

[56] The B. F. Goodrich Co. vs. Federal Trade Commission, 208 F. 2d 829 (D.C. Cir. 1953).
[57] FTC, File No. 203-1, Findings, Order, and Statement of Basis and Purpose, pp. 1–2.
[58] B. F. Goodrich vs. FTC, 208 F. 2d 829.
[59] B. F. Goodrich vs. FTC et al., 134 F. Supp. 39.
[60] FTC vs. B. F. Goodrich Co. et al., 242 F. 2d 31.

quantity-limit proviso . . . the Commission did not purport to base its order on the belief." [61] Thus, there was no finding of either fewness of available purchasers or of jeopardy to competition. The quantity limit for replacement rubber tires was set aside.

The quantity limits proviso has been criticized on four counts by the *Attorney General's National Committee to Study the Anti-Trust Laws*.[62] The committee contended first that the cost defense was adequate to determine if there were any undesirable concessions. Second, they pointed out that the quantity limits proviso complicated the Act with novel and perplexing criteria. For example, nothing defined the "fewness" of buyers on which the invoking of the proviso depended nor related an "unjustly discriminatory" quantity discount to the express price discrimination provisions of Section 2(a). Third, the proviso referred to fewness of buyers, not to size of discount, thus presenting the paradox of applying it when only a few rather than many purchasers received the discount, of which the others might complain. Fourth, the proviso necessarily aimed to threaten price differentials which reflected economies in efficient distribution, thereby offending the consumer interest which the cost defense was designed to preserve.

Territorial Price Discrimination. Territorial discriminations of price may occur through formulas or through the relation of prices to competitive situations in local or regional markets. Through formula such discriminations may be classified as a delivered price system. Delivered prices incorporate transportation charges and hence refer to the point of delivery, namely, the buyer's location. Quotations on delivered prices are computed customarily by recourse to four essential formulas. In single or multiple basing-point pricing, one or several mills serve as reference points for price. To this price is added the actual freight charge to the customer's door. Similarly, in freight equalization the most favorably located mill serves as the base to which the freight charge to the customer's door is added. In zone pricing, the country is carved into geographic sectors; within these sectors all buyers are charged the same price. Finally, a uniform delivered price system treats the entire nation as a single market, charging the identical price to all customers wherever they may be located.

Proceedings against the United States Steel Corporation culminat-

[61] 242 F. 2d 31, 36.
[62] 1955.

ing in a decision in 1924 were significant in the development of thinking about territorial price discrimination.[63] Big Steel based its delivered price on a concept of "Pittsburgh plus." Thus, if a shipment were made from a subsidiary near Chicago to a Chicago customer, the Chicago customer would be charged the phantom freight cost from Pittsburgh to Chicago. The case focused attention on competition in the secondary line of commerce and dramatically expressed the idea that such competition was damaged when buyers were systematically deprived of the advantages of their location. The Federal Trade Commission coupled its findings of injury in the secondary line with another that the discrimination through which the injury developed was a price-fixing device.

Under the Sherman Act delivered pricing has been considered a form of discrimination constituting conspiracy. Proceedings under the Act culminated in the Sugar Institute decision of 1936. In this case a scheme for regimenting prices and stifling competition featured the forced adherence of sellers to a basing-point formula as one means of maintaining industrywide collusive prices.[64] In several proceedings the Federal Trade Commission challenged the industrywide delivered pricing systems as a threat to price competition. It acted under Section 5 of the Federal Trade Commission Act which prescribed "unfair methods of competition" to get at the unreasonable restraints outlawed by Section 1 of the Sherman Act.

Several pricing plans were uniformly condemned by the courts, which inferred that illegal union of independent strands of commercial conduct constituted conspiracy.[65] With the exception of the Steel and Sugar Institute cases, no proceedings were instituted against formulated territorial price discrimination until passage of the Robinson-Patman Act. The Sugar Institute case dwelt on agreed price reporting. One of the many joint activities of the defendants had been to agree on the maintenance of a delivered price system. This was condemned by the lower courts as a restraint of trade.[66] A portion of the decrees in the case prohibited concerted determination of transpor-

---

[63] Docket 445 2 Rigid Steel Conduit Assoc., 168 F. 2d 175, 181.

[64] Sugar Institute vs. United States, 297 U.S. 553 (1936).

[65] E.g., Salt Producers Association vs. Federal Trade Commission, 134 F. 2d 354 (7th Cir. 1943); U.S. Maltsters Association vs. Federal Trade Commission, 152 F. 2d 161 (7th Cir. 1945); Milk & Ice Cream Can Institute vs. Federal Trade Commission, 152 F. 2d 478 (7th Cir. 1946); Fort Howard Paper Co. vs. Federal Trade Commission, 156 F. 2d 899 (7th Cir. 1946); Bond Crown and Cork Co. vs. Federal Trade Commission, 176 F. 2d 974 (4th Cir. 1949).

[66] 297 U.S. 553; 15 F. Supp. 817.

tation charges, concerted limitation of freight absorption, and agreement on a system of delivered prices or the refusal to sell f.o.b. refinery. This part of the decision was not appealed.

The Federal Trade Commission has treated cases concerning territorial price discrimination since passage of the Robinson-Patman Act under the amended Section 2(a) of the Clayton Act. Between July 1, 1946, and June 30, 1955, the Commission issued orders against price fixing in 46 cases in which it found a delivered pricing method of sufficient importance to be cited in the findings or in the order.[67] Not many cases were prosecuted under uniform price discrimination. The reason for this may be the logic expressed in the Staley case.[68] In this case, which we shall consider presently, the court held there was no discrimination in a uniform delivered price.

The Commission issued one order under zone pricing and this became the lead case.[69] The order forbade the respondents from concurring on a zone-price system or any other system resulting in identical price quotations. An appeal to the Seventh Circuit Court of Appeals resulted in a modification of the order and a dismissal of the charge of discrimination in the sale of dry white lead on the ground that there was no competition between buyers in the premium zone and those in the par zone. But it did sustain the Commission's findings of unlawful discrimination in the zone differentials for white lead-in-oil and lead oxides.[70] The Supreme Court reviewed the case only in reference to the Commission's right to issue on order against an individual company's matching of delivered prices on a zone basis, sustaining the Commission in its decision.[71]

Basing-point cases initiated by the Commission fell into two classes. First, there were seven cases, all pertaining to corn products, each concerned with discriminatory use of the basing-point system of a single manufacturer. Second, there were two cases, one involving corn products and the other involving cement, in which the charge of price discrimination was coupled with a conspiracy charge.[72] The Staley Corn Products case concerned the shipment of corn syrup from the base point of Chicago.[73] Like U.S. Steel, Staley charged phantom freight from Chicago even though deliveries were actually made from plants at locations nearer to customers. Staley maintained that it was meeting the prices of its competitors in good faith. Corn Products

[67] Edwards, *op. cit.*
[68] 324 U.S. 726.
[69] 227 F. 2d 825.
[70] *Ibid.*
[71] 352 U.S. 419–31.
[72] Edwards, *op. cit.*
[73] 34 FTC 1369.

Refining Company was accused of the same practice. Upon appeal of the Commission's order to these companies to cease their tactics, Judge Lindley of the Seventh Circuit Court of Appeals said: "In so far as the delivery price includes for freight more than the actual cost of transportation it measures a definite discrimination forbidden by statute. . . ." [74]

The Staley case came before the Seventh Circuit Court twice. The second time Judge Minton sustained the Commission's findings. He did so, he said, because the respondents had stipulated that "The higher prices paid for such syrup by such candy manufacturers located as aforesaid other than in the City of Chicago, Illinois, contribute to a greater or lesser degree in their having higher raw material costs than those candy manufacturers located in Chicago, Illinois . . . that the lower profits of those candy manufacturers paying higher prices for such syrup diminishes their incentive or desire to compete with those manufacturers paying the lower prices for such syrup and may deter potential new candy manufacturers from entering the industry in cities where they would pay the higher syrup costs." [75] Judge Minton, however, rejected the Commission's findings regarding good faith, saying: "The companies' competition was using the system when the companies entered the field. The companies merely followed the system and practices which had been established by their competitors. That this was done in good faith is not questioned in the evidence." [76]

The case then went to the Supreme Court which found ample evidence to support the Commission's inference of injury to competition from its findings that glucose was a principal ingredient of low-priced candy and that differences of a fraction of a cent in the price of the candy were sufficient to divert business.[77] On the matter of good faith, Justice Stone, however, said: "The test of good faith presupposes that the person charged with violating the Act would, by his normal, non-discriminatory pricing methods, have reached a price so high that he could reduce it in order to meet the equally low price." Justice Stone further rejected the contention that Staley was following other pricing systems in themselves illegal. The grounds for his rejections were that the statute did not concern itself with pricing systems but placed emphasis on individual competitive situations.

In its case against the Cement Institute, the Commission was concerned with a multiple basing-point.[78] The Commission charged that

[74] 144 F. 2d 211, 215–16.
[75] 144 F. 2d 221, 223n–24n.
[76] *Ibid.*

[77] 324 U.S. 726.
[78] 37 FTC 254–55.

the cement manufacturers' basing-point pricing formula occasioned discrimination. The actual prices of cement were mill-net realization, which differed according to the location of the customer. "The discrimination in mill-net by each respondent seller," the Commission said, "forms a systematic pattern that is the mathematical counterpart of the delivered price pattern resulting from the multiple basing-point delivered price system, which system is an expression of the effort of each respondent seller to match the delivered prices of other respondent sellers." [79]

In the Seventh Circuit Court of Appeals the ruling went against the Commission. Judge Major indicated that the Supreme Court had recognized that a seller may absorb freight charges when done in good faith to meet an equally low price of a competitor, even though a uniform delivered price at all points of delivery might result.[80] The Supreme Court reversed Judge Major. Referring to the Corn Products and Staley cases, Justice Black held that the combined effect of the cases was to prohibit the adoption for sales purposes of any basing-point system.[81] All basing-point systems were declared unlawful and the court rejected the suggestion that systematic absorption of freight charges could be regarded as meeting competition in good faith. Only pricing systems of f.o.b. mill were thus lawful. Departures could take place only in specific situations.

This decision provoked a bitter political discussion. Several bills were presented to Congress in an effort to obtain legal sanction for handling delivered pricing systems on a formula basis. The impact of this discussion was to tone down the emphasis placed by the Federal Trade Commission on proceedings covering territorial pricing formulas.

The Attorney General's Report expressed the opinion that Congress did not intend to make delivered pricing illegal per se.[82] In the National Lead and Chain Institute cases, it was found that both had been guilty of violating Section 5 of the Federal Trade Commission Act through collusive pricing conduct.[83] To the extent that these orders deny sellers the right independently to quote "delivered" prices in meeting rivals' offers, they not only fail to promote effective competition, but also may be vulnerable by blocking what the law permits. Under the Commission's "actual price" criterion, the Report held, only significant disparities in "laid-down cost" could sufficiently prejudice

[79] *Ibid.*
[80] 156 F. 2d 533, 560–61.
[81] 333 U.S. 683, 723, 725.
[82] Attorney General's Report, *op. cit.*
[83] National Lead, *op. cit.; Chain Institute vs. FTC*, 246 F. 2d 231.

the competitive vigor of individual buyers to invalidate a "delivered" price as discriminatory and therefore illegal. Thus, a zone pricing system would not discriminate among buyers *within each zone*, but might discriminate against buyers in *adjacent zones*. The discrimination inherent in single or multiple basing-point systems, the Report asserted, would be coextensive with the disparities in actual price paid by each buyer. The Report went on to say that it was the actual price paid by buyers which determined their competitive standing and thus became an index for legality.

Switching now from territorial price discrimination through formula to discrimination through relation of prices to local competitive situations, let us consider briefly discrimination in one local market while a company sells in a much wider area. One early case concerned Muller and Frank, vendors of chicory. The firm undercut prices in New Orleans to eliminate a competitor. The courts sustained the Federal Trade Commission's order directing Muller and Frank to cease restraining the competitor.[84] In a similar situation Page Dairy lowered its prices on milk in certain local areas. The Commission found that Page's price discrimination had the reasonable probability of damaging competition in the narrow sense of substantially lessening it or of tending to create a monopoly in the primary line of commerce.[85]

In other cases, the Commission ordered the American Brake Shoe Company to cease selling bearings to any purchaser in a grade area at different prices from those charged to other purchasers in the same area where the company was in competition with any other seller of such products. The order, however, did not prohibit the quotation of lower prices in the southeastern part of the United States where such competition was lacking.[86] The Maryland Baking Company had the avowed purpose of forcing a competitor out of business.[87] The Fourth Circuit Court of Appeals affirmed a lower court decision which held it unlawful to forbid price discrimination in any area of the United States in which a company did business while not requiring uniform prices throughout the country or prohibiting a company from making prices in good faith to meet competition.[88] In contrast to this case, the Commission ordered Anheuser-Busch, which had reduced prices

[84] 142 F. 2d 511, 518.
[85] FTC 395.
[86] 87 F. Supp. 484.
[87] Docket 6327, Maryland Baking Co.
[88] Maryland Baking Co. vs. FTC, 243 F. 2d 716.

in an area to become more competitive, to cease discriminating through price reduction in any market in which it was in competition with other sellers, unless it proportionately reduced prices everywhere.[89]

The position taken by the Commission in most of these cases has not been fully reviewed by the courts. The case against American Brake Shoe resulted in admissions and consent orders. Page Dairy did not appeal the Commission's order. In April 1959, the Seventh Circuit Court of Appeals set aside the Anheuser-Busch order declaring the company was under attack for price reductions in St. Louis, not for differentials in price between St. Louis and other markets. Such reductions might violate Section 3, under which the Commission had no jurisdiction, but not Section 2(a), under which it did.[90] Yet another court ruled that the Arden Farms Company, which had reduced prices in the Los Angeles area, was not guilty of predatory pricing in one local area. The reason given was that its prices were higher in other areas.[91] The court maintained that different market areas had different price structures. Furthermore, it noted that Arden was able to make a profit at this low price. Decisions apparently vary in accordance with human differences of opinion.

Brokerage. Section 2(c) of the amended Clayton Act contains the brokerage provision of the Robinson-Patman Act. This provision states:

> That it shall be unlawful for any person engaged in commerce, in the course of such commerce, to pay or grant, or to receive or accept, anything of value as commission, brokerage, or other compensation, or any allowance or discount in lieu thereof, except for services rendered in connection with sale or purchase of goods, wares, or merchandise, either to the other party to such transaction or to an agent, representative or other intermediary therein where such intermediary is acting in fact for or in behalf, or is subject to the direct or indirect control, of any party to such transaction other than the person by whom such compensation is so granted or paid.

In other words, a broker cannot receive a commission from both buyer and seller, or anything in lieu of commission. This has amounted to a per se ruling that only one party to a transaction may pay the broker's fee. Even if the broker takes the commission he receives from the supplier and passes it on to the buyer, the practice remains illegal.[92]

---

[89] Docket 6331, Anheuser-Busch, Inc.

[90] Anheuser-Busch, Inc. vs. FTC, CCH, *Trade Cases,* 1959, par. 69330.

[91] Balian Ice Cream Company vs. Arden Farms Company, CCH 68, 186 (CCa 9, October 1955).

[92] Biddle Purchasing Co., 96 F. 2d 687.

And even if the broker performs a service for the other party in the transaction he is not entitled to additional compensation. The courts ruled in a case involving the A & P:

> The agent cannot serve two masters, simultaneously rendering services in an arm's length transaction to both. . . . The record clearly requires the conclusion that the field buying agents of the petitioner were the agents of the petitioner and that such services as were rendered by them to sellers were purely incidental to such representative capacity. For such incidental services the petitioner may not be compensated.[93]

The Robinson-Patman law does not permit an exception when services are rendered. In this respect, the Fifth Circuit Court of Appeals has ruled that exceptions would destroy the statute and nullify its intent. By transfer of a comma, said the court, the words could be attached to those immediately preceding "or any allowance or discount in lieu thereof, except for services rendered." The statute would then prohibit "a commission, brokerage, or other compensation, or any allowance or discount in lieu thereof except for services rendered, in connection with sale or purchase, etc." As published the punctuation was confusing, the court noted. It suggested that the true meaning would become clearer by transposing the comma after *thereof* to after *render*.[94]

Many voluntary groups and cooperatives have been affected by this provision. Although paid by sellers they would pass the brokerage discount along to the buyers.[95] As applied to voluntary groups and cooperatives, Edwards indicated, this has a tendency to weaken them.[96] In addition, dummy brokerages have been declared illegal under this act.[97]

There seems to be no defense to receiving payments from both parties to a transaction. If a company employs a broker and ceases using him it cannot claim a larger discount because of lower distribution costs; nor can it claim proportionally equal allowances such as advertising in place of brokerage. Thus, the brokerage provision of the Robinson-Patman Act has tended to maintain a broker's monopoly. That is to say, a seller's discount would be illegal if it were discrimina-

[93] 106 F. 2d 667, 674.
[94] 102 F. 2d 763, 770.
[95] Docket 3221, United Buyers Corp.; Docket 5338, National Modes, Inc.; Docket 5482, Carpet Frosted Foods, Inc.
[96] Edwards, *op. cit.*
[97] Docket 3344, Atlantic Commission Co.

tory, if it might injure competition, if it failed to reflect a difference in cost, if there were no proof that it was made in good faith to match a competitor's price, or if its receipt were unlawful because the seller could not lawfully grant it and the buyer knew this to be so. If the discount is granted "in lieu of brokerage" it would be illegal irrespective of conditions.[98] In this regard, companies may not claim competitive injury [99] or maintain that the discount was justified by costs.[100]

Proportionally Equal Arrangements. Sections 2(d) and 2(e) of the Robinson-Patman Act forbid a seller to enter into cooperative promotional arrangements of any type except on "proportionally equal" terms with all competing customers. It is not necessary to prove injury to competition to establish a violation of these two sections.[101] The Commission says that the seller must notify all qualified customers, including retailers who purchase through wholesalers,[102] of his willingness to pay for such services as well as their entitlement to participation in them.[103]

The defense for providing services and facilities resides in Section 2(e). This section holds that the facilities furnished must be accorded to all purchasers on proportionally equal terms. Two other defenses are contained in Section 2(b). These are the now familiar defenses that the facilities were supplied in good faith to meet a competitor [104] and that the discrimination could be justified on the basis of cost.[105]

Buyer's Liability. Section 2(f) applies to buyers rather than to sellers and states that it is "unlawful for any person engaged in commerce, in the course of such commerce, knowingly to induce or receive a discrimination in price which is prohibited by this section." When the Robinson-Patman Act was passed it was thought that this section would receive vigorous prosecution. However, until 1953 it was little used. Since the Supreme Court's decision in the Automatic Canteen case, the Commission has not resorted to it at all.[106]

Said the Supreme Court in reviewing this section for the first time: "The Commission is, on this record, insisting that once knowledge of

[98] Docket 6366, Union Malleable Manufacturing Co.
[99] Docket 6230, Rocky Mountain Wholesale Co.
[100] 149 F. 2d 970.
[101] Great Atlantic and Pacific Tea Co. vs. FTC, 106 F. 2d 667 (34d Cir. 1939).
[102] Elizabeth Arden, Inc. vs. FTC, 156 F. 2d 132 (2nd Cir. 1946).
[103] Kay Windsor Frocks, FTC, Docket 5735 (1954).
[104] Elizabeth Arden, Inc., 39 FTC 288 (1944).
[105] Simplicity Pattern Co., Inc. vs. FTC (D.C. Cir. 1959).
[106] 346 U.S. 61, 74, 78–79.

a price differential is shown, the burden of introducing evidence shifts to the buyer. . . . We think the fact that the buyer does not have the required information, and for good reason should not be required to obtain it, has controlling importance. . . . We therefore conclude that a buyer is not liable under 2(f) if the lower prices he induces are such as the cost justification or not known to him not to be within one of these defenses." [107]

Meeting Competition in Good Faith. The most important decision on the good faith defense was the Supreme Court's ruling in 1958 in the Standard Oil case.[108] This was the first time that a seller succeeded in justifying a challenged price discrimination through use of Section 2(b), namely, that the price "was made in good faith to meet an equally low price of a competitor." Since 1936 the Federal Trade Commission had maintained that "good faith" was only a "qualified" defense and would afford the seller no protection if potential injury to competition were shown. The Supreme Court rejected this construction and ruled that the "meeting-competition" provision afforded a complete defense, incidental "injury" notwithstanding.[109] This now converted Section 2(b) into a substantive rule of law from a procedural rule of evidence.

In response to the contention of the Commission that a seller is precluded from competing in a local market unless he is willing to make an across-the-board reduction in each place where business is conducted, the Supreme Court said:

There is, on the other hand, plain language and established practice which permits a seller, through section 2(b) to retain a customer by realistically meeting in good faith the price offered to that customer without necessarily charging the seller's price to its other customers.[110]

Robbins stated that unless there were a legislative change, the "meeting-competition" defense would certainly become a more significant justification in future pricing cases.[111] Before the Standard Oil case the courts had spelled out certain limits to the "meeting-competition" defense. Both in 1956 and 1957 the Seventh Circuit Court

---

[107] *Ibid.*
[108] FTC vs. Standard Oil Co., 355 U.S. 396 (1958).
[109] Standard Oil Co. vs. FTC, 340 U.S. 231 (1951).
[110] FTC vs. Standard Oil Co., *op. cit.*
[111] W. David Robbins, "A Marketing Appraisal of the Robinson-Patman Act," *Journal of Marketing,* Vol. 24, No. 1, July 1959, p. 18.

of Appeals said that competitive price must be responsive to an actual rival or to specific lower prices.[112]

The Standard Oil decision was not concerned with entire markets, only with individual customers. Also it dealt with preventing the loss of present customers and not with gaining new ones. The competitive price, therefore, had to be defensive rather than aggressive.[113] Furthermore, the competitive price could not be set pursuant to a pricing system.[114] It had been held earlier that "equally low prices" meant prices for similar quantities.[115]

Although Section 2(b) does not expressly limit its application to competitors' lawful prices, the earlier opinion of the Supreme Court in the Standard Oil case made reference to such prices.[116] The "lawful" offer of a competitor was not mentioned in the 1958 Standard Oil case, however, other than in the dissent. The Commission had not determined that the competitive price cuts which Standard Oil was meeting were illegal. The "lawful" price was clearly expressed in the 1958 dissent which emphasized the "insurmountable obstacles" confronting the seller who sought to ascertain the legality of a competitor's price. Dealing with this problem two years before the Fifth Circuit Court of Appeals had held that "To establish this 2(b) defense, a seller does not have the burden of proving that the competing price was lawful. Section 2(b) should not be construed as if it were written 'was made in good faith to meet a lawful equally low price.' "[117]

Another related problem having to do with Section 2(b) is the "like-grade-and-quality" phrase of Section 2(a). In three different cases [118] the Federal Trade Commission rejected the "meeting-competition" defense when a seller of merchandise who normally sold at a premium because of a "superior public acceptance, unrelated to actual quality," reduced his prices to match a competitor. The meaning of like grade and quality has tended to signify only the purely physical character-

[112] E. Edelmann & Co. vs. FTC, 239 F. 2d 152 (7th Cir. 1956), cert. denied, 355 U.S. 951 (1958).

[113] Standard Oil Co. vs. FTC, 340 U.S. 231, 249 (1951 dictum).

[114] FTC vs. National Lead Co., 353 U.S. 419 (1957).

[115] FTC vs. Standard Brands, Inc., 189 F. 2d 510 (ed. Cir. 1951).

[116] FTC vs. Standard Oil Co., *op. cit.*

[117] Standard Oil Co. vs. Brown, d.b.a. Bob Brown's Standard Service, 238 F. 2d 54 (1956).

[118] Anheuser-Busch, Inc., FTC Docket 6331 (1957); Standard Brands, Inc., 46 FTC 1495 (1950), *aff'd on other grounds,* 189 F. 2d 510 (2d Cir. 1951); Minneapolis-Honeywell Regulator Co., 44 FTC 351, 371, 396 (1948), *rev'd on other grounds,* 233 F. 2d 649 (7th Cir. 1956).

istics of products and has not taken into consideration differences or unlikenesses in consumer preferences.

Refusals to Deal

Boycotts, strikes, and similar refusals to deal with others are commonly associated with disputes between labor and management. However, they also occur among the marketing activities of a company or a group of companies, and when they do, they may be subject to legal prosecution under the various federal statutes designed to prevent monopoly, restraint of trade, and unfair practices. Combination boycotts have long been condemned as unreasonable restraints under Section 1 of the Sherman Act. In the Eastern States Retail Lumber Dealers Association decision the Supreme Court invalidated an arrangement whereby members of a retailing group could boycott all suppliers who competed with them by selling directly to retail customers.[119] When members of the Fashion Originators' Guild conspired to boycott retailers who practiced "style piracy" by handling garments manufactured from copied designs and to circulate lists of retailers to be boycotted, the Supreme Court declared the practice an "unfair method of competition" proscribed by the Federal Trade Commission Act and found an offense under the Sherman Act as well.[120] In the view of the court, a concerted restraint by a powerful combination could not be justified legally even if designed to prevent admittedly insidious trade conduct or acknowledged commercial torts. In this and subsequent rulings the Supreme Court declared group action that coerced outside parties an undue restraint of trade and said that whatever its purpose, such action was likely to be unreasonable per se.[121]

In the absence of conspiracy or combination, refusals to deal by individual businessmen are generally safe from anti-trust prosecutions. This principle was developed shortly after the First World War in the Colgate case.[122] In this case a criminal indictment under the Sherman Act charged Colgate with employing tactics designed to coerce its distributors to adhere to a "suggested" resale price. The Supreme Court rejected the argument of combination or conspiracy and said that a company might select its own customers. However, enforce-

[119] 234 U.S. 600 (1914).
[120] 312 U.S. 457 (1941).
[121] United States vs. Frankfort Distilleries, Inc., 324 U.S. 293 (1945).
[122] United States vs. Colgate & Co., 250 U.S. 300 (1919).

ment of a resale price policy against resourceful, price-cutting dealers, the court ruled in a subsequent case, might invite joint policy efforts, tantamount to agreement, between a seller and distributors willing to adhere to his resale price.[123] This, of course, was a violation of Section 1 of the Sherman Act.

Section 2 of the Act may forbid refusals to deal for monopolistic ends. In the Eastman Kodak case, the Supreme Court held that discontinuance of photo supplies to a competitor who had previously resisted Kodak's desires to buy him out was an attempt to monopolize.[124] Conversely, threats to withhold purchases, if wielded by buyers with monopoly power to exact concessions detrimental to less favorably situated competitors, may violate the monopolization clause of Section 2.[125] Thus, the courts may penalize an exercise of the discretion to deal if it is used to achieve or extend a monopolistic market position. When "conceived in monopolistic purpose or market control"[126] even individual refusals can violate the monopolistic prohibitions of Section 2.

Refusal to deal may also constitute a violation of Section 2 of the Clayton Act if the services are not "proportionally equal." The ending of trade relations with one distributor who also handles products made by the manufacturer's competitors may confirm an implicit insistence of exclusive dealing arrangements with other distributors. This may show that sales to distributors who are retained by the company are conditioned by the distributors' exclusion of rival products, and therefore fall within the prohibitions of Section 3.[127] Moreover, a supplier's refusal to sell singly a particular item in his line, although of itself unexceptionable under any anti-trust provision, may imply joint sales of the product plus a forced combination or "tying" sale which is proscribed by Section 3 of the Clayton Act.[128]

A refusal to deal, in addition, may constitute an "unfair method of competition" prohibited by Section 5 of the Federal Trade Commission Act. In the absence of a fair trade exemption, any plan to control prices by withholding goods from price cutters may be found to be an "unfair method of competition" if it involves any understanding beyond a naked refusal to deal.[129] The decisions on all refusals to deal

123 United States vs. Bausch & Lomb Optical Co., 321 U.S. 707, 723 (1944).
124 Eastman Kodak Co. vs. Southern Photo Materials Co., 273 U.S. 359 (1927).
125 United States vs. Griffith, 334 U.S. 100 (1948).
126 Times-Picayune Publishing Co. vs. United States, 345 U.S. 594, 625 (1953).
127 Carter Carburetor Corp. vs. Federal Trade Commission, 112 F. 2d 722 (1940).
128 Times-Picayune Publishing Co. vs. United States, 345 U.S. 594 (1953).
129 Fashion Originators Guild vs. Federal Trade Commission, 312 U.S. 457 (1941).

have placed and evaluated refusals in the business context in which they appear. Although refusals in themselves are protected by other laws, they are examined with respect to marketing in the light of the broader business policies of which they form a part.

Exclusive Dealings

Manufacturers may wish to deal with certain dealers on an exclusive franchise basis. Frequently the manufacturer or creator of a service may require that the dealer or representative handle only his product or service to the exclusion of all others. On the one hand, this may contribute to more efficient selling effort and lower costs of distribution. On the other hand, this tends to exclude other forms of competition from obtaining some of this business. The legality of this practice is determined by Section 3 of the Clayton Act. This section forbids any person:

> to lease or make a sale or contract for sale of goods, wares, merchandise, machinery, supplies, or other commodities, whether patented or unpatented . . . or fix a price charged therefor, or discount from, or rebate upon, such price, on the condition, agreement, or understanding that the lessee or purchaser thereof shall not use or deal in the goods, wares, merchandise, machinery, supplies, or other commodity of a competitor or competitors of the lessor or seller, where the effect of such lease, sale, or contract for sale or such condition, agreement, or understanding may be to substantially lessen competition or tend to create a monopoly in any line of commerce.

A typical "tying" arrangement conditions the sale or lease of a machine on the consent of the buyer or lessee to use with it only supplies or services furnished by the seller or lessor. "Full-line forcing" binds the distributor of one item to accept a second or several additional products in the seller's line. In both types of arrangements, the supplier of the particular commodity foists on the purchaser something that the latter does not wish to buy at all. Outright exclusive dealing procedures may also concern the terms of sale for a single product. As a condition of doing business, a manufacturer might demand that his customers shun all rival merchandise. In addition, the same results might obtain temporarily in a manufacturer's insistence on a contract that obligated the buyer to fill all his needs from the single source for a specified time. The element common to all these practices is the exclusion of rival sellers, either by terms of the arrangement or its effects.

The United Shoe Machinery case was a good example of a company's having a tying arrangement which compelled buyers of its product to acquire their supplies from it.[130] This practice was condemned under Section 3 as obviously excluding any purchases from competitors. The probability of adverse effect on competition or a tendency toward monopoly was found in United's "dominant position in supplying shoe machinery of the classes involved." [131] Application of Section 3 to "tying" arrangements also appeared in the International Salt case in 1947.[132] Here the decision of the court condemned the arrangement as embracing a not "insignificant or insubstantial" volume of commerce in the "tied" supplies.[133] It was declared "unreasonable, *per se* to foreclose competitors from any substantial market." [134] In the *Times Picayune* case, the Supreme Court ruled that whenever a supplier "enjoys a monopolistic position in the market for the tying product, *or* if a substantial volume of commerce in the 'tied' product is restrained, a tying agreement violates the narrower standards expressed in Section 3 of the Clayton Act because from either factor the requisite potential lessening of competition is inferred." [135]

In connection with exclusive dealing the Standard Oil case raised the question of "quantitative substantiality." [136] At issue were contracts obligating filling stations to take all their gasoline as well as accessories, in some cases, from Standard Oil. The contracts covered 16 per cent of the existing retail gasoline outlets in the "western area" where Standard Oil, the largest marketer of the region, accounted for 23 per cent of the total gallonage. The District Court, conceding that Standard did not enjoy a "dominant" position, nevertheless invalidated the arrangements under Section 3 of the Clayton Act as well as under Section 1 of the Sherman Act by inferring the competitive consequences simply from the contracts which covered "a substantial number of outlets and a substantial number of products whether considered comparatively or not." [137] In the court's opinion the "quantitative substantiality" of trade flowing through exclusive marketing channels by itself constituted a "substantial lessening of competition" which the Clayton Act sought to eliminate.

Since the Standard Oil ruling both the courts and the Federal Trade

[130] 258 U.S. 451 (1922).
[131] *Ibid.*
[132] International Salt Co. vs. United States, 332 U.S. 392 (1947).
[133] *Ibid.* at 396.
[134] *Ibid.*
[135] 345 U.S. 594 (1953).
[136] Standard Oil of California vs. United States, 337 U.S. 293 (1949).
[137] *Ibid.* at 298.

Commission have refrained from a strict test of "quantitative substantiality." [138] Rather than subject exclusive dealing to rigid criteria, they have thoroughly scrutinized the specific factual pattern of each case. These inquiries have evidently been directed to determining whether the challenged practices have menaced competition in the distribution process by actually cutting off the access of competitors to a substantial share of the market. The Supreme Court has defined the ultimate issue under Section 3 of the Clayton Act as whether the challenged arrangement "would under the circumstances disclosed probably lessen competition or create an actual tendency to monopoly." [139] Tying arrangements that involve a "wielding of monopolistic leverage" [140] create the probability of economic harm whenever the seller occupies a dominant market position for the "tying" commodity, or when his arrangements cover a substantial volume of trade in the "tied" product.[141] Under the precedent-setting decisions, exclusive dealings or exclusive requirements contracts are illegal under Section 3 whenever they *in fact* "foreclose" rivals from access to a "substantial share of the line of commerce affected." [142] The heart of the matter, said the Attorney General's Report, was the ease with which rival suppliers could practically secure access to consumers through other ways.[143]

Resale Price Maintenance

In 1936, the matter of maintaining resale prices came to a head in the Old Dearborn case. In this case the Supreme Court interpreted the "Fair Trade" law of the state of Illinois as designed solely "to afford a legitimate remedy for an injury to the good will which results from the use of trademarks, brands or names" by price cutters at the retail level.[144] This law consequently did not transgress the due process and equal protection clauses of the Fourteenth Amendment, the court held. The case supplied the legal framework for passage

[138] Federal Trade Commission vs. Motion Picture Advertising Service Co., 344 U.S. 392, 394 (1953).

[139] 258 U.S. at 357.

[140] Instro-Gas Corp., FTC, Dkt. 5851 (October 6, 1954).

[141] Times-Picayune Publishing Co. vs. United States, 337 U.S. 293, 314 (1949).

[142] Standard Oil of California vs. United States, 337 U.S. 293, 314 (1949).

[143] Attorney General's Report, *op. cit.*

[144] Old Dearborn Distributing Co. vs. Seagram Distillers Corp., 299 U.S. 183, 198 (1936).

of the Miller-Tydings Act in 1937 which amended Section 1 of the Sherman Act to exempt from anti-trust prosecution:

Contracts or agreements prescribing minimum prices for the resale of a commodity which bears, or the label or container of which bears, the trade mark, brand, or name of the producer or distributor of such commodity and which is in free and open competition with commodities of the same general class produced or distributed by others, when the contracts or agreements of that description are lawful [in the state of resale].

In 1951, the Supreme Court construed the Miller-Tydings exemption as shielding from federal anti-trust laws only *consensual* contracts or agreements while placing enforcement against "nonsigning" distributors beyond the pale.[145] The court took the position that unless expressly exempt by Act of Congress all fixing of resale prices, whether consensual by agreement or coercive through "nosigner" controls, was illegal as an unreasonable restraint of trade. This opinion in the Schwegmann case jeopardized the fair trade concept.

To repair this damage the McGuire Act of 1952 added "nosigner" enforcement to the exemption previously granted by the Miller-Tydings Act. In addition, the McGuire Act expressly authorized "stipulated" as well as "minimum" resale prices and further exempted fair trade agreements that bound buyers to obtain fair trade conditions from those to whom they resold. The McGuire Act also said that neither fair trade agreements nor enforcements should be deemed an "unlawful burden or restraint upon, or interference with, commerce."

At present the factual content of the statutory requirement that goods in fair trade must be "in free and open competition with commodities of the same general class" lacks authoritative interpretation. Besides, the express statutory denial of the fair trade exemption to arrangements between competing companies creates unresolved issues when an integrated seller, operating his own distribution outlets, practices fair trade with independent distributors competing on the same market level. These issues similarly arise when a "dual" supplier who directly serves retail customers as well as distributors sets fair trade prices for distributors who vie with him for retail sales.

The Attorney General's Report recommended repeal of both the Miller-Tydings and McGuire Acts, thereby subjecting the maintenance of retail prices, along with other price-fixing practices, to those federal

---

[145] Schwegmann Bros. vs. Calvert Distillers Corp., 341 U.S. 384 (1951).

anti-trust controls that safeguard the public by keeping the channels of distribution free.[146]

A free economy depends on a healthy, competitive distribution system. This salubrious state is more likely to flourish when there is sound, rational, knowledgeable marketing management. To provide such management, as we have seen in the course of this book, the individual marketing man requires a thorough familiarity with the many diverse aspects of the marketing operation and the ability to apply them shrewdly to the marketing situation at hand. If the man interested in a career in marketing management can distill these numerous principles and practices, and fuse their best qualities into a code for his own efforts; if he can adapt the methodology of science to the professional problems confronting him; if he can draw usefully on the lessons of the behavioral sciences for insights into his own planning endeavors; and if, further, he can appreciate the temper of the political, social, and legal climate in which the marketing process operates, he should have no difficulty in performing a valuable economic service and contributing to the general well-being of his fellow-man and the preservation of his society. The opportunity beckons. The path has been clearly mapped. It is for him to choose to pursue it or not.

Summary

The laws relating to the maintenance of competition are the Sherman Act, the Clayton Act, and the amended Section 2 of the Clayton Act, or the Robinson-Patman Act. The philosophy of the Sherman Act is expressed in the "rule of reason" where a violation exists if there is intent to monopolize through excessive power of the company. The classical rules of competition have now been superseded by what is called "workable competition."

Mergers are important for marketing management because they represent a means of extending marketing strategy and because they have certain implications for public policy in regard to competition. Mergers were not successfully prosecuted under the Sherman Act. Section 7 of the Clayton Act was designed to remedy this situation. However, it was found that this section could not be effective because it limited prosecution to cases where there had been a stock transfer. The Celler Antimerger Act rectified this situation by making the transfer of assets illegal. Injury to competition exists if there is a reasonable probability that the merger would substantially lessen competition.

There is a difference of opinion regarding the relevant market. Some court rulings have taken the narrow view; some the broad. Market shares over 25 per cent have been ruled illegal.

[146] Attorney General's Report, *op. cit.*

Functional discounts are permitted if they are cost justified or meet competition in good faith. The same defense is allowed for quantity discounts. The quantity limits proviso permits the Federal Trade Commission to set a quantity limit beyond which no further discounts may be granted on the grounds that these would jeopardize competition.

Territorial price discrimination by formula is illegal if it denies sellers the right independently to quote "delivered" prices in meeting rival's offers. The decisions concerning territorial price discrimination without formula have been confusing in regard to the effects of competition in local areas as compared to the effects on competition throughout the country.

Once a seller has used a broker it is difficult to eliminate him because buyers may not receive any other payments in lieu of brokerage. In giving proportionally equal payments a seller must notify all qualified customers of his willingness to pay.

The buyer's liability section of the Robinson-Patman Act has been weakened by the recent Supreme Court decision that it is not necessary for the buyer to have the requisite information to prove or disprove discrimination. In the Standard Oil case the Supreme Court ruled that "meeting competition" in good faith was a complete defense against price discrimination.

Refusals to deal have been declared illegal if they have the tendency to lessen competition. The basis for determining whether exclusive dealing may be illegal is the ease with which rival suppliers can practically secure consumer access in other ways.

The McGuire Act made legal the "nosigners clause" for resale price maintenance. The Attorney General's Report suggested that this Act and the Miller-Tydings Act be nullified so that free competition might exert itself in the pricing system.

Suggested Cases

Milton P. Brown, Wilbur B. England, and John B. Matthews, Jr., *Problems in Marketing*, 3rd ed., McGraw-Hill, New York, 1961.

> Robinson-Patman Act, pp. 633–636.
>
> "Resale Price Maintenance: Fact and Fancy," pp. 644–645.

Harry L. Hansen, *Marketing: Text, Cases, and Readings*, rev. ed., Irwin, Homewood, Ill., 1961.

> Sherman Anti-trust Act, pp. 794–795.
>
> Detroit Gasoline Case, 803–816.

Kenneth R. Davis, *Marketing Management*, Ronald Press, New York, 1961.

> Great Atlantic and Pacific Tea Company, pp. 731–738.
>
> Simplicity Pattern, pp. 740–741.
>
> Prater Company, p. 742.

Intercollegiate Case Clearing House, Soldiers Field, Boston 63, Massachusetts.

> ICH 1635—The Cellophane Case.
>
> ICH 2M41—Lord's Service Station, Inc.

Index

IH 7m / 3 BS

Ao BS

Mi - 2m